MW01481873

The State of U.S. History

The State of U.S. History

Edited by
Melvyn Stokes

Oxford • New York

First published in 2002 by
Berg
Editorial offices:
150 Cowley Road, Oxford, OX4 1JJ, UK
838 Broadway, Third Floor, New York, NY 10003–4812, USA

Berg is an imprint of Oxford International Publishers Ltd.

Library of Congress Cataloging-in-Publication Data

The state of U.S. history / edited by Melvyn Stokes.
    p.cm.
Includes bibliographical references and index.
    ISBN 1-85973-596-7 -- ISBN 1-85973-502-9 (pbk.)
    1. United States--Historiography. 2. United States--Social conditions--
Historiography. I. Title: State of United States history. II. Stokes, Melvyn.
    E175 .S73 2001
    973'.07'--dc21

2001006568

British Library Cataloguing-in-Publication Data
A catalogue record for this book is available from the British Library.

ISBN 1 85973 596 7 (Cloth)
      1 85973 502 9 (Paper)

Typeset by JS Typesetting, Wellingborough, Northants.
Printed in the United Kingdom by Antony Rowe Ltd, Chippenham, Wiltshire.

Contents

Contents

Acknowledgements

All the chapters in this book were first presented as papers at the Commonwealth Fund Conference in American History held at University College London in 2000. They have since been revised for publication in the light of comments made at the conference, responses from colleagues not present at the conference, and subsequently-published work. I should like to thank all the contributors for meeting the sometimes very tight deadlines asked of them. I should also like to thank the four Commonwealth Fund Lecturers (Alan Brinkley, Daniel Feller, James T. Kloppenberg, and Patricia Nelson Limerick) for their contribution to the project as a whole. Finally, I am very happy to acknowledge the great assistance provided by Arlene Hui, first in helping to organize the conference itself and later as editorial assistant on this volume.

The conference itself was made possible through financial assistance, which is gratefully acknowledged, from the Commonwealth Fund of University College London, the British Academy, the Royal Historical Society, the British American Nineteenth Century Historians (BrANCH), the History Faculty of Cambridge University, the David Bruce Center for American Studies at Keele University, the London University Institute of United States Studies, and W. W. Norton and Co.

This book has been published with the help of a grant from the late Miss Isobel Thornley's bequest to the University of London and a grant from the Scouloudi Foundation in association with the Institute of Historical Research. The support of the Graduate School of University College London is also gratefully acknowledged.

Melvyn Stokes

Notes on Contributors

John Ashworth is Professor of American History at the University of Nottingham. He is the author of *Slavery, Capitalism and Politics in the Antebellum Republic, Vol. 1: Commerce and Compromise, 1820–1850* (1995) and is currently completing the second, concluding volume.

Alan Brinkley is the Allan Nevins Professor of History at Columbia University. Among his publications are *Voices of Protest: Huey Long, Father Coughlin, and the Great Depression* (1982); *The End of Reform: New Deal Liberalism in Recession and War* (1994); and *Liberalism and Its Discontents* (1998). He is currently completing a biography of Henry R. Luce.

Christopher Clark is Professor of North American History at the University of Warwick. He is the author of *The Roots of Rural Capitalism: Western Massachusetts, 1760–1860* (1990), *The Communitarian Moment: The Radical Challenge of the Northampton Association* (1995), and co-author of the first volume of *Who Built America?* (2nd edition, 2000). He is currently working on a book about U.S. social structures between the Revolution and the Civil War.

Adam Fairclough holds the chair of American Studies (History) at the University of East Anglia. His most recent books are *Teaching Equality: Black Schools in the Age of Jim Crow* (2001) and *Better Day Coming: Blacks and Equality, 1890–2000* (2001). He is currently writing a study of black educators in the Southern states during the segregation era.

Daniel Feller is Professor of History at the University of New Mexico and a specialist in Jacksonian America. He is the author of *The Public Lands in Jacksonian Politics* (1984) and *The Jacksonian Promise: America, 1815–1840* (1995) and the editor of Harriet Martineau's *Retrospect of Western Travel* (2000). He is currently writing a biography of Benjamin Tappan, antebellum politician, scientist, and social reformer.

Notes on Contributors

Robert A. Gross is Forrest D. Murden, Jr. Professor of History and American Studies at the College of William and Mary and book review editor of the *William and Mary Quarterly*. He is the author of *The Minutemen and Their World* (25th anniversary ed., 2001) and *Books and Libraries in Thoreau's Concord* (1988) and editor of *In Debt to Shays: The Bicentennial of an Agrarian Rebellion* (1993). His study of Concord, Massachusetts, in the era of Emerson and Thoreau will be published as *The Transcendentalists and Their World* in 2003.

Howell John Harris is Professor of History at the University of Durham. His most recent book is *Bloodless Victories: The Rise and Fall of the Open Shop in the Philadelphia Metal Trades* (2002). His current research is a study of economic growth, technical change, and social conflict in the U.S. metal-casting industry in the nineteenth and early twentieth centuries.

Michael J. Heale is Professor Emeritus of American History at Lancaster University. His books include *American Anticommunism: Combating the Enemy Within* (1990), *McCarthy's Americans: Red Scare Politics in State and Nation, 1935–1965* (1998), *Franklin Roosevelt: New Deal and War* (1999) and *The Sixties in America: History, Politics and Protest* (2001). He is currently writing a history of twentieth-century American politics.

S. Jay Kleinberg is Professor of American Studies and History at Brunel University. She is editor of the *Journal of American Studies* and the author of a number of books on women and families in the United States, including *Women in the United States, 1830–1945* (1999), *The Shadow of the Mills: Working Class Families in Pittsburgh, 1870–1907* (1989) and *Retrieving Women's History* (1988). Her most recent research is on widows, investigating the relationship between changes in the family economy and social welfare policy in the U.S. between 1870 and 1940.

James T. Kloppenberg is Professor of History at Harvard University. He is the author of *Uncertain Victory: Social Democracy and Progressivism in European and American Thought, 1870–1920* (1986) and *The Virtues of Liberalism* (1998) and co-editor, with Richard Wightman Fox, of *A Companion to American Thought* (1995). He is currently working on a history of democracy in America and Europe since 1630 and a study of history and critical theory.

Patricia Nelson Limerick is Professor of History and Chair of the Board of the Center of the American West at the University of Colorado. She is the author of *The Legacy of Conquest* (1987) and *Something in the Soil* (2000). She is currently at work on a book about ethnicity and environment.

Simon P. Newman is Director of the Andrew Hook Center for American Studies and Senior Lecturer in the Department of History at the University of Glasgow. He is the author of *Parades and the Politics of the Street: Festive Culture in the Early American Republic* (1997) and is currently completing *Embodied History: Reading the Bodies of the Poor in Early National Philadelphia*.

Mark A. Noll is McManis Professor of History at Wheaton College, Illinois. He is the editor of *God and Mammon: Protestants, Money, and the Market, 1790-1860* (2001), and the author of many books including the recent *The Old Religion in a New World: The History of North American Christianity* (2001). His history of early American religious thought, *America's God: From Jonathan Edwards to Abraham Lincoln*, will shortly appear.

Michael O'Brien is Lecturer in American History at the University of Cambridge and a Fellow of Jesus College. His books include *The Idea of the American South, 1920–41* (1979), *A Character of Hugh Legaré* (1985), *Rethinking the South* (1988), and *An Evening When Alone* (1993). He has just completed the manuscript of a two-volume intellectual history of the Old South.

Peter J. Parish is Emeritus Professor of American History, University of London, and is currently Mellon Senior Research Fellow in American History at the University of Cambridge. Author of books on the American Civil War and slavery, he edited *The Reader's Guide to American History* (1997). His current projects include a brief introduction to American history and a study of Abraham Lincoln's historical reputation.

Joy Porter is Senior Lecturer in American History at Anglia Polytechnic University, Cambridge. Her most recent publication is *To Be Indian* (2001). She is currently a Leverhulme Research Fellow and working on a book entitled *Masonic America*.

Melvyn Stokes teaches American history at University College London, where he has been principal organizer of the Commonwealth Fund

Conference on American History since 1989. His co-edited books include *Race and Class in the American South since 1890* (1994), *The Market Revolution in America* (1996), *The U.S. and the European Alliance Since 1945* (1999), *American Movie Audiences* (1999), *Identifying Hollywood's Audiences* (1999), and *Hollywood Spectatorship* (2001). He is currently writing a book on D. W. Griffith's *The Birth of a Nation*.

Michael Tadman is Senior Lecturer in History at the University of Liverpool. His publications include *Speculators and Slaves: Masters, Traders, and Slaves in the Old South* (1989, expanded 1996), a new edition of Frederic Bancroft's 1930s classic *Slave Trading in the Old South* (1996), and articles on slavery and the South in journals including the *American Historical Review*. He is at present working on a book on masters and slaves in the antebellum South.

David Turley is Professor of History at the University of Kent and Head of the School of History. His research and publications have been in the history of antislavery, slavery and emancipation as well as transatlantic reform. *American Religion* (1998) and *Slavery* (2000) have recently appeared. He is now completing a study of *Slave Emancipations and After* and researching a longer-term study of the development of African American social science in relation to the development of an African American intellectual class.

Introduction
Melvyn Stokes

U.S. history today reflects the social, cultural, and intellectual transformations of the past few decades. It has moved away from its traditional focus on the centers of political, economic, and social power and the doings of elite white men towards a new attempt at telling the history of groups (racial, ethnic, gendered, occupational, and class) who had until recently been largely ignored or misinterpreted. While historians have sought to include those formerly excluded, they have also embraced subject areas – such as popular culture – that were once disregarded or dismissed as trivial. As a consequence, American history itself has become increasingly fragmented while each year sees the publication of a vast amount of new scholarship. It is now virtually impossible for teachers and students at all levels to stay abreast of the latest developments across U.S. history as a whole.[1] This volume is intended to meet the needs of such readers, though it is hoped that it will also appeal to the general reader wishing to know more about the present state of U.S. history.

The last half of the twentieth century saw a number of surveys of this kind. Some initially arose from the attempts of scholars who were not Americans to explain the nature of American history to their own national audiences.[2] Often, such works were characterized by a defensive tone: American history was seen as rather new, rather short (at least in chronological terms), and rather simple (a fairly straightforward progression from early settlement to world power). A similar note of defensiveness was evident in John Higham's introduction to *The Reconstruction of American History* (1962), a collection of stocktaking essays by American scholars. Higham referred to "a fairly common view, particularly among European intellectuals, that American history is not very interesting and the achievement of American historians not very important." There was, Higham noted, more to be said for this view "than an American scholar likes to admit."[3]

The years immediately after the appearance of Higham's book, however, were exciting and productive ones in terms of American history. As the consensus paradigm associated with historians such as Louis Hartz and Richard Hofstadter broke down, many new studies – and new types of history – appeared. At the suggestion of the late Robert H. Wiebe, the Organization of American Historians devoted its 1969 conference to a general assessment of the existing state of American history. The published version of the conference proceedings demonstrated the growing preoccupation of American scholars with social concerns (education, social welfare, ethnicity), the emergence of new sub-fields (psychohistory and the study of science, technology, and the environment), and the growing salience of the "cliometric revolution."[4]

The changes within the discipline broadened and deepened over the following decade. Under the shadow of contemporary movements and events – the civil rights movement, the war in Vietnam, the Watergate scandal – and often influenced by the outlook of the *Annales* school of historians in France and the work of British social historians, notably E. P. Thompson and Eric Hobsbawm, American history was increasingly written "from the bottom up." Aided in some cases by techniques of quantification, themselves encouraged by the growing use of computers, scholars endeavored to shed light on the lives of "ordinary people." Much of this new work focused on women, African Americans, Indians, ethnic groups, or workers. Eclectic in its borrowing of methodologies from other social sciences, often informed by a restored-to-favor Marxism, and increasingly turning its back on politics in favor of more "private" spheres of human experience (family, recreation, housing, education, and work), this new scholarship played a part in creating within the American historical profession what Michael Kammen, in a survey published in 1980, hailed as "the most creative ferment of its entire lifetime."[5]

Following the collection of essays edited by Kammen (only part of which was principally concerned with American history), the 1980s saw only one major attempt by American historians to assess the state of their field. In 1982, to commemorate its tenth anniversary, *Reviews in American History* published a special issue devoted to twenty historiographical essays. That issue represented a reasonably comprehensive guide to many of the new fields – and new solutions to old problems – that were then emerging in American history.[6] Several of the essays it contained were to provide an essential basis for future work in their fields. Some predicted with fair accuracy the direction that work would take. Yet, in several cases, authors also expressed disappointment with the effect their field or sub-discipline had had in changing American history as a whole: Elaine Tyler May, for example, commented that, despite the wealth of new scholarship on women's history, the narrative of American history to be found in most textbooks paid little consideration either to gender issues or to women themselves.[7]

By the time another survey was published, eight years later, the situation May had deplored was changing rapidly. In *The New American History* (1990), edited by Eric Foner, Linda Gordon argued that not only was women's history the most productive field in American history, but that it was also helping to revise and reconceptualize other areas of history as well.[8] Foner's book as a whole was made up of thirteen chapters covering a mixture of periods and fields (a second edition in 1997 added three new fields[9]). It did an excellent job of covering these, but it did not attempt to offer a comprehensive review of the state of U.S. history.

The need for a review of this kind seemed increasingly clear as the twentieth century came to an end. In the last years of the century, many new tendencies were becoming evident in the writing of American history. Six of these seem especially significant. The first, already mentioned, was the rapid expansion and transforming influence of the history of women and gender. The second, which became clear for the first time in the 1980s, was the increasing salience of "cultural history." Using approaches and insights from a variety of sources (from the Frankfurt School to postmodern thinkers) and disciplines (including anthropology, semiotics, and literary theory), historians endeavored to study cultural phenomena as texts. At its most elementary level, this merely privileged popular culture over more elitist subjects. Scholars could now write seriously about the history of dime novels, pop music, vaudeville theater, or movies. A growing number of historians, however, began to see culture in terms of a network of institutions, practices, and representations that constructed different identities (such as those based on race, gender, ethnicity, or class). Since many groups and individuals resisted the identity constructed for them (and the subordination this often implied), culture itself became an analyzable site of struggle and contestation.

Closely related to the rise of cultural history was the third trend: the so-called "linguistic turn." As history became more and more concerned with the exploration of how meanings were produced and transmitted, the attention of historians was increasingly drawn to questions of language. Part of this new emphasis also derived from the work of French poststructuralist thinkers, notably Michel Foucault and Jacques Derrida. Foucault perceived language not so much as a reflection of reality but as constitutive of many different realities, each embodied in a particular discourse. Discourses, he argued, are themselves implicated in power relations: the manner in which they are constructed creates patterns of domination and subjection. Discourses, moreover, are unstable: they shift and change in ways that are often abrupt, arbitrary, and distinguished by unforeseen and paradoxical consequences. Derrida also highlighted the instability of linguistically-constructed meanings. There could be no final or authoritative interpretation of a text, he maintained, since texts all contain hidden contradictions that undermine their coherence. Derrida himself advocated a process of "deconstructing" texts, focusing on their marginalia, side-issues, inconsistencies, and key omissions in order to reveal both how language systems are constructed and the ways in which they contribute to the maintenance of patterns of domination. The stress placed by Foucault, Derrida, and other poststructuralist thinkers on the slipperiness of language as a conveyor of meaning, together with their distrust of all grand totalizing theories, also contributed to the fourth trend in recent American historical writing: the declining appeal of Marxist class-based interpretations of the past (a tendency further encouraged by the collapse of communism in eastern Europe and the former Soviet Union).

The fifth trend was the increasing attention paid to American regions, the West in particular. The sixth was the growing effort to see American history in comparative or internationalist perspective. On the face of it, these last two trends pulled in opposite directions: one directing new attention to American provincialism, the other recognizing that – in a world of transnational organizations and globalization – the claim that American national history was somehow distinctive and different had become far harder to sustain.[10] Yet, as Patricia Limerick notes later in this book, the "New Western History" – with its emphasis on environ-mentalism and the complex, multi-racial nature of society in the West – fits well with attempts to understand "frontier" or colonial societies in other parts of the world.

Some, at least, of these changes were addressed in two works appearing in the later half of the 1990s. In March 1998, *Reviews in American History* published fifteen historiographical essays.[11] In contrast to its 1982 predecessor, this issue was less comprehensive in coverage (a tendency increased by the attempt to cover a wide chronological range, with three chapters devoted mainly to colonial history) and, while most authors were conscious of the growing trend to internationalize American history, only two chapters came from contributors working outside the United States. Internationalization itself provided the main stimulus for the publication, also in 1998, of *Imagined Histories*, a collection of essays edited by Anthony Molho and Gordon S. Wood.[12] The principal aim of their book was to shed light on the ways in which American historians have presented their own past and that of other peoples in the last three or four scholarly generations. It rested squarely on the assumption that there *had* been a distinctive "American" approach to writing history. Consequently, all nineteen chapters of the book were by American scholars, though little more than a third were primarily concerned with American history itself. Underpinning the book also, however, was the conviction that, with the rapid decline during the last years of the twentieth century in belief in American exceptionalism, such a distinctive approach to historical scholarship was in the process of disappearance. *Imagined Histories*, therefore, had something of an elegiac tone: as Molho and Wood themselves observed, it could be "seen as a kind of requiem to an older provincial tradition of American historical writing."[13]

This volume, in contrast to the Molho and Wood collection, is an international (or at least a transatlantic) endeavor. Six of the chapters are by historians who teach at American universities; the remaining thirteen are by scholars who work in Britain (twelve of whom are British and one American). Yet, while all the contributors to this book are sympathetic to the movement to internationalize American history, and appreciate the insights conferred by viewing the American past in comparative or transnational perspective, the book itself consists in the main of essays analyzing issues and events relating to the American national experience. In an age of globalization, when some doubt whether "national" history is still an intellectually justifiable endeavor, the essays in this volume draw attention to the current vitality (and productiveness) of scholarly work addressing distinctly "American" themes. The book as a whole is devoted to the examination of "U.S." history and makes no apologies for this approach. (Perhaps, in the intellectual climate of today, insistence on the significance of certain themes and periods in domestic American history comes more convincingly in a work in which the majority of contributors are not American themselves, and therefore cannot be dismissed as mere parochial nationalists).

Because it is principally concerned with American history in the national period, colonial history as a separate field is not discussed in this volume (though Simon Newman, James T. Kloppenberg, Robert A. Gross, and Michael Tadman all mention aspects of colonial history of relevance to their chapters).[14] The book itself is divided into four parts: the first deals with themes and periods, from the American Revolution through the New Deal to the civil rights movement; the second is concerned with analyzing the state of a number of fields and sub-disciplines, including intellectual history, the history of women and gender, and aspects of popular culture; the third assesses the regional history of the West and South; the fourth analyzes some crucial problems and perspectives in U.S. history. Obviously, no single book of this kind could ever offer a completely comprehensive guide to all the current fields and specializations in U.S. history. Yet the present volume, it is hoped, will be seen to explore the state of historical scholarship in many crucial fields and to summarize a range of current debates.

The contributors to this volume were requested to assess the current state of their respective field or subject, to explain how that state was arrived at, and to indicate if possible likely areas for future investigation. Otherwise, as scholars who have themselves taken part – and continue to take part – in the rewriting of American history, they were free to advance their own views and to approach their subject in whatever way they deemed most appropriate. Some have opted to analyze the history of their field as a whole; others have preferred to concentrate their attention only on works published in recent years. All the chapters were first presented as papers, and discussed by a large, international group of scholars, at a Commonwealth Fund Conference held in London, England. They were later revised in the light of conference discussions, comments from colleagues not present at the conference, and subsequently published work in their respective fields.

Part I of this book is concerned with particular themes and periods in U.S. history. The first four chapters cover eighteenth- and/or nineteenth-century topics. Recent work on the American Revolution, according to Simon P. Newman, has emphasized its diversity. Earlier accounts, while usually disagreeing over the Revolution's causes, character, and consequences, had done so within the same broad conceptual framework. Modern scholars, however, looking through the prisms of class, race, and gender, have uncovered not just one revolution but many. The society of late eighteenth-century British North America now appears very complex and fragmented, with the Revolution itself little more than an umbrella beneath which a vast variety of local social and political conflicts played themselves out. Historians of the Revolution, Newman argues, even if they retain the political narrative centering on the birth of the American republic, must accept that the extraordinarily diverse society and culture of the time affected the Revolution at least as much as the Revolution itself affected them.

In terms of social and economic history, Christopher Clark comments, recent scholarship has largely redrawn our understanding of how change happened in American society between the Revolution and Reconstruction. Work in five main areas, he contends, has contributed to this revisionism. It is now clear, from research on the growing inequality of American society between the 1770s and the 1860s, that economic growth was to some extent driven by patterns of social exclusion and the maldistribution of wealth. Many economic changes after the Revolution were also heavily influenced by the progressive commodification of land. Relationships within households – including the economic contribution made by women – had a profound effect in shaping early American society and the processes of change emerging from it. Social networks, including kinship ties, that bound people together played a major role in shaping patterns of economic development, including Western settlement. Finally, this period saw the emergence of new organizations (such as banks – and freemasonry) that assumed some of the roles in economic support and assistance that had earlier been played by families. While other influences did exist, Clark argues, recent work on social history shows how the interaction of these five factors helped weave the fabric of change that characterized American society between 1780 and 1870.

In his chapter, Daniel Feller suggests that the "Jacksonian" period has lost its place at the center of the conventional master narrative of American history. Partly, this arises from the declining influence of that master narrative itself, with its periodization based on politics and concentration on elite white males. But it also reflects the too-frequent invocation, as interpretative tools, of broad concepts (liberalism, capitalism) or grand theory (the "market revolution" thesis). Feller finds two sub-fields, however, in which new scholarship is currently changing perceptions of the Jacksonian era. Gender historians are investigating the role of women as active participants in party politics, and historians of religion are not only establishing what many early nineteenth-century Americans believed, but also tracing the links (encouraged by the contemporary communications revolution) between religion and other social and political movements. Feller suggests that, in order fully to understand the politics of Jacksonian Democrats, it is necessary to view them (as still remains for historians to do) in an international perspective. Once compared to the British reformers from whom they derived much of their inspiration, they seem not so much fearful victims of the market revolution as optimists who, despite the defects of their existing society, believed in a democratic, non-aristocratic future.

Newman and Feller both emphasize, in their chapters, the importance of religion. Mark A. Noll, in his chapter, analyzes the scholarship on religious developments between independence and the Civil War. In the 1780s and 1790s, he observes, religion seems to have undergone a rather confused transition. This was followed by the most dramatic rise in religious adherence of any period of American history, most of it happening in the evangelical Protestant Churches. This evangelical surge has attracted considerable recent attention from scholars, who have variously examined how ordinary people appropriated religion for themselves, the changing meaning of religion for women in different American contexts, the Christianization of African Americans and Native Americans, and the ways in which religion encouraged sectional tensions. Despite such work, Noll argues, scholarly lacunae continue to exist. Moreover, while scholarship on the "surge" has established its importance, it has not yet succeeded in explaining *why* this should have been the case. Relatively little effort, Noll points out, has so far been made to integrate the history of nineteenth-century evangelical religion into the broader national story. In order to accomplish this, he believes, it is now necessary for scholars to investigate how the surge bore upon crucial issues such as economic development, political conflict, national expansion, gender definition, slavery, and war. Another important avenue for future scholarship, he suggests, will be to compare evangelical religion in the U.S. with that in relatively similar North Atlantic societies.

In the first of three chapters on twentieth-century themes, Alan Brinkley draws attention to the underlying stability of scholarly interpretations of the New Deal (William E. Leuchtenburg's synthesis, first published in 1963, is still the book most widely used by college teachers). This longevity, Brinkley argues, can be explained by the fact that Leuchtenburg preempted some left-wing criticisms of the New Deal – and by the relative absence of systematic critiques from left or right. Yet, Brinkley points out, recent scholarship has begun to transform perceptions of the New Deal. Some historians have applied gender considerations to the programs and movements of the time. Others have emphasized the array of limitations on the New Deal, including flawed state structures, 1930s political, social, and economic realities, and the ideological preconceptions of New Dealers themselves. There is increasing attention to the cultural side of the New Deal, to its unforeseen consequences, and to the attempt to see it in international perspective. In future, Brinkley suggests, it is likely that the New Deal will come to be seen both as part of a long-term evolution in bureaucratic structures and as a time when American public policy started to adapt itself to the needs of a society less preoccupied with problems of production than those of consumption.

In terms of interpreting the domestic anticommunist crusade of the 1940s and 1950s, Michael J. Heale observes, there is little agreement among contemporary historians. The initial view of scholars such as Daniel Bell and Richard Hofstadter that McCarthyism had been a populist insurgency against those in authority was succeeded, around 1970, by a different interpretation stressing the responsibility of the political elite. This tendency to see anticommunism as "made in Washington" was encouraged by discoveries under the Freedom of Information Act and revelations, after J. Edgar Hoover's death, concerning the FBI. Other perspectives emerged, however, in the late 1980s and the 1990s. Michael Rogin argued that McCarthyism was not unusual: political repression by white elites was endemic in American culture. Neoconservatives, sometimes aided by new material from U.S. and Soviet archives, contended that legitimate American anticommunism should not be confused with its bastard version, McCarthyism. Other scholars have expressed skepticism over the new evidence or continue to blame those in authority for anticommunist excesses. Heale suggests that more work is required on anticommunism in localities, its relationship both to 1940s liberalism and to later liberalism and conservatism, its gendered and racial aspects, its role as part of a long-established tradition, the ways in which it altered over time, the manner in which it received encouragement from the political system, and how it compared to anticommunism in other countries.

The next chapter, by Adam Fairclough, covers the racial strategies of African Americans in the twentieth century. Those strategies, he maintains, following John W. Cell, could broadly be identified as accommodation, confrontation, and separation. Yet he points out that there were many complexities and interactions between the three. Traditional civil-rights scholarship has presented the time before the mid-1950s as an era of accommodation, followed by a period of protest and confrontation. Recent scholarship, however, has thrown this clear division into doubt. Accommodation is being redefined as a form of resistance, stressing black agency rather than victimhood. Historians, moreover, are increasingly aware that the civil rights movement had its origins in the 1930s and 1940s, with some writers seeing union militancy and the communist party as the direct precursors of the movement (a theory Fairclough discounts) and others, more convincingly, emphasizing the pivotal role of the National Association for the Advancement of Colored People. Separatism of varying kinds is also now attracting considerable scholarly attention, from the analysis of Marcus Garvey and the Universal Negro Improvement Association to efforts at voluntary segregation arising out of the black tradition of self-help. The commitment to integration on the part of the civil rights movement, Fairclough notes, often concealed its organizational base in segregated black institutions. Sometimes, however, especially in the early days of the movement, blacks associated with conservative institutions did not support it. Such complexities in how African Americans viewed the civil rights movement seem likely to become increasingly well-documented, Fairclough suggests, since numbers of scholarly studies are now appearing on the movement's role in local communities.

Part II explores particular scholarly fields. Howell J. Harris's chapter deals with industrial history. He bases his analysis on a survey of articles published in the major journals covering each of the sub-fields of industrial history: business, economic, labor, and technological history. The use of such an approach, he suggests, has major advantages. It is in journals rather than in monographs that the earliest signs of new, research-based developments are likely to appear. Moreover, using periodicals makes it easier to make a quantitative (as well as qualitative) review of literature and draw conclusions based on hard data rather than general impressions. Based on this review, Harris concludes that most industrial history is chronologically limited, concerned for the most part with the classic years of high industrialism from approximately 1880 to 1940, and dealing mainly with the traditional industries of the old industrial belt. Vast areas of the economy, he notes, including the service and distribution sectors, are almost entirely ignored. In terms of the condition of the sub-fields of industrial history, Harris finds labor history in the most parlous state, torn apart by seemingly endless internal disputes and characterized by a falling quality of scholarly output. Technological history, having survived its own cultural wars, has attained methodological consensus, but tends to be sidelined. Economic historians, having absorbed the cliometric revolution of the 1960s and 1970s, now take its methods and approaches for granted, but are frequently concerned that historians in general do not show much interest in their work. Business historians, though themselves interested in a wide range of subjects, at times seem too uncritical of corporate capitalism.

James T. Kloppenberg argues that intellectual history, formerly believed to be in crisis, is now increasingly salient in American history as a whole. In our postmodern culture of irony, intellectual history directs attention to questions of meaning that are now at the center of historical enquiry. Many scholars, even those not thinking of themselves primarily as "intellectual" historians, are emphasizing in their work not merely what happened in the past but also what it meant for those involved. In the process, they are transcending traditional boundaries both within history itself and between history and other disciplines. As a focus for such efforts, Kloppenberg suggests an examination of the theme of democracy in American history, exploring how Americans' theory and practice of democracy have evolved over time. Such an approach, he maintains, would help provide an antidote to the "mindless reductionism" of much contemporary political and cultural debate. It would shed light on the origins of many current difficulties and demonstrate why complex, historically-rooted problems resist simple solutions. Rethinking American history as a single democratic cultural project with multiple dimensions, he believes, can help us understand better why "the American century" ended with a global embrace of the idea of democracy together with a general dissatisfaction in its practice. Moreover, Kloppenberg observes, since the hermeneutic approach of historians privileges critical distance as well as the close reading of texts, placing American intellectual history in general and democracy in particular in a comparative and international-ist framework may well help yield insights on U.S. history unavailable to those who see it only in a narrowly national perspective.

S. Jay Kleinberg, in her essay on women's history and gender, is markedly less optimistic than Kloppenberg regarding recent intellectual developments. Kleinberg identifies three stages in the process of including women in the historical record. The first stage – "contribution history" – concentrated on bringing to light the unheralded achievements of women in political and civic activities. The second stage – "feminist history" – put women's concerns at the center of attention and attempted to recon-struct women's worlds "on their own terms." Reorienting history in this way, Kleinberg notes, fundamentally alters both how we study the past and the nature of history itself. When women's interests and concerns are taken into account, traditional periodizations make little sense: winning the right to vote in 1920, for example, was more important to women generally than World War I (though it took far longer for minority women to be able to exercise that right). There was at first, indeed, a general tendency in feminist historical writing to privilege white, middle-class women. For example, the reigning paradigm for some time in women's history was that of "separate spheres," which initially developed out of the analysis of nineteenth-century didactic literature aimed at a bourgeois audience. It consequently marginalized women who were working-class, colored, or immigrant. Eventually, however, a more inclusive, multi-cultural approach developed. The third stage – gender history – arises in some respects from the "linguistic turn," since it focuses on the use of language to describe/inscribe meaning. Kleinberg appreciates that, by placing gender roles and how they are constructed at the center of their researches into the past, gender historians are effectively overturning key interpretations of that past by demonstrating how sex roles shaped society, politics, and economics. However, she also expresses anxiety that, trapped within a postmodern equivalent of Wittgenstein's inescapable "cage" of language, female agency and the historical specificity of women's experience – grounded on biological difference, influenced by class, race, region and other attributes, socially inflected, and changing over time – may be lost to sight.

Scholarship on popular culture became increasingly productive during the last years of the twentieth century. The next two chapters focus on two aspects of that expanding field. Robert A. Gross, through the medium of contemporary work on print culture, assesses the applicability of the ideas of Jürgen Habermas and Benedict Anderson to early America. For a brief period in eighteenth-century England and France, Habermas argued, the bourgeoisie had succeeded in carving out an autonomous "public sphere" for the rational discussion of public affairs. It was through the institutions of print culture that this public sphere took shape. According to Anderson, print media were crucial to the constitution of the modern world: through reading, people identified themselves as members of the "imagined communities" we call nations. Gross, however, maintains that the American press did not fulfill the principal requirements of Habermas's model during the early years of the republic. Newspapers rarely attempted to be impartial or make rational contributions to political discourse by analyzing all sides of disputes. Many, for financial reasons, became party organs: the imagined community they sought to create was one of party, not nation. Other print institutions (pamphlets, books) may have been closer in the late eighteenth century to shaping a public sphere characterized by openness and reasoned debate, but by the early nineteenth century they were starting to abandon such republican ideals for the more materialistic rewards of the literary marketplace. In any case, Gross argues, in the many small, face-to-face communities that characterized the early United States, print was simply too limited in its effects on daily life to be able to perform the specialized role of constituting an independent public sphere.

In my own chapter of this book, I discuss the growth of film history. There was very little scholarly history of this kind until comparatively recently. By the 1970s, however, the rapid expansion in cinema studies had created a demand for it. Aided by the discovery or increasing availability of archival materials, film history as a discipline was born. Yet it was constrained for several years by the fact that most of those drawn to cinema studies came from disciplines other than history, and their primary interest was in studying films as texts. For at least a decade after 1975, most academic debate concerning film concentrated on structuralist, psychoanalytical, and feminist explorations of how a theoretical spectatorship was positioned by the filmic text. Beginning around 1985, however, a new scholarship began to appear based on the premise that film texts could better be understood through the analysis of the particular circumstances (legal, economic, and political, as well as aesthetic) that governed their production. The last few years of the twentieth century also witnessed growing interest in how films were received. This expressed itself in two main sub-fields: first, "historical reception studies," which explore the interpretative strategies adopted by film critics and others in relation to individual films or groups of films; second, audiences studies, which have tried to investigate how audiences of the past responded to movies. In both cases, modern scholarship is shedding increasing light on the social and cultural history of movie-going.

Part III of this volume is concerned with the history of regions. During the 1970s and early 1980s, Patricia Nelson Limerick remarks, Western history was considered dead. At the end of the 1980s, however, it was resurrected as the "New Western History." Scholars associated with the new approach no longer assumed that the West lost its distinctiveness when the Turnerian frontier "closed" in 1890. They studied the twentieth century as well as the nineteenth, and noted many continuities between the two. The traditional history of the West concentrated on the doings of white people, especially men; the new history saw the region as one of the world's great racial and ethnic meeting-places. What Turnerians, moreover, regarded as a story of white settlement ("the frontier"), New Western historians have redefined in terms of conquest. The hallmark of the New Western history, Limerick maintains, is complexity. Inter-ethnic encounters were often far from simple (with black troops, for example, used in Indian wars and against Mexican-Americans). The tasks of constructing racial identities, classifying groups, and determining hierarchies, she contends, were often difficult and complicated. Under the influence of the New Western history, environmental history has evolved from an original concern with what white men did to protect the environment into a far more complicated study of the interrelations between places and all the people who have interacted with them. Increasingly, also, Limerick observes, historians are placing Western history in a global context of colonialism and imperialism, comparing U.S. methods of acquiring territory and treating native peoples to those of other nations.

Southern history, according to Michael O'Brien, has been influenced by the same trends as the rest of American history, though there have been local differences.[15] Historians of women, for example, expecting to uncover a female anti-racist tradition in the South, often find themselves dealing with conservative Southern women. In consequence, many face a crisis of purpose and their work is often marginalized within American women's history. The relationship of Southern history with African American history is also problematic. Black history, once a sub-set of Southern history, later became mainly preoccupied with blacks *outside* the South. Yet this in itself highlights a key issue of identification: since the South has no legally fixed boundaries, to be a Southerner means to be part of an invented tradition. Is, O'Brien asks, a black Mississippian living in Detroit a Southerner? In terms of the three most salient periods of Southern history, he finds a mixture of innovation and conservatism in recent work. First, antebellum studies have tentatively broken free of the model advanced by Eugene Genovese, in the main because attention has shifted away from the normative plantation. New scholarship, especially by younger historians, often foregrounds the fluid, multiple, and contingent nature of the Old South. Second, studies of the period between Reconstruction and World War I, despite the work of Edward Ayers, still revolve for the most part around the interpretation first advanced by C. Vann Woodward in the 1950s. Finally, O'Brien argues, the abundant scholarship on the civil rights movement has so far largely failed to break free from the partisan perspectives aroused by the movement itself.

Part IV of the book discusses a number of problems and perspectives concerning U.S. history. Michael Tadman's chapter is concerned with racism and ideology in the antebellum slave South. In particular, it examines how whites historically have constructed blacks. Scholars have disagreed over the point at which an explicitly racialized slavery emerged. Tadman contends that, since it was in the interest of owners to see blacks as suitable for enslavement, slaveholding society adopted a biological racism (the notion that blacks were innately inferior) with the arrival of the first African Americans in the colonies. Examining Eugene D. Genovese's thesis on the "web of paternalism" binding masters to slaves, Tadman finds the commitment of slaveowners to the notion of the family "white and black" to be considerably less firm than Genovese did. Most slaves, he believes, aware of the propensity of masters to break up black families by sale, probably rejected the idea of such paternalism. The existence of a number of "key slaves," however, according to Tadman, allowed the master to act (and think of himself) as generous and paternalistic, while treating other slaves badly or indifferently. Evaluating George M. Frederickson's "herrenvolk democracy" thesis – that the shared idea of being members of a "master race" encouraged all whites, poor as well as rich, to support planters and the system of slavery – Tadman cites recent work suggesting that the motivations of non-planter whites were more complex and also that there was more contact at the grass roots between poor whites and blacks (and possibly less racism) than the thesis allows.

Introduction

Joy Porter, exploring the ways in which historians have represented Native Americans, notes the remarkable persistence of stereotype and misunderstanding. Race itself, she argues in much the same way as Limerick and Tadman, was a European concept developed to rationalize the conquest or subjugation of particular populations. The treatment of Native Americans by historians, at least until the watershed years of the late 1960s and early 1970s, reflected – from the deployment of the term "Indian" to the assumption that such history could only be written on the basis of (non-Indian) written records – such European or Euro-American perceptions of race. Over the last three decades of the twentieth century, however, there was a significant shift in the scope, methodology, and perspective of scholarship on Native American history. Instead of Indians being dismissed as marginal "exotics," scholars began to look at the complexities of Indian-white relationships over time. Yet, Porter observes, there are still problems with this revisionism. It is chronologically unbalanced: Indian history in the twentieth century has still to receive its share of attention. Mainly white feminist scholars find it hard to deal sympathetically with Indian women, whom they often see as excessively domestic. Above all, perhaps, non-Native Americans have difficulty understanding the Indian view of history itself. Indians themselves tend to venerate their oral traditions far more than written records and privilege stories and cultural symbols over supposedly impartial "scientific" facts – which, Porter suggests, explains why most Indian writers prefer to produce novels and poetry, instead of history. Indeed, over those last three decades of the twentieth century, she points out, literary studies managed to assimilate Native American insights and perspectives. Historians, she maintains, could learn much from this precedent, and from two other fairly recent intellectual developments: the growing realization, by many museum specialists, of the limited ways in which museums had represented Native Americans and the emergence of World History, with its transnational standpoint and growing concern for peoples who recall their past in ways antithetical to conventional Western history.

Whereas gender and race are crucial considerations for contemporary historians of the United States, class – the third member of what, until the 1990s, at times appeared an inevitable trinity – has recently fallen from favor. As John Ashworth notes, Marxism, with its emphasis on the primacy of class in interpreting the past, has always faced particular problems in the United States, with its reputation for social mobility and dominant ideology centered on classlessness. Despite this, Marxist interpretations flourished in two periods: in the 1930s and later in the 1970s and 1980s. By the 1990s, however, Marxism as an interpretative tool was in sharp decline. Ashworth outlines some of the reasons for this: intellectual challenges from poststructuralism and feminism, the booming American economy, the collapse of communism in eastern Europe, and the disintegration of the Soviet Union. But it may also have been aided by the limited way in which American Marxists have traditionally understood the phenomenon of class. They have seen it either as a means of referring to an economic interest group or as synonymous with class-consciousness. Both these views, Ashworth argues, while helpful for the study of certain social groups at certain times, are not sufficient, either separately or in combination, to support the view that class should be a major – perhaps *the* major – factor in interpreting American history. For this to happen requires the adoption of a more structural view of class rooted in two specific assumptions: that the economy is of primary significance in determining the development of society (including its politics and belief systems) and that relations between classes at the point of production are of primary importance in determining its economic structure. To exemplify his thesis, Ashworth advances an interpretation of the origins of the Civil War in which primacy is given to class and the economy.

Peter J. Parish, reviewing contemporary scholarship, sees the coverage of the Civil War as uneven and compartmentalized. To link together a number of areas of current interest – work on the ordinary soldier, on the larger cities during the war, and on the responses to the war of various parts of the population – he proposes a common theme: an examination of how Northern civilian morale was preserved throughout the conflict. Without the strength and resilience of the bonds that bound localities to the nation, he argues, the North could not have won. That strength and resilience showed itself in the recruitment of large civilian armies, in the network of voluntary bodies sustaining life at community level, and in the constant propaganda campaign in support of the cause. The absence of such institutional support in the South meant that, under the pressures of the later stages of the war, ties between locality and nation shattered. Moreover, Parish contends, exploring themes of localism as nationalism and private activism for public purposes not only helps explain why the North won and the South lost: it encourages historians to regard the Civil War not simply as an exceptional event, to be "read out" of normal history, but as an episode that sheds considerable light on nineteenth-century American society and culture.

David Turley similarly approaches the topic of Reconstruction historiography through a unifying theme, in this case the role of African Americans. Black scholar W. E. B. DuBois, he notes, focused his 1935 book on the initiative shown by African Americans during the Reconstruction period. According to DuBois, slavery really came to an end (and a Northern victory became certain) when slaves abandoned their masters. After the success of this "general strike," DuBois contended, blacks began to cultivate liberated land in the way they preferred, demonstrating in the process a considerable capacity for self-government and economic self-management. Ultimately, however, the aspirations of blacks were blocked by the fact that they were positioned by landlords and employers in opposition to white labor. Later scholarly work on Reconstruction, from that inspired by the Freedmen and Southern Society Project to Eric Foner, has based itself on DuBois's assumption of black initiative and agency. Yet, as Turley shows, it has also revised DuBois's account in important respects. Recent scholarship has shown how slavery was succeeded by a diverse array of labor systems with many local variations. While little hint of the complexities of rural economic change emerged in DuBois's book, Turley comments that, in its discussion of the relationship between black and white labor, it opened the door to later work on social relations beyond those of blacks with their former masters, as well as comparisons with other post-emancipation societies.

The idea that there is such a thing as "U.S." history – the history of the American nation – has been undermined in recent years from several directions. Scholarship has investigated the nature and outlook of almost innumerable groups, and what were once perceived as "national" events and movements often appear very different when seen through the prisms of gender, race, ethnicity, sexual orientation, or locality. Influenced by poststructuralist assumptions, moreover, historians have chosen to ignore what could be seen as "mainstream" people and phenomena in order to concentrate attention on the marginal, the aberrant, and the transgressive. Other scholars have questioned the uniqueness (and significance) of U.S. history in an increasingly globalized environment – one in which finance and business, culture, and population movements all transcend national borders and the nation-state itself has started to seem in some respects outmoded. What the nineteen chapters in this book suggest, I believe, is that U.S. history – albeit a much more fluid and inclusive form of that history – is still a vibrant and productive area for scholarly investigation at the beginning of a new century. While assimilating fresh assumptions – including the conviction that perceiving American history in comparative or transnational perspective can contribute to many new insights – it remains an important, active, and, as always, highly contentious subject.

Notes

1. The June 2000 issue of the *Journal of American History*, for example, published reviews of 164 books and had a listing of "Recent Scholarship" extended to 63 pages under 43 different headings.
2. See for example H. Hale Bellot, *American History and American Historians: A Review of Recent Contributions to the Interpretation of the History of the United States* (London, 1952).
3. John Higham, "The Construction of American History," in Higham, ed., *The Reconstruction of American History* (London, 1962), p. 9.
4. Herbert J. Bass, ed., *The State of American History* (Chicago, 1970).
5. Michael Kammen, "Introduction: The Historian's Vocation and the State of the Discipline in the United States," in Kammen, ed., *The Past Before Us: Contemporary Historical Writing in the United States* (Ithaca, NY, 1980), p. 22.
6. Stanley I. Kutler and Stanley N. Katz, eds., *The Promise of American History: Progress and Prospects*, *Reviews in American History*, 10, no. 4 (December 1982).
7. Elaine Tyler May, "Expanding the Past: Recent Scholarship on Women in Politics and Work," in *Promise of American History*, p. 228.
8. Linda Gordon, "U.S. Women's History," in Eric Foner, ed., *The New American History* (Philadelphia, 1990), pp. 185–6.
9. Eric Foner, ed., *The New American History*, revised ed. (Philadelphia, 1997).
10. In 1992, *The Journal of American History* committed itself to the development of a more internationalist perspective on American history. See David Thelen's editorial, "Of Audiences, Borderlands, and Comparisons: Toward the Internationalization of American History," *The Journal of American History*, 79 (1992): 432–59. Also see the later special edition on the analysis and usefulness of "transnational" perspectives: *The Journal of American History*, 86 (December 1999).
11. The issue was later republished as a book. See Louis P. Masur, ed., *The Challenge of American History* (Baltimore, 1999).
12. Anthony Molho and Gordon S. Wood, eds., *Imagined Histories: American Historians Interpret The Past* (Princeton, 1998).
13. Molho and Wood, *Imagined Histories*, p. 17.
14. Since the main focus of the book, moreover, is on domestic U.S. history, foreign policy and international relations are not covered. For good summaries of scholarship on American foreign policy, see

Michael J. Hogan, ed., *Paths to Power: The Historiography of American Foreign Relations to 1941* (Cambridge, UK, 2000); idem, ed., *America in the World: The Historiography of American Foreign Relations since 1941* (Cambridge, UK, 1995).

15. For Southern history in international perspective, see Michael O'Brien, "The South in the World," *Southern Cultures*, 4 (Winter 1998): 1–83.

Part I
Themes and Periods

–1–

Writing the History of the
American Revolution

Simon P. Newman

In recent decades, the historiography of the American Revolution has flourished as never before. Each year sees the publication of many new articles, dissertations, and monographs. This process is both exhilarating and daunting. A generation ago, historians could keep abreast of a field producing a manageable scholarly output, but today's scholars of the Revolutionary period confront a bewildering variety of works addressing discrete areas, subjects, and approaches from a widely different array of methodological perspectives.[1]

In their own way, moreover, historians of the American Revolution have found that they are not immune to the stresses of contemporary life. The sense of fragmentation and dislocation in our modern world is shared by Revolutionary historians who, confronted by the incredible diversity of the lived experiences of late eighteenth-century Americans, are finding it ever more difficult to locate coherence, unity, and indeed sense within the American Revolution. The result is a wonderful richness and diversity in histories of revolutionary America, which is often, however, as dauntingly confusing as it is enlightening.[2] In reaction against a resulting sense of chaos, a distinct narrowing of focus – both in subject matter and in critical approach – defines the best recent Revolutionary historiography, and synthesis and coherent interpretations that bring order to our understanding of the Revolution appear ever more elusive.

At the beginning of the new millennium, the field resembles an enormous jigsaw puzzle, comprising an ever-growing number of pieces. Portions of the puzzle clearly belong together, fitting neatly and logically, and giving glimpses of a larger picture, but actually bringing together these clusters and the many smaller pieces that surround them is a Herculean task. Thus, although Revolutionary historiography is more lively and productive than ever before, its fractured nature defies comprehensive analyses that can accommodate a vast and often contradictory scholarship. This is perhaps best reflected by Linda Kerber's reliance upon fourteen headings and subheadings in her attempt to bring order to late twentieth-century Revolutionary historiography, employing such categories as "Republicanism," "Patriarchy," "Slavery," "Political Mobilization" and "Indian Relations."[3]

Gordon Wood's *The Radicalism of the American Revolution* (1992) represents the sole comprehensive explanatory overview of the Revolution produced in the last decade of the twentieth century. But Wood achieved synthesis only by ignoring much of the enormous diversity of belief, experience, and action in revolutionary America. His is a book in which great ideas and political movements loom large, but in whose pages it is hard to find people: the different experiences and objectives of women, African Americans, Native Americans, and rural and working Americans are largely absent from his pages.[4] Wood's argument that the War for Independence constituted a great and transformative social revolution ignores many of the actual participants, thus failing to acknowledge that late eighteenth-century America was home to many different groups and was a society awash with unresolved social conflict and dislocation.

With the apparent failure of synthesis, understanding the American Revolution has become increasingly difficult. Yet it is possible to make sense of the Revolution, and in the process learn something about America in the late twentieth and early twenty-first centuries. Each generation of Americans has approached and interpreted the history of the nation's founding from a unique perspective, with historians bringing the values and ideas of their era to the task of comprehending the birth of the United States. The same is true today. At the dawn of the twenty-first century, Americans are increasingly aware of the extraordinary diversity that characterizes their nation. While some celebrate this diversity, others find it confusing and even frightening. Yet an awareness of the nature of modern multicultural America offers us a unique vantage point from which to make sense of the American Revolution in ways that have eluded previous historians.

During the almost two-and-one-half centuries that have passed since American colonists began resistance and rebellion against British imperial rule, historians have struggled to come to terms with the conflict. Their narratives of the key actions and events have changed relatively little, and the chronology of Sugar Act, Stamp Act, Townshend Acts, Boston Massacre, Tea Act, Coercive Acts and so forth remains as familiar to the student of today as it was to the Patriot and Loyalist historians of the late eighteenth century.[5] Moreover, the same broad, conceptual questions have echoed through their works: why did the western world's least-taxed people revolt against a small increase in taxes? Was their revolution a radical or conservative event? How and when did such diverse colonies and discrete regions, long used to self-governance, cohere into a new nation?[6]

The change, of course, has been in the ways successive generations of historians have answered these questions and interpreted the American Revolution. While their accounts have focused upon much the same chronology of events, their interpretations of the Revolution have changed significantly. At the same time, for all of their diverse and distinct views, Revolutionary historians have founded their work upon familiar methodological imperatives and conceptual frameworks.[7] Only in the last generation of the twentieth century did the chaotic splintering of revolutionary historiography undermine these familiar frameworks.

The first historians of the Revolutionary era were the people who lived through the resistance against imperial policy, the War for Independence, and the construction of state and national republican governments. What is most striking about these early histories is the sense of surprise and awe with which the Whigs or Patriots regarded the history and results of their own actions. Mercy Otis Warren's magisterial *History of the Rise, Progress, and Termination of the American Revolution* (1805) was typical of these early accounts.[8] Like other members of the generation that lived through the 1760s and 1770s, Warren understood that the colonists had been proud and prosperous subjects of the British Empire. She believed that rebellion would not have occurred had the British government acted differently. Warren and the Patriots believed that their reactions against imperial policies were fueled by a fully justified desire to protect civil liberties and political freedoms.

The resulting histories embedded contingency theory within a moralistic context: contingency, in the belief that neither the Revolution nor its outcome was predictable, and moralistic in the explanations of why Americans fought, and how their leaders embodied these virtues. Thus, Warren included "Biographical, Political and Moral Observations" in the title of her history, and she argued that the Patriots, raised in an atmosphere of liberty, had engaged in a noble cause that might easily have been lost. Consequently, the betrayal by Benedict Arnold appeared particularly reprehensible, the sacrifices and achievements of men such as General Warren all the more heroic. Mason Weem's adulatory life of George Washington, based on sentimental half-truths, nonetheless tells us much about the ways these early histories embodied the hard-won success of liberty and republicanism in the noble lives of great Patriot leaders.[9] The Patriots' Whig interpretation of the Revolution as a great and good event was the first and indeed the most powerful and enduring interpretative model.

The generation that had lived through the Revolution was succeeded by the romantic historians of the early to mid-nineteenth century. Most were Yankees and, as sectionalism permeated the expanding republic, so too it colored their histories of a New England-centered War for Independence. George Bancroft, for example, was Massachusetts-born and Harvard-educated. For Bancroft, the driving force of the Revolution was what might be termed providential nationalism, a somewhat secularized version of the Puritan New Englanders' image of themselves as God's chosen people.[10]

During the nineteenth century, the United States and its people and economy expanded at a phenomenal rate, from a set of comparatively minor colonial outposts to a major world power. Many Americans accepted that it was the Manifest Destiny of the nation to enjoy such unrivaled growth and success, evidence of the divine blessing and mission of the United States. God had ordained the creation of this nation, Bancroft insisted, and it was to become the greatest and best the world had ever seen. Historians like Bancroft, therefore, kept alive the moralism of earlier writers such as Warren, but replaced their theories of contingency with a strong sense of providence and destiny.

The Civil War and the horrors of the Gilded Age sobered the people of the United States, not least their historians. As they took stock of hundreds of thousands of dead and maimed men, robber barons, immigrant ghettos, growing economic inequality, endemic political corruption, and the nation's first imperialist war, increasingly jaded historians were forced to admit that the United States was neither as great nor as good as prior generations had believed. Albion W. Small, for example, claimed that the Revolution did nothing more than create one new nation in the world. Only in the century that followed, Small argued, was American national identity slowly formed, most significantly in the bloody crucible of the Civil War. In short, Small argued, the United States was far from perfect when it was created and decades of growth and struggle were necessary to mould it into a strong and complete nation.[11] The moral certainties of the Patriots, and their pride in civic virtues and noble leaders, all but disappeared from histories of the Revolution, while contingency reappeared.

During the latter years of the nineteenth century, Johns Hopkins, Harvard, Wisconsin, and a succession of other universities began training the nation's first professional historians. This allowed the development of several competing schools of thought, including a continuing New

England-centered interpretation under Edward Channing.[12] A rival Southern School, championed by Thomas Jefferson Wertenbaker, began emphasizing the importance of the political culture of the Southern colonies, most especially Virginia, in the Revolution.[13] Increasing historical professionalization also encouraged the development of the Imperial and Progressive schools. As a leading luminary of the Imperial School, Charles Andrews took contemporary criticisms of the horrors of American society to an extreme: surveying the America he inhabited, he saw little or no evidence of moral supremacy, and thus concluded that it was futile to look for a special and unique creative process for the United States.[14] Andrews, Herbert Osgood, and others in the Imperial School were impressed, however, by what they saw as the very real achievements of the British Empire, then at its height.[15] Convinced by imperialist apologists who presented Britain as the world's greatest agent of civilization, and by Alfred Thayer Mahan and his American supporters, who proposed an imperial role for the United States, Andrews wrote the history of colonial and revolutionary America from the perspective of the British Empire.[16] His approach was very formalistic and legalistic, leaving little scope for social theory. The works of the Imperial School brilliantly explained and justified the British position, thus rendering the Revolution fairly inexplicable. In their insistence that the American Revolution could be understood only in the context of a larger Atlantic World, however, they propounded an interpretive model that has become increasingly salient in recent years.

The Progressive historians, like the group of reformers and the political party of the same name and era, emphasized social and class issues. Charles Beard claimed that the Revolution began as a conflict between colonial and British elites, and then evolved into a struggle between the American elite and the American people as a whole. Beard's *An Economic Interpretation of the Constitution* (1913) argued that the Constitution was a conservative document, written by a property-owning elite, to forestall social and political radicalism by forming a strong national government to protect their interests.[17] This somewhat simplistic interpretation, in which the Founders were motivated – if not driven – by no more than their immediate economic interests, was nevertheless tremendously powerful. Beard's vision of a financial elite pulling the political strings in late eighteenth-century America must have resonated with many of his contemporaries. The Progressive reformers of Beard's generation took on a similarly self-interested group of industrial magnates and tycoons, claiming that they manipulated the political process in pursuit of their own goals.

While Beard saw the revolutionary settlement as an attempt to end radicalism, Wisconsin's Carl Becker substituted a half-empty glass for one half-filled. In books on the Declaration of Independence and political parties in revolutionary New York, Becker agreed with Beard that the Revolution had begun as a struggle between colonial and British elites, but maintained that this imperial struggle had prompted an unexpected social revolution in America. Becker posited a Revolution that was comprised both of a "contest for home rule and independence, and . . . of who should rule at home."[18] John Franklin Jameson agreed with Beard and Becker that the social and political processes of resistance and revolution had opened a Pandora's Box of popular radicalism that could never again be closed.[19] Premised upon an acknowledgement of the existence and significance of class and economic differences within Revolutionary American society, the Progressive analysis added a third interpretative model to Revolutionary historiography.

The Imperial and the Progressive Schools dominated the writing and teaching of the American Revolution through the early twentieth century. Not surprisingly, however, the social, economic, and political transformations brought about by the Wall Street Crash, the New Deal, the end of the Depression, World War II, and the rise of the United States to world leadership combined to have a profound and lasting effect on historical thinking about the Revolution. Ever since the Civil War, many historians had been ashamed of aspects of their national past and present, seeing poverty, oppression, inequality, and injustice as betraying the ideals of the Revolution. During the mid-twentieth century, historians contemplated an America that had defeated German and Japanese racist imperialism, an America that had made a commitment in the New Deal to end poverty and want, and an America that was home to a nascent civil rights movement committed to equality for black Americans. With the start of the Cold War, and America's leadership of what became know as the "free world," it became imperative to understand American roots and principles, to make it possible adequately to define what America represented when defined against a Communist state that promised equality for all of humankind. Much of the energy of these scholars was devoted to defending America and its past against the threat of communism, and their histories highlighted an American past virtually free of class or racial conflict.

In many ways, this "consensus" history marked a return to the Patriots' Whig model of Revolutionary history. The Neo-Whigs of post-World War II America agreed with Thomas Paine, John Adams, Thomas Jefferson, and others that the Revolution had defended freedom against oppression, and that the nation it produced was forged in a crucible of liberty and equality. Led by Edmund S. Morgan, especially in *The Birth of the American Republic* (1956), the Neo-Whigs produced histories that celebrated the colonists for taking clear and consistent stands against Britain, and then employing the ideological foundations of this stand in their creation of the republic.[20] The studied self-interest and propaganda found by the Progressives and the Imperial School's focus on the Empire were rejected by Neo-Whigs, who found moderation and consensus to be defining characteristics of the Revolution. Concluding that the rhetoric of the Patriots had been based in real and realizable ideals, these historians wrote about the Revolution in overwhelmingly positive terms.

Along with the Whig model, the Atlantic World and progressive models also reappeared in the second half of the twentieth century. Bernard Bailyn, in *The Ideological Origins of the American Revolution* (1967), suggested that the colonists shared an ideology born in Europe that encouraged them to see the conflict with Britain as a struggle between power (embodying evil) and liberty (representing good). Perhaps drawing upon the Progressives' interest in propaganda, Bailyn studied the rhetoric of Patriot ideologues and revealed a powerful psychological Patriot dynamic. Obsessed by the threat of power overwhelming liberty, the Patriots saw enemies in every shadow. Thus, Bailyn's study of Massachusetts Governor Thomas Hutchinson demonstrated that the Loyalist was a rational man who cared deeply about his community and shared many of the political principles of the Whigs, but who also faced a driven and even paranoid group of Patriot ideologues.[21] The motivations and actions of the Loyalists seemed somewhat more understandable when contrasted to those of a seemingly paranoid Patriot elite.

Historians of Europe who were living and writing in the United States encouraged this development. R. R. Palmer in *The Age of the Democratic Revolution* (1959–64) and J. G. A. Pocock in *The Machiavellian Moment* (1975) saw the American Revolution as one stop on the long route taken by a set of republican ideas stretching all the way back to ancient Rome and Greece – ideas that had come to America via medieval Italy and seventeenth-century England before moving back to France and Continental Europe.[22] Gordon Wood, Bailyn's student, presented similar findings in *The Creation of the American Republic, 1776–1787* (1969). Wood viewed the Revolution as a triumph of liberty over oppression, a victory that was then partially betrayed by American Federalists in the Constitution.[23] In 1776, the United States had affirmed liberty and republicanism, and during the mid- to late twentieth century it furnished the military and economic might to keep them alive throughout the world.

Joyce Appleby complicated this Neo-Whig interpretation by arguing that a fascination for republican thought and ideology had obscured the basic fact that the Revolution – from Lockean ideology through to Jefferson's Declaration of Independence – was a thoroughly liberal defense of individual property rights and wealth, and (by implication) capitalism.[24] Classical republicanism was premised upon the sacrifice of personal interest for the good of the republic, while liberalism suggested that the republic would prosper by means of the pursuit of personal interest. However, whether republican or liberal in origins, the creation of the United States appeared in these histories as a unique and praiseworthy event. All of them, moreover, shared a conviction that the Revolution assumed shape and significance in the crucible of what would become known as the Atlantic World.

Such pride in the American past and present was bound, perhaps, to precede a fall. The period of the 1960s and 1970s – embracing the Civil Rights Movement, the Vietnam War, and the Watergate scandal – reshaped historical writing about the Revolution. It shattered many Americans' rosy glow of 1950s self-assurance – and also shattered the complacency of many Neo-Whig historians. Perhaps this is best seen in Edmund S. Morgan's *American Slavery, American Freedom: The Ordeal of Colonial Virginia* (1975), a powerful work in which, with considerable courage and great intellectual honesty, Morgan confronted his own realization of the symbiotic relationship between American liberty and racial slavery during the revolutionary era.[25] Such intuitions stretched beyond academia, as one can see in the rather muted Bicentennial celebrations of 1976, and in a popular series of Yale-educated Gary Trudeau's "Doonesbury" comics in 1975–76, showing the events and debates of the Revolutionary era through the prism of 1970s concerns about race and gender equality.

Led by John Shy, and informed by his appreciation of how the United States was fighting and losing a "hearts and minds war" in Vietnam, some historians reexamined a subject neglected by the Neo-Whigs: the War for Independence itself.[26] Studies of militia, army, and civilians have revealed a long and bloody war, in which many thousands of combatants and civilians were killed or injured. Pitting father against son, wife against husband, and slave against master, the war destroyed much of the new nation's infrastructure. It decimated ports, towns, crops, farms, and Native American communities, and made refugees of tens of thousands who had chosen one side over another. For all manner of late eighteenth-century Americans – from the urban "lower sort" to Southern planters, from yeoman farmers to mechanics, from slaves to Native Americans to educated white women – the war itself was the most traumatic and perhaps most significant event of their lives.

This assault upon neo-Whig histories, which might be labeled a Neo-Progressive reaction, is fueled by the imperative of a younger generation of historians to examine the American Revolution through the interpretative prisms of class, race, and gender. The Neo-Progressives, if such they may be termed, have moved in several different directions, although many share a broadly Marxist perspective and might just as easily be viewed as New Left historians. Historians such as Jesse Lemisch and Staughton Lynd were politically active in the 1960s and 1970s, leading them to reintroduce class, and to a lesser extent race and gender, into the history of the Revolution.[27] The resulting "new histories" drew upon methodologies and ideas from other disciplines, including race theory, feminist and gender theory, quantitative analysis, anthropology, and cultural studies.

One result of Neo-Progressivism is that the findings of the Neo-Whig consensus historians have not so much been disproved as rendered irrelevant. It was one thing to argue that Patriot leader John Hancock of Boston – the richest merchant in colonial America – had a clear and defensible set of political beliefs and economic and social principles that led him to become a revolutionary. But when historians began to examine the 1760s, 1770s, and 1780s from the perspective of such diverse groups as South Carolina slaves, free blacks in northern cities, poor urban laborers, and women of all classes and races, they found an incredible diversity of experience and opinion. Many varieties of history – especially social, economic and cultural, but also political and intellectual history – all broadened more in the last quarter of the twentieth century than in the preceding 200 years, incorporating the world of Americans from illiterate bondsmen and women to tenant farmers to seafarers.

Several of the leading Neo-Progressive and New Left historians of that quarter-century, particularly Gary Nash and Alfred Young, sought a bridge between the Whig and Progressive models by demonstrating that female, black, and poor Americans actually shared many of the political ideals and beliefs of the revolutionary elite, often pushing equality, freedom, and even democracy in ever more extreme directions. Plebeian biography has opened up the worlds of the revolutionary lower class, from the shoemaker George Robert Twelves Hewes to the Continental soldier Deborah Sampson to the farmer William Manning to the sailor William Widger, illustrating that such folk took revolutionary ideology in directions neither imagined nor countenanced by their social betters.[28] While such investigations have revealed multiple – often contradictory –

revolutionary impulses, they share the conclusion that slaves, women, and the poor seldom achieved a real improvement in their lives.

1980 saw the publication of books by Linda Kerber and Mary Beth Norton that heralded the beginning of systematic analysis of women's role in, and experiences of, the Revolution. Kerber, in particular, challenged Neo-Whig interpretations with a subtle study of the place of women in Enlightenment and Revolutionary ideology, and an exploration of the ways middle- and upper-class American white women attempted to capitalize on the Revolutionary settlement through the institution of Republican Motherhood.[29]

Others, such as Billy Smith, saw class as one of the most important factors in determining how Americans experienced the Revolution. Smith virtually ignored the political and ideological Revolution in his work, arguing that it meant and achieved very little for many Americans. As an event that ultimately benefited only white men with wealth and power, it was often far from revolutionary for those whose primary concerns were food, shelter, and work.[30]

Revolutionary history of the last half of the twentieth century saw the simultaneous reemergence of the three main interpretative frameworks of the past two centuries, namely, the Whig, Atlantic World, and Progressive models, each supported by a plethora of discrete and focused studies. By broadening the focus through the production of myriad studies of the experiences and actions of discrete groups within American society, the Revolution has become far more complicated. No longer is there *an* American Revolution but rather there are many rebellions and revolutions, for such variables as race, ethnicity, gender, class, vocation, region, and so forth all affected the impact of the Revolution on individuals or groups of people, creating enormous variety in their reactions to and expectations of the war and settlement. While such key concepts as liberty and the desire for greater self-determination retain some currency, these did not guarantee affiliation with the Patriot cause and, if shaped to fit all parties in late eighteenth-century America, become so amorphous as to fit much of human history.

The same is true of the War for Independence, for under this rubric there occurred a wide variety of armed conflicts. War was very different in the Southern backcountry, in the area surrounding Boston, out on the New York frontier, or in the countryside of New Jersey. Just as significantly, war was very different for runaway slaves, impoverished Philadelphia militiamen, the officers of the Continental army, and women left to fend for themselves and their families. The War for Independence may well have been the defining event for a generation of Americans, yet it was experienced in different places by different peoples in such very different ways as to appear now as a series of related yet different struggles, each of which assumed local shape and character. The resistance, rebellion, revolution, and warfare characterizing late eighteenth-century British North America could and did take markedly different forms among different groups in different contexts. What greater social and political revolution could there be for a black slave than to abandon slavery and fight for liberty under the flag of George III? What, too, of the rebellion of women such as Abigail Abbott Bailey, whose challenge to patriarchy and an abusive husband was fueled by the spiritual revolution of the Great Awakening?[31] The thousands of jigsaw pieces display not one Revolution but many different rebellions and revolutionary transformations, sometimes connected but often unrelated, yet all contributing to a great transformation of people, society, and government.

For many late eighteenth-century Americans, religious belief and practice were of far greater significance than politics. For some, like the Quaker diarist Elizabeth Drinker, the political revolution was an unfortunate and rather distasteful episode in a long life in which religion was central.[32] For others, the ongoing series of religious revivals that comprised the Great Awakening completely changed their own lives and those of their descendants. John Murrin has argued that the Great Awakening neither caused nor in any tangible way affected the American Revolution, but he is surely correct in asserting that it still transformed America in a truly revolutionary manner. American evangelical Christianity assumed shape in this seismic shift, with consequences that eventually extended from the spirituals of the plantations to the sermons of modern-day televangelists.[33]

Rural rebellions were perhaps the most constant form of insurrection in late eighteenth-century America, taking place before, during, and after the political revolution. The Neo-Whig historians astutely observed that many of the late eighteenth-century Americans who worked the land shared a fear of excessive taxes, debt, and a consequent loss of property and thus "independence." Those who worked and owned the land divided over the Revolution just as others did, however. A fierce sense of independence characterized rural Americans – an independence that could place them almost anywhere on the revolutionary spectrum.[34]

Class conflict, which many Whig scholars ignored, permeated urban America. Tension, and even open conflict, flowed from the natural conservatism of merchants and the urban elite, the desperate attempts of skilled craftsmen to maintain an artisan system that allowed property ownership and independence, and the ongoing and desperate struggle for survival among the ever-growing ranks of unskilled laborers, seafarers, free and enslaved African Americans, and women and children. Struggles between members of these different groups characterized American towns and cities before, during, and after the Revolution.[35] In Boston, for example, the revolutionary struggle profoundly affected the conflict between extremely wealthy and successful members of the merchant elite and myriad members of the working poor, whose situation had steadily worsened in the wake of the Seven Years War.[36] Similarly, as Steven Rosswurm has demonstrated, Philadelphia experienced a highly politicized class conflict during the Revolution.[37]

Even in the abiding hopes and desperate struggles for liberty shared by African Americans, there was remarkable diversity. The rural Stono Rebellion was aimed against the white planter class; the rebellion in New York City in 1741 (like Gabriel's Rebellion of 1800) was an urban affair that transcended simple racial divides, uniting different racial and ethnic groups and shaped by the politics and economics of class. The greatest single black rebellion to occur in and around the American Revolution was fostered by Virginia's last Royal Governor, Lord Dunmore. Thousands of slaves secured their freedom or died by dropping their tools and running to the King's armies.[38]

For Native Americans, the Anglo-American acquisition of French Canada in 1763 marked the beginning of the final struggle to stem the racist tide of Western settlement. There remained enormous diversity within the Native American populations, from the slave-worked plantations of assimilationist Cherokee to the fierce and abiding resistance of the Iroquois Confederacy. However, the American War for Independence represented just one more eighteenth-century war in which Indians sought to protect their lands, their culture, and their lives. Native American peoples effectively lost their independence, for white Americans secured the right to displace Indians from the lands they coveted. If Native Americans experienced one positive development in the Revolutionary era, it was a series of religious revivals that brought an unprecedented degree of intertribal unity.[39] This enormous coalition was unable, however, to prevent white Americans from destroying Native American independence.

In a very real way, contemporary historiography appears to invert the observation of J. Franklin Jameson that the revolution, once started, "could not be confined within thin narrow banks, but spread abroad upon the land."[40] Rather, the incredible diversity of American society and culture continued its movement in myriad directions regardless of a larger and almost abstract event labeled the American Revolution, sometimes touching and running with it, but often meandering along an independent course. For generations of American historians, the Revolution was an event that opened Pandora's Box, but modern historians are beginning to appreciate that the escaped spirits of an already long-opened box shaped the revolution in many different ways, in different places, with often starkly different results. British North America was a complex and fractured society, rent with social, political, economic, cultural, racial, and political divisions. It was a collection of societies well used to conflict and even rebellion and revolution, and these traditions helped carve out the road taken by the American Revolution.

This recognition has the unexpected result of restoring a degree of agency, although not necessarily power, to the many different types and groups of people who experienced and in various ways participated in the Revolution. Their objectives might range from a deep desire to free themselves from slavery, a wish to protect farms and loved ones from the depredations of British and Hessian soldiers, or an attempt to wrest rented land from mighty Hudson Valley landlords who supported the Patriot cause. All contributed to the ferment and unrest that underlay the American Revolution.

Moreover, the conservative fears expressed by Madison and Hamilton in the Federalist Papers, and later analyzed by Gordon Wood in his two books, now become more comprehensible. To the Federalists, late eighteenth-century American society was in danger of being torn apart by divisions of all sorts. Even a successful war for independence had not united Americans – it seemed only to have divided them more deeply. That conservative elites and, indeed, many others found solace in a common effort to create a strong central government, of and by the better sort, says as much about the rebellious nature of late eighteenth-century American society as it does about a reaction against the leveling radicalism of Paine and Jefferson.

Such a backlash might have occurred without the war for independence. The Revolution was less a form of political contagion, fostering a coherent and inclusive ideology of liberty, than it was an umbrella under which social and political conflicts played themselves out, albeit often in new contexts and with a renewed sense of significance. To argue, as Whigs and Neo-Whigs alike do, that the Revolution was radical because it occasioned social and political change is a reversal of the true situation: the rich diversity of the thirteen colonies, and the ongoing social conflict, rebellion, and revolution that they housed, affected the Revolution at least as much as it affected them.

The challenge facing historians of the American Revolution in the early twenty-first century is a difficult one. If they write histories that are framed by the desire to explain the causes, nature, and result of the political struggle with Britain that resulted in the creation of the United States, either they must ignore all the historiography that does not fit their interpretation, or they must depend upon headings, sub-headings, exceptions, caveats, qualifications, and disclaimers. Alternatively, historians may avoid the issue entirely, researching and writing ever more focused studies of the experiences of a particular class, race, or gender in a specific region.

None of these approaches is satisfactory. Neo-Whig synthesis succeeds by papering over the experiences of all that do not fit the paradigm. Alternatively, many practitioners of the "new" histories express a sense of the chaos and lack of connections in postmodern society in their work, separating groups, places, and events in their studies and then failing to connect them in an overall picture of late eighteenth-century America. To once again make some sense of the American Revolution, we must rid ourselves of aspects of the approaches of both the Neo-Whigs and the "new" historians. Building upon our recognition of the extraordinary diversity of society and culture in contemporary America, we must accept that the late eighteenth century was an era of many different rebellions and revolutions that were fought, lost, and won at different times and places by different combatants and with differing results.[41] Among issues that are now urgently in need of reappraisal are changes in political systems (at both the local and new, national level), the profound and widespread changes in American society itself (which may or may not have been linked to changes in political systems), and the manner in which either or both of these forms of change were experienced by the various elements of the American population.

The enduring popularity of political history is surely the result of the revolution's creation of the American nation-state, which has enabled historians and students to construct a coherent narrative of the founding and subsequent development of the United States. However, this political narrative is increasingly isolated from developments in social and cultural history, which have demonstrated that many Americans were excluded from and, indeed, little affected by the political transformation that gave life to the new republic. Some, such as Native Americans and many African Americans, might well have stood a greater chance of realizing the ideals of life, liberty, and the pursuit of happiness by aligning themselves with the British against the American Revolution. Others, such as many white women, urban poor, and tenant farmers, remained most concerned with the struggle to keep their families clothed, fed, and sheltered: political allegiances and transformations disrupted their lives with few tangible benefits.

As both teachers and scholars, we face real problems in doing justice to the history of the founding of the United States. Throughout the United States and beyond, many historians teach the American Revolution by assigning a text that chronicles the political history of the revolution, supplementing this core reading with supplemental readings and lectures based upon a half-century of scholarship on African Americans, Native Americans, women, the poor and other groups, showing in different sections of the course the often radically different objectives and experiences of various late eighteenth-century Americans. This approach characterizes the ways in which most historians continue to think about the American Revolution. Unfortunately, it over-privileges the political history of the founding of the nation by inadvertently marginalizing the revolutionary-era experiences of African Americans, Native Americans, poor white Americans and so forth, people who – when taken together – constituted the great bulk of the population.

As we enter a new millennium, with Americans more aware than ever before of the ways in which enormous ethnic, racial, social, and cultural diversity characterize the past, present, and future of the United States, synthetic studies of the American Revolution have to reverse this imbalance. While retaining the political narrative that traces the creation of the American polity, it must be the diverse and often contradictory experiences of the Americans who lived through that era that occupy center stage. In such histories, liberty would be seen to transcend the pamphlets and literary sources of traditional political history, taking far more diverse forms in the very real search for self-determination and liberty of Native Americans, enslaved and free African Americans, farmers and agricultural workers, and the urban laboring classes.

The result would be histories of late eighteenth-century America in which the overturning of British rule and the creation of a republican polity would appear as important yet often peripheral events. We shall neither see nor understand the scale, the significance and, indeed, the very soul of late eighteenth-century America until the extraordinarily diverse and often contradictory experiences of the men and women of this era become central to histories of the American Revolution. In such histories, the political narrative that has dominated two centuries of historiography will fade into the background where it belongs. And thus we shall come closer to understanding the world of late eighteenth-century Americans, in whose personal struggles for freedom and self-determination the contest with Britain, independence, and the creation of a republic were frequently marginal rather than central events.

Acknowledgements

I am very grateful to Simon Ball, Laura Edwards, Tom Humphrey, Allan Kulikoff, Billy Smith and especially Sally Gordon for their comments on earlier drafts of this chapter.

Notes

1. A search of the *America: History and Life* bibliographic database employing the keywords "American Revolution" generated 463 hits for 1955–64, 1,645 hits for 1965–74, and 3,484 hits for 1975–84. Both the increasing size and the growing diversity of scholarship is further indicated by the growth in numbers and categories of essays, articles and dissertations appearing in the "Recent Scholarship" listings of the *Journal of American History*. During the late 1950s, "Recent Articles" was divided into a "General" section, and then several regional categories, which in 1959–60 (vol. 46) contained 13 pieces relating to the American Revolution. In the 1979–80 Journal (vol. 66), the expansion of scholarship was reflected in some 124 articles. The 1999–2000 *Journal of American History* (vol. 89) featured a comprehensive listing of "Recent Scholarship" sub-divided into a set of forty-three categories. The 127 items listed under "Colonial and Revolutionary Period" were supplemented by many more listed under varied thematic and topical listings.

2. American historians have been lamenting the loss of "synthesis" for more than a decade. See, for example, Bernard Bailyn, "The Challenge of Modern Historiography," *American Historical Review*, 87 (1982): 1–24; Michael Zuckerman, "Myth and Method: The Current Crisis in American Historical Writing," *The History Teacher*, 17 (1984): 219–45; Herbert Gutman, "The Missing Synthesis: Whatever Happened to History?" *The Nation*, November 21, 1981: 521, 553–4; Hayden White, *The Content of the Form: Narrative Discourse and Historical Representation* (Baltimore, 1987); Thomas Bender, "Wholes and Parts: The Need for Synthesis in American History," *Journal of American*

History, 73 (1986): 120–36; David Thelen, "A Round Table: Synthesis in American History," *Journal of American History*, 74 (1987): 107–30; Fred Anderson and Andrew R. L. Cayton, "The Problem of Fragmentation and the Prospects for Synthesis in Early American Social History," *The William and Mary Quarterly*, 50 (1993): 299–310.

3. Linda K. Kerber, "The Revolutionary Generation: Ideology, Politics, and Culture in the Early Republic," AHA Pamphlet in "The New American History" series, ed. Eric Foner (Washington, DC, 1990).

4. This point has been made most effectively by Barbara Clark Smith and Michael Zuckerman, in a forum discussing Wood's book held at the 1993 meeting of the Organization of American Historians. These papers were reprinted as Smith, "The Adequate Revolution," and Zuckerman, "Rhetoric, Reality and the Revolution: The Genteel Radicalism of Gordon Wood," *The William and Mary Quarterly*, 3d. ser., 51 (1994): 684–702.

5. Robert A. Gross has made a similar argument, suggesting that the United States has been defined "by the myth of the Revolution . . . originating in Whig propaganda . . . [which was then elaborated] into a full-dress historical interpretation." See Gross, "White Hats and Hemlocks: Daniel Shays and the Legacy of the Revolution," in Ronald Hoffman and Peter J. Albert, eds., *"The Transforming Hand of Revolution": Reconsidering the American Revolution As A Social Movement* (Charlottesville, 1996), pp. 287–8.

6. Here I am paraphrasing Kerber's insightful AHA pamphlet, "The Revolutionary Generation," p. 1. Among other attempts to make sense of the historiography of the American Revolution are Jack P. Greene in the introduction to *The Reinterpretation of the American Revolution, 1763–1789* (New York, 1968); Edmund S. Morgan, ed., *The American Revolution: Two Centuries of Interpretation* (Englewood Cliffs, NJ, 1965); and Alfred F. Young, "Afterword: How Radical Was the American Revolution," in Young, ed., *Beyond the American Revolution: Explorations in the History of American Radicalism* (De Kalb, IL, 1993), pp. 317–64 and idem, "American Historians Confront the 'Transforming Hand of Revolution,'" in *The Transforming Hand of Revolution*, pp. 346–492.

7. While many American historians have presented various forms of American exceptionalism in their histories, a great many American Revolutionary histories are methodologically derivative. As with British, French, and other historians, there has been widespread importation and adaptation of existing conceptual frameworks, from Mercy

Otis Warren's employment of classical genres to the New Social historians' use of mid-twentieth century British and French social history.

8. Mercy Otis Warren, *History of the Rise, Progress, and Termination of the American Revolution. Interspersed with Biographical, Political and Moral Observations*, 3 vols., (1805, reprinted New York, 1970).

9. Mason Locke Weems, *A History of the Life and Death, Virtues and Exploits of General George Washington* (Philadelphia, 1800).

10. George Bancroft, *History of the American Revolution*, 7 vols. (Boston, 1852–74); idem, *History of the Formation of the Constitution of the United States of America* (New York, 1885); idem, *History of the United States of America from the Discovery of the Continent*, 6 vols. (Boston, 1834–75).

11. Albion Small, *The Beginnings of American Nationality; the Constitutional Relations between the Continental Congress and the Colonies and States from 1774 to 1789* (Baltimore, 1890).

12. Edward Channing, *A History of the United States* (New York, 1905); idem, *Town and County Government in the English Colonies of North America* (Baltimore, 1884).

13. Thomas Jefferson Wertenbaker, *The Shaping of Colonial Virginia* (New York, 1958); idem, *Give Me Liberty; The Struggle for Self-Government in Virginia* (Philadelphia, 1958); idem, *Planters of Colonial Virginia* (Princeton, 1922); idem, *The Old South* (New York, 1942).

14. Charles M. Andrews, "The American Revolution: An Interpretation," *American Historical Review* 31 (1926): 219–32.

15. Herbert Levi Osgood, *The American Colonies in the Seventeenth Century*, 3 vols. (New York, 1904–1907); idem, *The American Colonies in the Eighteenth Century* (New York, 1924–1930).

16. Alfred Thayer Mahan, *The Interest of America in Sea Power, Present and Future* (Boston, 1898).

17. Charles A. Beard, *An Economic Interpretation of the Constitution of the United States* (1913, reprinted New York, 1935); idem, *Economic Origins of Jeffersonian Democracy* (New York, 1927); Charles A. Beard and Mary R. Beard, *The Rise of American Civilization* (New York, 1933).

18. Carl Becker, *The History of Political Parties in the Province of New York, 1760–1776* (Madison, 1909), p. 5. See, also, Becker, *The Declaration of Independence, a Study in the History of Political Ideas* (New York, 1922).

19. John Franklin Jameson, *The American Revolution Considered as a Social Movement* (Princeton, 1926).
20. Edmund S. Morgan, *The Birth of the American Republic, 1763–89* (Chicago, 1956). See also idem, *The Meaning of Independence: John Adams, George Washington, Thomas Jefferson*(Charlottesville, 1976) and Morgan and Helen M. Morgan, *The Stamp Act Crisis: Prologue to Revolution* (New York, 1963).
21. Bernard Bailyn, *The Ordeal of Thomas Hutchinson* (Cambridge, MA, 1974).
22. R. R. Palmer, *The Age of the Democratic Revolution*, 2 vols. (Princeton, 1959–64); J. G. A. Pocock, *The Machiavellian Moment: Florentine Political Thought and the Atlantic Republican Tradition* (Princeton, 1975).
23. Gordon S. Wood, *The Creation of the American Republic, 1776–1787* (Chapel Hill, 1969).
24. Joyce Appleby, *Capitalism and a New Social Order: the Republican Vision of the 1790s* (New York, 1984).
25. Edmund S. Morgan, *American Slavery, American Freedom: The Ordeal of Colonial Virginia* (New York, 1975).
26. John Shy, *A People Numerous and Armed: Reflections on the Military Struggle for American Independence* (New York, 1976). For further examples of this genre of military history, see Charles Royster, *A Revolutionary People at War: The Continental Army and American Character, 1775–1783* (Chapel Hill, 1979); Ronald Hoffman and Peter J. Albert, eds., *Arms and Independence: The Military Character of the American Revolution* (Charlottesville, 1984); Richard H. Kohn, *Eagle and Sword: The Federalists and the Creation of the Military Establishment in America, 1783–1802* (New York, 1975); E. Wayne Carp, *To Starve the Army at Pleasure: Continental Army Administration and American Political Culture, 1775–1783* (Chapel Hill, 1984).
27. Jesse Lemisch, "Jack Tar in the Streets: Merchant Seamen in the Politics of Revolutionary America," *The William and Mary Quarterly* 3d. ser., 25 (1968): 371–407; idem, "Listening to the 'Inarticulate': William Widger's Dream and the Loyalties of American Revolutionary Seamen in British Prisons," *Journal of Social History*, 3 (1969): 1–29; idem, "The American Revolution Seen from the Bottom Up," in Barton J. Bernstein, ed., *Towards A New Past: Dissenting Essays in American History* (New York, 1967), and *Jack Tar vs. John Bull: The Role of New York's Seamen in Precipitating the Revolution* (New York, 1997); Staughton Lynd, "Freedom Now: The Intellectual Origins of American Radicalism," in Alfred F. Young,

ed., *Dissent: Explorations in the History of American Radicalism* (De Kalb, IL, 1968), and idem, *Anti-Federalism in Dutchess County, New York: A Study of Democracy and Class Conflict in the Revolutionary Era* (Chicago, 1962).

28. Alfred F. Young, *The Shoemaker and the Tea Party: Memory and the American Revolution* (Boston, 1999): the original version was published as "George Robert Twelves Hewes (1742–1840): A Boston Shoemaker and the Memory of the American Revolution," *The William and Mary Quarterly* 3d. ser., 38 (1981): 561–623; Michael Merrill and Sean Wilentz, ed., *The Key of Liberty: The Life and Democratic Writings of William Manning, "A Laborer"* (Cambridge, MA, 1993); Lemisch, "Listening to the 'Inarticulate.'" Alfred F. Young is currently completing a study of Deborah Sampson.

29. Linda K. Kerber, *Women of the Republic: Intellect and Ideology in Revolutionary America* (Chapel Hill, 1980); Mary Beth Norton, *Liberty's Daughters: The Revolutionary Experience of American Women, 1750–1800* (Boston, 1980). For a useful, albeit somewhat dated survey on work in this field, see Kerber, "'History Can Do It No Justice': Women and the Reinterpretation of the American Revolution," in Ronald Hoffman and Peter J. Albert, eds., *Women in the Age of the American Revolution* (Charlottesville, 1989), pp. 3–42.

30. Billy G. Smith, *The "Lower Sort": Philadelphia's Laboring People, 1750–1800* (Ithaca, NY, 1990).

31. Ann Taves, ed., *Religion and Domestic Violence in Early New England: The Memoirs of Abigail Abbot Bailey* (Bloomington, 1989).

32. Elaine Forman Crane, ed., *The Diary of Elizabeth Drinker*, 2 vols. (Boston, 1991).

33. John M. Murrin, "No Awakening, No Revolution? More Counterfactual Speculations," *Reviews in American History*, 11 (1983): 161–71. Perhaps the most striking study of the impact of evangelical revivals is Rhys Isaac, *The Transformation of Virginia, 1740–1790* (Chapel Hill, 1982). More recent works include Jon Butler, *Awash in a Sea of Faith: Christianizing the American People* (Cambridge, MA, 1990); Patricia Bonomi, *Under the Cope of Heaven: Religion, Society, and Politics in Colonial America* (New York, 1986); Ronald Hoffman and Peter J. Albert, eds., *Religion in a Revolutionary Age* (Charlottesville, 1994).

34. Classic studies include Edward Countryman, *A People in Revolution: The American Revolution and Political Society in New York, 1760–1790* (Baltimore, 1981); Sung Bok Kim, *Landlord and Tenant in*

Colonial New York Manorial Society, 1664–1775 (Chapel Hill, 1978). Recent new approaches include Allan Kulikoff, *The Agrarian Origins of American Capitalism* (Charlottesville, 1992); Alan Taylor, *Liberty Men and Great Proprietors: The Revolutionary Settlement on the Maine Frontier, 1760–1820* (Chapel Hill, 1990); and Michael Belle-siles, *Revolutionary Outlaws : Ethan Allen and the Struggle for Independence on the Early American Frontier* (Charlottesville, 1993).

35. Recent examples of the diverse approaches to these various urban groups include Barbara Clark Smith, "Food Rioters and the American Revolution," *The William and Mary Quarterly*, 3d. ser., 51 (1994): 3–38; Alfred F. Young, "The Women of Boston: 'Persons of Conse-quence' in the Making of the American Revolution," in Harriet B. Applewhite and Darlene G. Levy, eds., *Women and Politics in the Age of Democratic Revolution* (Ann Arbor, 1990), pp. 181–226; and Marcus Rediker, "A Motley Crew of Rebels: Sailors, Slaves, and the Coming of the American Revolution," in Hoffman and Albert, eds., *The Transforming Hand of Revolution*, pp. 155–98.

36. See, for example, Alfred F. Young, "The Crowd and the Coming of the American Revolution: From Ritual to Rebellion in Boston," paper presented to the Shelby Cullom Davis Center for Historical Studies, Princeton University, January 23, 1976; Gary B. Nash, *The Urban Crucible: Social Change, Political Consciousness, and the Origins of the American Revolution* (Cambridge, MA, 1979); and Allan Kulikoff, "The Progress of Inequality in Revolutionary Boston," *The William and Mary Quarterly*, 3d. ser., 28 (1971): 375–412.

37. Stephen Rosswurm, *Arms, Country, and Class: The Philadelphia Militia and the "Lower Sort" During the American Revolution* (New Brunswick, NJ, 1987).

38 See, for example, Gerald W. Mullin, *Flight and Rebellion: Slave Resistance in Eighteenth-Century Virginia* (New York, 1972); Peter H. Wood, *Black Majority: Negroes in Colonial South Carolina from 1670 through the Stono Rebellion* (New York, 1974); Sylvia Frey, *Water From The Rock: Black Resistance in a Revolutionary Age* (Princeton, 1991); Douglas Egerton, *Gabriel's Rebellion: The Virginia Slave Conspiracies of 1800 and 1802* (Chapel Hill, 1993); Eugene Genovese, *From Rebellion to Revolution: Afro-American Slave Revolts in the Making of the Modern World* (Baton Rouge, 1979).

39. Gregory Evans Dowd, *A Spirited Resistance: The North American Indian Struggle for Unity, 1745–1815* (Baltimore, 1992).

40. Jameson, *The American Revolution Considered as a Social Move-ment*, p. 9.

41. Kerber and Young have both drawn attention to the existence of a variety of different rebellions and revolutions. See Kerber, "The Revolutionary Generation," p. 2; Young, "Introduction," *Beyond the American Revolution*, p. 3.

–2–

Reshaping Society: American Social History from Revolution to Reconstruction

Christopher Clark

In 1780 a force of Continental troops under General Benjamin Lincoln of Massachusetts led the defense of Charleston, South Carolina, against a British attack. Eighty-five years later, Yankee soldiers were again in Charleston – this time as attackers themselves, visiting the Union's wrath on the city that had started the war against it.

The two events shared some similarities. In each case, the city fell to its attackers and, in each case, slavery contributed to its fall. Southern leaders' fear of arming slaves hindered their defense of places and institutions they cherished. In 1780 this fear had a bizarre effect. Outnumbered by the British, Lincoln urged South Carolina's leaders to strengthen the militia units that were supporting his force by recruiting slaves to join them. When the leaders refused, Lincoln prepared to withdraw from Charleston, but the South Carolinians compelled him to remain, threatening to use their militia – effectively in alliance with the British – to keep the Continentals in place. Their action ensured that, when the British captured Charleston, they also captured Lincoln and his men, dealing a serious blow to the American cause.[1] In 1865, Charleston suffered the destruction that Sherman's armies visited upon much of the Southeast, which was overwhelmed by Union muscle and numbers. As with the British before them, the Yankees' strength lay partly in the South's divisions. White Southerners wanted to defend slavery, but could not use the two-fifths of their population who were slaves to help them. Even in the quite different circumstances of revolution and civil war, social structures ensured a degree of continuity.

However, these two episodes also reflected the profound social changes that had occurred between 1780 and the 1860s. Within months of the second fall of Charleston, slavery was legally abolished. The two "Yankee" armies engaged there had been recruited in contrasting circumstances. Raising armies in the Revolution posed difficulties, because many men's labor was essential to the production of basic economic necessities. In a largely rural economy, extensive military service could undermine society itself. By the Civil War, however, the North had enough wage-earners and immigrants to recruit a large army without heavy reliance on conscription. Farm output and mechanization were sufficient to sustain production and also support a large army. The difference was not simply due to increased population. The structure of American society itself had shifted, making possible in the 1860s what eight decades earlier would have been improbable.[2]

The outlines of this shift have long been familiar. American society, of course, expanded dramatically, in size and in geographical extent. From being, at Independence, a rural society rooted in agricultural production, the U.S. by 1870 was both an expanding agricultural producer and emerging as a leading industrial economy. In the century after independence, the proportion of Americans living in "urban" places (with populations of 2,500 or more) more than trebled, and the number of such places multiplied by roughly forty times. The U.S. became noted not only for the scale and rapid growth of its greatest cities, but also for its proliferation of small and medium-sized towns.

At first glance the new social historians of the last three decades of the twentieth century did little to alter this outline of the reshaping of America. Because locally-focused studies and "microhistories" have remained among social history's dominant genres, it has often been difficult to keep a broad picture of change in view. The abundance of microhistories has uncovered an extraordinary variety of patterns that seems to lead us away from generalized explanations of change. Yet, gradually, historians are realizing that in this very variety lie important keys to understanding social change. The U.S. developed and was reshaped in a multiplicity of ways, whose interconnections helped drive the process of change itself. Although social history has complexified the categories with which we can explain social change, this greater complexity helps us more readily to capture the subtle and powerful influences on Americans' lives in this period.

Some changes can be called *extensive*. Both Northern and Southern societies expanded prodigiously across the land, extending the reach both of slavery and of household-based rural production. Meanwhile, in the late eighteenth and early nineteenth centuries, the U.S. had rebuilt and deepened its connections to the Atlantic world, disrupted by the Revolution. Agriculture was by far the largest occupation, followed by maritime work, and many Americans envisaged the U.S. as an agrarian republic served by commerce.

Yet there were also increasingly important patterns of *intensive* change in American society. Migration from farm regions to coastal and interior towns helped fuel rapid urban growth, especially in the North. Meanwhile, rural societies themselves, particularly in older regions, underwent substantial internal development, intensifying farming and in certain places also laying the foundations for an industrial economy.

These patterns of extensive and intensive change underscored American society's multivariant character. During the century after Independence, freehold farming, tenancy, and (until 1865) slave-based agriculture all expanded. Until the Civil War, although the proportion of slaves in the population declined, the absolute number of slaves rose dramatically. Meanwhile the wage-labor force and nonagricultural employment grew too. By 1870, about half the workforce was employed for wages. After 1840, there also emerged, especially in towns and in the Northeast, a growing salaried middle class. By the 1880s, half the workforce was employed outside agriculture, and in some places this proportion had been exceeded long before. These shifts marked important discontinuities with the past. They shaped and help explain the contrasting circumstances under which the Revolutionary War and the Civil War were fought.

We can grasp how recent scholarship is altering the ways we understand American social change by looking at five themes: the distribution of wealth; the acquisition and possession of land; households, and particularly the economic contributions of women; the analysis of social networks; and the emergence of new institutions and groups associated with them. These themes form just part of a more complex mosaic, but by examining them we can reach some propositions about the processes of change, which were propelled by the relationships and tensions between different individuals and groups.

Patterns of social exclusion and the maldistribution of wealth and resources helped drive American economic growth and development. Yet, until slavery came under assault, these imbalances were not so great as to be socially or politically crippling. Aspirations for social equality informed political ideology during and after the Revolution. The principle that "all men are created equal" and the near-adoption for the Declaration of Independence of Locke's prescription of "life, liberty, and property" reflected the connection between revolutionary republicanism and the hope that access to economic resources could sustain social equality. While Jeffersonian Republicans regarded landholding as a guarantee of such aspirations, Federalists such as John Adams were sure that economic inequalities were permanent and ineradicable. Recent work on wealth distribution largely confirms Adams's perspective, but also explains why the Jeffersonian vision seemed plausible to the many white male voters who gave it credence. Though historians disagree on the extent and trend of inequality, they portray a society whose white citizens at least enjoyed significant chances of access to property, but whose structural inequalities were sharp enough to enable certain groups to accumulate capital and wealth in their own hands.

Wealth distribution, already unequal in the colonial period, became less equal in the new country's first century. In 1774, the richest 10 percent of the population controlled about 53 percent of wealth. By 1860, the share of the richest tenth had reached 73 percent of wealth and would continue to rise for the rest of the century. Eighteenth-century wealth inequality was greatest in towns and in areas with large slave plantations. The average 53 percent share of wealth held by the top tenth in 1774 was exceeded in Boston and Philadelphia, at 63 percent and 72 percent respectively. The differential between urban areas and rural regions without large plantations persisted in the nineteenth century. By 1828, half of New York City's wealth was owned by just 4 percent of taxpayers, and by late in the century the top tenth in several large cities controlled well over nine-tenths of wealth.[3]

Several characteristics of urban life help explain these large inequalities. Recent studies have noted that urban tax records undercounted the poor, and have revised upwards estimates of the rate of poverty in cities. By 1860, while perhaps one in three Americans lived in poverty, up to one-half of urban Americans did so. One facet of this was gender inequality. Women had, to say the least, unequal access to resources, while certain cities and towns had high proportions of female-headed households. In ports such as Boston and Salem, where many men were employed at sea, the long absence and frequent disappearance of wage-earning men exacerbated the poverty of the families they left behind.[4] But urban growth and population migration from rural areas or overseas also contributed to poverty by increasing competition between workers in urban labor markets. Poverty levels were high not only in established cities such as Philadelphia but also in newly grown towns. In Cincinnati, the proportion of wealth held by the lower half of property owners fell steadily, from 12.1 percent in 1799 to 9.8 percent in 1817, and 8.1 percent in 1838. Many towns became pools of underemployed and low-paid workers of both sexes. As urban areas grew in size and relative importance, their contribution to the unequal distribution of wealth grew also.[5]

Yet urban growth only partly explains the persistence of inequality in the nation as a whole. Rural inequality also contributed. First, there was population pressure on land settlement in older regions throughout the eastern seaboard. In Delaware, where tenancy was common, concentration of land ownership was increasing in the early nineteenth century. In Chester County, Pennsylvania, the ratio of landless laborers to house-holders rose from 0.56:1 in 1756 to 0.81:1 in 1820. In Worcester County, Massachusetts, relatively widespread property distribution in the eighteenth century quickly became more unequal in the early nineteenth, as population pressed on the resources of a settled rural area.[6]

Second, despite the expansion of population onto new "frontier" land throughout this period, inequalities abounded in new rural regions as well as in old ones. In 1798, house values varied more widely in frontier regions than they did in seaboard rural areas, and as much as in large towns. The activities of land speculators or large landowners skewed property distribution. Many parts of Appalachia were subject to large-scale accumulation of land, a circumstance which kept poor settlers from owning property and sowed the seeds of the region's lasting poverty. In Western Pennsylvania in the early years of settlement, only small minorities of households held land of their own. In Ohio, speculators engrossed large amounts of land from the holders of military land warrants; in the 1790s, as few as one hundred men between them owned title to almost 1.5 million acres in the territory.

Third, further factors determined the trajectory of inequalities as these new regions were settled and cultivated. In the Appalachians, landlords' determination to retain timber and mineral rights prevented much redistribution to small property-owners. In fertile parts of the South, meanwhile, slavery enabled wealthy landholders readily to clear land and plant cash-crops and, as in Kentucky in the 1790s, to outstrip small farmers in gaining control of land. The extension of slave-based agriculture across the Old Southwest extended this zone of rural inequality, where the propertyless included considerable numbers of poor whites dependent on casual work. Where slavery was weak or nonexistent, distribution of land to small farmers was more common. In the large parts of western New York State that had been purchased by land companies, much depended on their policies for attracting settlers. Areas where farms could be purchased tended to develop more rapidly and less unequally than those whose owners established tenant farming. The sale of lands to farmers made Ohio the most egalitarian of the newly opened Western states, yet even here only 54 percent of household heads were property owners by 1835. Evidence from various frontier regions also confirms that early settlers usually secured most advantage in gaining property, and that latecomers were less likely to acquire land or wealth on the same scale as they had.[7]

The early U.S. was quite egalitarian by European standards, but nevertheless bore out John Adams's opinion that inequalities were inevitable. Poverty, gender, slavery, and other factors limited individuals' access to resources and created systematic differences that shaped nineteenth-century development. The U.S. was driven by a pattern of "egalitarian inequality": there was enough equality to create opportunity for many, but enough inequality to ensure that many others were subject to domination and exploitation.

Because property inequality was well established in the eighteenth century, and the proportion of households owning property did not decline markedly before the Civil War, some historians have argued that developments such as early industrialization did not make American society more unequal. Yet an examination of property-ownership and its connections with production, wealth, and power suggests that, for many people, the significance of property-holding changed during the period.

The Revolution unleashed several structural changes that helped reshape society in the two generations that followed. Its opening-up of access to Western lands and the U.S. Constitution's guarantee of a common market without interstate tariff barriers together made a substantial difference to former colonies whose economic structures had reached certain limits. There were also important shifts in the maritime economy, in migration patterns to towns, and in the development of new activities in settled regions of the countryside. Society underwent an extraordinary multi-path expansion. During the two or three generations following the Revolution, the U.S. became simultaneously a continental and an Atlantic power, an agricultural and industrial nation, and both more rural and more urban.

Underpinning these changes was a process by which land became progressively commodified. Colonial settlers and their descendants had relied heavily on cultivation. By the Revolution, various pressures were causing landholders in older regions to regard property less as an ancestral possession than as a resource that could be exchanged, or traded for cash. Demographic pressure led many families to migrate to new regions. Larger families and traditions of partible inheritance led many farmers to transfer or bequeath property to children not just as means of support, but as capital that might be realized in various ways.[8]

This commodification was reflected in the growth of land-markets in older rural regions from the later eighteenth century onwards. But the greatest commodification of all took place on unsettled land, as speculators and settlers moved into the trans-Appalachian West. They bought, seized, or occupied Indian land and projected grand designs for obtaining, dividing and settling territory yet to be gained. Expansion across the continent rested on inequality, and on the destruction of well-articulated patterns of cultural interaction, diplomacy and trade over what Richard White called the "middle ground" between Indian and settler societies. The "frontier," formerly a zone of interaction, now came to be seen as a line of settlement. Commodified land was its hallmark.[9]

Trans-Appalachian settlement did not follow an inevitable pattern. Political, structural, and historical factors shaped it. Popular participation in politics pressed governments toward greater liberality to settlers, as Congress lowered the purchase price and minimum acreage of federal lands, and many states passed preemption laws favoring the claims of squatters over those of landlords. Nevertheless, land settlement was often a contest. White migrants and squatters struggled both with Indians and with wealthy proprietors who sought to profit from development. There were also cultural struggles between the values of pioneers and those of elite groups – planters, land developers or merchants. In New York and elsewhere it took popular protests against land companies to influence their development policies, and against landlords' agents and public officials to reform manorial property-rights.[10]

The connections between land, power, and social status were rooted in peoples' relationships to labor. Accordingly, the significance of land to social elites came to vary from region to region. Southern planters acquired and cultivated land because their ownership of slaves permitted them to control directly the labor required for crop production. Northern elites, largely unable to use coerced labor on any scale, enjoyed a less direct relationship to land. Without slave labor, and with wages for farm labor high, wealthy Northerners profited either from land speculation or from the marketing and supply of the produce and goods that small rural landowners and farmers sold and purchased. In the parts of the South where there were large slave plantations, there was a substantial congruence between landownership and political leadership.[11] Elsewhere, the overlaps between landholding, wealth, and political power were looser.

The effects of slavery and frontier inequality helped underpin a reversal by the 1840s and 1850s of post-revolutionary attitudes to property distribution. Though Democrats continued to profess the ideal of equality, their party was increasingly swayed by Southern planters who defended slavery with the argument that inequality was inevitable and should therefore be borne by a supposedly-inferior "mudsill" class. Whigs, free-soilers, and Republicans, meanwhile, based their critique of slavery on the argument that it supported aristocratic dominance. Instead, they advocated "free soil" and the distribution of land to family farmers as a measure for social equality. By the late 1850s, Abraham Lincoln explicitly claimed the Jeffersonian mantle, rejecting the notion that a social "mudsill" was inevitable or justifiable.

Northern speculators in land for farming settlements rarely made the fortunes that they hoped for. However, those who possessed land that could support urban development often did achieve wealth, local influence or both. Small developers such as David Hudson, who had migrated to Ohio early in the nineteenth century, found themselves holding key lots in successful small towns, and a luckier few obtained property in towns that turned into cities. Though there were many other sources of wealth in large urban centers, property holding was a significant basis for fortunes. The most valuable dwellings in Boston in 1798 occupied city lots that averaged 51 times the size of those of the poorest dwellings, with commensurate potential for later subdivision. An 1846 survey of rich Philadelphians found that at least one in eight had made some or all of their fortunes from property. Wealthy New York City landowners used their influence to shape the city's physical landscape, pressing for the development of parks and other facilities in locations that would optimize their property values.[12]

For a growing urban population, real estate provided security and the opportunity for an owned, rather than rented, home. But, increasingly, this property was not a source of productive value. Meanwhile, many farmers, who did own productive property, were finding themselves marginalized in an integrated national market as they became dependent on prices dictated in distant cities, and on transportation links whose tariffs and schedules they could do little to influence. These disparities would lead to both industrial and agricultural protest and class conflict in the postbellum decades. The changing composition of wealth altered relationships between property and power, and between property and production. These were among the keys to broader social changes.

Households were the central social institutions and units of production in early America. Social historians have done much to explore the implications of this for broader patterns of social change. Households carried forward the expansion of American agriculture and much of the settlement of the newly-opened West. They also lay at the roots of American industrialization. Though industrial development was conventionally associated with towns, to which it often gave rise, recent social historians have stressed that many of its origins lay in rural areas, in the needs and skills that arose there, and in the organization of rural households to participate in manufacturing activity.[13]

The notion of the family farm as normative had strong roots in the revolutionary republican tradition, and evolved in the antebellum period among various claimants to that tradition's legacy. Jeffersonians stressed the importance of independent farm households as the guarantee of equality. Federalists stressed the importance of families, along with churches and schools, as the basis of social order. Both attached importance to the variety of activities that households conducted. Transmitted through their Jacksonian and Whig heirs, this attachment to the vision of the farm household remained strong in the divided politics of the 1850s.

There were, however, important differences of emphasis. Southerners, especially, regarded independent farms of any kind as morally and politically equivalent to one another. Slaveholders on their plantations were just as much "family farmers" as yeomen on their backcountry homesteads. According to Stephanie McCurry, even in some of the most class-divided segments of the Old South – the rice-plantation regions of South Carolina and Georgia – planters and yeomen were bound together both by local ties of patronage and obligation and by a common identity as household patriarchs. Each of them had authority over his dependents – wife, children, or slaves. This elision contributed to the evolution of Southern ideology as the sectional crisis deepened, and to the decision of small farmers in plantation areas to support secession in 1860 and 1861.[14]

To free-soilers, however, the modest family farm represented a way of life that rebutted slaveholders' claims to share equality with their poorer neighbors. Slavery created aristocracy, both because it consisted in a class relationship rooted in tyranny and because it enabled the accumulation and cultivation of large landholdings. Free-soilers attacked the South's apparent thralldom to a planter aristocracy, and urged the avoidance of large-scale landholdings elsewhere. James Warren and his son John, Massachusetts nurserymen who settled in California in the 1850s, criticized the new state's large *ranchos*, held under Mexican land grants. John Warren suggested that if these were "divided into smaller farms, and improved and cultivated by enterprising, persevering men . . . the wealth of the . . . State would materially increase." It was in these same terms that Abraham Lincoln, addressing farmers and other groups in 1859 and 1860, attached himself to the legacy of the Jeffersonian tradition as the protector of the laboring small-farmer against the aristocratic planter who used the labor of others.[15]

Most idealizations of family farming embodied another elision, however. The family was usually assumed to be a unit, little subject to scrutiny, whose members shared the same interests. It was regarded either as a patriarchy, which subsumed women and children under the authority of a male household head, or as a moral shelter from the dangers and uncertainties of the (male-dominated) marketplace. Yet relationships within households were specifically unequal. Men, women, children, servants, and slaves all had quite different legal rights and obligations.[16] The structures of work and authority within households, and the struggles and tensions that these could produce, had a profound effect on the shaping of early American society and on the processes of change that emerged from it.

Households were the primary location for women's work. This was once almost invisible to historians, partly because they rarely considered it, partly because the conventions and ideological assumptions of the past caused it to be omitted from much of the written record. Most commentators and political economists from the eighteenth century onward systematically underrated women's contributions. Alexander Hamilton, in his 1791 report on manufactures, advocated the setting up of factories and workhouses to employ women and children who, he took it for granted, were under-occupied. Proponents of domestic silk manufacture advocated it as a suitable activity for women and children who, they were confident, had too little else to do. The subsequent growth of wage-labor and the separation of much wage-earning from the domestic environment contributed to the undervaluing of labor (undertaken mostly by women and children) that took place outside the cash system. Only recently have social historians recovered a sense of the contribution of women's work to the shaping of American society in general.[17]

The undercounting of women's tasks and their economic value potentially alters calculations about the scale and growth-rates of the U.S. economy. This is so, especially, in relation to the late eighteenth and early nineteenth centuries, after which significant structural shifts from household-based to nondomestic forms of employment would have altered the relative contribution of unmeasured women's work.[18] Moreover, certain fairly recent studies have revealed significant regional variations in household production and the organization of women's work, which had a profound effect on patterns of agricultural and industrial development in the nineteenth century.

In parts of the mid-Atlantic region, for instance, the labor demands of wheat production and the availability of immigrant male labor combined to make late colonial and early national household textile production a mixed-gender affair, in which women spun yarn for weaving by male weavers. In New England, by contrast, with its different crop mixes, both spinning and weaving had become women's work by the late colonial period.[19] These patterns were linked to the composition of labor in households. Farming families in Pennsylvania and adjacent regions were more likely than those in New England to employ servants or dependent wage-workers. Such patterns in turn strongly influenced their regions' respective industrial development. Farm families in New England became increasingly engaged in rural manufactures, including outwork done at home by women for merchants and factories, and rural women became a significant proportion of New England's first factory workforces. Mid-Atlantic rural regions became less involved in manufacturing; outwork was rarer, and the proportion of women workers in early industry considerably lower. Women and children were, as Barry W. Levy has noted, New England's first working class. Working-class formation in the mid-Atlantic region followed somewhat different patterns, due in part to the different composition and orientation of rural households.[20] Across the U.S., household patterns, their relationships to production and consumption, gender roles and relationships, helped determine the character of class and race in different regions.

Attention to the history of women has led to further developments in the understanding of social processes. From early studies of women's experience in early America, by Carroll Smith Rosenberg, Nancy Cott, and others in the 1970s, emerged an appreciation of the social networks and interconnections that threaded individuals and families together. Materials long unknown or disregarded bear clues, not just to patterns of everyday life, but to relationships between the open and hidden character-istics of social life.[21]

Historians have long been attentive to patterns of kinship, lineage, and social networks when analyzing elite groups, and this focus has continued. Groups of merchants, with kin and friendship connections, were among the primary actors in transatlantic trade. Family and kinship provided much of the connection, knowledge, and mutual interest that enabled bonds based on trust to be maintained over great distances, and such connections often also provided the channels along which capital flowed to finance commercial innovations. Rural and provincial elites, too, were often bound by kinship ties. Delaware's eight leading Federalist families at the turn of the nineteenth century have been described as "one extended cousinage," whose connections spread into Maryland and New Jersey as well. Perhaps half of the hundred richest Virginia families were connected to one another by marriage.[22]

Yet extension of network analysis to other social groups has done much to reveal broader patterns of interconnection in early America. It has helped define and explain exclusion and inclusiveness. Recent studies of post-revolutionary politics and ideology have uncovered the rich symbolism of late eighteenth-century political culture and what Simon Newman has called the "politics of the street."[23] Yet as Newman and others have recognized, this culture was not merely symbolic, but underwent structural changes, as politics shifted from "the street" into the world of clubs, caucuses and political meetings associated with the creation of a party system. At one level, this shift entailed exclusion: politically marginal groups, including the poor, women, and African Americans were often robbed of what little political role they had had by being denied the chance for informal public participation in ritual events. In another sense, however, post-revolutionary politics reflected the revolution's legacy in admitting once-excluded groups to political participation. White working-men, in particular, had been able to force their way into the political arena, and their sustained pressure for participation was met by the widespread and progressive reduction of property qualifications and other restrictions on their voting during the first quarter of the nineteenth century. It was also reflected in marked increases in participation in politics. Voting turnouts, long known to have reached high levels during the Jacksonian period, have now been found to have risen from early in the century.[24]

Analysis of social networks has, however, also reshaped our understanding of the positions of men and women in social groups. Recent attention to Jürgen Habermas's conception of a bourgeois public sphere in the civic life of towns has focused on its gendered character. The public sociability associated with coffeehouses, exchanges, and other informal public arenas was overwhelmingly male. Yet as Mary P. Ryan, Elizabeth Varon, and others have shown, women also came to occupy quasi-public roles in the conduct of political and civic life, although excluded from power or voting. Churches, too, especially in the revivals of the Second Great Awakening, became complex terrains which women profoundly influenced even as they remained under formal male leadership. From these sprung many of the reform movements that would markedly affect public life and political debate over everything from education and the consumption of alcohol to the abolition of slavery. Other historians have uncovered the interactions, shared by men and women closer to home, which helped shape these quasi-public roles. Karen V. Hansen traced patterns of sociability among rural New Englanders, identifying the arena of the "social" as a middle ground between the "public" world and the "private" sphere of family intimacy. Nancy Grey Osterud has stressed the shared character of men's and women's roles in the development of northern farming communities.[25]

Social networks profoundly influenced patterns of economic development. Rural historians have underscored the importance of household exchanges of goods and labor, and the role of kinship and neighborhood in shaping education, apprenticeship, employment, courtship, and marriage. New ventures in crop-raising and marketing, in rural handicraft manufacturing, and in emigration to new regions frequently drew on these patterns of exchange and interconnection. Above all, they formed many of the channels along which credit flowed in the antebellum economy.

Frontier settlement, for example, was rarely an individual activity. Family connections and chain migration helped structure the westward movement, which was usually centered not on individuals but on households. Young men might travel west to seek out places to settle, but often their families, and perhaps kin and neighbors too, subsequently gathered around them, or were guided by their presence to settle near them. Though census evidence suggests that individual settlers and families were often highly mobile, analysis of social networks reveals patterns of kinship and neighborhood that shaped their actions, and provided a degree of geographical stability. Family and neighborhood credit and assistance was frequently instrumental in setting up new farms. Friendship and kinship also structured frontier trade, not least because they promised fewer risks than dealing with strangers. When Johann Sutter (later famous as the owner of the land on which California gold was discovered in 1848) started trading on the Santa Fe trail in 1835, one of his Missouri neighbors noted that "several Germans are joining him, since he is a clever man of good character, one you can believe and trust; also because we have known him for a long time." Ties of family, region, and religion strongly influenced settlement patterns and community-building by European migrants to the Middle West, but they were often important to American-born migrants too.[26]

The California Gold Rush itself, that great symbol of male escape and aspiration, owed much to the influence of social networks. Though it attracted young men pursuing visions of wealth and adventure, it drew particularly from regions and groups where kinship and neighborhood networks could sponsor gold-seeking. Among the tens of thousands of 'Forty-Niners, migrants from the Northeastern states were particularly prominent, while those from the Old Southeast were often conspicuous by their absence. Men organized emigrant companies or traveled to California in groups based on local patterns of connection and affiliation. Even though many of these groups had dissolved by the time they reached the goldfields, they played a crucial role in organizing the effort to get there. Gold-digging itself was in many respects a cooperative venture, and returning gold-seekers frequently had to face the expectations of the kin and neighborhood sponsors they had left behind.[27]

Yet the importance of family and neighborhood networks for shaping patterns of debt and credit also formed part of the process of social exclusion on racial, gender, or other grounds. The collapse of the "middle ground" between Indian and white societies entailed in part the cutting off of trading and credit relationships across cultural boundaries. In older-settled regions such as New England, Native Americans became increasingly separated from most social networks, living with few connections to white society, or working in ways that kept them out of the records generated by white households and institutions. But, for people of color who sought to operate in white society, race and exclusion from social networks could still bring vulnerability. Between 1815 and 1830, Elleanor Eldridge, an African American woman in Providence, Rhode Island, built a profitable business as a house decorator and landlord. However, as the racial atmosphere in Providence became poisonous in the 1830s, Eldridge became exposed to white vindictiveness. Traveling through Massachusetts, she fell ill and stayed for some time with relatives to recuperate. In her absence, rumors spread in Providence that she was dead, and creditors stepped in to secure their assets. She returned home to find her properties sold off at auction and her (black) tenants evicted, and she faced a long, unsuccessful effort to recoup her losses through a court system resolutely deaf to her remonstrances.[28]

Chain migration, family connections, and community settlement shaped the social contexts for some of the major issues in nineteenth-century American development. Benedict Anderson has written of the sense of affinity between strangers that weave the "imagined communities" of nationhood, and identified the emergence of capitalist print-culture as one of the means by which this sense of affinity could be cultivated. Undoubtedly, such a process occurred in the antebellum U.S., which became preeminently a nation of readers and of avid devourers of newspapers and other printed media.[29] But because of its heavy reliance on social connections, migration also literally stretched the webs of kinship far across the continent. By 1858, when President James Buchanan spoke of ties that bound Americans from ocean to ocean, he was referring not just to symbolic bonds, but to real connections that many thousands of people felt through personal experience.

A society of migrants was also a culture of letter-writers. The "community" that many Americans imagined was constructed of kinship ties as well as more abstract concepts of affinity. Indeed, private letters from kin were often channels for the circulation of print media, as families sent newspapers to friends and relatives living at a distance. And though Buchanan sought to stress the unity such bonds established among a scattered people, it was by then clear that they were also vectors of division. When New England and southern migrants clashed in Kansas after 1854 over the extension of slavery, their respective positions were nurtured by men and women back East who not only supported their principles, but recognized direct kinship and other ties with them. Social networks, in other words, such as those around kinship and migration, underpinned profound political conflicts. The expansion of slavery to the West would have remained a largely abstract issue had it not been for kinship ties that made it of tangible personal concern for many people across the nation.

Important as they were in shaping patterns of behavior, however, household, familial, and social networks also constrained individuals, and provoked efforts to break with them. The tropes of individual adventure and breaking the bonds of society figured strongly in nineteenth-century writing, particularly in male self-representations. This abandonment or reshaping of social networks was an important force for change.

Again, much depended on the ability to control labor. Historian Jean Cashin has suggested that, for slaveholding planters moving from the Carolinas and Georgia to new cotton lands in Alabama and Mississippi, escape meant stepping beyond wider family relationships altogether. Owning slaves liberated a handful of wealthy Southerners from the social ties that bound most people.[30] In the North, many successful nineteenth-century men from rural backgrounds wrote autobiographies that stressed their escape from family ties and household obligations – though the more respectable took care to pay tribute to the influence of their mothers. The escape was often from the labor or tedium of farming itself. For Horace Greeley, it was a removal from rural poverty to cosmopolitan opportunity, in his case through apprenticeship and hard labor in the printing trade. For James Guild, peddler from Vermont, escape meant the pursuit of personal ambition, removal from friends who were content to continue a modest way of life, and a hard – though ultimately triumphant – struggle with the dark forces of loneliness that accompanied the abandonment of neighbors and kin.[31]

This theme of escape from family and local ties was deeply gendered. Men sought it more often than women, and stressed it in memoirs to a greater degree than women did in letters or diaries. Though men's and women's attitudes to migration varied across a broad spectrum, women often found the decision to move taken for them and the breach with family and kin a brutal wrench. Cashin's study of migrant planter families emphasizes the contrast between men who longed to break with family ties and their wives who found themselves committed to frontier isolation without the support of now-distant connections. Rarely, however, did this male escape from old ties entirely succeed. Cashin has suggested that the absence of banks on the Southern frontier led newly-settled planters to fall back on their Eastern families and resources when hard times struck, and connects this with relatively high rates of bankruptcy and instability among cotton planters.[32]

Yet the breaking of family and kinship ties had analogies to the early nineteenth-century expansion of markets. The parallel is not straight-forward. Increased market involvement often rested on personal ties and the access to labor and credit that they bought. But some men, especially, sought new types of institutional affiliation to which they could transfer from their families, kin, and neighbors some or all of their reliance for economic support or assistance. New organizations came to play some of the roles of families, kin, and neighborhood.

A preeminent example was freemasonry, which expanded rapidly after the Revolution. Steven Bullock has shown that in urban areas, where it was already established, freemasonry was transformed as new groups struggled for control of the movement. Meanwhile, it spread geographic-ally, into small towns and country areas where it had not previously existed, becoming an important element in male sociability and affiliation and successfully inserting itself into civic and political life. Not least, it supplemented the personal bonds that structured debt and credit relation-ships in the early republic's economy. Membership of a lodge could provide not only opportunities for business, but also channels of access to credit and special consideration unavailable to those outside masonic circles.[33]

Coupled with the secrecy of its rituals and behavior, these facets of masonic affiliation brought the movement into collision with other religious and political groups in the 1820s. Attacks on freemasonry following the Morgan case in 1826, which resulted in the formation of the Antimasonic party, operated on several levels. Politically, it was feasible for masonry's opponents to portray its secrecy as a threat to the republic while they dismantled patterns of intrigue, affiliation or patronage that they rejected or had been excluded from. At the economic level, suspicion of closed arrangements and business deals undermined public confidence in a movement that had functioned in part as a substitute for private financial networks. At the religious level, freemasons found themselves attacked by evangelicals for their rituals, and for their associations with deism. Moreover, there was a gendered character to antimasonry. While evangelical churches became important institutional affiliations for women outside the home, masonic lodges remained exclusively male. Because part of the spiritual process of evangelical reform was to rescue and convert male souls, freemasonry found itself under attack as a bastion of male privilege, unreachable by female influence.

More gradually, but in much of the North at least more permanently, banks also emerged as affiliations giving access to credit and resources hitherto provided through family or kin networks. Groups of men with means formed banks in part to take advantage of the capital and savings of others, but also to create institutions that could assume their personal borrowing and lending obligations. An important role for early nineteenth-century banks was to lend money to the men who founded them or to their close associates. Rhode Island banking commissioners reported in 1836 that the state's banks were "to a considerable extent mere engines to provide the directors with money." Massachusetts and New Hampshire reports reached similar conclusions.[34] The political controversies over banking that flared in some states in the antebellum period were shaped in part by attitudes to the social relationships within which banks operated. New institutions helped reshape American society as they provided solutions to the tensions and problems of social networks.

The interactions of the issues discussed above – inequality, property, households, social networks, and institutions – helped weave the fabric of change that altered American society between the Revolution and Reconstruction. There were myriad other influences, too, from religion, the law, and politics to technological change and the development of markets. Yet the intersections of social structures and people's agency made cultural and material circumstances into powerful forces of conflict and change.

Because this was particularly so in periods of economic distress, financial panics such as those of 1819 and 1837 and the depressions that followed them were important turning-points in the evolution of social structures.[35] Entrepreneurs, picking up after the 1819 panic, intensified efforts they had already begun in order to exercise control over craft skills, and to increase their systematic use of waged employees. It is no coincidence that some of the first organized labor movements, industrial strikes, and labor periodicals emerged in the 1820s. Still, the ideology of the 1820s and 1830s remained deeply rooted in the Revolutionary era's concept of propertied independence. Mechanics' and trades' associations, and the "middling interest" parties that sprang up in Boston and other centers, urged that property used in the production of goods should be the basis for freedom and equality. Suspicion of large organizations or corporations centered on the fear that they would subvert these hopes. "The liberty our fathers sought," wrote the Rhode Islander Thomas Man in 1833, "the factory system sets at nought." Economic expansion and diversification lay primarily in the hands of small businesses, independent craftsmen, and households. Journeymen carriage-makers in Massachusetts, protesting against the incorporation of a carriage-building company in 1838, wrote of their aspirations to become masters of their own shops. Women factory operatives on strike at Lowell, Massachusetts, in the 1830s took their stand as "the daughters of free men."[36]

The panic of 1837 and subsequent depression had a more profound effect. It speeded institutional shifts, particularly in the North, emphasizing the role of corporations and large investors, and introducing commercial innovations such as credit-reporting and new accounting methods. Moreover, as Edward Balleisen has suggested, the shattering experience of bankruptcy reshaped the aspirations of small producers, many of whom now sought salaried positions that could provide security without great financial risk. They moved into clerkships, brokerages, insurance, the offices of commercial and transportation companies, or undertook management functions in newly-growing railroads and manufacturing firms. This marked the inception of a new middle class that by the postbellum period would be identified with the term "white-collar."[37]

As salaried work came to be interpreted by the 1850s as the ideological equivalent of propertied independence, important similarities and differences with manual waged employment also emerged over the next two decades. On one hand, the insistence that a salary conferred independence and full standing as a citizen of the republic helped shape the ideological coalition between farmers, wage-workers, and businessmen who entered the Republican Party after 1854. The new middle class could claim equal standing with the nation's farmers. As salaried employees, however, they occupied similar relationships to business as wage-workers, though perhaps with greater status or influence. The respectability of a salary helped legitimize the growing respectability of the wage, and so the shift of the 1840s did some of the work of bringing wage-work firmly within a newly aligned republican vision.

There was also, however, a significant ethnocultural dimension to this ideological shift. Access to "white-collar" work was at first skewed towards the American-born, who predominated among those "independent" traders and craftsmen hit by the panic of 1837 and its aftermath. Family contacts, kinship, and neighborhood all contributed to the finding of clerical and other employment, just as they had previously guided the finding of apprenticeships and clerks' positions in stores. Meanwhile, the growing influx of wage workers from Europe – including British textile and pottery workers fleeing depression and Irish families fleeing famine – began to solve the North's chronic shortages of hired labor. Here were men and women who did not have the same networks of social contacts as their American-born neighbors, and who were at first heavily reliant on finding waged employment. The forging of an "ethnic" American working class was under way.[38]

Meanwhile, just as the North was solving its chronic labor scarcities, the South was undergoing the opposite process. The geographical expansion of the plantation system, underscored by the annexation of Texas in 1845, bid up the price of slave labor and increased the concentration of slaveholding in the hands of wealthy planters. Northern free-soil ideologists, congratulating themselves at the fluidity of their own society, looked southward to see growing inequalities, both as between slave and free, and as between slaveholders and nonslaveholding whites.[39]

The creation of new hierarchies of white-collar work in the North enabled a new social mobility myth to be erected alongside the traditional "agricultural ladder" of progression from hired hand to tenant to land-owning farmer that was an important part of Whig, and then free-soil Republican ideology. One result was a breach with the revolutionary generation's association of worthiness with manual work. Among the new middle class, the conclusion became easier to reach that manual employment was to be avoided if possible. A Union officer, Jerry Remington, writing to his family during the Civil War about his postwar plans, noted that "of all kinds of labor that of the hands gets the least pay. . . . Body and sinew the world over are cheap," and he resolved not to become a farmer like his father. This observation would frame the post-Civil War fragmentation of the Republican alliance of farm, work, and business, and pointed to a growing Northern indifference to the position of former slaves in the post-Reconstruction South.[40]

We can only grasp the full range and power of social changes by understanding the complexities of individual and institutional relationships. Over time, these relationships altered social structures and reshaped society itself. We have always known that, with its rapid demographic growth and geographical expansion, the early United States underwent dramatic change. But recent social history, in its very exposure of the myriad varieties of change, is providing us with a subtler appreciation of the power of social structures and relationships to reshape an entire nation. If social historians have not entirely altered the outline of the story, their work should profoundly affect our understanding of how change came about.

Notes

1. David B. Mattern, *Benjamin Lincoln and the American Revolution* (Columbia, 1995), chapter 6.
2. Allan Kulikoff, *From British Peasants to Colonial American Farmers* (Chapel Hill, 2000), pp. 256–75; Matthew Gallman, *The North Fights the Civil War* (Chicago, 1996), p. 65.
3. Alice Hanson Jones, *Wealth of a Nation to Be: The American Colonies on the Eve of the Revolution* (New York, 1980). The Boston figure of 63.4 per cent was for 1771. See Gary B. Nash, *The Urban Crucible: Social Change, Political Consciousness, and the Origins of the American Revolution* (Cambridge, MA, 1979), p. 395. On wealth distribution generally, see James L. Huston, *Securing the Fruits of Labor: The American Concept of Wealth Distribution, 1765–1900* (Baton Rouge, 1998) and Lee Soltow, *The Distribution of Wealth and Income in the United States in 1798* (Pittsburgh, 1989).
4. On the prevalence of poverty, see Billy G. Smith, *The "Lower Sort": Philadelphia's Laboring People, 1750–1800* (Ithaca, 1990) and Richard Oestreicher, "The Counted and the Uncounted: The Occupational Structure of Early American Cities," *Journal of Social History*, 28 (1994): 351–61; on gender and poverty, Daniel Scott Smith, "Female Householding in late 18th-century America and the Problem of Poverty," *Journal of Social History*, 28 (1994): 83–107, and Elaine Forman Crane, *Ebb Tide in New England: Women, Seaports, and Social Change, 1630–1800* (Boston, 1998).
5. Steven J. Ross, *Workers on the Edge: Work, Leisure, and Politics in Industrializing Cincinnati, 1788–1890* (New York, 1985).
6. David J. Grettler, "Environmental Change and Conflict over Hogs in Early Nineteenth-Century Delaware," *Journal of the Early Republic*, 19 (1999): 197–220; Paul G. E. Clemens and Lucy Simler, "Rural Labor and the Farm Household in Chester County, Pennsylvania, 1750–1820," in Stephen Innes, ed., *Work and Labor in Early America*

(Chapel Hill, 1988), pp. 113–14; John L. Brooke, *The Heart of the Commonwealth: Society and Political Culture in Worcester County, Massachusetts, 1713–1861* (Cambridge, UK, 1989), pp. 42–3.

7. Soltow, *Distribution of Wealth and Income*, p. 74. On the Old Southwest, see Stephen J. Aron, *How the West was Lost: The Transformation of Kentucky from Daniel Boone to Henry Clay* (Baltimore, 1996); on Appalachia, Wilma A. Dunaway, *The First American Frontier: The Transition to Capitalism in Southern Appalachia, 1700–1860* (Chapel Hill, 1996); on Western Pennsylvania, R. Eugene Harper, *The Transformation of Western Pennsylvania, 1770–1800* (Pittsburgh, 1991); on Ohio, Daniel M. Friedenberg, *Life, Liberty, and the Pursuit of Land: The Plunder of Early America* (Buffalo, 1992), p. 277.

8. David Jaffee, *People of the Wachusett: Greater New England in History and Memory, 1630–1860* (Ithaca, 1999); Toby L. Ditz, *Property and Kinship: Inheritance in Early Connecticut, 1730–1860* (Princeton, 1986); Winifred B. Rothenberg, *From Market-Places to a Market Economy: The Transformation of Rural Massachusetts, 1750–1850* (Chicago, 1992).

9. Edward Countryman, *Americans: A Collision of Histories* (New York, 1996); Richard White, *The Middle Ground: Indians, Empires and Republics in the Great Lakes Region, 1650–1815* (Cambridge, UK, 1991); Gregory H. Nobles, *American Frontiers: Cultural Encounters and Continental Conquest* (New York, 1997).

10. Alan Taylor, *Liberty-Men and Great Proprietors: The Revolutionary Settlement on the Maine Frontier, 1760–1820* (Chapel Hill, 1990); idem., *William Cooper's Town: Power and Persuasion on the Frontier of the Early American Republic* (New York, 1995); Charles E. Brooks, *Frontier Settlement and Market Revolution: The Holland Land Purchase* (Ithaca, 1996); Reeve Huston, *Land and Freedom: Rural Society, Popular Protest and Party Politics in Antebellum New York* (New York, 2000).

11. James Oakes, *Slavery and Freedom: An Interpretation of the Old South* (New York, 1990), pp. 75–7.

12. Soltow, *Distribution of Wealth and Income*, p. 64; on David Hudson, see Gerald W. McFarland, *A Scattered People: An American Family Moves West* (1985; reprint ed., Amherst, MA, 1991), pp. 71–7. *Memoirs and Auto-biography of Some of the Wealthy Citizens of Philadelphia, with a Fair Estimate of their Estates* (Philadelphia, 1846), compiled 1,132 entries, of which 942 gave details of sources of wealth. Of these 12.8 per cent held urban property. Roy Rosenzweig

and Elizabeth Blackmar, *The Park and the People: A History of Central Park* (Ithaca, 1992).

13. Kulikoff, *From British Peasants to Colonial American Farmers*, chapter 5; Christopher Clark, *The Roots of Rural Capitalism: Western Massachusetts, 1780–1860* (Ithaca, 1990), chapter 3; David S. Landes, *The Wealth and Poverty of Nations: Why Some are so Rich and Some so Poor* (New York, 1998), pp. 297–8.

14. Stephanie McCurry, *Masters of Small Worlds: Yeoman Households, Gender Relations, and the Political Culture of the Antebellum South Carolina Low Country* (New York, 1995); John Ashworth, *Slavery, Capitalism and Politics in the Antebellum Republic: Volume I: Commerce and Compromise, 1820–1850* (Cambridge, UK, 1995).

15. Paul W. Gates, ed., *California Ranchos and Farms, 1846–1862, including the Letters of John Quincy Adams Warren of 1861* (Madison, WI, 1967), p. xv.

16. Michael Grossberg, *Governing the Hearth: Law and the Family in Nineteenth Century America* (Chapel Hill, 1985).

17. Jeanne Boydston, *Home and Work: Housework, Wages, and the Ideology of Labor in the Early Republic* (New York, 1990); Laurel Thatcher Ulrich, *Good Wives: Image and Reality in the Lives of Women in Northern New England, 1650–1750* (New York, 1982).

18. N. Folbre and B. Wagman, "Counting Housework: New Estimates of Real Product in the United States, 1800–1860," *Journal of Economic History*, 53 (1993): 275–88.

19. Laurel Thatcher Ulrich, "Wheels, Looms, and the Gender Division of Labor in 18th Century New England," *William and Mary Quarterly*, 55 (1998): 3–38; Adrienne D. Hood, "The Gender Division of Labor in the Production of Textiles in 18th Century Rural Pennsylvania (Rethinking the New England Model)," *Journal of Social History*, 27 (1994): 537–61; idem., "The Material World of Cloth Production and Use in 18th Century Rural Pennsylvania," *William and Mary Quarterly*, 53 (1996): 43–66.

20. Clark, *The Roots of Rural Capitalism*, chapter 5; Thomas Dublin, *Transforming Women's Work: New England Lives in the Industrial Revolution* (Ithaca, 1994); Philip Scranton, *Proprietary Capitalism: The Textile Manufacture at Philadelphia* (Cambridge, UK, 1984); Barry Levy, paper presented to the Annual Conference of the Society for Historians of the Early American Republic, Nashville, TN, July 1996.

21. Carroll Smith Rosenberg, "The Female World of Love and Ritual," *Signs* (1975); Nancy F. Cott, *The Bonds of Womanhood* (New Haven,

1977); Laurel Thatcher Ulrich, *A Midwife's Tale: The Life of Martha Ballard, Based on her Diary, 1785–1812* (New York, 1990); Catherine E. Kelly, *In the New England Fashion: Reshaping Women's Lives in the Nineteenth Century* (Ithaca, 1999).

22. Philip H. Burch, Jr., *Elites in American History,* 3 vols. (New York, 1980–1981), vol. I, p. 46.

23. Simon P. Newman, *Parades and the Politics of the Street: Festive Culture in the Early American Republic* (Philadelphia, 1997); David Waldstreicher, *In the Midst of Perpetual Fetes: The Making of American Nationalism, 1776–1820* (Chapel Hill, 1997).

24. Andrew W. Robertson, *The Language of Democracy: Political Rhetoric in the United States and Britain, 1790–1900* (Ithaca, 1995).

25. Jürgen Habermas, *The Structural Transformation of the Public Sphere* (1962; trans. ed. Cambridge, UK, 1989); Elizabeth R. Varon, "Tippecanoe and the Ladies Too: White Women and Party Politics in Antebellum Virginia," *Journal of American History*, 82 (1995): 494–521; Karen V. Hansen, *A Very Social Time: Crafting Community in Antebellum New England* (Berkeley, 1994); Nancy Grey Osterud, *Bonds of Community: The Lives of Farm Women in Nineteenth Century New York* (Ithaca, 1991).

26. Walter D. Kamphoefner et. al., eds., *News from the Land of Freedom: German Immigrants Write Home* (Ithaca, 1991), p. 100; Jon Gjerde, *The Minds of the West: Ethnocultural Evolution in the Rural Middle West, 1830–1917* (Chapel Hill, 1997).

27. Malcolm J. Rohrbough, *Days of Gold: The California Gold Rush and the American Nation* (Berkeley, 1997).

28. Donna Keith Baron, J. Edward Hood, and Holly V. Izard, "They Were Here All Along: The Native American Presence in Lower-Central New England in the Eighteenth and Nineteenth Centuries," *William and Mary Quarterly*, 53 (1996): 561–86; [Frances H. Green] *Memoir of Elleanor Eldridge* (Providence, RI, 1838), pp. 63–93.

29. Benedict Anderson, *Imagined Communities: Reflections on the Origin and Spread of Nationalism* (1983; revised edition London, 1991).

30. Jean V. Cashin, *A Family Venture: Men and Women on the Southern Frontier* (Baltimore, 1991).

31. Joyce O. Appleby, ed., *Recollections of the Early Republic: Selected Autobiographies* (Boston, 1997); Horace Greeley, *Recollections of a Busy Life* (New York, 1868). See also Joyce Appleby, *Inheriting the Revolution: The First Generation of Americans* (Cambridge, MA, 2000).

32. Cashin, *A Family Venture*, pp. 85–6.

33. Steven C. Bullock, *Revolutionary Brotherhood: Freemasonry and the Transformation of the American Social Order, 1730–1840* (Chapel Hill, 1996), chapter 7.
34. Naomi Lamoreaux, "Information Problems and Banks' Specialization in Short-Term Commercial Lending: New England in the 19th Century," in Peter Temin, ed., *Inside the Business Enterprise: Historical Perspectives on the Uses of Information* (Chicago, 1991), p. 163; see also Naomi R. Lamoreaux, *Insider Lending: Banks, Personal Connections and Economic Development in Industrial New England* (Cambridge, UK, 1994).
35. Charles Sellers, *The Market Revolution: Jacksonian America, 1815–1846* (New York, 1991) emphasizes the significance of the panic of 1819.
36. Gary Kornblith, "Cementing the Mechanic Interest," *Journal of the Early Republic*, 8 (1988); Thomas Man, *The Factory Store: A Poem* (Providence, RI, 1833); Remonstrance of George W. Cushing and Others (1838), in Oscar Handlin and Mary Flug Handlin, *Commonwealth: A Study of the Role of Government in the American Economy: Massachusetts, 1774–1861*, revised edition (Cambridge, MA, 1969), p. 266; Thomas Dublin, *Women at Work: the transformation of work and community in Lowell, Massachusetts, 1826–1860* (New York, 1978).
37. Edward J. Balleisen, *Navigating Failure: Bankruptcy and Commercial Society in Antebellum America* (Chapel Hill, 2001); see also Alfred D. Chandler, *The Visible Hand: The Managerial Revolution in American Business* (Cambridge, MA, 1977).
38. Herbert G. Gutman, *Power and Culture: Essays on the American Working Class*, ed. Ira Berlin (New York, 1987), Introduction.
39. Gavin Wright, "'Economic Democracy' and the Concentration of Agricultural Wealth in the Cotton South, 1850–1860," in William N. Parker, ed., *The Structure of the Cotton Economy of the Antebellum South* (Washington, DC, 1970), especially pp. 73–9.
40. Eric Foner, *Free Soil, Free Labor, Free Men: The Political Ideology of the Republican Party before the Civil War* (New York, 1970); Joseph P. Reidy, *From Slavery to Agrarian Capitalism in the Cotton Plantation South: Central Georgia, 1800–1880* (Chapel Hill, 1992). Heather Cox Richardson, *The Death of Reconstruction: Race, Labor, and Politics in the Post-Civil War North, 1865–1901* (Cambridge, MA, 2001).

–3–

Rediscovering Jacksonian America
Daniel Feller

My purpose here is to assess the state and prospects of scholarship on Jacksonian America, the period extending roughly from the War of 1812 to the Mexican War and centering on the 1820s and 1830s. It is customary to begin a historiographic review by applauding the vitality of one's field – the parade of fine monographs, the emergence of new insights, the exciting work in progress. Yet candor in this case compels a different course. In the closing years of the twentieth century, Jacksonian scholarship, strictly so-called, fell into the doldrums. Both in popular perception and in college courses, the period has become something of a dead zone between the founding era and the Civil War. The ranks of self-described Jacksonian scholars are thinning, while the label "Jacksonian" has become increasingly rare and problematic, often appearing only within quotation marks. In the early 1970s the *Journal of American History* ran six articles featuring "Jacksonian" in the title, culminating with Ronald P. Formisano's historiographic essay in June 1976. In the quarter-century that followed, there were none. Meanwhile the vaguer term "antebellum" grew from two appearances in article titles in the 1970s to nine in the 1990s.

Yet only a generation earlier the Jacksonian era had stood prominent and even preeminent, at least among political historians. In dual polls in 1976 and 1977, scholars named the five most influential works in American political history to appear since World War II. Two of them were Arthur M. Schlesinger Jr.'s *The Age of Jackson* and Lee Benson's *The Concept of Jacksonian Democracy*, while a third, Richard Hofstadter's *The American Political Tradition*, had important chapters on Jackson and John C. Calhoun. No book from the colonial, Revolutionary, Federalist-Jeffersonian, or Civil War eras made the list.[1]

No one would expect the same results today. Yet why should a subject once seen as central in the American story have lost its salience so quickly? Declining general interest in political history cannot be the whole answer, for studies of the founding era and its personalities have never thrived so well. Jacksonian America has dropped from our consciousness not because we lost interest in politics, but because it lost its once-proud place in the master narrative of American history, even as the very idea of a master narrative came into question. Work continues on the years from 1815 to 1848, but its prevailing thrust is not to reinforce but to challenge the presumption of "Jacksonian America" as an epoch with coherent boundaries and distinctive content.

Beginning with Alexis de Tocqueville, master narratives pinpointed the Jacksonian era as the time when America really became American, when its defining qualities emerged, whether those qualities be freedom and democracy (as in the subheadings to Robert V. Remini's Jackson biography) or something less savory such as acquisitiveness, materialism, ethnocentrism, and racism (as argued most forcefully by Edward Pessen).[2] One enduring approach has been to link the era's political distinctiveness (the emergence of Jacksonian Democracy) to its economic innovations (the transportation revolution). In its latest incarnation, this fusion produced the "market revolution" synthesis, as expounded in Charles Sellers's 1991 opus of the same name, in Sean Wilentz's 1990 historiographic essay, in the Commonwealth Fund conference of 1994, and in works by Harry L. Watson and others.[3]

Taken at face value, the market revolution thesis ought to have put the Jacksonian era at the forefront of scholarly attention, for it pinpoints it as the pivotal turning point in all of American history, the moment when America went capitalist, or perhaps was conquered by capitalists. Yet despite a flurry of publicity surrounding Sellers's book, a general reawakening of interest in the period of this supposedly vital transformation seems not to have happened. To discuss the most significant reasons for this failure requires clearing away some linguistic debris, for, as with "republicanism," the market revolution has achieved a certain ubiquity and utility largely by losing specific meaning. Some historians use the term as an undifferentiated label for change after 1815, while others tie it down in a variety of ways.[4]

The interpretative forebear of the market revolution was the transportation revolution, a phrase to which its creator, George Rogers Taylor, gave precise content: the inauguration of new means of transportation and communication and their impact upon patterns of production, distribution, and consumption. This event was revolutionary, but in economic capabilities rather than social purposes. Taylor acknowledged clashes of group-interest generated by rapid development, but he made no claim of overarching class conflict or cultural transformation, and indeed his scheme left little room for it. His discussion of government, for instance, assessed the instruments Americans used to promote economic growth, but did not posit a fundamental disagreement over the nature of economic organization or the basic power relationships in society. Americans' ambition to get ahead was already there in 1815; the transportation revolution provided the means. It was an acceleration down an existing path, not a turning away from it.[5]

Despite a superficial resemblance that has led some users to employ them interchangeably, the market revolution thesis is very different. It sees the changes described by Taylor as contested, not consensual; as discontinuous from previous experience, revolutionary not only in material effects but in cultural essence. The market revolution did not merely extend and quicken the operation of markets. It created, or imposed, a market society and a market culture. It marked either the penetration of capitalist values among the people at large or the conquest of those who held them over their foes – in Charles Sellers's terms, the advent of bourgeois hegemony. It was a revolution not only in economic instruments, but in *mentalité* and in power.[6]

A major article by Harry L. Watson typifies the argument. Watson interprets controversies between fishermen and millers over damming Southern streams in terms of a "deep clash of values" between "the emergent culture of the marketplace ... celebrating hard work and personal advancement," and "the culture of an older subsistence community ... depending on natural abundance, the rhythms of nature, and the consumption needs of its members to regulate its work life." Where a consensus historian might see the play of interests, or a conventional Marxist a conflict of classes, the market revolution scholar finds a clash of cultures, of "power and ideology." There are clear winners and losers: the "transforming power of the market revolution" spells "an end to the independence and empowerment that had once been established by republican government and the subsistence economy. ... What the American Revolution had granted, the market revolution was taking away." The "frustrated yeoman" could only submit or "retreat" to the American West, there to fight and lose the same battle again and again to the end of the century. In this scheme the American West is always a refuge of oppression, never a land of opportunity, for people going there do not want to better their lives but only to preserve their "independence." They are not conquerors but refugees, not carriers of capitalism but victims of it.[7]

Market-revolution historians track what they see as a pervasive political-social-cultural-religious resistance to the intrusion of the market. Curiously, they have not found much sign of it in economic practice.

Some have hardly felt it necessary to look: as one critic observed, the economic content of the essays in *The Market Revolution in America* was "surprisingly light." Though economic historians may have their own ideological blinders and limiting presumptions, still their techniques are useful in testing propositions about economic activity. Thus far, those techniques have not borne out claims of anti-market behavior even among groups supposedly most hostile to the market revolution. Nor, on the other side, has anyone shown or seriously tried to show that the revolution's supposed spear-carriers – bankers, merchants, entrepreneurs – were really as singlemindedly self-aggrandizing as Charles Sellers and others would suggest. Thus the empirical foundations for the market revolution as a "deep clash of values" remain in doubt.[8]

The evidence for Taylor's transportation revolution lies in canals, railroads, telegraph lines, freight rates and tonnages, factories, banks and credit agencies, prices current, store and household inventories. The proof of the market revolution, conceived not as a quickened stage in development but as a cultural conquest, is – where? As one critic notes, the idea that Americans had become more "materialistic, competitive, and self-interested" by the 1830s "appears in almost every book on post-revolutionary America published in the last thirty years," yet "has never been defended empirically." On the other side, one would think that European visitors could not help but notice the anxiety and misgiving, to say nothing of "the fury, the suspicion, and the terror," that supposedly possessed those millions of Americans who "felt themselves in the grip of monsters" as the market revolution overwhelmed them. Yet one looks in vain in travellers' accounts for evidence of these gripping fears. Instead they complain of ordinary Americans' insufferable exuberance and confidence.[9]

It is indeed easy to find in Jacksonian America (or today) expressions of unease with the quickening pace of life, resentment at the wealth and extravagance of others, and nostalgia for a simpler time, along with complaints against business corporations, stock-jobbing and speculation, and currency manipulation. But to elevate these into resistance to the market revolution (without which the market revolution, conceived as a culture war, ceases to exist) requires force-feeding them into a reified scheme whose categories are at once oversimplified and anachronistic. A characteristic article on "Religious Tracts, Evangelical Reform, and the Market Revolution in America" shows where this may lead. While noting that technological and organizational improvements made possible the American Tract Society's mass production and distribution of its pamphlets, the author claims that their message "stood in opposition to the values and priorities of the market revolution" by "celebrating a traditional world of reciprocal social obligations, community harmony, and religious duty" – "a vision strikingly at odds with the individualism of liberal economic thought." Here is an anthropomorphized market revolution with its own values and priorities; liberalism and individualism reduced to plain selfishness; and all the complexities of human motivation and aspiration arrayed in simple dichotomy. Surely the idea that his business practices contravened his social, community, and religious concerns would have baffled Arthur Tappan, the Tract Society's chief sponsor. Is chopping him up into opposing pro- and anti-capitalist impulses really the best way to make sense of him?[10]

One sign of the difficulty in nailing down the market revolution is that those who posit it cannot agree when it happened, though its pernicious effects seem always the same. Viewed from outside the Jacksonian prism, the market revolution appears as another incarnation of the ubiquitous transition to capitalism, which, like the collapse of community, the death of virtue, and the end of the simple life, seems to have been going on at least since the beginning of time. "A subsistence, peasant-based economy was being subverted by mercantile capitalism." A Carolina hamlet in 1830? No, this is Salem Village, Massachusetts, in 1692. Citizens "were buffeted by a world of unstoppable social and economic change. . . . The terms of life were tightening. If some enjoyed a heady freedom in the opportunities for choice and gladly seized the chance to make their way on their own, others floundered without a settled social place" – Concord, Massachusetts, 1775. "Our business men are madly striving in the race for riches"; even "the farmer's son, not satisfied with his father's simple and laborious life, joins the eager chase for easily acquired wealth. . . . The gulf between employers and the employed is constantly widening, and classes are rapidly forming, one comprising the very rich and powerful, while in another are found the toiling poor." Andrew Jackson in 1832? No, Grover Cleveland in 1888.[11]

Whatever one thinks of the transition to capitalism, the case for it as a distinctively Jacksonian phenomenon has not been made. No one has succeeded in tying this broader cultural transformation to its supposed specific reflection in political events of the 1820s and 1830s. To an early-republic specialist, the Jacksonian market revolution appears as a pale echo, a historiographic copycat, of changes that really centered around or preceded the American Revolution. Many scholars find the transition to capitalism under way or even complete before 1815; still others see it stretching well past 1848.[12]

Like its republicanism forerunner, the market revolution with its analogues of liberalism and capitalism once served a useful purpose by alerting historians to things they had not seen. Yet these constructs now stand as blinders and filters between us and the evidence, self-referential archetypes with a life of their own, demanding that the varieties of human experience be diced and trimmed to fit them. This is especially true of capitalism, an anachronism and pernicious abstraction, used often nowadays to fix upon our subjects a purpose of achieving ends they never dreamed of. Capitalism, as a historian's term, gains its utility, its power, its very meaning not so much from what it is (for on definitions there has been much disagreement) as from what it negates and excludes, i.e. from what it is not – socialism, harmonious community, the moral economy, the Garden of Eden. What could take its place in our narratives? Eric Hobsbawm has remarked that "the one element of directional change in human affairs which is observable and objective, irrespective of our subjective or contemporary wishes and value-judgments," is "the persistent and increasing capacity of the human species to control the forces of nature by means of manual and mental labor, technology and the organization of production." This seems unarguable. And hence Hobsbawm declares the indispensability of Marx, for "he built his conception and analysis of history on this basis – and so far no one else has."[13]

I would like to see us try. For if what Hobsbawm calls "a materialist conception of history" is a necessary bow to reality, one that relies on Marxian categories of class to organize its narrative is not. Indeed, to do this is very largely to predetermine the shape of one's story before gathering the evidence to tell it, and there is no better proof of that than the tendentious framing of early American history within the paradigm of capitalist consolidation. By breaking free of it, historians could shed the dualisms that now entrap them, and escape the declensionism – the longing for the lost alternative, the lament for the fatal wrong-turning – that marks so much recent Jacksonian scholarship.

Still, while relinquishing the market revolution may free historians to understand the complexities of Americans' aspirations and actions on their own terms, it may also leave Jacksonian scholars grasping for a unifying theme. Jacksonian America has no banner event, a revolution or war or great national crisis, on which to hang grand narratives. And the tags it once had – the flowering of democracy, the rise of the common man – have fallen into disrepute. The idea that America really became American in Andrew Jackson's day loses force if to be American itself no longer carries a distinctive meaning.

Indeed, scholarship on the period 1815–1848 now runs toward dis-aggregating Jacksonian America and scrutinizing the pieces rather than the whole. In political history this trend is clearly marked, as is the general atrophy of Jacksonian scholarship. The avalanche of major monographs has slowed to a trickle; and while political historians a generation ago struck boldly toward the nexus of politics and society, more recent studies mainly fill out the internal dynamics of the party system. These works amplify and codify our knowledge of Jacksonian politics, but they hardly strike new ground. Further, their opening dates in the 1820s and 1830s show how far straight political history, still pegged to the rise of the party system, has diverged from historians working within the framework of the market revolution, for whom this would be beginning *in media res*.[14]

Journal articles on Jacksonian politics likewise convey an air of *déjà vu*, as scholars re-mine the republican paradigm, dispute whether those high levels of voter turnout really signify participatory democracy, and argue the validity of the "party period" as an organizing tool for political history. While sometimes instructive, these debates are not new. It may say something about the state of Jacksonian political scholarship that the only article the *American Historical Review* chose to run on the subject in the 1990s scolded historians for not reading Lee Benson more carefully. The agenda of Jacksonian political history seems mired in the questions of the 1970s.[15]

In two areas, however, recent work not only revises the picture of poli-tics but casts it in a wider light. The first is gender. In American political history, this clearly is where the action is. Within the period 1815–1848, studies including Elizabeth R. Varon's on Virginia and Ronald and Mary Zboray's on Massachusetts are revealing women as active enthusiasts in party politics. Studies of campaign styles and rhetoric and of certain spe-cific episodes, most notably the Margaret Eaton scandal during Jackson's presidency, are exposing the gendered nature of partisan discourse.[16]

Building on earlier work that highlighted women's benevolent, charit-able, and religious activities, historians are also uncovering evidence and pushing theories that challenge the boundaries around the word "political." Aside from those who demanded the vote, many women were engaged in providing social services and in agitating for a broad array of causes, including Sabbatarianism, temperance, and antislavery. These endeavors, which undercut the image of a separate "woman's sphere," have encou-raged historians to look at the way gender ideology molded perceptions by erecting boundaries between male and female, or public and private, realms of activity – boundaries that now appear more rhetorical (and permeable) than real.[17]

All this adds a new dimension to our picture of Jacksonian civic life. Women were everywhere, not only in public forums but in overtly partisan ones, in discourse and in fact, as symbols and as people. Analysis of gendered party rhetoric fills out the ideological contrasts sketched by earlier political historians: what Elizabeth Varon calls "Whig womanhood" fits neatly into the associative and benevolent Whig ethos described by Daniel Walker Howe and others, just as Democratic notions of male chivalry and protectiveness, as shown in the Eaton affair, confirm our images of the party's rugged masculinity and chauvinism. Henry Clay always yearned to shake hands with opponents; Jackson longed to slit their throats. Given this, Varon's intriguing suggestion of a gender gap in Jacksonian politics might well be true.[18]

Still, despite its freshness and creativity, in several ways the gender approach to politics tends to overplay its hand. The reasons are obvious: as one author declares, "the stakes are high" – not analytical stakes, but political ones. Scholarship which appears to limit the historical agency of white women, like that which circumscribes the initiative of slaves or free blacks, is not very welcome within the historical profession. The demand for a usable past is ever present. It is good that it is; without it, historians would know less than they do, and would have less reason to care. But it does not relieve them of the obligation to ask hard questions.[19]

For one thing, when we talk about women in politics we still have very little idea how many women we are talking about, or how well they typified the wider female population. And at some point, we ought to be moved to find out. That some women were politically engaged is significant, especially if we had once thought there were none. But a following question, for women just as for men, must be: how many and how common were they?[20]

This question, which was high on scholars' agenda a couple of decades ago, seems to have passed into disfavor. Practitioners of yesterday's "new social history" and "new political history" sought out the typical, the everyday, the common. They wore with pride their love of ordinary people. Today, we often aim to gain a critical vantage on the common by seeing it from the outside, and for this perspective we seek out the atypical, the extraordinary, even the bizarre and deviant. As an extreme example, Robert Matthews, also known as Matthias the Prophet, an obscure cultist with a handful of followers, was too insignificant to rate a mention in Alice Felt Tyler's thorough 1944 survey of antebellum religion and reform. Yet now historians use him, or try to, to cast a revelatory light on all of Jacksonian society and culture.[21]

Numbers are not the only measure of significance. Yet they are an important one, as political historians have long realized. The question of who and how many really cared about parties and policies has properly been at the center of political history's agenda for some time now. Historians need to be wary of totalizing generalizations about "women" just as they have learned to be about men. Fascination with women who were feminists or political activists can lead historians to equate the exemplary with the ordinary. Yet to do this without convincing evidence is to make again the same error (or commit the same elitist sin) from which the plain people's history of the last generation of the twentieth century sought to liberate us.

A related point concerns the boundaries of the political. It may be true, as Jean Baker suggests, that "from a broader perspective, parties and high politics are only one expression of a rich, diverse arena . . . of civic life." What gives pause is that word "only." Politics were a special expression, a uniquely powerful expression. They determined who governed, and how. They could, as in 1860–61, start a war. There was a reason why women seeking equality fastened on the vote: it had power. The title of Elizabeth Varon's book suggests the problem: *We Mean to be Counted*. But whatever else they were, women were not counted, in a game where counting determined winners and losers.[22]

The linguistic approach to politics can enlighten, but it can also obscure. An analysis of the controversy over Andrew Jackson's marriage in the 1828 presidential campaign decodes its gendered imagery in creative ways, but is less successful in relating it to issues, policies, or the results of the election itself. Approaching politics as a form of discourse risks losing sight of who said something, why and where they said it, who heard it, and what effect it had on them. The discourse itself becomes the salient fact.[23]

In short, it is not clear that a gendered perspective really changes the old political narrative very much. The places where historians have found gender intruding most clearly into party politics – in formulaic rhetoric and rituals and in certain fairly confined episodes – are ones of arguable significance for politics, if not for gender. The very language which historians now scrutinize so minutely for its gendered inflections was, not long ago, summarily dismissed as "campaign claptrap."[24] From one point of view, the Eaton affair casts a revealing light on the gendered structuring of the Jacksonian political universe. From another point of view, and one with strong scholarly defenders, it was a sideshow. About the main issues of Jacksonian party conflict – the tariff, internal improvements, and above all banking – the gender approach has had little to say, other than to point up that they were male debates, and perhaps therefore not really as consequential as believed by political historians of either the market revolution or party-system schools. Yet the discovery of women as partisans points in the opposite direction – toward reaffirming, rather than undermining, the importance of old-fashioned political history by buttressing its claims to broad popular interest.

The other thriving arena of Jacksonian scholarship is religion. Until recently, political as well as social and labor historians tended to look at religion from the outside only. Even while highlighting its importance, the ethnocultural approach to politics essentially reduced religion to denominational labels and categories, deployed as determinants of party affiliation: evangelical/pietist/puritan/Arminian Whigs versus anti-evangelical/liturgical/nonpuritan/antinomian Democrats. In social and labor history, religion figured as little more than the hegemonizing tool of the capitalist class.[25]

We are far beyond that now. At the beginning of the 1990s, Nathan Hatch and Jon Butler, looking at religion from the inside, brought home the depth and volatility of Americans' Christian faith. An avalanche of scholarship followed. This is not the place to explore this literature (reviewed by Mark A. Noll in Chapter Four of this volume), but only to give a sense of the myriad directions in which it points. Indeed, religion is at once the most expansive and the most integrative force at work within Jacksonian scholarship today.[26]

In *Cosmos Crumbling*, Robert Abzug showed how what he calls the "religious imagination" energized Americans to sacralize and purify their lives, their communities, and their country through a host of campaigns including Sabbatarianism, temperance, body reforms, and abolitionism. Richard Carwardine revealed how evangelicalism permeated antebellum political culture. Challenging much of the last generation's "new labor history," Jama Lazerow and others uncovered Protestantism as "the handmaiden, rather than the saboteur, of labor protest," the authentic "voice of a self-consciously Christian working class."[27]

All this work approaches religion respectfully on its own terms, not as a cover for something else. It treats religious motives and impulses as equal, not subsidiary, to considerations of material or class interest. It also tends to re-highlight the generation after 1815 as having a distinctive character, marked by accelerating participation and escalating organization, enhanced energy and widening senses of responsibility. In doing this it restores the sense of fluidity and hopefulness which seems so transparently to stamp the era, and which the market-revolution school either disparaged or denied.

Within the scheme of explanation laid out by Thomas Haskell in the famous *American Historical Review* debate on capitalism and humanitarianism, religion can also solve the conundrum on which market-revolution historians have foundered: the relation, not oppositional but symbiotic, between business and benevolence. Broadening communication networks awakened Americans to the existence of a wider world and their ability to influence it, offering new scope for their enterprise yet also making the sufferings of faraway people their sufferings, the sins of strangers their sins. Fervent post-1815 nationalism and Christian impulses of universal benevolence both activated this awareness and prescribed its field of operations. Previously, people far removed from slavery might entertain a sense of wrong in it, but they could hardly, as did Theodore Weld and Angelina Grimké, feel it so immediately as to sign their love letters with "Farewell in the love of the Lord and the bonds of the poor broken hearted slave." Nor, without the printing press, the mails, and the funds of Arthur Tappan, would they have been in position to try to right the wrongs they now considered their own. In Tappan's case, if one must rule the other, his enterprise clearly subserved his benevolence. But in truth there was no contradiction to be resolved. Haskell's scheme fits Tappan so perfectly it might have been devised for him.[28]

New tools of organization and publicity elevated abolitionism and other reforms from isolated and inert individual sentiments into potent crusades. The training and dispatch of agents, the mass production and dissemination of literature, the gathering of signatures on petitions and of goods for sale at fairs, the summoning of conventions, the endless coordination between local, state, and national societies, all would have been cumbersome and difficult operations in 1815. By the mid-1830s they were nearly routine. The same instruments, adapted to suit circumstances, served all the proliferating movements of the Jacksonian years, including the political parties. This shrinking of distances worked both ways. In November 1831, the Georgia legislature offered five thousand dollars for the apprehension of William Lloyd Garrison. Who in Georgia, only a few years before, would have known or cared about the fulminations of an obscure Boston editor?

This recalls Taylor's transportation revolution in its original form, as an enabling event – and one clearly centered in the 1820s and 1830s, the heart of the Jacksonian era. Amplifying Taylor, Richard John has traced the creation of a national communications network that came into working order around 1828, the year of Andrew Jackson's election to the presidency. It is surely no coincidence that Benevolent Empire propagandizing and the Sabbatarian and abolition controversies all exploded at about the same time, for the means to conduct or even conceive those campaigns on a national scale previously did not exist. The same is true for the Democrats and Whigs who organized in these years and also for trade unions and labor parties, which spread rather through emulation and imitation than through spontaneous local combustion. The objectives of these movements might have been at cross-purposes, but what made them all possible was the same. A newly functioning system of gathering and disseminating information made people aware of a larger world and gave them the power to change it. Here is a materialism without Marx, and without the presumed primacy of class.[29]

Still, what about the Bank War and other Jacksonian political issues, or even Andrew Jackson himself? So far they have hardly appeared. Yet without them the label "Jacksonian America" cannot stand.

The transportation revolution was itself a made event, a product of Americans' aspirations and purposeful actions. Yet in pursuing their developmental goals, questions arose about the balance between local and national advantage, between liberty and direction, and between federal and state authority. Those questions, which stood at the center of Jacksonian party politics, were both self-interested and ideological. They addressed the welfare of particular constituencies along with their broader conceptions of American democracy and their hopes of American destiny. As one critic of central control put it:

> It is contrary to all sound republican principle that the general government of a nation, widely spread over regions, and separated into sections diversified in their productions, occupations, and interests, should use its power of legislating for the whole to provide for the particular interests of a part. The principle of perfect political and social equality is violated. . . . The government of a republic has no business with distinctions among its subjects. . . . If America had been as free, from the beginning, in all respects, as a young country ought to be, – free to run her natural course of prosperity, subject only to the faithful laws which regulate the economy of society as beneficially as another set of laws regulates the seasons, we might never have heard of the American system.[30]

To anyone intimate with Andrew Jackson's state papers, this language looks familiar. It could easily come from the Maysville Road Veto or the famous core passage of the Bank Veto, which uses even the same metaphor. But it does not. It comes from *Society in America* by Harriet Martineau, an Englishwoman who toured the United States in 1834–36.

One way to appreciate the significance of Jacksonian America is to see it for a moment through her eyes.

Harriet Martineau was a radical: a democrat, a free trader, a dissenting Christian (Unitarian), an abolitionist, and a women's-rights advocate. Interestingly, she saw no contradiction between these postures. She saw them all as perfectly harmonious – and she was a person who cared a great deal about consistency. She did not, however, consider herself an agent of capitalism or bourgeois hegemony, nor of Victorianism; and while we might think of her that way, we are not going to understand her very well if we start off by importing these constructs into her psyche.

Looking through the eyes of an English radical, Martineau thought she could make immediate and perfect sense of America and its politics. Believing the fundamental question to be, as in Britain, the principle of aristocracy against the principle of democracy, she sided instinctively with the Democrats. (This had nothing to do with personalities. She got on famously with Henry Clay and Joseph Story, while she found Martin Van Buren evasive and Jackson simply appalling.) She had no difficulty linking the Jacksonians' laissez-faire economics to their egalitarian politics and also their anti-clericalism. All were part of the same liberating attack on entrenched power and privilege – on "aristocracy" – that she and her radical friends were mounting in England. Granted, most Democrats were not abolitionists or proponents of women's rights. Still the abolitionists, she thought, were naturally democratic; the plain people (at least in the North) were fundamentally abolitionist; and once attention was drawn to these topics the end was foreordained. To Martineau, slavery and women's subjugation were vestiges of aristocracy, incompatible with America's democratic foundations and therefore doomed to extinction as its civilization matured. We might laugh at her naivety, except that she turned out to be right.

How would Jacksonian politics look if seen from Martineau's perspective? Historians have searched out the transatlantic connections of American labor and social and religious and reform movements, without which their timing and even their existence make no sense. The British affiliations of Whiggery extended even to the party's name. But historians' approach to Andrew Jackson's Democracy of late has been strictly indigenous. They look for its inspiration in revolutionary republicanism, in spontaneous reaction against the market revolution, in farmsteads and artisan workshops. Most histories of Jackson's administration barely mention the great Reform Bill of 1832 or those British writers from whom Democrats imbibed their ideas of political economy.[31]

Perhaps historians assume that, having secured white male democracy, the United States had left the Old World's political struggles behind. America's reforms might proceed in tandem with Britain's, but her electoral politics were *sui generis*. Principles still in contest there were already settled here. Yet this is a retrospective judgment, reflecting the same tendentious view of history of which one might accuse Martineau. There was reason, in the 1830s and even later, to believe that issues we now consider settled by then were in fact not settled. The word that Jacksonians used to characterize their enemy was "aristocracy," and they used it with sufficient vehemence, in private as well as in public, to suggest they meant it. Not that they saw real danger of a landed hereditary nobility in America; but they did see, not only in prospect but in fact, a closed coterie, whose claims to power and authority were buttressed by exclusive political and economic privilege. They also saw a clerical phalanx yearning and striving to become an official establishment. It was their consequent anti-clericalism that defined the Democrats' point of view on religion, linking together their response to the Eaton affair, Indian removal, Sabbatarianism, temperance, and abolition. Jacksonians were not anti-Christian or even anti-evangelical, but they all hated what they called "priestcraft," the clerical arm of aristocracy.

Democrats conceived their mission in world-historic terms. Looking at England and at Europe, it would be impossible for anyone in the 1830s to think that the battles against aristocracy (in its most literal sense) and for economic, political, and religious liberty – that is, for free trade and laissez-faire, universal male suffrage, and separation of Church and State, all knit together in the Democratic ethos – had finally been won. There were powerful forces bent on reversing them, both abroad and, Jacksonians believed, at home. British admirers encouraged them to think so. Throughout his presidency, Andrew Jackson waged a bitter war against the United States Senate, marked by struggles over appointments, the Senate's censure of Jackson, and its subsequent expunction. Democrats branded the Senate as an anti-republican anachronism, a bulwark of aristocracy. Harriet Martineau agreed, as did political philosopher Jeremy Bentham. In 1830 Bentham wrote Jackson to compliment him on "the coincidence between your ideas and my own on the field of legislation." He applauded Jackson's first message to Congress, condemned the entire Senate as "superfluous functionaries," and dedicated to Jackson a tract he called *Anti-Senatica*.[32]

Resetting Jacksonian Democracy in this context invites reinterpretation of its political program, its economic philosophy, its stance toward religion and reform, and its ideas of progress. Yes, Democrats did use that word.

Once we stop thinking of them as fearful traditionalists huddled for protection against "capitalism" and begin to see them as they saw themselves – as heralds of a better and freer future – then the old conundrums that the market-revolution approach merely compounded will melt away. Historians will no longer wonder why a party could preach equality and practice laissez-faire, or why so many Democrats – representatives of what might be called the Jacksonian Enlightenment – could also be champions of scientific progress, educational reform, and social experiment.[33]

To apprehend the Democratic outlook need not mean to accept it. Believing themselves locked in Manichean struggle against reactionary Whig "aristocracy," Democratic partisans viewed their world in terms that were narrow and incomplete. They held no monopoly on progressive principle, though they assumed they did. Equality, freedom, even democracy itself were malleable concepts, employed by different people in different ways and to sometimes contradictory ends. Labor radicals and entrepreneurs, evangelicals and freethinkers, Democrats and Whigs all trumpeted liberty and assailed "aristocracy." What should strike our notice, along with the varying meanings attached to these labels, was their universal use. If the means of eradicating privilege and advancing equality were very much at issue, the goals had become (except among proslavery theorists and other frank reactionaries) nearly unchallengeable. Armed with the new tools of the transportation revolution, Americans in the 1820s and 1830s embarked on a multifaceted, contentious quest to fulfil the promise of the American Revolution by working out the implications of its precepts.

Beyond the blinkered partisanship which led her too easily to equate American Whiggery with British aristocracy, this democratizing impulse is precisely what Harriet Martineau, a dedicated believer in human progress, saw in Jacksonian America, and it is why she found it so irresistibly cheering a place despite its deformities of slavery and sexual subjugation. She understood just what was new about it, and what its example foretold: a human empowerment, economic and moral as well as political, beyond all previous imagining. Yet to many today, this is simply incomprehensible, so steeped are we in the image of Jacksonian America as a place of exclusion, deprivation, and dependence. Our historiography speaks relentlessly of decline and defeat, of winners (the capitalists) and losers (everyone else, but especially women and blacks). As one scholar declares, "republicanism was defined by the principle of exclusion. The exclusion of women, or slaves, or propertyless workers, or any other so-called dependent class marked not simply the limits of republicanism but one of its defining characteristics."[34]

I think this is not true. That some were excluded is certain. But there was nothing new in that exclusion. The reason to erect new, highly visible, boundaries was precisely that the category of those who were included was being broadened, thrown open in unheralded ways – ways that could justify, by simple extrapolation, as Harriet Martineau and the abolitionists and the Seneca Falls conventioneers understood so well, a still further opening to include not those newly excluded, but those not yet included. As a principle, democracy did not underwrite exclusion but undercut it. Proslavery ideologues recognized this and warned of racial and sexual leveling as democracy's natural consequence.[35]

If the Jacksonian era saw the rapid expansion of the slave system, it also gave rise to a mass antislavery movement, armed with the means to mount an opposition to slavery on a scale undreamed of a generation before. And if it saw a sharpening of the boundaries between newly enfranchised white men and unenfranchised white women, it also, at the same time *and in the same way*, provided women with the arguments to challenge those boundaries. Harriet Martineau understood this: to establish her case for political equality, all she had to do was quote the Declaration of Independence. It seems strange to chalk off as losers people whose rights to a share of protection and power were now being effectively promulgated for the first time.

One might accept all this and yet question the word "Jacksonian" as a label for the era. Why, even indirectly, associate a man and his party with changes many of which he and they deplored? Yet the significance that Harriet Martineau and others attached to Andrew Jackson as a democratic symbol was surely in some sense correct. For all the caveats we might enter about racial and sexual subordination, inequalities of wealth and disparities of status, the salient fact was that a man of obscure origin had been elevated to the chief magistracy of the American republic, not by revolutionary upheaval but by peaceful suffrage, and once there had proceeded to govern in the name of "the humble members of society – the farmers, mechanics, and laborers" against the "selfish purposes" of "the rich and powerful." No matter why and in what context they were uttered, these words from Jackson's Bank Veto message were freighted with future portent.[36]

It is easy to miss their novelty if our point of reference is not the nineteenth century but the early twenty-first. Yet here is an irony worth contemplating: that very standard by which historians judge and often condemn Jacksonian America is itself a legacy of Jacksonian America. It is by his own democratic professions that we assess Andrew Jackson's sincerity and consistency. Yet not until goals of equality and democracy had been proclaimed, and the tools of forwarding them devised, could a society be measured against them and found wanting. Though clearly forecast by the American Revolution, it was in the Age of Jackson that those aspirations were first fully embraced and campaigns to achieve them set into motion. Like Harriet Martineau, we can only condemn Jacksonian practice by affirming what was in her day recognized, on both sides of the Atlantic, as a novel and distinctively American democratic ideal. In setting a standard by which to judge both their professions and our own, perhaps Andrew Jackson and his contemporaries left something worthy of our continuing attention, and respect, after all.

Notes

1. Allan G. Bogue, *Clio and the Bitch Goddess: Quantification in American Political History* (Beverly Hills, 1983), pp. 113–14. The other two books were Richard Hofstadter's *The Age of Reform: from Bryan to F.D.R.* (New York, 1955) and C. Vann Woodward's *The Origins of the New South 1877–1913* (Baton Rouge, 1951).
2. Robert V. Remini, *Andrew Jackson and the Course of American Freedom* (New York, 1981); idem, *Andrew Jackson and the Course of American Democracy* (New York, 1984); Edward Pessen, *Jacksonian America: Society, Personality, and Politics*, revised ed. (Homewood, IL, 1978). For a synopsis of major Jacksonian interpretations since Tocqueville, see Daniel Feller, "Jacksonian Era," in Peter J. Parish, ed., *Reader's Guide to American History* (London, 1997), pp. 356–9.
3. Charles Sellers, *The Market Revolution: Jacksonian America, 1815–1846* (New York, 1991); Sean Wilentz, "Society, Politics, and the Market Revolution," in Eric Foner, ed., *The New American History* (Philadelphia, 1990), pp. 51–71; Harry L. Watson, *Liberty and Power: The Politics of Jacksonian America* (New York, 1990); Christopher Clark, *The Roots of Rural Capitalism: Western Massachusetts, 1780–1860* (Ithaca, NY, 1990). For commentary on the thesis, see "A Symposium on Charles Sellers, *The Market Revolution*," *Journal of the Early Republic*, 12 (1992): 445–76; Melvyn Stokes and Stephen Conway, eds., *The Market Revolution in America: Social, Political, and Religious Expressions, 1800–1880* (Charlottesville, 1996); Richard Lyman Bushman, "Markets and Composite Farms in Early

America," *The William and Mary Quarterly*, 55 (1998): 351–74; and Daniel Feller, "The Market Revolution Ate My Homework," *Reviews in American History*, 25 (1997): 408–15.

4. On the expansion and dilution of republicanism, see Daniel T. Rodgers, "Republicanism: The Career of a Concept," *Journal of American History*, 79 (1992): 11–38. For varying usages of the market revolution (often capitalized), see Donald B. Cole, *The Presidency of Andrew Jackson* (Lawrence, KS, 1993), Charles E. Brooks, *Frontier Settlement and Market Revolution: The Holland Land Purchase* (Ithaca, NY, 1996), and Paul Goodman, *Of One Blood: Abolitionism and the Origins of Racial Equality* (Berkeley, 1998). One sign of the haziness of the concept is that those who use it disagree on who its friends and foes were. Michael Paul Rogin's *Fathers and Children: Andrew Jackson and the Subjugation of the American Indian* (New York, 1975), one of the first to deploy the term, shows Andrew Jackson spearheading the market revolution, while Charles Sellers's *The Market Revolution* has him rallying its opponents.

5. George Rogers Taylor, *The Transportation Revolution, 1815–1860* (New York, 1951).

6. For a précis of the argument, see Paul E. Johnson, "The Market Revolution," in Mary Kupiec Cayton, Elliott J. Gorn, and Peter W. Williams, ed., *Encyclopedia of American Social History* (New York, 1993), vol. 1, pp. 545–60. Johnson calls the market revolution "the central, transforming process in American social history between the Revolution and the Civil War." His account teems with compulsory phrasings ("decisions were coerced," "farmers were forced," families were "constrained" and "relinquished control over economic choices," producing a "vastly increased dependence") and ends with a section on "Winners and Losers."

7. Harry L. Watson, "'The Common Rights of Mankind': Subsistence, Shad, and Commerce in the Early Republican South," *Journal of American History*, 83 (1996): 13–43; quotes from pp. 32, 16, 17, 39–40, 42.

8. John Majewski, "A Revolution Too Many?," *Journal of Economic History*, 57 (1997): 476–80. See also Winifred Barr Rothenberg, *From Market-Places to a Market Economy: The Transformation of Rural Massachusetts, 1750–1850* (Chicago, 1992); Naomi R. Lamoreaux, "Accounting for Capitalism in Early American History: Farmers, Merchants, Manufacturers, and their Economic Worlds," paper delivered at the Society for Historians of the Early American Republic, Lexington, KY, July 1999; Diane Lindstrom, H-NET review of

"Special Issue on Capitalism in the Early Republic," [in *Journal of the Early Republic*, 16 (1996), 159–308], March 7, 1997.

9. Randolph Roth, "Liberalizing Vermont," *Reviews in American History*, 25 (1997): 406; Harry L. Watson, book review in *Journal of the Early Republic*, 16 (1996): 522. Americans' smug self-satisfaction maddened foreign visitors from Frances Trollope to Charles Dickens.

10. Mark S. Schantz, "Religious Tracts, Evangelical Reform, and the Market Revolution in America," *Journal of the Early Republic*, 17 (1997): 425–66; quotes from pp. 429, 433.

11. Paul Boyer and Stephen Nissenbaum, *Salem Possessed: The Social Origins of Witchcraft* (Cambridge, MA, 1974), p. 178; Robert A. Gross, *The Minutemen and Their World* (New York, 1976), p. 107; Grover Cleveland Fourth Annual Message, December 3, 1888, in James D. Richardson, ed., *A Compilation of the Messages and Papers of the Presidents*, vol. 8 (Washington, 1898), p. 774.

12. Stephen Hahn and Jonathan Prude, ed., *The Countryside in the Age of Capitalist Transformation: Essays in the Social History of Rural America* (Chapel Hill, 1985); Alan Kulikoff, *The Agrarian Origins of American Capitalism* (Charlottesville, 1992); Paul A. Gilje, ed., *Wages of Independence: Capitalism in the Early American Republic* (Madison, WI, 1997).

13. Eric Hobsbawm, *On History* (New York, 1991), p. 31. The word "capitalism" to describe an economic system was unknown in Jacksonian America, though "capitalist" was already common. The first usage of "capitalism" in the *Oxford English Dictionary* is from 1854.

14. Joel H. Silbey, *The American Political Nation, 1838–1893* (Stanford, 1991); Michael F. Holt, *The Rise and Fall of the American Whig Party* (New York, 1999); William G. Shade, *Democratizing the Old Dominion: Virginia and the Second Party System, 1824–1861* (Charlottesville, 1996). For a longer view, see Donald J. Ratcliffe, *Party Spirit in a Frontier Republic: Democratic Politics in Ohio, 1793–1821* (Columbus, 1998); idem, *The Politics of Long Division: The Birth of the Second Party System in Ohio, 1818–1828* (Columbus, 2000).

15. "Political Engagement and Disengagement in Antebellum America: A Round Table," *Journal of American History*, 84 (1997): 855–909; "Round Table: Alternatives to the Party System in the 'Party Period,' 1830–1890," *Journal of American History*, 86 (1999): 93–157; Ronald P. Formisano, "The Invention of the Ethnocultural Interpretation," *American Historical Review*, 99 (1994): 453–77.

16. Elizabeth R. Varon, *We Mean to Be Counted: White Women and Politics in Antebellum Virgina* (Chapel Hill, 1998); Ronald J. Zboray and Mary Saracino Zboray, "Whig Women, Politics, and Culture in the Campaign of 1840: Three Perspectives from Massachusetts," *Journal of the Early Republic*, 17 (1997): 277–315; Kirsten E. Wood, "'One Woman So Dangerous to Public Morals': Gender and Power in the Eaton Affair," *Journal of the Early Republic*, 17 (1997): 237–75; John F. Marszalek, *The Petticoat Affair: Manners, Mutiny, and Sex in Andrew Jackson's White House* (New York, 1997).

17. The literature on women's public activity includes Mary P. Ryan, *Cradle of the Middle Class* (New York, 1981); Kathryn Kish Sklar, *Catharine Beecher: A Study in American Domesticity* (New York, 1976); Nancy Hewitt, *Women's Activism and Social Change: Rochester, New York, 1822–1872* (Ithaca, 1984); Lori D. Ginzberg, *Women and the Work of Benevolence* (New Haven, 1990); Mary P. Ryan, *Women in Public* (Baltimore, 1990); and Julie Roy Jeffrey, *The Great Silent Army of Abolitionism: Ordinary Women in the Antislavery Movement* (Chapel Hill, 1998). A useful synthesis of this literature down to 1990 is Anne M. Boylan, "Women and Politics in the Era Before Seneca Falls," *Journal of the Early Republic* 10 (1990): 363–82.

18. Daniel Walker Howe, *The Political Culture of the American Whigs* (Chicago, 1979).

19. Stephanie McCurry, "The Two Faces of Republicanism: Gender and Proslavery Politics in Antebellum South Carolina," *Journal of American History*, 78 (1992): 1245.

20. Paula Baker, "The Midlife Crisis of the New Political History," *Journal of American History* 86 (1999): 164.

21. Alice Felt Tyler, *Freedom's Ferment: Phases of American Social History from the Colonial Period to the Outbreak of the Civil War* (Minneapolis, 1944). Paul E. Johnson and Sean Wilentz's *The Kingdom of Matthias: A Story of Sex and Salvation in Nineteenth-Century America* (New York, 1994) today is often the only Jacksonian reading assigned in college American history courses.

22. Jean Harvey Baker, "Politics, Paradigms, and Public Culture," *Journal of American History*, 84 (1997): 898.

23. Norma Basch, "Marriage, Morals, and Politics in the Election of 1828," *Journal of American History*, 80 (1993): 890–918. See also Nancy Isenberg, *Sex and Citizenship in Antebellum America* (Chapel Hill, 1998); Kimberley K. Smith, *The Dominion of Voice: Riot, Reason, and Romance in Antebellum Politics* (Lawrence, KS, 1999).

24. Lee Benson, *The Concept of Jacksonian Democracy: New York as a Test Case* (Princeton, 1961), p. 81.

25. Paul E. Johnson, *A Shopkeeper's Millennium: Society and Revivals in Rochester, New York, 1815–1837* (New York, 1978); Sean Wilentz, *Chants Democratic: New York City and the Rise of the American Working Class, 1788–1850* (New York, 1984).

26. Nathan O. Hatch, *The Democratization of American Christianity* (New Haven, 1989); Jon Butler, *Awash in a Sea of Faith: Christianizing the American People* (Cambridge, MA, 1990). See also Daniel Walker Howe, "The Evangelical Movement and Political Culture in the North during the Second Party System," *Journal of American History*, 77 (1991): 1216–39; and idem., "Protestantism, Voluntarism, and Personal Identity in Antebellum America," in Harry S. Stout and D. G. Hart, eds., *New Directions in American Religious History* (New York, 1997), pp. 206–35.

27. Robert H. Abzug, *Cosmos Crumbling: American Reform and the Religious Imagination* (New York, 1994); Richard J. Carwardine, *Evangelicals and Politics in Antebellum America* (New Haven, 1993); Jama Lazerow, *Religion and the Working Class in Antebellum America* (Washington, 1995), pp. 3, 10. See also Teresa Anne Murphy, *Ten Hours' Labor: Religion, Reform and Gender in Early New England* (Ithaca, 1992) and William R. Sutton, *Journeymen for Jesus: Evangelical Artisans Confront Capitalism in Jacksonian Baltimore* (University Park, PA, 1998). Recent work on religion stresses the depth of popular feeling over slavery, which some party-system historians continue to deny. See Mitchell Snay, *Gospel of Disunion: Religion and Separatism in the Antebellum South* (New York, 1993); John R. McKivigan and Mitchell Snay, *Religion and the Antebellum Debate over Slavery* (Athens, GA, 1998).

28. Thomas L. Haskell, "Capitalism and the Origins of the Humanitarian Sensibility," in Thomas Bender, ed., *The Antislavery Debate* (Berkeley, 1992), pp. 107–60; Grimké to Weld, February 16, 1838, in Gilbert H. Barnes and Dwight L. Dumond, ed., *Letters of Theodore Dwight Weld, Angelina Grimké Weld, and Sarah Grimké* (New York, 1934), p. 554.

29. Richard R. John, *Spreading the News: The American Postal System from Franklin to Morse* (Cambridge, MA, 1995).

30. Harriet Martineau, *Society in America* (London, 1837), vol. 2, pp 236–8. On Jacksonian political economy, see Daniel Feller, *The Public Lands in Jacksonian Politics* (Madison, 1984) and John Lauritz Larson, *Internal Improvement: National Public Works and*

the Promise of Popular Government in the Early United States (Chapel Hill, 2001).

31. On Anglo-American reform, see Frank Thistlethwaite, *The Anglo-American Connection in the Early Nineteenth Century* (Philadelphia, 1959); Robert Kelley, *The Transatlantic Persuasion* (New York, 1969); David Brion Davis, *Slavery and Human Progress* (New York, 1984); Betty Fladeland, *Men and Brothers: Anglo-American Anti-slavery Cooperation* (Urbana, IL, 1972); and Jamie L. Bronstein, *Land Reform and Working-Class Experience in Britain and the United States, 1800–1862* (Stanford, 1999). The neglect of Jacksonianism's broader influences and aspirations in Sellers's *Market Revolution* and Watson's *Liberty and Power* marks a retreat from the insight in Schlesinger's *Age of Jackson*, pp. 314–21. On Jacksonian economic thought, see Paul K. Conkin, *Prophets of Prosperity: America's First Political Economists* (Bloomington, IN, 1980) and James L. Huston, *Securing the Fruits of Labor: The American Concept of Wealth Distribution, 1765–1900* (Baton Rouge, 1998). On America's meaning to contemporary Europeans, see Hugh Brogan, "Alexis de Tocqueville and the Liberal Moment," *The Historical Journal*, 14 (1971): 289–303.

32. Charles Warren Everett, ed., "Jeremy Bentham's 'Anti-Senatica,'" *Smith College Studies in History*, 11 (1926): 209–67.

33. William Stanton, *The Great United States Exploring Expedition* (Berkeley, 1975); Josephine Mirabella Elliott, ed., *Partnership for Posterity: the Correspondence of William Maclure and Marie Duclos Fretageot, 1820–1833* (Indianapolis, 1994); Nathan Reingold, ed., *Science in Nineteenth-Century America: A Documentary History* (New York, 1964); Daniel Feller, "Democratic Science: The Politics of Knowledge in Jacksonian America," paper delivered at the Organization of American Historians, Indianapolis, April 1998. Scientists and social reformers who were also active Democrats included the Owenites at New Harmony, a large cadre of Philadelphians, and such leading party men as George Bancroft, Joel Poinsett, Levi Woodbury, and Benjamin Tappan.

34. McCurry, "Two Faces of Republicanism," p. 1264. Nancy Isenberg puts it more arrestingly: "Simply stated, democracy, at its core, is essentially undemocratic, because divestment and exclusion are too obviously a mainstay of 'democratic' practice." H-SHEAR Digest, March 7, 2000. Paralleling feminist attacks on male democracy, a burgeoning literature on "whiteness" puts racial exclusivity at the foundation of white Americans' self-definition. Alexander Saxton,

The Rise and Fall of the White Republic (New York, 1990); David R. Roediger, *The Wages of Whiteness: Race and the Making of the American Working Class* (New York, 1991); "Special Issue on Racial Consciousness and Nation-Building in the Early Republic," *Journal of the Early Republic*, 19 (1999): 577–775.

35. Gordon Wood makes this point for an earlier period in *The Radicalism of the American Revolution* (New York, 1991).
36. Richardson, *Messages and Papers*, vol. 2 (1896), p. 590.

–4–

The Evangelical Surge and the Significance of Religion in the Early United States, 1783–1865
Mark A. Noll

During the 1780s and 1790s religion in the new United States existed in a state of confusing transition. The colonies' one total religious system, New England Puritanism, survived only in fragments, its integrative force destroyed by the pietism of revival and the secularization of the Revolution. The main colonial alternative to Puritanism – established Anglicanism in the South – was even more thoroughly discredited through its association with the repudiated rule of King and Parliament. Local religious revivals promoted by evangelical Protestants were taking place in many locations throughout the 1770s and 1780s, but these revivals were at work on frontiers, among African Americans, as a result of Methodist itineration, and in response to Baptist lay preaching – in every case, that is, far from the new country's geographical or social centers of power.

From this parlous base there followed an explosion of religion, especially of evangelical Protestant religion in almost every conceivable shape and style.[1] No other period of American history has ever witnessed such a dramatic rise in religious adherence. One careful estimate suggests that the proportion of the national population actively associated with Churches (which were overwhelmingly evangelical Protestant in character) rose from 17 percent of the population in 1776 to 34 percent in 1850, and that during a period when no other value system or wide-spread form of organization (including the American government) came anywhere close to the size and cultural weight of the Churches.[2]

After decades in which historians studiously avoided confronting the size and significance of this evangelical surge, writing about religion in the United States (especially the religion of the evangelical kaleidoscope) between the War for Independence and the Civil War is now expert, thorough, insightful, and prolific.[3] This chapter analyses some of the areas where unusually productive research has recently been published. It goes on to contend that this scholarship, despite its considerable breadth and depth, has sharpened the sense of religion's importance in these decades of American history far more than it has explained the whys and wherefores of that importance.

A great deal of the best writing in the last fifteen years or so of the twentieth century treated aspects of the expansion of evangelical religion, either by illuminating how the new era emerged, exploring what evangelical religion, in all of its great variety, meant for different regions, classes, the two sexes, intellectual life, and institution-building, or showing why evangelical faith became so critical for the sectional crisis of the 1840s and 1850s and the Civil War itself.

Against this broader landscape, Nathan Hatch's *The Democratization of American Christianity* is the single most important study of its time because of the way it promotes a fresh understanding of religion in relationship to national culture. It is perhaps the one book for this era that, because of its broad implications, most nearly resembles contemporary work on British history such as J. C. D. Clark's *English Society, 1688–1832* and Boyd Hilton's *Age of Atonement*. These two books, while very different from one another, both make critical use of religion for construing, respectively, the conservative character of the long eighteenth century and the political economy of Britain's early industrial era.[4]

Hatch's title, as it happens, is imprecise, for rather than democracy as such, he describes an anti-elitist populism where it was relatively common for the iron rule of new exhorters to replace the institutionalized authority of old pastors. Hatch may also have given too little attention to the speed with which upstart religions began to take on some of the formal characteristics of the establishments they had so vigorously opposed. Details notwithstanding, however, the book is unusually persuasive in describing how upstart Methodists, Baptists, Disciples, Mormons, and African Americans exploited a "crisis of authority in popular culture" and a "cultural ferment over freedom" to fashion new, socially-dynamic variations of Protestant Christianity.[5] This new religion was anti-traditional, anti-elitist, and anti-Catholic. While at the same time being anti-Calvinist, biblicistic, individualistic, and down-to-earth, it also led to the creation of tightly knit, intentional Church communities. In those communities of the converted, the organizational genius of self-appointed founders was fully on display. Hatch's achievement was to replace the proprietary-minded churchmen of Victorian urban Protestantism as the central religious figures of the age with the much less respectable parvenus who refounded American Christianity in the wake of social and political revolution. In Hatch's view, itineration, lay-preaching, polemical tracts by the self-taught, and the popular religious press constituted the center of American religion in the early national period and hence contributed to the centering of the new nation itself. What Hatch provides is a religious variation on interpretations of the post-revolutionary era by Robert Wiebe and Gordon Wood that view the radicalism of the Revolution as leading to a break with the forms of society in which the Revolution occurred (which patriot leaders thought they were preserving) and then to a momentous opening-up of American society.[6]

In the wake of Hatch's prize-winning study has come a flourishing of scholarship on early American Methodism, a subject where previous treatments mostly did not chart the full dimensions of early Methodist expansion or account for the meaning of that expansion in broad national terms.[7] Hatch's work, including his own direct appeal for more attention to the Methodists,[8] prompted a different climate in which, during the 1990s, at least six consequential studies appeared.[9] These books are exemplary in charting the incredible speed of Methodist expansion, the efficiency of Methodist connectionalism, and the civilizing effects of Methodist advance. The only complaint to be made about this new wave of scholarship is that some of its practitioners concentrate more on problems arising when Methodists began to seek respectability (Schneider especially) or on situations when Methodists fomented cultural antagonism (Heyrman especially) than on what surely must be the most important task for a historian, succinctly stated by David Hempton as getting "to the heart of the Methodist *experience* by answering the basic questions: what is it and why did it grow where and when it did?"[10]

Apart from these studies of the Methodists, however, other late twentieth-century scholarship on the American denominations did better at showing how national history influenced religion than at showing how religion affected the nation. One notable exception is a fine book by Jenny Franchot on the freighted cultural significance of Protestant conversions to Catholicism. Franchot's study shows, in particular, why Rome was attractive to a number of alienated Victorians, mostly from New England, while at the same time a fear of Rome as the liberty-destroying whore of Babylon remained vigorous among lay and clerical Protestants, especially in New England.[11] Other scholarship on Adventists, Baptists, Episcopalians, Lutherans, Mennonites, Mormons, and Restorationist Churches, while impressive in itself, lays the ground for integrating the Churches into the national story more than actually addressing that task.[12] Of special regret is that so little probing work has been done on the Baptists, who remain the major American religious group least integrated into national historiography.[13]

Hatch's emphasis on ordinary people appropriating religion for themselves is but one instance of how religion can be approached. Several studies, for example, have shown in careful detail how religious revival in individual localities enlisted individuals and families for the Churches. According to Terry Bilhartz, Baltimore in the 1790s was a place with a full "supply of [religious] goods" from "competing vendors" that created an eager market of church-going consumers. David Kling argues that northwestern Connecticut, in the early decades of the new century, saw old-style Congregationalists remake themselves in response to a demand for audience-focused preaching. In the view of Kathryn Long, major northern cities in 1857 and 1858 were a venue where Presbyterian and Dutch Reformed businessmen astonished themselves with the results from revival practices that Methodists had been refining into high art for over half a century.[14]

Not as directly related to Hatch's particular concerns, but sharing his conviction that developments among non-elite audiences represented the truly central religious story, are a wealth of other significant works. Several scholars have researched the religious dimensions of social transformation in small towns and the countryside. Exemplary studies by Randolph Roth on the Connecticut River Valley in Vermont, by Curtis Johnson on upstate New York, and by Alan Taylor on the Maine frontier are only three of the books showing how much inherited Protestant faiths contributed to the shaping of new communities, but also how much life in those new communities moderated, laicized, or even radicalized (in Taylor's rural Maine) the shape of Protestantism. These books are especially convincing as they trace moves away from Calvinism in theology and deference in religious institutions towards various degrees of self-assertion in both.[15]

Significant books on women include studies on religion in both public and private spheres. Susan Juster's reading of congregational records from New England Baptists led her to conclude that, when Baptist men began to join the public defense of freedom against imperial Britain, the result within their congregations was to stifle the egalitarian impulses of revivalist religion, restrict the freedom of evangelical women from speaking in meetings, and encourage gender models towards an ideal of separate spheres.[16] By contrast, and also illustrating how much cultural difference separated the 1780s from the 1810s, a careful monograph from Catherine Brekus shows that the burst of anti-establishmentarian evangelicalism in the early decades of the new century propelled more than 100 women into public life as itinerating preachers and pastors. Brekus's female preachers were Methodist, Free Will Baptist, and African American rather than from the colonial established Churches, and the opportunities they enjoyed for exhorting in public were mostly closed down by the 1830s. But her work still offers strong confirmation of the real differences that separated early-national religion from the religion of the late colonial period.[17]

Books by Laurel Thatcher Ulrich and Elizabeth Fox-Genovese also represent exemplary efforts at depicting the daily rounds of women in the very different worlds of a rural New England midwife and Southern plantation residents – rounds that included a full, unselfconscious integration of the era's evangelical beliefs and practices.[18] The early chapters of Dana Robert's history of women in missionary work brings public and private together, especially in revealing what women contributed as domestic managers, active co-laborers, and even theorists of evangelization to the missionary movement that took off as a by-product of rapid Protestant expansion.[19]

Scholarship on minority populations shows some of the same evidence of tumultuous times. Mechal Sobel's careful account of blacks and whites in Virginia during the eighteenth century finds more evidence for genuine religious fellowship across racial lines, especially following the evangelical revivals in the 1750s, than is revealed in Fox-Genovese's work on the 1830s and 1840s.[20] A remarkably effective synthesis of recent scholarship on black religion by Sylvia Frey and Betty Wood has the added advantage of comparing developments on the American mainland with those in the Caribbean. The greater proportion of Africans in the latter environment, the larger presence in the Caribbean of Moravians (the era's most effective Protestant missionaries), and, especially, the ending of slavery throughout the British empire made for different conditions in a narrative featuring the rise of evangelical faiths and the enduring importance of women's spirituality in black communities.[21] William G. McLoughlin's outstanding series of books on the mission to the Cherokee represents one of the most notable efforts ever made in American historical writing to track the complexity of cross-cultural (and cross-racial) religious exchange. In several volumes, McLoughlin underscores the paradigm outlined in Brekus and several of the Methodist books – a period of evangelistic breakthrough and significant Church formation in the decades immediately after the ratification of the Constitution followed, in the Jacksonian era, by a definite restriction of religious as well as social freedom. In this tragic case, the freedom-loving Jacksonians of Christian America stripped freedom-constituting Cherokees of almost everything they had struggled to achieve in constructing their own version of Christian America.[22]

Studies of religion and economic life have not prospered as well as studies of other subjects, perhaps because the populist drift of much late 1990s religious scholarship is so directly against the grain of older interpretations. Those interpretations had posited, in the words of Paul Johnson's influential study of revivalism in Rochester, New York, that evangelical religion provided "powerful social controls" to a rising class of bourgeois entrepreneurs eager to exploit opening market possibilities during the early stages of American industrialization.[23] A volume edited by Melvyn Stokes and Stephen Conway gave full attention to Charles Sellers' *The Market Revolution*, including his effort to link economic attitudes with specific religious styles. Sellers was certainly correct in targeting religion as critical for economic exchange in Jacksonian America. But, as Daniel Walker Howe and Richard Carwardine pointed out, Sellers' use of the terms "Antinomian" and "Arminian" was muddled, his depiction of religion as superstructure driven by economic deep structure was inadequate to what had actually taken place, and he misread the economic behavior of Methodists, which for this period is an insurmountable mistake.[24] Still, efforts are going forward to illuminate the economic-religious synergies of the age. The most impressive recent work reverses earlier depictions to argue that, in some localities and under certain conditions, artisans, factory workers, and even union organizers freely chose the new evangelical faiths as fulfilment of their most authentic personal desires.[25] It was also the case that quite a few Protestants sincerely felt that they could use expanding market possibilities to better serve God, their fellow creatures, and themselves.[26]

Other significant areas of recent scholarship are not tied as directly to the populist focus. A series of path-breaking works on what might be called the institutions of religious practice show how thoroughly elite projects could be integrated into the lives of ordinary people. Two books on the Bible – which remained far and away the most-purchased title of the era and almost certainly also the most read – explore the nature of that popularity. Peter Wosh's account of the American Bible Society (ABS), considered as a business, concentrates on the way that the ABS's trustees gradually added rational market reasoning to its earlier dedication to Christian service, and may therefore shortchange the story of what it took for the ABS to get the Scriptures out in the staggering quantities it achieved.[27] Paul Gutjahr's history of printed Bibles has a tendentious thesis – that multiplying formats and printing styles undercut the traditional deference accorded to what the Bible actually said. Whether that argument fits with what happened or not, his beautifully illustrated volume is the best account to date of what was at once the publishing, religious, artistic, and literary phenomenon of the age.[28]

Harry Stout's powerful argument, in his study of colonial Puritanism, that paying attention to another Protestant institution, the sermon, is the best way to gauge over time the spiritual condition of preacher and parishioner receives impressive support from two recent works on this later period. Mark Hanley treats more than sermons, but his account of the many ministers who resisted the era's mixture of Christianity and republicanism draws substantially on sermonic literature. An even more comprehensive use of that resource enables Kenneth Startup to show how fixated Southern clergy were on money, but also how vigorously they stuck to older Protestant scruples about the misuse of lucre and the abuse of economic power.[29]

Working against modern trends in historical scholarship generally, the best recent books on religion and intellectual life are more concerned with traditional elites than with commoners.[30] Daniel Walker Howe's *Making the American Self* is as admirably well-balanced in its argument as the book's subjects sought to be in their own persons. To Howe, balance is the key to understanding what the era's major thinkers sought to do: to mediate between Enlightenment and Protestant values, between public service and self-help, between polite culture as a vehicle for social betterment and faculty psychology as a vehicle for understanding human motivation.[31]

The other notable recent studies emphasizing the importance of religion for elite intellectual endeavor concern the South. Robert Calhoon's meditation on evangelicalism and conservative social values effectively outlines both the tensions and harmonies that figures such as John C. Calhoun found between these two previously antagonistic systems.[32] Harmony of a different sort is advocated by Eugene Genovese in a series of provocative statements aimed at convincing modern skeptics that antebellum Southern slaveholders really believed what they said, seeing Christianity as absolutely true, slavery as a good system for promoting social harmony, and Yankee capitalism as slavery without Southern ameliorations.[33]

Unfortunately, theology as such remains a subject of far less interest to historians than it was to huge numbers of ordinary and elite citizens of the time. (Besides the Methodist Harper brothers, Presbyterians Moses W. Dodd [of Dodd, Mead, and Co.] and Charles Scribner began their successful publishing houses in large part to meet the demand for accessible theological reading.[34]) Scholarly exceptions that link streams of theological exposition with streams of national development include Allen Guelzo's account of debates over Jonathan Edwards' construal of human free will, Bruce Kuklick's continued championing of New England's New Divinity theologians as consequential thinkers, and Bruce Mullin's sterling account of the extensive American debate over the subject of miracles.[35] In general, however, most of the good books on theology remain focused inward on the meaning of theology for the theologians rather than for the society in which they exerted considerable influence.[36]

In the present golden age of biography, books written about individuals often become vehicles for reflecting more broadly on an era's tensions and achievements. For American religious history of this period, a crop of 1990s biographies is exceptionally luxuriant. It includes solid studies on the familiar leaders of the evangelical movement (Timothy Dwight, Charles Finney), on significant but previously neglected populist evangelicals (Elias Smith), and on the comparison between nineteenth-century American evangelicals leaders and their peers in Britain and continental Europe.[37] The line-up of noteworthy biographies also includes impressive studies of an evangelical luminary (Harriet Beecher Stowe) whose evangelical commitments are backgrounded in an effort to speak to modern feminist concerns, and of a non-evangelical luminary (Emily Dickinson) whose evangelical environment is featured as a way of understanding her major interests.[38] There are now careful studies of individuals at the fringes of modern sympathy, including defenders of Southern slave society (J. H. Thornwell) and antinomian despisers of all social proprieties (Mathias).[39] The list of impressive books on African American figures includes David George (who founded Churches in South Carolina, Nova Scotia, and Sierra Leone) and Sojourner Truth.[40] A significant set of first-person narratives from four African American women exhorters are among the most revealing biographical writings now in print.[41] And as a gesture of fair play to religious sentiments that were rapidly going out of favor in the era, E. S. Gaustad has written an appreciative religious biography of Thomas Jefferson.[42]

The most impressive late 1990s biography touching religious themes, however, is Allen Guelzo's new treatment of Abraham Lincoln entitled *Redeemer President*.[43] This is a particularly important book, not only because it is now the most judicious account of Lincoln's religion available, but also because Guelzo succeeds so well in placing Lincoln's religion in the context of his Whig political commitments. For Guelzo, Lincoln was able, without himself ever embracing evangelicalism, fully to internalize the evangelicals' dynamic push for spiritual – but also cultural, social, and material – betterment. The book is a particular triumph for illustrating the great effect of the evangelical surge on public life in the United States. Eighty years before Lincoln became president, all of the new country's major political leaders were Church members, yet none employed Scripture in public speech. Their view of God was of a beneficial Artificer. Lincoln, by contrast, never joined a Church, yet used Scripture in public speech with profound subtlety. His God, especially as the War Between the States rolled on, became once again the Wholly Other of earlier, more orthodox centuries.

American historical scholarship has long suffered from a misappropriation of energy in treating religion during this period's two great public events: the American Revolution and the Civil War. Even though the Revolutionary era was ambiguous about traditional religion, issues of religion and the Revolution have been studied to death. This is probably because of the weight that, since the 1940s, has fallen on interpretations of the Constitution's First Amendment, which naturally stimulates scholarship, both tendentious and curious, about the "founding of America." By contrast, although the era of the Civil War was ardently religious, and in forms resembling much of the religion that continues to be practiced in the United States, questions of religion and the great division of North and South have been relatively neglected. This may be because the forms of faith in the Civil War are too close – as both positive ideal and negative reference – for scholars to treat with the engaged detachment they deserve. In recent years, thankfully, this situation has begun to change.

The recent past has witnessed a steady stream of solid works on religious life and thought in the Revolutionary era, but not of the agenda-setting sort that appeared from Alan Heimert's *Religion and the American Mind* (1966) through Thomas Curry's definitive study of Church-State relations to the passage of the First Amendment (1986), taking in seminal studies by Nathan Hatch, Ruth Bloch, Steven Marini, and a number of others.[44] There have also been, fairly recently, a solid group of works on the historical setting of the Constitutional settlement with respect to religion.

The most important of the books on the Revolutionary era is a wide-ranging and expertly introduced collection of sermons by Ellis Sandoz. This lengthy volume has the added advantage of including considerable numbers of British, Loyalist, and uncertain, as well as patriot, sermons.[45] But there have also been many other useful studies, including a long list of thoughtful books that begin with events in the 1770s before moving on to either normative political science or provocative civic meditation.[46]

Of more self-consciously historical work, the most helpful are Mark Valeri's account of how Jonathan Edwards's closest student negotiated the ideological and practical turmoils of the Revolutionary age, a collection of essays from the U.S. Capitol Historical Society on the religious lives of ordinary people in the Revolutionary era, and a new book demonstrating through extensive documentation how relatively unorthodox and unevangelical, if not exactly irreligious, the major founding fathers actually were.[47]

In the 1980s and 1990s, there was a great deal of writing aimed at retrieving the essential meaning of the Revolutionary and Constitutional period in relation to contemporary preoccupations. Much of that material is associated with the concerns of the New Christian Right and represents the triumph of hope over research.[48] One or two salvos from the other political direction could be called the triumph of academic exasperation over historical balance.[49] On quite another level is the careful work of legal scholars such as John Witte who are working hard at separating what can be understood with reference to the past from what may be argued in the present.[50] One of the best contributions to that project is Jonathan Sarna and David Dalin's volume of sources on Jewish attitudes toward Church and State which shows that American Jews have always mixed a healthy dose of religious accommodation with the better-known stance of strict separation.[51]

An unusually effective bridge between the actual historical circumstances of the Revolutionary era and the relations of Church and State in the early national period has been offered by John West's *The Politics of Revelation and Reason*.[52] The great merit of his book is to show why it was so relatively easy to move from the religiously cool world of the founding fathers to the religiously hot world of the revived evangelicals. The reason was the agreement shared by almost all Americans – once the Loyalists were safely dispatched to Nova Scotia, Upper Canada, or the mother country – that the new United States was supposed to promote religious liberty but not dictate any specific set of religious beliefs and practices. West shows that the surprising degree of agreement among those whose own religious convictions differed so considerably rested on two shared assumptions: first, that the moral goods promoted by the Churches largely coincided with the moral goods promoted by the government, and, second, that the Churches had a unofficial, informal, but still important role to play in making the moral calculus of republicanism actually work. The politically-minded believers of the nineteenth century, after misconstruing the presidential candidacy of Thomas Jefferson as an effort to install an old-style ruler with establishmentarian powers, hit their stride in voluntary mobilization against Sunday mails and for Cherokee protection, before entering into the era of their greatest political influence in the sectional divisions leading to the Civil War. With West and a few others as possible exceptions, however, historical work on religion and politics in the Revolutionary era and then on issues of Church and State arising from that era seems to have entered a period in which scholars fill out paradigms determined by previous scholarship and current political exigencies rather than embarking upon fresh historical reevaluations.

It is quite otherwise with religion and the Civil War. At last the seriousness of faith in and for that conflict has begun to be matched with a seriousness of scholarship. As indicated by the works by Farmer, Fox-Genovese, Genovese, Guelzo, and Startup mentioned above, many aspects of religion in the antebellum and Civil War years are now receiving serious attention. For the way in which religion, especially evangelical religion, helped create the heightened sectional antagonism that led to war, a significant collection of essays on moral (including biblical) debate over slavery, edited by John McKivigan and Mitchell Snay, was published in 1998.[53] Substantial as this volume is, however, it does not have the reach of the most important book on religion in the antebellum decades: the meticulous 1993 study by Richard Carwardine explaining how evangelical practices and beliefs infused the entire political process from the campaign of 1836 through the election of Lincoln in 1860. Carwardine's care in charting local as well as national relationships between evangelical mobilization and political activity prevents him from making sweeping generalizations. There are too many evangelical Whigs who remain loyal to their Southern states, too many instances of vicious public polemics between evangelical Baptists and evangelical Methodists, too much interdenominational carnage following the North-South division of the Methodists in 1844 to affirm unequivocally that evangelicals as such pushed national politics in a single direction. But Carwardine is unusually effective in showing how a mode of perception and a style of discourse that had received a tremendous boost from the evangelical surge eventually became the norm for the nation's public realm. In his words: "Evangelicalism helped to shape thinking about national mission and purpose; about entrepreneurialism and economic individualism; about the relationships between men and women, parents and children, blacks and whites, immigrants and native Americans, rich and poor; about public and private morality; and . . . about the political responsibilities of the moral individual in a democracy and a republic."[54]

Carwardine's book has been joined by several other outstanding studies, especially Mitchell Snay's account of the impact exerted by evangelical institutions, theology, and discourse in pushing the South toward division.[55] David Cheseborough published in the 1990s significant collections of documents that feature the central role of sermons in providing divine commentary on the great national events of the era.[56] And Robert Abzug offers a thoughtful meditation on the reach (and also limits) of evangelically-driven social reform.[57]

If the scholarship on religion leading up to the war still remains far in advance of scholarship on religion in the war itself, it is significant that good work has begun to appear on that latter subject. Anne Rose's sensitive reading of records from mostly elite families is one of the most convincing accounts of why the war left evangelical Protestantism seriously weakened in the decades that followed.[58] Most auspiciously, a weighty collection of papers edited by Randall Miller, Harry Stout, and Charles Reagan Wilson has recently provided the fullest, if not necessarily the most cohesive, examination of what it meant to serve as chaplains to Catholic troops in the Northern army, to preach and publish in war-torn Richmond, or (among other subjects) to adjust as editors of Southern religious papers to the fickle hand of divine providence.[59]

The most obvious complaint against this welcome efflorescence of scholarship is that it is much more revealing about the South than about the North. What religion meant to the eager Whig-Republicans, reluctant Democrats, Irish and German immigrants, the 35,000 or so mostly-Protestant clergymen who included both jingoistic war-mongers and cautious casuists, the wives and parents and children whose menfolk went off to battle – for these Northerners who won the war, the bearing of religion has only just begun to be explored.[60]

That judgment about historical treatment of religion during the Civil War may stand more generally for much late twentieth-century scholarship on the entire period. An extraordinary range of solid studies has appeared, but the cumulative effect of that scholarship has been to notice, or underscore, the general importance of religion in the early history of the U.S. rather than to try to explain the nature of that importance. The need to probe more deeply was emphasized by Michael O'Brien in his 1999 review of three books already mentioned (Frey and Wood; McKivigan and Snay; Miller, Stout, and Wilson). While acknowledging that such scholarship has succeeded at one level in making religion central to American historical consciousness, O'Brien wondered about the nature of the religion that was now receiving this attention: "Almost everyone worshipped close to the same God; the opposing forces [in the Civil War] were mostly Protestant, mostly evangelical, so the analytical significance of a religion that was everywhere and so nowhere in particular, is unclear. At best, one is left with a sense that religion explains who fought, not why."[61]

A similar query has been raised by scholars concerning whether modern historians are willing to enter sympathetically into the religious worldviews of early Americans. Susan Juster, for example, has suggested that the historical actors' accounts of their own spiritual experience deserve to be treated with as much seriousness as modern interpretations of them: "What price [epistemological and moral] do we pay when we insist on translating the supernatural into modern analytical terms – like illness, or psychoanalytical conflicts, or even cultural practices and textual signs?"[62]

Finally, the great boom in recent scholarship fairly cries out for placement in comparative perspective. The struggle to break through artificial conceptions of American exceptionalism has been largely won for the colonial period.[63] It remains more of a problem for the national and antebellum periods where, to take only the closest geographical example, the results of Canadian scholarship are relatively infrequently brought to bear on American interpretations. Yet the ability to understand the motive power, the elective affinities, or the denominational trajectories in the early United States could only be strengthened by making the effort to understand such questions as: why radically antiformalist evangelicalism may have been stronger in certain parts of the Maritimes and Canadian West before 1812 than in the United States, but weaker almost everywhere after 1815; what role the Churches played in reshaping Canadian conceptions of the whig notion of "virtue" in the early nineteenth century; what forces drove early Canadian Methodism away from fellowship with nearby American co-religionists and toward cooperation with British Methodists; why Canadian evangelical theologians did not rely so thoroughly on the scientific Baconianism that prevailed nearly everywhere in the United States; how Methodist dissent and Anglican establishmentarianism moved rapidly toward each other during the middle decades of the nineteenth century in what is now Ontario; and what accounted for the anti-slave, pro-South sentiments that were so common in the Maritime Provinces during the Civil War?[64] Similar efforts to read religion in the United States against religion in all regions of Britain offers the prospect of even further reward.[65]

Pressing questions remain for historians who recognize the need to incorporate religion into broader American narratives: what went into the religions that expanded so rapidly in the early United States? In particular, how did the great surge of evangelical Protestant faiths come to bear on the standard issues (economic development, political conflict, national expansion, gender definition, slavery, and war) that have dominated historical interest for the period? What can be learned concerning the workings of religion in America by comparing their effects with those of relatively similar religions in relatively similar North Atlantic societies? It is a tribute to the extraordinary achievements of recent scholarship in American religious history that these questions may now be raised. It remains an agenda for the future to answer them.

Notes

1. A good preliminary survey is provided by Curtis D. Johnson, *Redeeming America: Evangelicals and the Road to Civil War* (Chicago, 1993).
2. The estimate is from Roger Finke and Rodney Stark, "How the Upstart Sects Won America: 1776–1850," *Journal for the Scientific Study of Religion*, 28 (1989): 30.
3. Of many colloquia in American religious history that have appeared over the last several years, the most helpful for background to the subjects treated in this chapter is Harry S. Stout and D. G. Hart, eds., *New Directions in American Religious History* (New York, 1997).
4. J. C. D. Clark, *English Society, 1688–1832* (Cambridge, UK, 1985); Boyd Hilton, *The Age of Atonement: The Influence of Evangelicalism on Social and Economic Thought, 1785–1865* (Oxford, 1988).
5. Nathan O. Hatch, *The Democratization of American Christianity* (New Haven, 1989), pp. 17, 22. For even sharper statement of his thesis, see Hatch, "The Whirlwind of Religious Liberty in Early America," in *Freedom and Religion in the Nineteenth Century*, ed. Richard Helmstadter (Stanford, 1997), pp. 29–53.
6. Robert Wiebe, *The Opening of American Society: From the Adoption of the Constitution to the Era of Disunion* (New York, 1984); Gordon S. Wood, *The Radicalism of the American Revolution* (New York, 1991).
7. Merits of that earlier work are on display in *Perspectives in American Methodism: Interpretive Essays*, eds. Russell E. Richey, Kenneth E. Rowe, and Jean Miller Schmidt (Nashville, 1993). An exception for earlier studies that did connect Methodists to the broader national picture was Donald G. Mathews, *Slavery and Methodism . . . 1780–1840* (Princeton, 1965).

8. Hatch, "The Puzzle of American Methodism," *Church History*, 63 (1994): 175–89.
9. Russell E. Richey, *Early American Methodism* (Bloomington, IN, 1991); A. Gregory Schneider, *The Way of the Cross Leads Home: The Domestication of American Methodism* (Bloomington, IN, 1993); Christine Leigh Heyrman, *Southern Cross: The Beginnings of the Bible Belt* (New York, 1997); John H. Wigger, *Taking Heaven By Storm: Methodism and the Rise of Popular Christianity in America* (New York, 1998); Cynthia Lynn Lyerly, *Methodism and the Southern Mind, 1770–1810* (New York, 1998); and Dee E. Andrews, *The Methodists and Revolutionary America, 1760–1800* (Princeton, 2000).
10. David Hempton, "'Motives, Methods, and Margins': A Comparative Study of Methodist Expansion in the North Atlantic World, c. 1770–1850," in Hempton, *The Religion of the People: Methodism and Popular Religion, c. 1750–1900* (London, 1996), p. 5.
11. Jenny Franchot, *Roads to Rome: The Antebellum Protestant Encounter with Catholicism* (Berkeley, 1994). Also insightful on the interplay of internal Roman Catholic history and the external history of American society are Patrick W. Carey, *People, Priests, and Prelates: Ecclesiastical Democracy and the Tensions of Trusteeism* (Notre Dame, 1987); Dale B. Light, *Rome and the New Republic: Conflict and Community in Philadelphia Catholicism between the Revolution and the Civil War* (Notre Dame, 1996); Charles P. Hanson, N*ecessary Virtue: The Pragmatic Origins of Religious Liberty in New England* (Charlottesville, 1998); and the early chapters of Robert N. Bellah and Frederick E. Greenspahn, eds., *Uncivil Religion: Interreligious Hostility in America* (New York, 1987).
12. See as examples Ronald L. Numbers and Jonathan M. Butler, eds., *The Disappointed: Millerism and Millenarianism in the Nineteenth Century* (Bloomington, IN, 1987), on Adventists; Gregory A. Wills, *Democratic Religion: Freedom, Authority, and Church Discipline in the Baptist South, 1785–1900* (New York, 1997); Robert Bruce Mullin, *Episcopal Vision/American Reality: High Church Theology and Social Thought in Evangelical America* (New Haven, 1986); Diana Hochstedt Butler, *Standing Against the Whirlwind: Evangelical Episcopalians in Nineteenth-Century America* (New York, 1995); David A. Gustafson, *Lutherans in Crisis: The Question of Identity in the American Republic* (Minneapolis, 1993); Theron F. Schlabach, *Peace, Faith, Nation: Mennonites and Amish in Nineteenth-Century America* (Scottdale, PA, 1988); Richard L. Bushman, *Joseph Smith*

and the Beginnings of Mormonism (Urbana, IL, 1984); Jan Shipps, *Mormonism: The Story of a New Religious Tradition* (Urbana, IL, 1985); and Richard T. Hughes, *Reviving the Ancient Faith: The Story of Churches of Christ in America* (Grand Rapids, 1996). A good recent collection outlining possibilities for denominational history is Robert Bruce Mullin and Russell E. Richey, eds., *Reimagining Denominationalism* (New York, 1994).

13. The potential for that study is suggested in Bill Leonard, ed., *Dictionary of Baptists in America* (Downers Grove, IL, 1994).
14. Terry D. Bilhartz, *Urban Religion and the Second Great Awakening: Church and Society in Early National Baltimore* (Madison, NJ, 1986), p. 139; David Kling, *A Field of Divine Wonders: The New Divinity and Village Revivals in Northwestern Connecticut, 1792–1822* (University Park, PA, 1993); Kathryn Teresa Long, *The Revival of 1857–58* (New York, 1998).
15. Randolph Roth, *The Democratic Dilemma: Religion, Reform, and the Social Order in the Connecticut River Valley of Vermont, 1791–1850* (New York, 1987); Curtis D. Johnson, *Islands of Holiness: Rural Religion in Upstate New York, 1790–1860* (Ithaca, 1989); Alan Taylor, *Liberty Men and Great Proprietors: The Revolutionary Settlement on the Maine Frontier, 1760–1820* (Chapel Hill, 1990).
16. Susan Juster, *Disorderly Women: Sexual Politics and Evangelicalism in Revolutionary New England* (Ithaca, 1994).
17. Catherine Brekus, *Strangers and Pilgrims: Female Preaching in America, 1740–1845* (Chapel Hill, 1998).
18. Laurel Thatcher Ulrich, *A Midwife's Tale: The Life of Martha Ballard, Based on Her Diary, 1785–1812* (New York, 1990), pp. 7, 295–6, and *passim*; Elizabeth Fox-Genovese, *Within the Plantation Household: Black and White Women of the Old South* (Chapel Hill, 1988), pp. 16–20, 327–8, and *passim*.
19. Dana Lee Robert, *American Women in Mission* (Macon, GA, 1996).
20. Mechal Sobel, *The World They made Together: Black and White Values in Eighteenth-Century Virginia* (Princeton, 1987).
21. Sylvia R. Frey and Betty Wood, *Come Shouting to Zion: African American Protestantism in the American South and British Caribbean to 1830* (Chapel Hill, 1998). Frey prepared the way for this synthesis with an unusually effective study that also paid sensitive attention to religion, *Water from the Rock: Black Resistance in a Revolutionary Age* (Princeton, 1991).
22. William G. McLoughlin, *Cherokees and Missionaries, 1789–1830* (New Haven, 1984); idem, *Cherokee Renascence in the New Republic*

(Princeton, 1986); idem, *Champions of the Cherokees: Evan and John B. Jones* (Princeton, 1990); idem, *The Cherokees and Christianity, 1794–1870* (Athens, GA, 1994)

23. Paul E. Johnson, *A Shopkeeper's Millennium: Society and Revivals in Rochester, New York, 1815–1837* (New York, 1978), p. 138. For a summary of this once standard picture, which serves as prelude to a very different interpretation, see Winifred Barr Rothenberg, *From Market-Places to a Market Economy: The Transformation of Rural Massachusetts* (Chicago, 1992), pp. 2–3.

24. Daniel Walker Howe, "The Market Revolution and the Shaping of Identity in Whig-Jacksonian America," and Richard Carwardine, "'Antinomians' and 'Arminians': Methodists and the Market Revolution," in Melvyn Stokes and Stephen Conway, eds., *The Market Revolution in America: Social, Political, and Religious Expressions, 1800–1880* (Charlottesville, 1996), pp. 259–81, 282–307.

25. Outstanding recent works include Jama Lazerow, *Religion and the Working Class in Antebellum America* (Washington, DC, 1995); and William R. Sutton, *Journeymen for Jesus: Evangelical Artisans Confront Capitalism in Jacksonian Baltimore* (University Park, PA, 1998). Important assistance for understanding connections between religious and economic spheres is provided by the early sections of R. Laurence Moore, *Selling God: American Religion in the Marketplace of Culture* (New York, 1994). A number of sociologists have shown how theories from the late twentieth century can be applied to questions of markets and religion in early U.S. history – for example, George M. Thomas, *Revivalism and Cultural Change: Christianity, Nation Building, and the Market in the Nineteenth-Century United States* (Chicago, 1989); and Roger Finke and Rodney Stark, *The Churching of America, 1776–1990* (New Brunswick, NJ, 1992). The sociologists Robert Wuthnow and Tracy L. Scott have contributed a helpful bibliographical essay, "Protestants and Economic Behavior," in Stout and Hart, *New Directions in American Religious History*, pp. 260–95.

26. This is a point made by Daniel Walker Howe and several of the other contributors to *Protestants, Money, and the Market, 1790–1860*, ed. Mark A. Noll (forthcoming), which includes essays from John Walsh, David Hempton, Richard Carwardine, David Paul Nord, Richard Pointer, Kenneth Startup, and Kathryn Long, as well as the Carwardine and Howe essays mentioned in note 24 above.

27. By the late 1840s, Harper and Brothers (founded by four Methodist brothers primarily to produce religious literature) had become one

of the largest publishers in the world; in that period it was printing 2,000,000 books per year. By comparison, from 1842 to 1848, the ABS distributed an average of 426,293 Bibles and testaments annually, with over 600,000 each in 1847 and 1848. See John Tebbel, *A History of Book Publishing in the United States: Vol. 1, 1630– 1865* (New York, 1972); Henry Otis Dwight, *The Centennial History of the American Bible Society* (New York, 1916), p. 577.

28. Peter J. Wosh, *Spreading the Word: The Bible Business in Nineteenth-Century America* (Ithaca, 1994); Paul C. Gutjahr, *An American Bible: A History of the Good Book in the United States, 1777–1880* (Stanford, 1999).

29. Harry S. Stout, *The New England Soul: Preaching and Religious Culture in Colonial New England* (New York, 1986); Mark Y. Hanley, *Beyond a Christian Commonwealth: The Protestant Quarrel with the American Republic, 1830–1860* (Chapel Hill, 1994); Kenneth Startup, *The Root of All Evil: The Protestant Clergy and the Economic Mind of the South* (Athens, GA, 1997).

30. Solid efforts at synthesizing a wide range of elite and commoner intellectual histories are found in Jean V. Matthews, *Toward a New Society: American Thought and Culture, 1800–1830* (New York, 1990); and Anne C. Rose, *Voices of the Marketplace: American Thought and Culture, 1830–1860* (New York, 1995).

31. Daniel Walker Howe, *Making the American Self: Jonathan Edwards to Abraham Lincoln* (Cambridge, MA, 1997). A similar ideal of balance attended the labors of mid-state Presbyterians during and after the War for Independence, as explained in Mark A. Noll, *Princeton and the Republic, 1768–1822: The Search for a Christian Enlightenment in the Era of Samuel Stanhope Smith* (Princeton, 1989).

32. Robert M. Calhoon, *Evangelicals and Conservatives in the Early South, 1740–1861* (Columbia, SC, 1988). Roughly the same trajectory has been traced by Bertram Wyatt-Brown in *Southern Honor: Ethics and Behavior in the Old South* (New York, 1982).

33. Eugene D. Genovese, *The Slaveholders' Dilemma* (Columbia, SC, 1992); idem, *The Southern Tradition* (Cambridge, 1994); idem, *The Southern Front* (Columbia, MO, 1995); idem, *A Consuming Fire: The Fall of the Confederacy in the Mind of the White Christian South* (Athens, GA, 1999).

34. Charles A. Madison, *Book Publishing in America* (New York, 1966), pp. 32–3.

35. Allen C. Guelzo, *Edwards on the Will: A Century of American Theological Debate* (Middletown, CT, 1989); Bruce Kuklick,

Churchmen and Philosophers: From Jonathan Edwards to John Dewey (New Haven, 1985); Robert Bruce Mullin, *Miracles and Modern Religious Imagination* (New Haven, 1996). A book that details the lingering effect of the eighteenth century's most influential American theologian is Joseph Conforti, *Jonathan Edwards, Religious Tradition, and American Culture* (Chapel Hill, 1995).

36. As examples, see Charles D. Cashdollar, *The Transformation of Theology, 1830–1890: Positivism and Protestant Thought in Britain and America* (Princeton, 1989); Gary K. Pranger, *Philip Schaff (1819–1893): Portrait of an Immigrant Theologian* (New York, 1997); Stephen R. Graham, *Cosmos in the Chaos: Philip Schaff's Interpretation of Nineteenth-Century American Religion* (Grand Rapids, 1995); William DiPuccio, *The Interior Sense of Scripture: The Sacred Hermeneutics of John W. Nevin* (Macon, GA, 1998); and Richard E. Wentz, *John Williamson Nevin: American Theologian* (New York, 1997).

37. John R. Fitzmier, *New England's Moral Legislator: Timothy Dwight, 1752–1817* (Bloomington, IN, 1998); Charles Hambrick-Stowe, *Charles G. Finney and the Spirit of American Evangelicalism* (Grand Rapids, 1996); Michael G. Kenny, *The Perfect Law of Liberty: Elias Smith and the Providential History of America* (Washington, DC, 1994), with significant treatment of Elias Smith also in Hatch, *Democratization of American Christianity*; Ulrich Gäbler, *Auferstehungszeit: Erweckungsprediger des 19. Jahrhunderts* (Munich, 1991).

38. Joan D. Hedrick, *Harriet Beecher Stowe* (New York, 1994); Roger Lundin, *Emily Dickinson and the Art of Belief* (Grand Rapids, 1998).

39. James Oscar Farmer, Jr., *The Metaphysical Confederacy: James Henley Thornwell and the Synthesis of Southern Values* (Macon, GA, 1986); Paul E. Johnson and Sean Wilentz, *The Kingdom of Mathias: A Story of Sex and Salvation in Nineteenth-Century America* (New York, 1994).

40. Grant Gordon, *From Slavery to Freedom: The Life of David George, Pioneer Black Minister* (Hantsport, Nova Scotia, 1992); Nell Irvin Painter, *Sojourner Truth: a Life, a Symbol* (New York, 1996).

41. Sue Houchins, ed., *Spiritual Narratives* (New York, 1988), contains the autobiographical writings of Maria W. Stewart, Jarena Lee, Julia A. J. Foote, and Virginia W. Broughton.

42. Edwin S. Gaustad, *Sworn on the Altar of God: A Religious Biography of Thomas Jefferson* (Grand Rapids, 1996).

43. Allen C. Guelzo, *Abraham Lincoln: Redeemer President* (Grand Rapids, 1999).

44. Alan Heimert, *Religion and the American Mind From the Great Awakening to the Revolution* (Cambridge, MA, 1966); Thomas J. Curry, *The First Freedoms: Church and State in America to the Passage of the First Amendment* (New York, 1986); Nathan O. Hatch, *The Sacred Cause of Liberty: Republican Thought and the Millennium in Revolutionary New England* (New Haven, 1977); Ruth H. Bloch, *Visionary Republic: Millennial Themes in American Thought, 1756–1800* (New York, 1985); Stephen A. Marini, *Radical Sects of Revolutionary New England* (Cambridge, MA, 1982). For ripple effects from this body of work, see Philip Goff, "Revivals and Revolution: Historiographic Turns since Alan Heimert's *Religion and the American Mind*," *Church History* 67 (1998): 695–721.

45. Ellis Sandoz, ed., *Political Sermons of the American Founding Era, 1730–1805* (Indianapolis, 1991); with the useful Sandoz, *Index to Political Sermons of the American Founding Era* (Indianapolis, 1997).

46. John Patrick Diggins, *The Lost Soul of American Politics: Virtue, Self-Interest, and the Foundations of Liberalism* (New York, 1984); William Lee Miller, *The First Liberty: Religion and the American Republic* (New York, 1985); A. James Reichley, *Religion in American Public Life* (Washington, DC, 1985); Ellis Sandoz, *A Government of Laws: Political Theory, Religion, and the American Founding* (Baton Rouge, 1990); Daniel L. Dreisbach, *Religion and Politics in the Early Republic: Jasper Adams and the Church-State Debate* (Lexington, KY, 1996); James H. Hutson, *Religion and the Founding of the American Republic* (Washington, DC, 1998); and James H. Hutson, ed., *Religion and the New Republic: Faith in the Founding of America* (Lanham, MD, 2000).

47. Mark Valeri, *Law and Providence in Joseph Bellamy's New England: The Origins of the New Divinity in Revolutionary America* (New York, 1994); Ronald Hoffman and Peter J. Albert, eds., *Religion in a Revolutionary Age* (Charlottesville, 1994); Derek H. Davis, *Religion and the Continental Congress, 1774–1789: Contributions to Original Intent* (New York, 2000). Donald Weber's effort to exploit contemporary theories of language in interpreting the stance of New Divinity ministers toward the Revolution was only partially successful. See Weber, *Rhetoric and History in Revolutionary New England* (New York, 1988).

48. For example, John Whitehead, *The Second American Revolution* (Elgin, IL, 1982); Peter Marshall and David Manuel, *From Sea to Shining Sea: Discovering God's Plan for America in Her First Half-Century of Independence, 1787–1837* (Old Tappan, NJ, 1986); David

Barton, *Spirit of the American Revolution* (Aledo, TX, 1994); Gary Amos and Richard Gardiner, *Never Before in History: America's Inspired Birth* (Dallas, 1998).

49. See especially R. Laurence Moore and Isaac Kramnick, *The Godless Constitution: The Case Against Religious Correctness* (New York, 1996).
50. John Witte, Jr., *Religion and the American Constitutional Experiment: Essential Rights and Liberties* (Boulder, CO, 2000).
51. Jonathan D. Sarna and David G. Dalin, eds., *Religion and State in the American Jewish Experience* (Notre Dame, 1997).
52. John G. West, Jr., *The Politics of Revelation and Reason: Religion and Civic Life in the New Nation* (Lawrence, KS, 1996).
53. John R. McKivigan and Mitchell Snay, eds., *Religion and the Antebellum Debate over Slavery* (Athens, GA, 1998). This work carries further the solid work begun in John R. McKivigan, *The War Against Proslavery Religion: Abolitionism and the Northern Churches, 1830–1865* (Ithaca, 1984); and Larry E. Tise, *Proslavery: A History of the Defense of Slavery in America, 1701–1840* (Athens, GA, 1987).
54. Richard J. Carwardine, *Evangelicals and Politics in Antebellum America* (New Haven, 1993), p. 48.
55. Mitchell Snay, *Gospel of Disunion: Religion and Separatism in the Antebellum South* (New York, 1993).
56. David B. Cheseborough, *God Ordained this War: Sermons on the Sectional Crisis* (Columbia, SC, 1991); *"No Sorrow like Our Sorrow": Northern Protestants Ministers and the Assassination of Lincoln* (Kent, OH., 1994); *Clergy Dissent in the Old South, 1830–1865* (Carbondale, IL, 1996).
57. Robert H. Abzug, *Cosmos Crumbling: American Reform and the Religious Imagination* (New York, 1994).
58. Anne C. Rose, *Victorian America and the Civil War* (New York, 1992).
59. Randall M. Miller, Harry S. Stout, Charles Reagan Wilson, eds., *Religion and the American Civil War* (New York, 1998).
60. James McPherson's brilliant general study, *Battle Cry of Freedom: The Civil War Era* (New York, 1988), covers religion only lightly. Perhaps reflecting the recent boom in scholarship, some of his more recent volumes, such as *For Cause and Comrades: Why Men Fought in the Civil War* (New York, 1997), pause longer on religious motivations and consequences (see especially pp. 62–75).
61. Michael O'Brien, "Did the truth make them free?" *Times Literary Supplement*, 23 July 1999, p. 29.

62. Susan Juster, "Tales of the Supernatural: Historians and Witches," *Intellectual History Newsletter* 21 (1999): 54; a similar concern is voiced by Allen C. Guelzo, "God's Design: The Literature of the Colonial Revivals of Religion, 1735–1760," in *New Directions in American Religious History*, p. 148.

63. The significant contribution of editors and contributors to the *William and Mary Quarterly* is probably the single most important reason for the awareness among colonialists of the North Atlantic region as a whole.

64. Respectively, G. A. Rawlyk, *The Canada Fire: Radical Evangelicalism in British North America, 1775–1812* (Kingston and Montreal, 1994); Cecilia Morgan, *Public Men and Virtuous Women: The Gendered Languages of Religion and Politics in Upper Canada, 1791–1850* (Toronto, 1996); Neil Semple, *The Lord's Dominion: The History of Canadian Methodism* (Kingston and Montreal, 1996); Michael Gauvreau, *The Evangelical Century: College and Creed in English Canada from the Great Revival to the Great Depression* (Kingston and Montreal, 1991); William Westfall, *Two Worlds: The Protestant Cultures of Nineteenth-Century Ontario* (Kingston and Montreal, 1989); and Greg Marquis, *In Armageddon's Shadow: The Civil War and Canada's Maritime Provinces* (Kingston and Montreal, 1998).

65. One of the reasons why Richard Carwardine's work on religion in antebellum America is so insightful is that it has been carried out alongside significant efforts to understand religious forces in Britain as well. See for example his *Transatlantic Revivalism: Popular Evangelicalism in Britain and America, 1790–1865* (Westport, CT, 1978); "Religion and Politics in Nineteenth-Century Britain: The Case Against American Exceptionalism," in *Religion and American Politics From the Colonial Period to the 1980s*, ed. Mark A. Noll (New York, 1990), pp. 225–52; and "Evangelicals, Politics, and the Coming of the American Civil War: A Transatlantic Perspective," in *Evangelicalism: Comparative Studies of Popular Protestantism in North America, the British Isles, and Beyond, 1700–1990*, eds. Mark A. Noll, David W. Bebbington, and George A. Rawlyk (New York, 1994), pp. 198–218.

–5–

The New Deal in American Scholarship
Alan Brinkley

More than most episodes in the recent American past, the New Deal of the 1930s has a curiously complicated relationship to the interplay between history and memory, for the image of Franklin Roosevelt and the image of the administration over which he presided have moved in sharply different directions. In popular memory, Roosevelt himself has become an American icon, the only twentieth-century figure who can stand alongside Washington, Lincoln, and Jefferson in the pantheon of great American heroes, the only modern leader to have – like Washington, Lincoln, and Jefferson – a memorial on the Mall in Washington. In his own time, Roosevelt was intensely controversial – both beloved and loathed with extraordinary passion. Today, he is a kind of secular saint, of whom no one dares speak negatively. Historians chronicling Roosevelt's life have been generally admiring, but have presented him as not just a visionary leader, but also as a consummate politician – wily, often cynical, sometimes duplicitous. Their work has had little or no impact on Roosevelt's image in popular culture.

The interplay of history and memory has been very different in assessments of the New Deal itself. The image in popular memory of the achievements of the New Deal has evolved from being a revered model of enlightened government to become a widely (if not universally) repudiated symbol of obsolete statism. Its image in historical scholarship, by contrast, has been remarkably stable. For more than fifty years – through liberal triumphs and liberal failures, through the rise of an anti-liberal left to the resurgence of an anti-liberal right, from Truman to Johnson to Reagan to Clinton – most historians have continued to present the New Deal as a bold and largely successful moment of political innovation. The raging currents of political change, which have had such profound effects on many other areas of scholarship, seem to have penetrated New Deal history hardly at all.

Not that New Deal scholarship has been static. There has been considerable variation in the evaluation of the New Deal within the basic framework of liberal interpretation – and some significant, although never terribly influential, challenges to the framework itself. This chapter will attempt to explain how, despite its underlying stability, New Deal scholarship has evolved over the last generation or so.

The first effort by a historian to explain the New Deal was probably the small book published in 1938 by Arthur M. Schlesinger, the father of the Arthur Schlesinger now more commonly associated with the age of Franklin Roosevelt. Schlesinger Sr. was what we now call a "progressive" historian, and he looked at the New Deal as he did the rest of American history: as part of a long, ever unfinished struggle between democracy and plutocracy, between the "people" and the "interests." The New Deal, perhaps needless to say, was the democratic force in Schlesinger's admiring study – just as it was in the much more substantial three-volume study by his son, *The Age of Roosevelt*, published in the late 1950s. The two Schlesingers, father and son, thus established the New Deal as a field of scholarship, and established as well a liberal/progressive framework for understanding it.[1]

But the most influential and durable product of the liberal/progressive generation of New Deal historians is almost certainly William E. Leuchtenburg's *Franklin D. Roosevelt and the New Deal*, published in 1963. Leuchtenburg's book was a masterpiece of synthesis, grounded in an exceptional mastery of sources and written in clear and elegant prose. But it was also an interpretation of the New Deal that departed in modest ways from that of the Schlesingers. It was, on the whole, supportive of the many things the New Deal tried and achieved, but it also introduced a critical element to the previously uncritical liberal interpretation by discussing the many social problems the Roosevelt administration failed to address or failed to solve, most notably the Depression itself, which the New Deal was unable to end. Leuchtenburg also took note of the absence of significant structural reform in the industrial economy, the limits of the new welfare state, the failure of government relief measures to help those groups most in need of assistance, and the New Deal's modest record on racial issues. The New Deal was, Leuchtenburg claimed, a "half-way revolution" (not the Third American Revolution that his more ebullient contemporaries Eric Goldman and Carl Degler claimed it was).[2]

Today, more than a third of a century later, Leuchtenburg's book remains the most widely-used history of the New Deal among college teachers; and the interpretation that shaped it is still the basis of most New Deal scholarship. It is difficult to think of any other field in American history where a large, interpretive synthesis has remained so dominant for so long. One reason Leuchtenburg's book has survived so successfully is that the very thing that distinguished it from the earlier classics of New Deal scholarship also ensured its longevity. The skepticism, the mild criticisms, the faint whiff of disappointment made Leuchtenburg's book more palatable for the era of political disillusionment that soon followed its publication. He preempted some of the criticisms of the left, while retaining the core of the liberal analysis.

The durability of Leuchtenburg's interpretation raises another, particularly perplexing, question about New Deal scholarship: the relative absence of a well-developed left-wing critique of the New Deal. In the 1960s and 1970s, when so much of the historical profession was engaged in revisionist scholarship from the left on almost every conceivable subject, the New Deal received only cursory attention. There were suggestive articles – by Barton Bernstein, Ronald Radosh, Howard Zinn, and others – that suggested the outlines of a simple and rather obvious left critique: that the New Deal left many important problems unsolved and even unaddressed, most notably problems of racial injustice and economic inequality; that it failed to challenge, and did much to buttress, corporate capitalism; that its real instincts were far more conservative than its reputation suggests. But none of these things added very much to Leuchtenburg's muted criticisms, and the creation of a significant left interpretation of the New Deal remained one of the unfinished projects of this otherwise fruitful, and controversial, period of scholarship.[3]

More recently, there have been some more serious and sophisticated critiques from the left: Thomas Ferguson's challenging essays connecting the New Deal to new forms of capitalist internationalism; Colin Gordon's important book showing the connections between the early New Deal and the efforts of financiers and industrialists to shape government policy in the service of their own long-term interests. But even these much more significant challenges to the liberal paradigm have failed to shift the way most scholars (and teachers) discuss the New Deal.[4]

Nor has there been much serious criticism of the New Deal from the right. That is less surprising, perhaps, than the absence of criticism from the left. Conservative and right-wing views are not very well represented in mainstream historical scholarship. There has never been a thorough going conservative reappraisal of American history in any way comparable to the reappraisal by the left. Still, conservative forces have become increasingly important in many areas of American life in recent decades, including the world of scholarship and intellectual life, and one might expect to have seen a more serious effort than there has been to challenge the standing of the New Deal – the great fount of modern liberalism.

Instead, conservative reservations about the New Deal have crept slowly into liberal interpretations in much the same way that left reservations crept in a generation ago. One example of that is the important and much-honored recent book by David Kennedy, *Freedom from Fear*, a volume in the Oxford History of the United States. Kennedy is, at heart, an admirer of the New Deal, and he concludes his long and impressive account of its complicated history with an approving evaluation of what it did to save capitalism and provide new layers of security for many Americans. But, while earlier narratives of this kind are peppered with criticisms from the left, Kennedy's is peppered with criticisms from the right: that the New Deal egregiously and gratuitously meddled with capitalist institutions; that it carried on a destructive war against producers that undermined their confidence and discouraged investment (here reviving a long-forgotten contemporary critique of the New Deal for destroying "business confidence"); that the great achievement of the New Deal was, in fact, the very thing that the left saw as its greatest failure – its success in laying the groundwork for an unfettered capitalist expansion in the years after the war; its refusal, in the end, to impose very much new additional regulation on the private economy.[5]

Another major challenge to traditional interpretations of history has had a slightly larger, but still not profound, impact on the understanding of the New Deal: the role of gender. Historians of women and gender have reinterpreted the New Deal in two related, but essentially separate ways. The first, and more extensive, is to examine the role of women within the New Deal. That has included extensive attention to the important part Eleanor Roosevelt played in her husband's administration, and in the public life of the nation in the 1930s and 1940s. It has also involved examination of the extensive network of women who held office in the New Deal and operated, often in concert, to promote various elements of a women's agenda. The second, more complex, and so far less fully developed area of reinterpretation is to look at New Deal programs and actions in gendered terms – to try to understand the assumptions about men and women that went into the making of the New Deal state. This approach has had its greatest impact on the discussion of the welfare state, but it has also become visible in accounts of the labor movement, the New Deal's cultural projects, the conduct of World War II, and many other areas. It seems reasonable to assume that gendered interpretations will eventually change our understanding of the New Deal as profoundly as they have changed our understanding of progressive reform and many other areas of history, but they have not yet done so.[6]

What I have described so far is the story of an important area of American historical scholarship in which a reasonably centrist, liberal interpretation has reigned largely unchallenged since it emerged in the 1930s, with only a small amount of largely ineffectual nibbling around the edges by the left and the right. But that is not the entire story of New Deal scholarship. There were, in fact, considerable changes in the field during the 1980s and 1990s – changes that were far less ideological than the changes occurring in those same years in the larger political culture, but ones that are significant by the standards of the academic world.

Historians have paid most attention, perhaps, to the question of constraints, to defining the limits imposed on New Deal reform by the political, social, and economic realities of the 1930s and by the ideological preconceptions of the New Dealers themselves. This is not surprising, perhaps, given the nature of American public life since the 1960s and the great difficulty modern leaders have had in winning support for ambitious goals. The first scholars to consider this question focused primarily on political constraints and argued that Franklin Roosevelt, despite his enormous personal popularity, was never able fully to overcome powerful opposition to his policies both within the government and in the electorate at large. James MacGregor Burns, in his notable biography *The Lion and the Fox,* criticized Roosevelt for his failure to make full use of his popularity to challenge this opposition and for his failure genuinely to reshape the party system and provide a secure home for progressives within it. Most scholars, however, have suggested that such a reshaping was never within Roosevelt's power. They have revealed ways in which conservative opposition to the New Deal in Congress was an important factor in the administration's calculations almost from the beginning and became more powerful as time went on. They have also shed light on the way in which the conservatism of the South (and the Southern representatives in Congress) helps explain the failure of the administration to take more active measures on behalf of racial equality.[7]

More recently, scholars have given renewed attention to the role of the courts – and the Supreme Court in particular – in shaping the contours of the New Deal. The obstructionism of the Court in the early years of the New Deal, when it invalidated legislation creating the National Recovery Administration (NRA), the Agricultural Adjustment Administration (AAA), and other New Deal programs, has been a part of the scholarly picture of the New Deal from the start. The president's ill-fated "court-packing" scheme of 1937, according to this account, preceded a real and important change in the behavior of the Court, which subsequently – because of its fear of Roosevelt's efforts at court reform and changes in its composition as justices died and retired – began to uphold New Deal measures. But more recent scholarship suggests a more complicated story, in which the court was evolving toward a more flexible view of interstate commerce before the court-packing controversy, and in which the New Deal itself precipitated many of its own problems by drafting important legislation sloppily and without sufficient attention to constitutional guidelines. The constraints the Court provided, according to these newer accounts, were not simply a result of the tired old men whom Roosevelt tried to demonize, but of the slow pace of constitutional change and the enduring problems that American federalism creates for all progressive governments.[8]

Other scholars have emphasized ideological constraints: the degree to which Roosevelt and those around him operated in response to the economic and political orthodoxies of their time. Here too it is possible to see a recognition – spurred by the political changes of the last two decades of the twentieth century – of the enduring power of conservative belief and conservative activism in American political life. Although the New Deal proved more flexible and less ideological than the administrations that preceded it, it too was constrained by powerful conservative assumptions: the belief in a balanced budget, the mistrust of the "dole," the reluctance to intrude the federal government too deeply into the field of microeconomic management, and others.

The clumsy, jerry-built, welfare state that emerged from the New Deal (of which the expensive and inefficient Social Security System remains the centerpiece) was in large part a product of the strong ideological opposition, even among many of the most committed liberals, to an overt system of direct government assistance to the poor. It reflected the racist assumptions of much of the political world through its careful initial exclusion from coverage of those occupations in which African Americans (and women) were most heavily represented. It was also a product of highly gendered assumptions about the proper distribution of benefits. Both men and women involved in the creation of Social Security retained a strong belief in the centrality of the "family wage" and offered the most secure and generous benefits of the system to men. Women were left with the frail Aid to Dependent Children (later Aid to Families with Dependent Children) program, which was based on an assumption of female vulnerability and incapacity.[9]

Nowhere has the argument for the New Deal's ideological conservatism been more forcefully advanced than in the field of labor history. New Deal labor laws and the growth of trade unionism they helped to promote – phenomena liberals have long considered among the most important progressive triumphs of the 1930s – have received withering reassessments by a host of scholars. Indeed, this is perhaps the only area of New Deal scholarship in which there is a serious and well-developed critique from the left. These scholars argue that the events of the 1930s mark a highly limited victory (if not an actual defeat) for labor; that the large hopes for creating a lasting basis for genuine industrial democracy were not achieved; that the New Deal was never fully committed to seeing them achieved. Some labor historians have seen in the great working-class struggles of the 1930s a striking (if short-lived) effort to redefine democracy and create a central place in it for labor. Among such scholars are Gary Gerstle and Lizabeth Cohen, both of whom chronicle ways in which labor radicalism helped ethnic workers overcome their immigrant backgrounds and become wholly a part of a class-based movement. But such work does not challenge the argument of the left, that New Deal labor laws (both in their conception and in their administration) gradually deradicalized the labor movement and forced it to limit its aims to conventional wage and benefit issues.[10]

Starting in the 1980s, a new body of scholarship began to identify some previously lightly examined constraints on the New Deal: constraints imposed by the nature of American governmental and political institutions. In doing so, it made a case for considering the structure of the state itself as a crucial factor in the actions of government (as opposed to models of state behavior that emphasize the influence of party systems, social forces, or constellations of interest groups). These "state-centered" scholars argue that one reason the New Deal did not do more was because of the absence of sufficient "state capacity"; most of the federal bureaucracy in the 1930s was too small and inexperienced to be able to undertake large tasks. The failure of the NRA, according to Kenneth Finegold and Theda Skocpol, was in large part a result of the absence within the government of institutions capable of supervising the industrial economy. That absence made it almost inevitable that control of the experiment would fall into the hands of businessmen themselves. The relative success of the AAA, in contrast, is attributable to the far more highly developed bureaucratic capacity of the Agriculture Department, with its close relationship to powerful farm organizations and its several generations of experience in attempting to manage the farm economy.[11]

Another reflection of this growing interest in institutions is increasing scholarly attention to the way the consequences of policy initiatives often depart from the intentions behind them. In the broadest sense, the unexpected outcomes of New Deal efforts can be seen in the emergence in the 1930s of the so-called "broker state." As Ellis Hawley demonstrated in *The New Deal and the Problem of Monopoly*, his landmark history of economic policy in the 1930s, by the end of the Depression, important new groups – workers, farmers, and others – were beginning for the first time to exercise meaningful political and economic power. The federal government, in the meantime, had largely rejected the idea of trying to impose any central design on the economy or promoting a transcendent national goal. Its policies worked, rather, to guarantee the rights of particular interest groups and oversee pluralistic competition in the national marketplace. It had become a broker state.

The rise of the broker state is arguably one of the most significant political developments of the New Deal era, and some historians – in talking about the "second New Deal" that emerged in 1935–1936 – have argued that it was the result of a deliberate ideological choice by Roosevelt and those around them. But the broker state was to a large degree an unintended result of government policies designed to advance other ends. The NRA, for example, has been seen by some scholars as part of a broad corporatist impulse powerful at least within the early New Deal. Yet it failed in its avowed goal of stabilizing prices and markets and harmonizing industrial relations. Its most important legacy may have been a partially unintended one: the organization of industrial workers into an important competitive actor in the marketplace (which the National Industrial Recovery Act's (NIRA) Section 7a – precursor to the 1935 Wagner Act – did much to promote). Other initiatives designed to promote a planned, harmonious economic world failed in their larger goals but similarly left behind newly organized groups capable for the first time of effectively defending their claims. Hawley termed this process "counter-organiza-tion," the mobilization of weaker groups to allow them to confront stronger ones – an alternative New Dealers gradually came to prefer to the more politically difficult effort to curb the influence of existing centers of power directly.[12]

Another important shift in the scholarly approach to the New Deal is the tendency to see its achievements less as the result of the political and intellectual impulses of the moment and more as the product of long-term social transformations. This is not, of course, the *longue durée*. But by the standards of twentieth-century history, these interpretations are evidence of an increasing effort to look beyond the preoccupations of the moment (which modern historians have often had great difficulty doing) and to see large changes that were not clearly visible at the time but are somewhat more visible now.

One broad approach to the history of the New Deal, which still has not attracted very much scholarly attention, is the effort to see it in a global perspective. Daniel T. Rodgers's *Atlantic Crossings* has recently demonstrated the importance of the trans-Atlantic migration of ideas between American and Europe in shaping social policies on both sides of the ocean in the first third of the twentieth century. Most New Dealers were less avowedly internationalist in their approach to policy than their progressive predecessors had been, but there is much in what the New Deal did that could fruitfully be explored less parochially than has so far been the case. A few scholars have pointed to some uncomfortable analogies between New Deal economic and social programs in the early and mid-1930s, and vaguely similar programs in Germany, Italy, and the Soviet Union. But those analogies are so provocative and disturbing that no one has chosen to explore them in any detail. There are other, less visible links between American and British social policy in the late 1930s and early 1940s – through the simultaneous work of the Beveridge commission in Britain and the National Resources Planning Board in the United States, both of which produced ambitious planning documents toward the end of the war (even though only the British plan led to real changes in social policy). Still other scholars have seen in the increasingly internationalist aspirations of American capitalism an important clue the behavior of many corporate leaders in supporting important aspects of the New Deal. And historians interested in gender – among them Linda Gordon and Theda Skocpol – have suggested fruitful ways of linking the development of American and European welfare states and their treatment of women.[13]

Another longer-term approach to the New Deal has emerged from historians of American culture, who see the Roosevelt years not simply as a political or economic or institutional event, but also as an important moment in the evolution of American culture. Much of the cultural history of the 1930s can, of course, be understood without direct reference to the New Deal. But the enormous impact both of Roosevelt's personality and of his programs on the popular imagination of his time cannot be ignored in any attempt to characterize Depression culture. Out of the crucible of Depression and New Deal emerged a complicated interplay of cultural changes, which at one and the same time reinforced and challenged inherited values. Among many Americans, the 1930s – in part because of their frightening image of a world unraveling – created a desperate effort to shore up traditional values and attitudes, an effort reinforced in many ways by Roosevelt's effort to assure Americans that the pre-Depression world could be restored by the use of traditional methods. Among others, the Great Depression created a vigorous culture of dissent, expressed most visibly in the world of the Popular Front. It had an ambiguous relationship with the New Deal. The failure of the Roosevelt administration to end the Depression, and to move as vigorously against corporate power as the left wished, was one of the spurs to the growth of the American Communist Party and its Popular Front allies. But in some of its guises, most famously the Federal Theater Project and other explicitly cultural projects of the Roosevelt government, the New Deal actually embraced and promoted the culture of the left. The Great Depression also strengthened the yearning among many Americans for the idea of community – as an alternative to the harsh, individualistic, acquisitive culture that they believed had failed them; the New Deal reinforced that impulse as well with some its rhetoric and with such programs as the Farm Security Administration and the Resettlement Administration. The cultural impact of the New Deal, in short, was as varied as its political impact.[14]

Looking beyond the immediate to longer-term processes has also been the avowed aim of the so-called organizational historians, who see the New Deal as a reflection of the long-term evolution of managerial systems in both private and public life. The engine that drove both the New Deal and much of twentieth-century history, they have argued, is the rise of large-scale bureaucratic institutions in all areas of American life – business, finance, government, education, philanthropy – and the consequent adaptation of society to their existence. The commitment of the organizational historians to a Weberian model of modern historical change has led them to look at the New Deal as a part of a long-term evolution in bureaucratic structures much more than an ideological event defined by its own time.[15]

A related argument sees many New Deal achievements as the result of the emergence in the twentieth century of coherent interest groups, who were steadily gaining influence at the expense of political parties. Some scholars have suggested that urbanization, and the growing political power of the city, shaped New Deal programs far more than the ideological inclinations of its leaders; the gradual shift in political attention in the 1930s from rural issues toward such matters as public housing, fair labor standards, and public health is evidence of the mobilization of powerful urban forces. Others, among them Jordan Schwarz, see the New Deal as both a cause and a product of the rising power of the South and the West. He suggests that one of the principal legacies of the New Deal was its embrace of an effort, spanning several decades, to use the power of government (what Schwarz calls "state capitalism") to develop these previously underdeveloped areas of the country; vast public-works projects in the South and the West, he claims, were the fulfilment of a regional effort to use public investment to create a basic infrastructure for those regions that stretched back to early in the century.[16]

Still other scholars, myself among them, argue that the New Deal was a reflection of the rising emphasis on consumption in American culture and the American economy alike, and that both the economic and welfare policies of the Roosevelt administration were part of a broad political adaptation to that shift, which moved public policy in significantly new directions. From the emergence of large-scale corporate industrialism in the late nineteenth century, to the first years of the New Deal in the 1930s, the "problem of monopoly," as it was widely known, preoccupied the political agenda of almost everyone who could fairly be called a progressive and a reformer. The great problem facing the nation, virtually all reformers agreed, was the concentration of corporate power. The solution to that problem was to find some way to limit, redirect, or regulate that power so that it did not threaten the public good. The central question of public life was, in other words, the problem of production – and the distribution of power among producers.

By the end of the New Deal, and certainly by the end of World War II, that great question had been quite substantially redefined. No longer were reformers or progressives or (as most by now called themselves) liberals very much concerned about production. Capitalism, they had concluded, was the most efficient system for producing and distributing goods, and it should be largely (although not completely) left alone to do its work. The great problem now was consumers. How would the fruits of industrial capitalism be widely enough distributed to produce a market for the economy's goods and create a decent life for most of the American people? As with the question of production, there were disagreements about how to deal with the problem of consumption. The allure of Keynesian economics was only one – albeit the most powerful one – of the many prescriptions being promoted in the early 1940s.[17]

This shift in outlook from an explanation of economic (and political economic) life focusing on production to one focusing on consumption is, of course, part of a much larger social, cultural, and economic transformation in the middle and later years of the twentieth century: the conquest of scarcity, the discovery of abundance, the redirection of human and social aspiration toward the achievement of a new level of material existence – a kind of existence now visible all around us, in America, in Britain, in much of continental Europe, in virtually every nation that has successfully entered the modern industrial (and now post-industrial) world.

What this suggests is that the New Deal can best be understood as part of a large transition in American (and Western European) life from its rural, pre-industrial past to its urbanized, industrialized, bureaucratized, and fantastically affluent (if often troubled) postwar future. The New Deal was not, of course, simply a mechanical response to social change. It was a product of the sensibilities, ideologies, and political abilities of Franklin Roosevelt and the men and women he brought into government with him; and it was similarly a product of the political institutions and partisan interests that shaped public life in those years. But the New Deal did not exist in a social and economic vacuum. It emerged during a critical moment in American life; a moment in which all the great social changes of the industrial era – industrialization, bureaucratization, urbanization, and the growth of a consumer-centered culture and economy – collided in a crisis of epic proportions. Understanding the New Deal requires understanding its own, complicated internal life – as historians have been trying to do for more than sixty years. But it also requires understanding its relationship to the great social and cultural changes of which it was in part a product and which it struggled, sometimes successfully and sometimes unsuccessfully, to master.

Notes

1. Arthur M. Schlesinger, Sr., *The New Deal in Action, 1933–1938* (New York, 1939); Arthur M. Schlesinger, Jr., *The Age of Roosevelt* (Boston, 3 vols., 1956–1960).
2. William E. Leuchtenburg, *Franklin D. Roosevelt and the New Deal* (New York, 1963); Carl N. Degler, *The New Deal* (Chicago, 1970); Eric F. Goldman, *The Crucial Decade: America, 1945–1955* (New York, 1956).
3. Barton J. Bernstein, "The New Deal: The Conservative Achievements of Liberal Reform," in *Towards a New Past: Dissenting Essays in American History*, ed. Barton J. Bernstein (New York, 1967); Ronald Radosh, "The Myth of the New Deal," in Ronald Radosh and Murray Rothbard, eds., *A New History of the Leviathan: Essays on the Rise of the Corporate State* (New York, 1972); Howard Zinn, *New Deal Thought* (Indianapolis, 1966); Thomas Ferguson, "From Normalcy

to New Deal: Industrial Structure, Party Competition, and American Public Policy in the Great Depression," *International Organization*, 38 (1984); Theda Skocpol, "Political Response to Capitalist Crisis: Neo-Marxist Theories of State and the Case of the New Deal," *Politics and Society*, 10 (1980).

4. Ferguson, "From Normalcy to the New Deal"; idem, "Industrial Conflict and the Coming of the New Deal: The Triumph of Multinational Liberalism in America," in Steve Fraser and Gary Gerstle, eds., *The Rise and Fall of the New Deal Order, 1930–1980* (Princeton 1989); Colin Gordon, *New Deals: Business, Labor, and Politics in America, 1920–1935* (New York, 1994).
5. David M. Kennedy, *Freedom from Fear: The American People in Depression and War* (New York, 1999).
6. Susan Ware, *Beyond Suffrage, Women in the New Deal* (Cambridge, MA, 1981; idem, *Partner and I: Molly Dewson, Feminism, and New Deal Politics* (New Haven, 1987); Blanche Wiesen Cook, *Eleanor Roosevelt, vol. 1, 1884–1933* (New York 1992); Theda Skocpol, *Protecting Soldiers and Mothers: The Political Origins of Social Policy in the United States* (Cambridge, MA, 1992); Linda Gordon, *Pitied but Not Entitled: Single Mothers and the History of the Welfare State* (New York, 1994).
7. James MacGregor Burns, *Roosevelt: The Lion and the Fox* (New York, 1956); James T. Patterson, *Congressional Conservatism and the New Deal: The Growth of the Conservative Coalition in Congress, 1933–1939* (Lexington, 1967); idem, *The New Deal and the States: Federalism in Transition* (Princeton, 1969).
8. Leuchtenburg, *The Supreme Court Reborn: Constitutional Revolution in the Age of Roosevelt* (New York, 1995); idem, "The Origins of Franklin D. Roosevelt's 'Court-Packing' Plan," *Supreme Court Review*, 1966; idem, "Franklin D. Roosevelt's Supreme Court 'Packing' Plan," in Harold M. Hollingsworth and William F. Holmes, eds., *Essays on the New Deal* (Austin, 1969); Leonard Baker, *Back to Back: The Duel Between FDR and the Supreme Court* (New York, 1967); Joseph Alsop and Turner Catledge, *The 168 Days* (Garden City, 1938).
9. Linda Gordon, *Pitied but Not Entitled*; idem, "Social Insurance and Public Assistance: The Influence of Gender in Welfare Thought in the United States, 1890–1935," *American Historical Review*, 97 (1992): 19–54; idem, "Black and White Visions of Welfare: Women's Welfare Activism, 1890–1945," *Journal of American History*, 78 (1991): 559–90; idem, ed., *Women, the State, and Welfare* (Madison, 1990).

10. Gary Gerstle, *Working Class Americanism: The Politics of Labor in a Textile City, 1914–1960* (New York, 1989); Lizabeth Cohen, *Making a New Deal: Industrial Workers in Chicago, 1919–1939* (New York, 1990).
11. Kenneth Finegold and Theda Skocpol, *State and Party in America's New Deal* (Madison, 1995); Skocpol and Finegold, "State Capacity and Economic Intervention in the Early New Deal," *Political Science Quarterly* 97, no. 2 (1982).
12. Ellis W. Hawley, *The New Deal and the Problem of Monopoly* (Princeton, 1966); Kennedy, *Freedom from Fear*.
13. Daniel T. Rodgers, *Atlantic Crossings: Social Politics in a Progressive Age* (Cambridge, MA, 1998); John A. Garraty, "The New Deal, National Socialism, and the Great Depression," *American Historical Review*, 78 (1973); Colin Gordon, *New Deals*; Theda Skocpol and Margaret Weir, "State Structures and the Possibilities for Keynesian Responses to the Great Depression in Sweden, Britain, and the United States," in Peter B. Evans, Dietrich Rueschemeyer, and Theda Skocpol, eds., *Bringing the State Back In* (New York, 1985).
14. Warren I. Susman, *Culture and Commitment, 1929–1945* (New York, 1973); idem, *Culture as History: The Transformation of American Society in the Twentieth Century* (New York, 1984); Richard Pells, *Radical Visions, American Dreams: Culture and Social Thought in the Depression Years* (New York, 1973); Barbara Melosh, *Engendering Culture: Manhood and Womanhood in New Deal Public Art and Theater* (Washington, 1991); Alan Brinkley, *Voices of Protest: Huey Long, Father Coughlin, and the Great Depression* (New York, 1982).
15. Louis Galambos, *Competition and Cooperation: The Emergence of a National Trade Association* (Baltimore, 1966); idem, "The Emerging Organizational Synthesis in Modern American History," *Business History Review*. 44 (1970): 279–90; idem, *The Rise of the Corporate Commonwealth: United States Business and Public Policy in the Twentieth Century* (New York, 1988); idem, "Technology, Political Economy, and Professionalization: Central Themes of the Organizational Synthesis," *Business History Review*, 57 (1983): 471–93; Brian Balogh, "Reorganizing The Organizational Synthesis," *Studies in American Political Development*, 5 (1991): 119–72; Alfred D. Chandler, Jr., *Strategy and Structure: Chapters in the History of American Industrial Enterprise* (Cambridge, MA, 1962); idem, *The Visible Hand: The Managerial Revolution in American Business* (Cambridge, MA, 1977).

16. Jordan A. Schwarz, *The New Dealers: Power Politics in the Age of Roosevelt* (New York, 1993); Samuel P. Hays, "Politics and Society: Beyond the Political Party," in *The Evolution of American Electoral Systems* (Westport, CT, 1981).
17. Herbert Stein, *The Fiscal Revolution in America* (Chicago, 1969); Dean L. May, *From the New Deal to New Economics: The American Liberal Response to the Recession of 1937* (New York, 1981); Alan Brinkley, *The End of Reform: New Deal Liberalism in Recession and War* (New York, 1995); Theodore Rosenof, *Patterns of Political Economy in America: The Failure to Develop Democratic Left Synthesis, 1933–1950* (New York, 1983).

– 6 –

Beyond the "Age of McCarthy": Anticommunism and the Historians
Michael J. Heale

With the ending of the Cold War it might have been thought that scholarly interest in the Age of McCarthy would wither away. But something like the reverse has occurred. The Cold War "victory" of the United States has been followed by an intensification of academic warfare, at least on the related issues of the place of communism and anticommunism in American life.[1] Even Senator McCarthy himself, whom modern historians had for the most part consigned to a bit part in the drama, has lately been shouldering his way back onto the stage. A 1998 editorial in the *New York Times* saw signs of a "rehabilitation of Senator McCarthy" in recent scholarship and, as if on cue, a largely exculpatory biography of the senator appeared two years later. The Cold War evidently smolders on.[2]

Most scholars acknowledge that anticommunism was a protean creature, encompassing very different and often mutually antagonistic elements, from the pragmatic liberalism of Americans for Democratic Action (ADA) to the paranoid patriotism of the John Birch Society. The existence of several varieties of anticommunism has not been conducive to synthesis. Indeed, there is probably at the moment less agreement than there has ever been on how to interpret domestic anticommunism. In the 1950s, there was a rough consensus on the nature of McCarthyism shaped by scholars such as Daniel Bell and Richard Hofstadter. By the 1970s, in the wake of New Left historiography, there also seemed to be broad if not universal agreement on its main characteristics. But in the same way that the Soviet empire was sundered by centrifugal pressures, so too has been the historiography of American anticommunism.

It is unnecessary to linger on the early studies of McCarthyism. Journalistic contemporaries were often tempted to treat McCarthy as a "one-off," an adventurer who could be explained largely in terms of his own demagogic talents and charismatic personality.[3] Contemporary scholars were also inclined to see McCarthy as something of an aberration, though they also believed that there were potent social forces behind him, as was made clear in *The New American Right* (1955), edited by Daniel Bell. One of the contributors to that volume was Richard Hofstadter, who made use of the concept of status anxiety. Behind the brutal assaults of Senator McCarthy on the political establishment, Hofstadter (and other scholars who would come to be labeled "pluralist") maintained, were the populistic suspicions of groups who were either declining or rising. Their resentments tended to be displaced onto some elite group, such as senior government officials. Here was a form of right-wing activism with support in the grass roots and directed against the privileged, in some measure a rerun of the Populist uprising of the 1890s. In this scenario, McCarthyism was seen as a popular insurgency against those in authority or, alternatively, as a moralistic or authoritarian mass protest against modernity. One implication of these approaches was that such insurgency would pass as the social order adapted to progress; another, however, was that a sustained mass movement could prove immensely destructive to American democratic institutions.[4]

In the decade and a half after the publication of *The New American Right*, a number of studies appeared furthering this kind of interpretation. They tended to depict McCarthyite conservatism as aberrant, irrational, and extremist. The McCarthyites were at once disruptive of a free society and marginal to the political mainstream.[5] But this approach did not go unchallenged, even by other "pluralist" scholars, and by about 1970 was being replaced by a very different understanding. Nelson Polsby made an early attack on the Bell-Hofstadter position, pointing to the role of party politics in generating McCarthyism. Earl Latham also stressed the significance of Republican partisanship in the McCarthy assault on the Truman administration, especially the Republicans' determination to use the issue to avenge their unexpected defeat in the presidential election of 1948. Most significant was Michael Paul Rogin's *The Intellectuals and McCarthy* (1967), which demonstrated the strength of McCarthyism in traditional Republican constituencies and the responsibility of various elites. Rogin, explicitly distancing himself from what he regarded as pluralist elitism, excoriated the scholars of the 1950s for allowing their fear of the masses to distort their understanding of history. A number of subsequent studies also located the main responsibility for McCarthyism in Republican partisanship. In this perspective, McCarthyism was neither populist nor irrational, and it was close to the mainstream, little more than a variety of Republican politics in a Cold War age.[6]

A variant on this was Robert Griffith, *The Politics of Fear* (1970), which located McCarthyism in the dynamics of American party politics, although it also emphasized the centrality of conservative Republicans. Both Democrats and Republicans deployed the communist issue as they competed for ascendancy in the anxious postwar years, and between them they fashioned the environment in which Senator McCarthy flourished. Despite McCarthy's vicious attacks on the administration, abetted by Republican allies, the larger phenomenon of McCarthyism was, in a sense, bipartisan.[7]

As New Left historiography took firmer hold in the 1970s, the tendency to locate responsibility for McCarthyism at the top increased. The revisionist reevaluation of the origins of the Cold War also militated against the temptation to assign main responsibility to the Republicans. Athan Theoharis and Richard Freeland, in particular, related the escalation of domestic anticommunism to the Truman administration's anti-Soviet rhetoric and policies. David Caute's substantial study, *The Great Fear* (1978), placed major responsibility on the Truman administration and Cold War liberals. Targeting such liberals too was Mary S. McAuliffe, who found them fearful of being labeled soft on communism and consequently ready to compromise civil liberties.[8] Republican intransigence, these authors tended to imply, was to be expected, and it was the failure of liberal Democrats and intellectuals to defend civil libertarian principles that allowed the anticommunist tendency to reach center stage. Further, when the Truman administration itself sought to exclude domestic communists from American life, it was legitimizing and enhancing the anticommunist cause.[9] This approach shared at least one characteristic with the "pluralist" writers – the patriotic right, as personified by Joseph McCarthy, was marginalized.

While there were interpretative differences in the writings of the liberal and New Left historians of the 1970s, they had established a new orthodoxy. The roots of McCarthyite politics were now only rarely associated with populist insurgency or grass-roots anxieties, and there was little discussion of the irrational. The emphasis was on the role of elites operating within the parameters of conventional politics and, as such, subject to pressure from conservative interest groups. The main division occurred between those authors who located the primary causal influence in the Cold War foreign and domestic policies of the Truman administration, abetted by self-protective liberal intellectuals, and those who emphasized the resurgence of Republican and conservative politics.

Both these perspectives directed attention to the formative role of the federal government. In the 1980s, as use of the Freedom of Information Act allowed greater access to official archives, further studies appeared which for the most part reinforced the notion that the Frankenstein's

Monster of McCarthyism was created in Washington. One focus of attention was the Federal Bureau of Investigation, presided over by J. Edgar Hoover. Kenneth O'Reilly and Athan Theoharis uncovered in disturbing detail the activities of the FBI in disseminating anticommunist propaganda, expanding political surveillance, and cooperating with McCarthyite figures. This approach made it possible to place Hoover himself at the center of red-scare politics; Joe McCarthy became little more than one of his puppets, to be discarded when it began to act on its own. McCarthyism, it seemed, might better be termed "Hooverism." Individual responsibility was yet again being reassigned. Where some early commentators had heaped blame on McCarthy himself, others on Republican leaders such as Robert Taft, New Left scholars on Truman, in the 1980s J. Edgar Hoover was often found to be holding the smoking gun. But Hoover was head of a powerful federal agency, and so responsibility was still located at the top.[10]

The disinclination to associate McCarthyism with grass-roots pressures can be seen as part of a larger historiographical movement to look with suspicion on elites. As already noted, the revisionist perspective on the Cold War focused responsibility on Democratic administrations, and the demands of an anti-Soviet foreign policy carried repressive implications for domestic policy. For scholars who became disenchanted in the 1960s with the John Kennedy and Lyndon Johnson variety of liberalism, a resilient corporate power and the growth of the national-security state seemed to go hand in hand. New Left scholars, who sympathized with the popular protests of the decade, were reluctant to attribute to populism the authoritarian traits perceived by Hofstadter and Bell, and were uneasy about the ready resort to explanations that labeled people "extreme" or "paranoid." With the 1970s, and the revelations about the Nixon White House following Watergate and about the FBI following Hoover's death, it became easier for liberals and leftists to believe that if there were paranoids in the American polity, they were to be found in positions of high command.

Nonetheless, the scholars of the 1970s and 1980s for the most part shifted attention away from the sociological and the psychological and towards the political and institutional. Whether domestic anticommunism and its McCarthyite excesses were linked to Democrats or Republicans or to the very dynamics of the two-party system, political processes and partisan motives were central, and intertwined with interest group and bureaucratic pressures. Ironically, this shift was occurring at a time when other American historians were moving their attention from political to social history, and this served to impede the integration of the new perspectives into the broader framework. (The "new social historians" for the most part were not inclined to study right-wing movements.) The McCarthy industry, in consequence, has sometimes seemed a rather isolated one, pursuing its preoccupations at some remove from major historiographical currents.

One exception to the emphasis on high politics and interest groups was a provocative 1987 essay by Michael Rogin, restoring the socio-psychological dimension. According to this view, the counter-subversive impulse is related to the historic repression of those symbols of disorder, Native Americans and African Americans, who had to be controlled by state violence. From the early days of an expansive white settlement, a fear of subversion turned conflicts of interest between races into profound and pervasive "psychologically based dangers to personal and national identity." A similar process later impelled Americans to employ state power against an immigrant working class that was held to be importing subversion and, later again, concerns about personal and national identity also served to legitimize the measures of the national-security state against "the invisible agents of a foreign power." While Rogin had no wish to resurrect the status anxiety thesis he had once demolished, his new analysis did emphasize the insecurities historically experienced by Americans (especially white elites) in their new and changing environment, and their related need to assert a sense of identity. Political repression, it seemed, was not the work of a paranoid or right-wing fringe but was central to American political culture.[11]

By the 1980s, historians were also reassessing the history of American *communism* in ways that carried implications for its adversaries. Early Cold War historians such as Theodore Draper had tended to treat the American Communist Party (CP) as little more than a creature of the Soviet Union.[12] Younger scholars, however, began to present it in more favorable light: Maurice Isserman, in examining the World War II period, conceded the damage caused by Moscow's dominance but also showed that many party members were moved by traditional progressive ideals; other scholars similarly saw party members as operating within the tradition of an authentic American radicalism. These studies often focused on particular communities and labor groups, developing a social-history perspective in which party members strove to strengthen working-class institutions.[13] But this approach was sharply criticized by other young scholars, who upheld the earlier view that American communism was subject to Soviet control. Harvey Klehr found this to be the case even in the popular-front years of the 1930s. Klehr and John Earl Haynes later asserted that "American Communists always strove to do what Moscow wanted, no more, no less." In 1985, battle broke out in the *New York Review of Books*, poising the stern view of scholars such as Draper and Klehr against the sympathetic approach of Isserman and other New Left historians.[14] Neither side convinced the other, but both were operating at a time when archives were still opening and each could look forward to having the last word.

The modern scholars who took an unsympathetic view of American communism risked being labeled neoconservative, and in the 1990s a strong neoconservative challenge also emerged to the liberal and New Left tendency to berate political elites for unnecessarily unleashing McCarthyism. Again this may be seen as part of a more general shift in the intellectual climate. The heyday of New Left writing was over. By the 1980s, some conservative episodes in American history were receiving more sympathetic treatment than had been the case earlier (and not exclusively by "conservative" scholars). Illustrative of the new perspectives was the celebrated scholarly reevaluation of the presidency of Dwight Eisenhower. Far from being a bumbling innocent who preferred the golf course to the Oval Office, Eisenhower now became a shrewd operator who always remained in command of his administration, although he liked to manage it with a "hidden hand."[15] He also possessed a coherent and defensible political philosophy.[16] While the opening of new archives helped make this re-evaluation possible, it was easier – in the light of Vietnam, the inflationary 1970s, and the yawning federal deficits of the 1980s – to perceive virtue in the prudent foreign and fiscal policies of the Eisenhower administration.

Conservative politics then received a boost with the ending of the Cold War and the "victory" of the United States. As shrewd a journalist and historian as Godfrey Hodgson described Ronald Reagan as "impressively right and courageous on the big issues." Despite his conspicuous failings, "in the end he was a massively successful President," who restored American self-confidence. The rehabilitation of Reagan, the sometime FBI fink, following that of Eisenhower, had implications for interpretations of the Age of McCarthy. Richard Nixon, too, has recently enjoyed something of an upgrade. Conservative presidents have not come too badly out of recent scholarship, while "liberal" presidents Kennedy and Johnson have for the most part remained consigned to the sin bin, in which Bill Clinton seems destined to join them.[17]

It is against this kind of background that scholars have returned to a study of McCarthyism. Some have been keen to redress the imbalance that they perceived in a historiography that downplayed both the role of the Soviet Union in promoting the Cold War and the threat presented by the American CP. An important example is Richard Gid Powers, *Not Without Honor* (1995), which is eloquent on the horrors perpetrated by Communist regimes and insistent that legitimate American anticommunism should not be confused with the bastard of McCarthyism. "The history of anticommunism is not the same as the story of anticommunist extremism," Powers observes, "any more than the history of malpractice is the history of medicine."[18]

The opening of archives in the United States and Russia in the 1990s strengthened the neoconservative perspective. Harvey Klehr, John Earl Haynes, and Fridrikh Igorevich Firsov used archives from the old Soviet Union to show that the American CP accepted Soviet subsidies and some of its members engaged in espionage activity for the Soviet Union. They agreed that Senator McCarthy's own behavior was "the vicious partisanship of a political bully," but concluded that "the belief that the American Communist movement assisted Soviet intelligence and placed loyalty to the Soviet Union ahead of loyalty to the United States was well founded." This thesis was boosted in 1995 with the revelation by the U.S. government of the Venona Project, involving thousands of Soviet espionage telegrams intercepted by American intelligence during World War II, but only partially decoded. The release of some of these allowed Haynes and Klehr to produce another volume presenting further evidence of the ways in which the American CP aided Soviet espionage during the 1930s and 1940s. In particular, spies for the Soviets were to be found in the new government agencies hastily erected in wartime. For these scholars, the anticommunist programs of the American government were thus vindicated. Corroborative evidence came with the publication of *The Haunted Wood* (1999) by Allen Weinstein, who was given translated notes from KGB files via former KGB agent Alexander Vassiliev. While this material is not available to other scholars, it apparently confirms that several Americans did function as Soviet informants. These espionage operations, however, were largely closed down by the Soviets and the FBI following Elizabeth Bentley's defection in 1945, and little survived by the time that Joe McCarthy began pursuing spies.[19]

Meanwhile, other scholarship of the 1990s also took Soviet espionage seriously and developed an argument that might be summarized on these lines: for the United States, communism was both a foreign and a domestic threat to which American anticommunism was often a realistic and reasonable response, and, while the antics of Senator Joseph McCarthy were wholly despicable, such excesses might have been averted or contained had American liberals and policy-makers themselves shown more wisdom and discretion at crucial moments.[20]

This is an argument that has been energetically disputed. Some major scholars remain committed to the kind of revisionist interpretation associated with the New Left. Ellen Schrecker, in a series of studies, has carefully documented the extensive manner in which those in authority were implicated in anticommunist activity. "In order to eliminate the alleged threat of domestic Communism," she writes in *Many Are the Crimes* (1998), "a broad coalition of politicians, bureaucrats, and other anticommunist activists hounded an entire generation of radicals and their associates, destroying lives, careers, and all the institutions that offered a left-wing alternative to mainstream politics and culture." While stressing its variety, she is clear that anticommunism was "primarily a top-down phenomenon." Influential sectors of the federal government placed considerations of national security above respect for civil liberties and carried the bulk of Americans with them. In the climate prevailing at the end of the 1990s, Schrecker's book was not universally welcomed. Another specialist charged her with a "strident partisanship" that made her book no more than "the best example of the many leftist tirades against 'the great fear' that have become commonplace." Schrecker, for her part, has been cited as saying that recent revisions of McCarthyism are part of "a continuing effort to discredit the left."[21]

Such exchanges and the revelation of the Venona Project have attracted the attention of the media. Much of the new archival evidence has been represented even in the quality press as vindicating Joe McCarthy's crusade, and there has been a fierce crossfire over this and related issues. One observer has characterized these various hostilities as a war between "red diaper babies," who had grown up and were now to be found arrayed on both sides, determined either to vindicate or to redeem their family reputations.[22]

The new evidence confirmed that the Soviet Union wielded substantial influence over the leaders of the American CP and that it had agents or informers scattered through the agencies of the American government in the 1930s and 1940s. But there is disagreement over how much the various files establish. Some scholars see the evidence as proving that the CP was the obedient agent of the Soviet Union and that Soviet agents had seriously penetrated the Roosevelt and Truman administrations. Others have been skeptical of its value, pointing out that the most important Moscow archives have remained closed and that the new information is not very startling, is often ambiguous, and relies on the claims of agents who had a vested interest in exaggerating their own importance.[23]

Furthermore, the new evidence does not go far in explaining American *anticommunism*. It may continue to press questions about the internal security measures of the Truman administration (which have been variously condemned as either damaging or inadequate). But most of the evidence is related to the period before 1950, that is *before* Joseph McCarthy took up the cause, and in any case it does little to explain the intensity and pervasiveness of anticommunism. Also, the thrust of the argument is that the moderate anticommunism of the political elites was legitimate; it does not dispose of the leftist view that the actions taken by the elites did more harm than good to American life.

It remains the case that the greater part of the writing on McCarthyism from the 1960s to the 1990s pointed to the responsibility of those high in the polity. McCarthyism was mostly seen as a "top-down phenomenon." Intriguingly, the direction taken by McCarthy research has been the opposite to that adopted by other historians. The civil rights movement, in particular, was initially seen as led from the top, but gradually the focus shifted away from the national scene and towards the role of local activists. At much the same time that McCarthy scholars were shifting responsibility from the grass roots to national elites, civil-rights scholars were doing the reverse. An explanation might be found in their common political sympathies, but the two positions are not necessarily incompatible. It is perfectly possible that civil rights was more a grass-roots phenomenon and McCarthyism more an elitist one. Demand for rights is likely to come from the bottom, from those who are denied them; political repression, almost by definition, comes from the top.

The comparison itself, however, again suggests that not enough has been done to reconcile scholarship on McCarthyism with other historical writing on the mid-twentieth century. Several scholars, for example, in examining the trajectory of American liberalism from the New Deal to the 1960s, have argued that a crucial change of direction occurred in the 1940s. In that decade, it is said, the radical aspirations that could be found in New Deal thought finally disappeared, as liberals ceased to contest capitalist structures, lost interest in directly controlling the economy, and settled for Keynesian-style management and growth. While the scholarship to this effect has been substantial, the role of anticommunist pressures in bringing about this conservative turn in the 1940s has remained unclear. To Alan Brinkley, for example, the essential changes of attitude in liberal circles had already occurred by 1945, largely because of the war, although other scholars have emphasized the impact of the Cold War in the late 1940s.[24]

Whatever effect the communist issue had on American liberalism during the Truman years (and the CP made its own weighty contribution to the disruption of the liberal-left), the longer-term consequences also remain speculative. It is at least arguable that McCarthy's disgrace assisted the recovery of liberalism, at least in the form of anticommunist Democrats of the John Kennedy and Hubert Humphrey variety (and of liberal Republicans too). It is not impossible that Kennedy's hairbreadth victory in 1960 owed something to the McCarthyite baggage carried by his opponent.[25] Still, as has often enough been pointed out, Kennedyite liberalism can sometimes be difficult to distinguish from conservatism.

Similarly, an issue rarely pursued in detail is the relationship between McCarthy and the later resurgence of conservative politics. In the late 1950s and early 1960s, McCarthyism could be seen as an aberration by scholars who were confidently awaiting the full flowering of American liberalism, but since then the flow of American history has hardly seemed leftward. Did McCarthyism have anything to do with the ending of "the New Deal Order," the strengthening of the Republican party, and its swing to the right? Was McCarthy a way station in the journey of some Americans from the Democratic to the Republican party? Some scholarship on the 1960s and 1970s has focused on the detachment of urban ethnic Catholics from the Democratic coalition by Republicans. Were these the same unhappy citizens who had once given McCarthy and his like some support in such cities as Detroit and Boston, and who perhaps later flirted with George Wallace before being drawn into the "new Republican majority"? Shards of evidence for some process of this sort have sometimes been cited, but a systematic examination remains to be attempted.[26]

Whatever other influences gave rise to McCarthyism, a major characteristic of its more virulent forms was hostility towards New Deal politics, as well as towards New Deal allies in the industrial unions. (Labor historians have extensively explored the disruptive impact of the communist issue on the trade-union movement.)[27] Scholarly research has suggested that many working- and middle-class whites in the cities in the 1940s and 1950s were not particularly comfortable with reform politics, at least if African Americans seemed to be among the beneficiaries.[28] Some of them betrayed McCarthyite attitudes. McCarthyism similarly played a role in exacerbating tensions between Northern and Southern Democrats. Many formerly Democratic voters in the South did eventually join the Republican party. How far did the strident patriotism associated with McCarthyite politics ease this transition? Arguably, a major function of McCarthyism was to expose the fragility of the New Deal coalition. The success of Richard Nixon and Ronald Reagan owed at least something to support garnered from both Southern whites and Northern urban ethnics, groups that had not been wholly immune to McCarthy's appeal.

This hints at the influence of race, a dimension of McCarthyism that has yet fully to be examined, as does that of the role of the South more generally. In 1955 Seymour Lipset and Nathan Glazer pointed to polling evidence that the South was "the most anti-McCarthy section of the country."[29] Yet the South was surely more deeply implicated than this statement allows. A Republican and a Roman Catholic such as McCarthy might indeed be an unlikely hero there, but the section helped to sustain the larger cause of reactionary anticommunism. Texan Martin Dies had first chaired the House Un-American Activities Committee (HUAC), which was made into a permanent committee on the motion of John Rankin of Mississippi. In Texas, McCarthy enjoyed the financial support of a number of oil barons and significant popular support in communities such as Houston. Even in the Deep South, he had influential admirers, such as Senator Herman Talmadge of Georgia, and McCarthy's anti-communist crusade was in significant part taken over by Senator James Eastland of Mississippi when he assumed the chairmanship of the Senate Internal Security Sub-committee in 1955. It may not be possible to understand the intensity and longevity of anticommunism without reference to the peculiar condition of the South.[30]

If racism – whether in the South or in Northern cities such as Detroit – was one of the springs of popular anticommunism, there are other aspects of ethnicity that remain to be fully examined. Modern analyses of right-wing movements (not necessarily McCarthyism) have draw attention to the role of evangelical and fundamentalist Protestantism, while a number of recent scholars (like some earlier ones) have emphasized the relatively strong support given to McCarthyite politics by Roman Catholics.[31] Some form of the Bell thesis may yet be viable, if McCarthyism can in some measure be shown to attract support from conservative Protestants and Catholics, often mingling uneasily in the nation's cities and suspicious of the processes of modernization and secularization.[32]

The dimension of gender should also not be neglected. The broad backlash which reasserted traditional gender roles after World War II may have had something to do with the macho posturing of red-hunters such as Joe McCarthy and J. Edgar Hoover. But women joined the counter-subversive cause too, and it may be that they played a significant role at local level, although information is fragmentary. We know little, for example, of the Minute Women of the U.S.A., who surfaced in several cities to mobilize campaigns against socialism and communism. Are we to conclude that women's traditional responsibility for home and moral order led some into a fervent embrace of patriotism? Were these among the unhappy suburbanites to whom Betty Friedan would soon draw attention, giving meaning to their lives by attaching themselves to a cause? And what of Detroit's Women's Crusade Against Socialism, whose members in the early 1950s apparently believed that the whole male sex was genetically soft on communism and that the republic would be safe only when it was ruled by "Women real Women"?[33]

One reason for the neglect of the dimensions of race and gender has been the relative absence of social historians in anticommunist scholarship. Another reason for the limitations in the field itself has been the preoccupation with causation. The impulse to assign responsibility has been irresistible, and the question has often been put in the simplified form: who supported McCarthy? While the attempt to explore causation is legitimate, it is hardly the sole concern of the historian. Much of the historiography of the New Deal, for example, concerns the way in which it changed over time, but this is rarely an issue raised about domestic anticommunism. This partly explains why there have been so many competing interpretations – different scholars have focused on different parts of the phenomenon.[34]

To suggest that insufficient account has been taken of change over time is also to suggest that the study of anticommunism may benefit from a reconsideration of its place in the American system of politics. Scholars interested in bringing together historical and political-science approaches have been active in elucidating the course of the labor movement and the development of welfare, but as yet have said little about how the political system abetted McCarthyism. The Founding Fathers, after all, had intended that the system of divided government should function to protect liberty. What gave McCarthyism its potency was the anticommunist consensus in the early 1950s among the three branches of government, not to mention the fourth estate. It was the iron lock resulting from the agreement between the executive, legislature, and judiciary that domestic communism was a threat that allowed dissidents little escape. Just how and why was it that these branches failed to constrain one another in these vital years?[35]

Another aspect of American political culture often overlooked is the influence that culture allows individual actors to exercise. Several studies have stressed the peculiar traits of Joseph McCarthy's shameless personality. But, as modern students have made clear, he was not the only actor in a drama in which several figures had opportunities to nudge the course of events. When he first sought to explain the "pseudo-conservative revolt," Hofstadter made much of the fluidity of American society and the democratic nature of its political institutions. We need not return to theories of status anxiety to consider the implications for the role of individuals in an "open" polity. With Pat McCarran and Joe McCarthy in the Senate, with J. Edgar Hoover at the FBI, with a clumsy Truman or a cautious Eisenhower in the White House, is it any wonder that the anticommunist right won victories from time to time? In a polity with a more disciplined party system or a stronger permanent civil service or a more cohesive ruling class, individuals in high office might have less room to indulge their own propensities. As the example of J. Edgar Hoover best illustrates, one characteristic of the American system is the opportunity it affords for individuals to further their personal agendas. The fortuitous combination of a number of individuals at a particular time could be fateful.

One essay which did reflect on the distinctiveness of American politics was Herbert Hyman's contribution to *The Radical Right*, which suggested that the particular character of the official security programs in Britain, with their relatively limited reach and unpublicized application, helped to explain the relative weakness of the McCarthy style there. It also speculated that the British public was more deferential than the American.[36] It is surprising that Hyman's lead in conducting comparative studies has not been more widely followed. The United States, after all, sent the Rosenbergs to the chair. In Britain the admitted spy Klaus Fuchs went to jail for nine years. Fuchs never became a party issue and his treason did not seem to touch populist nerves. Fuchs's spying, of course, began while Winston Churchill was Prime Minister; when his guilt was revealed, Churchill was Leader of the Opposition. The Conservatives were hardly in a position to exploit this issue, even had they wanted to, which may point to the salience of party politics in the United States.

The Rosenbergs, of course, denied their guilt, as did Alger Hiss. Apart from Theodore Hall and the atom spies, on present evidence Soviet success in recruiting dedicated agents among American citizens in the highest and most sensitive circles was not that impressive, especially during the Cold War itself. Judith Coplon hardly compares with the likes of Klaus Fuchs, Kim Philby, Donald Maclean, Guy Burgess, Anthony Blunt, and George Blake. Whatever the murky role of American fellow travelers, the substantial pipeline to Moscow via British traitors has been glaringly exposed. Some of these spies had been students together at Cambridge in the 1930s, and it is not altogether surprising that they were disenchanted with the British establishment's feeble response both to the depression and to the rise of Hitler. In the United States, on the other hand, young men of Alger Hiss's generation thrilled to the New Deal and made a hero of Franklin Roosevelt. Some of them also aided the Soviet Union (a wartime ally) before the onset of the Cold War, although just how far remains unclear. But to the end of his life Hiss represented himself as a committed New Dealer and it is possible that he saw himself both as a patriotic American and as a well-wisher towards Soviet attempts to improve the lot of the masses and to resist fascism. The Republican right has frequently charged the New Deal with permitting the penetration of Soviet spies, but it is at least arguable that the New Deal actually reduced the incidence of spying. Without it, yet more well-born young men destined for high office might have been tempted to follow the example of their Cambridge contemporaries.[37]

As has been periodically pointed out though often enough ignored, external pressures as well as internal political dynamics need to be addressed in any explanation of McCarthyism. At the very least, the foreign crises of the period lent credibility to the nation's dedicated anticommunists. The Korean War, in particular, was roughly coincident with the heyday of McCarthyite politics, but only rarely have scholars suggested that the phenomenon might be more aptly termed the Korean War Red Scare.[38] The governmental anticommunism under way in the 1940s doubtless encouraged the popular demonization of the radical left, but, without the Korean War McCarthy's own charges would likely have fallen flat and other excesses have been avoided.

As noted earlier, the scholarly terrain of the Age of McCarthy seems now to be occupied by an array of mutually hostile camps. In part, this may be an unfortunate heritage of the evolution of McCarthy studies. The first students of the phenomenon seemed eager to stress that it was a bottom-up movement, leading their critics to look instead at the role of elites, a tendency that was reinforced with the emergence of New Left scholarship. Similarly, scholars of communism have been divided between those who see the American CP as an obedient agent of Moscow and those who emphasize the autonomy and authentic progressivism of American communists. This tendency to deal in polarities has not lent itself to the process of synthesis.

But synthesis is surely needed. Is it impossible to believe, if traditional categories must be used, that both populism and elitism had something to do with anticommunist and McCarthyite politics, and that the CP was both an agent of Moscow and a fellowship in which many Americans hoped to further their own priorities? Domestic anticommunism, like any other significant American political movement, consisted of many elements and changed over time. Scholars have established clearly enough the responsibility of successive political administrations, of the party system, and of the FBI in the spawning of the ill-controlled creature of McCarthyism. What has been less satisfactorily delineated is the popular dimension, and how popular politics interacted with elite and governmental actions.

Modern scholarship has given the grass-roots or popular dimension of McCarthyism only fitful attention, despite suggestive studies in cognate areas. In 1982, Alan Brinkley located the source of support for Huey Long and Father Coughlin in attempts to protect the autonomy of the individual and of the local community from the growing demands of centralized authority. Leo Ribuffo, in examining other nativist figures, similarly emphasized their traditional bourgeois and mainstream values rather than their supposed aberrant qualities. Recent work on the Ku Klux Klan of the 1920s has presented it as the product of localized resistance to the growing power of distant authorities. For a later period, Ronald Formisano has examined the community-based resentments of ordinary people towards a liberal elite in the anti-busing controversy in Boston. These various studies suggest an approach to an understanding of grass-roots McCarthyism, one that is related to the anxieties to be found in local communities, which were perhaps attempting to preserve traditional values and individual autonomy in an increasingly bureaucratic world.[39] For many citizens who were not otherwise "extreme" or "aberrant," communism could stand for a variety of forces (national unions, big government, feminism, civil rights) capable of invading a locality and subverting its folkways. (The Georgia segregationist Lester Maddox attributed the civil rights movement to an intriguing alliance between "big capitalists" and "Communists"!)[40] Suspicion of cosmopolitan values, itself a feature with a long tradition in American history, may also have helped to bond the anticommunist cause. But, as yet, depictions of McCarthyism as a community-based "populist" movement have surfaced only in a few broad works of synthesis rather than in research studies.[41]

The difficulty of the first generation of scholars in establishing clear connections between social ("status") groups and McCarthyism has perhaps discouraged others from exploring the "populist" dimension. The word "populist," freighted as it is with a variety of meanings, is itself unhelpful. When the popular dimension is inspected, the bodies that come most conspicuously into view are the American Legion and other veterans' organizations, patriotic societies such as the Daughters of the American Revolution (DAR), some business groups, and a range of Catholic and other religious organizations. Are these what is meant by "grass roots"? Another approach is to regard this activity as part of the American voluntary tradition, one that Alexis de Tocqueville was among the first to notice. Tocqueville emphasized the importance, in Jacksonian America, of associational activity, from temperance societies to commercial companies, and "associations of a thousand other kinds, religious, moral, serious, futile, general or restricted, enormous or diminutive."[42]

In the United States the voluntary principle early became bound up with notions of citizenship. Ideas of republicanism were sufficiently diffused for individuals to have some sense of ownership of their country, and the voluntary association provided a means through which such proprietorship might be expressed. Exercising the rights of citizenship was an obligation, and certainly a legitimate activity, one variously expressed through the bible societies of the 1830s, the women's groups of the late nineteenth century, and the veterans' organizations of the twentieth century. Hyman, in the essay cited above, noted the virtual absence of such groups when national security issues emerged in Britain. McCarthyism in the United States cannot adequately be explained without according a significant role to such activity.

But it was not the only source of domestic anticommunism. It is surely the coexistence of influential elites with energetic associational or "grass-roots" activity in the United States that is important. It is the intertwining of the two that needs attention, a dynamic interaction that produced the phenomenon popularly known as McCarthyism. A complementary way in which McCarthyism can be conceived is as a cycle. HUAC came into existence in 1938, and a number of "little HUACs" appeared at the end of that decade too, not to mention the Smith Act and its state counterparts. HUAC itself maintained a separate existence for thirty years, and it was not until the late 1950s that the Smith Act began to be dismantled. Somewhere in between came Senator McCarthy, riding a wave unleashed by both governmental decisions and voluntary activity. Viewing the phenomenon as a cycle makes it possible to accommodate at least some of the contrasting interpretations that have appeared. In my own analysis of McCarthyism in Massachusetts, for example, I argued that extra-legislative pressures, which in that particular context could be called populist, were important in driving the phenomenon in the early stages. But as they gained buoyancy because of the Cold War, political elites abandoned their resistance and accommodated to these populist currents, in the hope of controlling them. By doing this, the elites strengthened the anticommunist cause. They won control of a sort, and what had once been "populist" pressures were redirected away from elite institutions (such as Harvard) and downwards and outwards towards the politically marginal, such as hapless trade unionists, teachers, and old CP members. The end result was a strengthening of the national security state, as instruments of political surveillance became more firmly institutionalized.[43]

In this model, populist pressures (or voluntary activity), international tensions, and elite (or governmental) decisions all play a part, and none can be removed from the equation without destroying it. Another necessary element in Massachusetts, as elsewhere, was the visible presence of a Communist party that was responsive to the Soviet Union, even though the red-baiters exaggerated the threat it represented. Such amplification again brings us back to the "open" and "democratic" nature of the American polity, which breeds a form of insecurity both among elites and among those who seek to exercise their citizenship rights within it.

No doubt more plausible models can be constructed to explain the nature and course of Cold War anticommunism. And a synthesis is not necessarily correct by virtue of being a synthesis. But one wonders whether the tension that exists between the armed camps of American scholars of communism and anticommunism is any longer creative. A less polarized historiography is surely needed if a deeper understanding of the Age of McCarthy is to be achieved. Such a historiography will have to find a place for the distinctive American tradition of an active citizenry and its interaction with powerful, if insecure, authorities, for the disturbing impact of the Cold War (and the hotter Korean War) and the visible presence of a Soviet-aligned Communist party, and for the very design of the American political system itself. And if historians need to draw on social-science methodology to construct a multivariate explanation for the nature of McCarthyism, they will need also to be mindful that they are historians and that any synthesis must pay close attention to the evolution and possible transformation of their subject. Finally, they need to reflect on the fact that the United States was not the only polity subject to a "red menace."

Notes

1. Discussions of the historiography of McCarthyism to around 1990 include the "Introduction to the Second Edition," in Robert Griffith, *The Politics of Fear: Joseph R. McCarthy and the Senate* (2nd edn., Amherst, 1987), and the essays in Richard M. Fried, *Nightmare in Red: The McCarthy Era in Perspective* (New York, 1990), M. J. Heale, *American Anticommunism: Combating the Enemy Within, 1830–1970* (Baltimore, 1990), and Ellen Schrecker, *The Age of McCarthyism: A*

Brief History with Documents (Boston, 1994). William B. Hixson, Jr., *Search for the American Right Wing: An Analysis of the Social Science Record, 1955–1987* (Princeton, 1992) is a study of the literature on right-wing movements.

2. *New York Times*, October 23, 1998; the factual errors in Arthur Herman, *Joseph McCarthy: Reexamining the Life and Legacy of America's Most Hated Senator* (New York, 2000) render it unreliable.
3. Richard H. Rovere, *Senator Joe McCarthy* (New York, 1959).
4. Daniel Bell, ed., *The New American Right* (New York, 1955). An updated edition, *The Radical Right*, appeared in 1963 (Garden City, NY) An elegant analysis of the Bell thesis is Kendrick Oliver, "'Post-Industrial Society' and the Psychology of the American Far Right, 1950–74," *Journal of Contemporary History*, 34 (1999): 601–18.
5. Note the titles of these works: Richard Hofstadter, "The Pseudo-Conservative Revolt," in Bell, ed., *Radical Right*; Hofstadter, *The Paranoid Style in American Politics* (New York, 1964); Alan C. Elms, "Psychological Factors in Right-Wing Extremism," in Robert A. Schoenberger, ed., *The American Right Wing: Readings in Political Behavior* (New York, 1969), pp. 143–63; Robert W. Sellen, "Patriotism or Paranoia? Right-Wing Extremism in America," *Dalhousie Review*, 43, 3 (1963). A late entry taking some account of the critics of this approach was Seymour Lipset and Earl Raab, *The Politics of Unreason: Right-Wing Extremism in America, 1790–1970* (New York, 1970).
6. Polsby, "Towards an Explanation of McCarthyism," *Political Studies*, 8 (Oct., 1960): 250–71; Latham, *The Communist Controversy in Washington: From the New Deal to McCarthy* (Cambridge, MA, 1966); Rogin, *The Intellectuals and McCarthy: The Radical Specter* (Cambridge, MA, 1967); Michael Miles, *The Odyssey of the American Right* (New York, 1980); David Reinhard, *The Republican Right since 1945* (Lexington, 1983). Rogin's concern was to show that there was no connection between the agrarian Populism of the 1890s and support for McCarthy. While targeting conservative Republicans, his analysis did not exclude the possibility that McCarthy enjoyed some "populistic" support in the country at large.
7. Griffith, *The Politics of Fear*. Also focusing responsibility on elites were the essays in Griffith and Athan Theoharis, eds., *The Specter: Original Essays on the Cold War and the Origins of McCarthyism* (New York, 1974).
8. Theoharis, *Seeds of Repression: Harry S. Truman and the Origin of McCarthyism* (New York, 1971); Freeland, *The Truman Doctrine and the Origins of McCarthyism* (New York, 1972); Caute, *The Great Fear:*

The Anti-Communist Purge Under Truman and Eisenhower (New York, 1978); McAuliffe, *Crisis on the Left: Cold War Politics and American Liberals, 1947–1954* (Amherst, 1978).

9. ADA-type liberals have regularly been accused of doing the bidding of the national security state, promoting anti-Soviet ideology and in effect of legitimizing McCarthyism through their own rejection of communism. A recent contribution in this vein is Frances Stonor Saunders, *Who Paid the Piper? The CIA and the Cultural Cold War* (London, 1999).

10. O'Reilly, *Hoover and the Un-Americans: The FBI, HUAC, and the Red Menace* (Philadelphia, 1983); Theoharis and John Stuart Cox, *The Boss: J. Edgar Hoover and the Great American Inquisition* (Philadelphia, 1988); see also Richard Gid Powers, *Secrecy and Power: The Life of J. Edgar Hoover* (New York, 1987). Two useful biographies of McCarthy also appeared in the 1980s: Thomas C. Reeves, *The Life and Times of Joe McCarthy* (Melbourne, FL, 1982) and David Oshinsky, *A Conspiracy So Immense: The World of Joe McCarthy* (New York, 1983).

11. Rogin, "Political Repression in the United States," in Rogin, *Ronald Reagan, the Movie, and Other Episodes in Political Demonology* (Berkeley, 1987), pp. 55, 68. Similarly placing some emphasis on the insecurities inseparable from American political culture, including inherited assumptions about the frailty of republican institutions, was Heale, *American Anticommunism*. A later study from a leftist perspective that more explicitly resorted to psychological theory was Joel Kovel, *Red Hunting in the Promised Land: Anticommunism and the Making of America* (New York, 1994).

12. For the early Cold War perspective see Theodore Draper, *The Roots of American Communism* (New York, 1957) and *American Communism and Soviet Russia: The Formative Period* (New York, 1960); Irving Howe and Lewis Coser, *The American Communist Party: A Critical History, 1919–1957* (Boston, 1957).

13. Isserman, *Which Side Were You On? The American Communist Party during the Second World War* (Middletown, 1982); Paul Lyons, *Philadelphia Communists, 1936–1956* (Philadelphia, 1982); Mark Naison, *Communists in Harlem During the Depression* (Urbana, 1983); Ronald W. Schatz, *The Electrical Workers: A History of Labor at General Electric and Westinghouse, 1923–1960* (Urbana, 1983); Robin D. G. Kelley, *Hammer and Hoe: Alabama Communists during the Great Depression* (Chapel Hill, 1990).

14. Klehr, *The Heyday of American Communism: The Depression Decade* (New York, 1984); Klehr and Haynes, *The American Communist Movement: Storming Heaven Itself* (New York, 1992), p. 179; *New York Review of Books*, May 9, 30, August 15, 1985; Isserman, "Three Generations: Historians View American Communism," *Labor History*, 26 (Fall 1985): 517–45.
15. Among others, see Fred I. Greenstein, *The Hidden-Hand Presidency: Eisenhower as Leader* (New York, 1982).
16. Robert Griffith, "Dwight D. Eisenhower and the Corporate Commonwealth," *American Historical Review*, 87 (1982): 87–122.
17. Hodgson, "White House, white lies," *The Independent* (London), Weekend Review, October 30, 1999: 10; David Mervin, *Ronald Reagan and the Presidency* (London, 1990); Irwin F. Gellman, *The Contender: Richard Nixon, the Congress Years, 1946–1952* (New York, 1999); Melvin Small, *The Presidency of Richard Nixon* (Lawrence, 1999).
18. Powers, *Not Without Honor: The History of American Anticommunism* (New York, 1995), p. 427. If the neoconservative interpretation of domestic anticommunism has been gaining ground among academics, it seems to have missed the Hollywood community, where a kind of defiant New Left view remains strong, to judge by its celebratory 1997 production "Hollywood Remembers the Blacklist," and by the protests when the Film Academy gave a lifetime achievement award to Elia Kazin in 1999. A "neoconservative" treatment of Hollywood is Kenneth Lloyd Billingsley, *Hollywood Party: How Communism Seduced the American Film Industry in the 1930s and 1940s* (Rocklin, CA, 1998). There have been many studies of the impact of the communist issue on American intellectual and especially popular culture; see for example Stephen J. Whitfield, *The Culture of the Cold War* (Baltimore, 1991).
19. Harvey Klehr, John Earl Haynes and Fridrikh Igorevich Firsov, *The Secret World of American Communism* (New Haven, 1995), pp. 325, 326; Haynes and Klehr, *Venona: Decoding Soviet Espionage in America* (New Haven, 1999); Allen Weinstein and Alexander Vassiliev, *The Haunted Wood: Soviet Espionage in America – The Stalin Era* (New York, 1999).
20. See for example Powers above and Harvey Klehr and Ronald Radosh, *The Amerasia Spy Case: Prelude to McCarthyism* (Chapel Hill, 1996); Guenter Lewy, *The Cause That Failed: Communism in American Political Life* (New York, 1990); Klehr and Haynes, *American Communist Movement*. John Earl Haynes, *Red Scare or*

Red Menace? American Communism and Anticommunism in the Cold War Era (Chicago, 1996) argues that much of anticommunism was a reasonable response to a clear and present danger.

21. Ellen Schrecker, *No Ivory Tower: McCarthyism and the Universities* (New York, 1986); idem, *Age of McCarthyism;* idem, *Many Are The Crimes: McCarthyism in America* (Boston, 1998), pp. x, xiii; Thomas C. Reeves, *New York Times Book Review,* June 14, 1998; "Was Joe McCarthy Right?" *To The Best of Our Knowledge*, Wisconsin Public Radio, www.wpr.org/book/981108a.htm.

22. Ethan Bronner, "Rethinking McCarthyism, If Not McCarthy," *New York Times*, October 18, 1998.

23. Ibid.; "Beware the rehabilitation of Joseph McCarthy," *New York Times*, October 23, 1998; Christopher Lehmann-Haupt, "Romantics and Hustlers With Gloves, Cloaks and Daggers," *New York Times*, January 18, 1999; Ellen Schrecker, "The Spies Who Loved Us?", *The Nation*, May 24, 1999.

24. Brinkley, "The Idea of the State," in Steve Fraser and Gary Gerstle, eds., *The Rise and Fall of the New Deal Order, 1930–1980* (Princeton, 1989), pp. 85–121. Essays by Nelson Lichtenstein and Ira Katznelson in this collection similarly argue that "social democratic" options were closed off in the 1940s, although they attach significance to postwar developments. See also Michael Denning, *The Cultural Front: The Laboring of American Culture in the Twentieth Century* (London, 1996), p. 464, and David Plotke, *Building a Democratic Political Order: Reshaping American Liberalism in the 1930s and 1940s* (Cambridge, UK, 1996), pp. 293–97, 310–26.

25. It would have been ironic if this were the case, given the Kennedy family's friendship with McCarthy.

26. Some students have examined the late twentieth-century growth of right-wing politics in a longer perspective, e.g. Hixson, *Search for the American Right Wing* and Jerome L. Himmelstein, *To the Right: The Transformation of American Conservatism* (Berkeley, 1990). There have been a number of studies of the erosion of New Deal or Democratic dominance and the resurgence of the Republican party, e.g. Thomas Byrne Edsall with Mary D. Edsall, *Chain Reaction: The Impact of Race, Rights, and Taxes on American Politics* (New York, 1991); William C. Berman, *America's Right Turn: From Nixon to Bush* (Baltimore, 1994).

27. Among others, see Harvey Levenstein, *Communism, Anti-Communism, and the C.I.O.* (Westport, 1981). For some scholars McCarthyism was directed primarily at the labor movement.

28. See, for example, contributions by Arnold R. Hirsch, Thomas J. Sugrue and Gary Gerstle to the "Round Table" in *Journal of American History*, 82 (September 1995): 522–86.
29. Glazer and Lipset, "The Polls on Communism and Conformity," in Daniel Bell, ed., *The New American Right* (New York, 1955), p. 160.
30. For recent studies taking account of McCarthyism in the South see Adam Fairclough, *Race and Democracy: The Civil Rights Struggle in Louisiana, 1915–1972* (Athens, GA, 1995); Patricia Sullivan, *Days of Hope: Race and Democracy in the New Deal Era* (Chapel Hill, 1996); George Lewis, "The Uses and Abuses of Anti-Communism by Southern Segregationists as a Weapon of Massive Resistance, 1948–65," (PhD dissertation, University of Newcastle, 2000). Scholars have also been slow to examine McCarthyism as a regional or sectional phenomenon. The communist issue seems to have worked its way differently through the various regional political cultures. See for example James Truett Selcraig, *The Red Scare in the Midwest, 1945–1955* (Ann Arbor, MI, 1982); M. J. Heale, *McCarthy's Americans: Red Scare Politics in State and Nation, 1935–1965* (London and Athens, GA, 1998).
31. Leonard J. Moore, "Good Old-Fashioned New Social History and the Twentieth-Century American Right," *Reviews in American History*, 24 (1996): 558; Hixson, *Search for the American Right-Wing*, p. 326; Steve Rosswurm, "The Catholic Church and the Left-Led Unions," in Rosswurm, ed., *The CIO's Left-Led Unions* (New Brunswick, 1992), pp. 119–37; Schrecker, *Many Are The Crimes*, pp. 72–5.
32. I have tried to draw attention to the role of the metropolitan environment in nurturing nativist and fundamentalist tensions in *McCarthy's Americans*, especially pp. 282–88. If Catholics were often new-stock immigrants, many of the Protestant residents of Midwestern and Western cities were often recent migrants possessed of traditional religious values. For both, forms of cultural resistance may have been intertwined with Americanizing impulses.
33. Heale, *McCarthy's Americans*, p. 130.
34. The focus on causation has risked overlooking effects. The discussion of consequences has often been by analysts of subjects other than McCarthyism, e.g. David Halberstam on Vietnam: *The Best and the Brightest* (New York, 1972).
35. New Left and liberal historiography has tended to emphasize the responsibility of the executive branch of government, slighting the role of the judiciary. There have been several studies of the various

"cases" associated with McCarthyism – Hiss, the Rosenbergs, etc. – but little in the way of a sustained examination of the role of the legal system. The Supreme Court in particular played a critical part in first endorsing red-scare politics and later in dismantling the apparatus of suppression. The focus on the executive has also been at the expense of the legislative branch. It was the legislative branch that tended to take the initiative with respect to programs to combat Communist subversion. Earl Latham pointed this out with respect to Congress several years ago, and the same was true in several state governments. The energy of the legislative branch does not sit overly comfortably with the notion that McCarthyism was a top-down phenomenon, it being the branch (especially the lower houses) that could most readily be invaded by populist pressures.

36. Hyman, "England and America: Climates of Tolerance and Intolerance," in Bell, ed., *Radical Right*, pp. 269–306.
37. The passions unleashed by "spy cases," stronger in the U.S. than in Britain, might suggest that some Americans believe that the U.S. ought to be immune to such Old World deformities.
38. Philip Jenkins, *The Cold War at Home: The Red Scare in Pennsylvania, 1945–1960* (Chapel Hill, 1999), p. 9, does make this point; similarly emphasizing the impact of the Korean War is Heale, *McCarthy's Americans*.
39. Alan Brinkley, *Voices of Protest: Huey Long, Father Coughlin, and the Great Depression* (New York, 1982); Leo Ribuffo, *The Old Christian Right: The Protestant Far Right from the Great Depression to the Cold War* (Philadelphia, 1983); Leonard J. Moore, "Historical Interpretations of the 1920s Klan: The Traditional View and the Populist Revision," *Journal of Social History* 24 (Winter 1990): 341–57; Ronald P. Formisano, *Boston against Busing: Race, Class, and Ethnicity in the 1960s and 1970s* (Chapel Hill, 1991).
40. Heale, *McCarthy's Americans*, p. 270.
41. An important treatment in this vein is Michael Kazin, *The Populist Persuasion: An American History* (New York, 1995), chapter 7, which suggests how right-wing activists drew on the rhetoric of community (a community said to be under attack by a liberal and modernizing elite) to promote a form of popular anticommunism. See also Hixson, *Search for the American Right Wing*, pp. 42–3.
42. Alexis de Tocqueville, *Democracy in America*, ed. Phillips Bradley (New York, 1945), I, p. 114.
43. Heale, *McCarthy's Americans*, Part III.

7

Segregation and Civil Rights: African American Freedom Strategies in the Twentieth Century

Adam Fairclough

According to the historian John W. Cell, blacks in America have adopted "three main approaches" to the problem of racial oppression: "accommodation," or submitting to white supremacy with a view to securing improvements inside the system; "militant confrontation," or outright opposition to all forms of racial discrimination; and "separatism," or seeking to create an all-black nation or community, either inside the United States or on another continent. However, Cell cautions that black strategies were rarely self-contained or mutually exclusive; moreover, they cannot be neatly divided into "conservative" or "radical" camps. Accommodation, militant confrontation, and separatism, he writes, "were not so much distinct schools as they were philosophies in a state of continual tension, interaction, and adaptation. The variations and combinations were virtually endless."[1]

These are useful categories and important qualifications. They contradict the tendency to analyze black history in terms of bipolar opposites: DuBois versus Washington; the Communist party versus the NAACP; separatism versus integration; Martin versus Malcolm; violence versus nonviolence. They also resist the notion that confrontation, or protest, was morally and politically superior to accommodation.

Perhaps the most significant development in the historiography of what may loosely be called the "black freedom movement" of the twentieth century is a reappraisal of the pre-*Brown* decades – the classic "Age of Segregation" – using the kind of analytical framework suggested by Cell. In the 1960s and 1970s, many historians took *Brown* and the Montgomery bus boycott as decisive turning points in Southern race relations, events that divided the twentieth century into a period of accommodation and a period of protest. Moreover, impressed by the militancy of the boycotts, sit-ins, and demonstrations of their own time, they generally took a dim view of the accommodationist tactics of the pre-*Brown* era. Idus A. Newby's study of blacks in South Carolina and Louis Harlan's biography of Booker T. Washington, for example, portrayed accommodation as a flawed strategy which, far from promoting racial equality, played into the hands of white supremacists and further ensnared blacks in the oppressive web of segregation. Meanwhile, the burgeoning literature on the civil rights movement told heroic stories of a younger generation that confronted Jim Crow with a moral certainty and physical courage lacking in their predecessors.

As might be expected, however, when the historiography of the civil rights movement reached a certain maturity and critical mass, scholars became more impressed by continuities between the pre-*Brown* decades and the Montgomery-to-Selma years. Although Martin Luther King, Jr. continues to be the focus of public interest and scholarly attention – witness the popularity and critical acclaim enjoyed by Taylor Branch's work on King – many historians are now examining the civil rights movement at the state and local level, as well as tracing the roots of mass protest to the labor, left-wing, and NAACP activism of the 1930s and 1940s. In a similar vein, recent books about the Roosevelt era – including Patricia Sullivan's study of Southern radicals and John Egerton's treatment of Southern liberals – argued that political forces unleashed by the New Deal foreshadowed the civil rights movement.[2]

Revisionist studies of the Old Left, especially the Communist Party, strengthened the notion that the civil rights movement had an important precursor, demonstrating that more "militant confrontation" occurred during the supposed era of accommodation than was hitherto recognized. Mark Naison's book on black Communists in Harlem, Robin Kelley's study of the Communist Party in Alabama, Michael Honey's account of the labor unions in Memphis, Roger Keeran's work on the United Auto Workers Union, Gerald Horne's study of the Civil Rights Congress, and Robert Korstad's history of the Food, Tobacco and Agricultural Workers Union all contend that the Communist Party was in the vanguard of the struggle against racism during the 1930s and 1940s. Even historians otherwise critical of the CP, such as Harvey Levenstein and George Fredrickson, have praised its commitment to racial equality. Indeed, it is not implausible to suggest that the seminal event in the birth of the modern civil rights struggle was the worldwide campaign in defense of the Scottsboro boys mounted by the Communist-controlled International Labor Defense in the early 1930s.[3]

The birth and dynamic growth of the Congress of Industrial Organizations (CIO), in which Communist organizers played a vital role, created an alliance of black and white workers that presented another profound challenge to Southern racism. Indeed, some historians depict the labor militancy of the Roosevelt era as a direct antecedent of the civil rights movement. In the words of an influential article by Robert Korstad and Nelson Lichtenstein, "the civil rights era began, dramatically and decisively, in the early 1940s," when the left-led, interracial unions of the CIO challenged the socio-economic structure of the Jim Crow South. These unions, Rick Halpern agrees, forged "long-lasting ties with community groups which allowed the CIO to become a general social movement." In places like Bessemer, Alabama, and Winston-Salem, North Carolina, black unionists revived local NAACP branches, furnishing energy for voter registration drives and other civil rights activities. Citing the case of the Packinghouse Workers, whose commitment to racial equality endured long after 1945, Halpern echoes the Korstad-Lichtenstein thesis that the CIO had the potential to become a major force in the civil rights struggle.[4]

The main problem with this thesis, however, is the singular *lack* of continuity between the Old Left and the civil rights movement. The ossifying labor movement and the virtually defunct Communist Party made scant contribution to the civil rights struggle of 1955–68. "[L]ittle, if any, memory of the New Deal years informed the civil rights movement of the 1960s," writes Patricia Sullivan, even though "activists of the earlier decades tilled the ground."[5]

Seeking to explain why the budding civil rights coalition of the late 1930s and 1940s came to grief, leaving so few traces, historians of the Old Left have blamed McCarthyism. The virulent anticommunism of the Truman years, they argue, not only suppressed the CP but also destroyed the Southern Conference for Human Welfare, decimated the CIO, purged the NAACP of its more militant elements, and undermined black opposition to colonialism. To quote Steve Rosswurm, McCarthyism "destroyed a growing southern civil rights movement that was . . . grounded in the trade unions." As a consequence, the civil rights movement that re-emerged in the mid-1950s had few links to organized labor, failed to challenge American foreign policy, and "posed no threat to capitalism."[6]

This long overdue re-evaluation of the Old Left has contributed more than any other recent scholarship to our understanding of what John Egerton called the "generation before the civil rights movement." There is a danger, however, of greatly overstating the possibilities of radical change in the 1930s and 1940s, and making McCarthyism a scapegoat for the failures and weaknesses of the Old Left. The interracialism of the CIO, for example, was highly pragmatic and did not easily translate into a direct attack upon racial discrimination. The organization and survival of interracial unions usually depended upon sidestepping issues of segregation and discrimination. Michael Honey provides copious evidence of deep racial divisions that prevented unions in Memphis, Tennessee, from attacking segregation. Bruce Nelson found that in Mobile, Alabama, unions had to soft-pedal national anti-discrimination policies in order not to alienate white workers. According to Rick Halpern, even an advanced union such as the United Packinghouse Workers acquiesced in workplace segregation below the Mason-Dixon line. The left-led CIO unions tended to be far more egalitarian in their rhetoric than in their practices.[7]

Hence racism and self-interest among white workers often nullified the CIO's racially egalitarian ideals. Although McCarthyism took its toll on the unions, writes Robert J. Norrell, "The failures of organized labor in the South . . . were due in equal, if not greater, measure, to the militant white supremacy of many southern workers." Outside the workplace, the CIO often failed to have much political clout. Union strength in Birmingham and Detroit did not necessarily lead to the election of racial liberals; nor did it foster opposition to racial segregation among working-class voters.[8]

Even if the CIO had vigorously attacked Jim Crow, it would scarcely have mustered the strength to defeat it. As Allan Draper argues, historians who believe that organized labor had the potential to create a powerful civil rights movement "have built their case on marginal unions." The South was precisely the region where labor was weakest, and where the left-led CIO unions claimed the smallest proportion of union membership. There was no window of opportunity: the supporters of white supremacy had a stranglehold on Southern politics and a veto on national policy. And they were relatively impervious to assault from interracial unions, even in alliance with liberals and civil rights organizations. It is wishful thinking to argue, as do Korstad and Lichtenstein, that anticommunism aborted the growth of an "autonomous, labor-oriented civil rights movement," if by that they mean a movement that might have reformed the South by confronting and destroying racial segregation. As Honey concedes, "CIO hopes for transforming the postwar South seem in retrospect almost a mirage."[9]

Still searching for roots of the civil rights movement in the 1930s and 1940s, other historians stress the pivotal role of the National Association for the Advancement of Colored People (NAACP). The history of the NAACP is so long, rich, and diverse that it is impossible to set down between two covers; nevertheless, book-by-book, like a gigantic jig-saw puzzle, the outline of that history is taking shape. Richard Kluger, Genna Rae McNeil, and Mark V. Tushnet have explored the NAACP's campaign against segregated education, launched by Charles Houston and continued by Thurgood Marshall, which undermined the constitutional foundations of Jim Crow. Robert Zangrando, Richard C. Cortner, and Kenneth R. Goings have described the NAACP's fights against lynching, "legal lynchings," and racist judges. Michael Gillette, Adam Fairclough, John Kirk, and Steven Tuck have traced the activities of the NAACP in Texas, Louisiana, Arkansas, and Georgia, noting its dynamic expansion in the late 1930s and 1940s.[10]

If the NAACP's national leaders failed to make the best use of its membership – which increased tenfold during World War II – the strength of its grass-roots organization nonetheless made the NAACP a force to be reckoned with. Local branches filed lawsuits, organized voter registration campaigns, supported strikes, complained to the Fair Employment Practices Committee, and investigated lynchings and police brutality. Although the NAACP attracted criticism for being conservative and stolidly middle-class, it was actually diverse in both membership and political viewpoint. If the NAACP was so lacking in militancy, one wonders why NAACP members were fired, beaten, jailed, and murdered, and why, in 1956, state authorities throughout the South tried to suppress the organization completely. Michael Honey described the labor militancy of the late 1930s and 1940s as the "missing link in the evolution of the black freedom struggle." However, the NAACP has a stronger claim to be that "missing link": it, more than the CIO or the CP, developed a realistic and effective strategy for attacking Southern racism.[11]

It was the NAACP's principled but pragmatic opposition to white supremacy that enabled it to eclipse the Communist Party during World War II. In 1939, the NAACP actually had fewer members than the CP. Six years later, harnessing and encouraging wartime militancy over racial discrimination, the NAACP had acquired more than 400,000 new members, decisively overtaking its rival. The Communist Party, by contrast, seriously damaged its standing with blacks by endorsing the Hitler-Stalin pact, opposing the March on Washington Movement, and, after Germany attacked the Soviet Union, urging unconditional support for the war effort. By subordinating the civil rights cause to its loyalty to the Soviet Union, the CP allowed the NAACP to seize the initiative and forge ahead.[12]

Why, then, did the NAACP play such a subsidiary role in the civil rights movement that emerged after *Brown*? One reason was the state-sponsored repression that all but wiped out the NAACP's Southern branches in 1956. The other was the NAACP's anti-communism, enthusiastically championed by long-serving executive secretary Walter White, which played into the hands of racists and conservatives. White's anti-communism was dogmatic and ruthless; his attempts to curry favor with J. Edgar Hoover misguided. Refusing to stand up for civil liberties during the Cold War, the NAACP helped to split the Old Left. Purging its own ranks of alleged communists, it cut itself off from grass-roots militancy, rendering itself even more vulnerable to right-wing attacks. Disavowing mass action or even mass agitation, it placed too much faith in lawsuits, a strategy that yielded diminishing returns in the face of white Massive Resistance to *Brown*.

By the 1950s, *Brown* notwithstanding, the NAACP cut a sorry figure. Internal wrangling and unimaginative tactics made the organization ill-equipped to defend itself against persecution by the Southern states. Black Southerners yearned for bold leadership, but the NAACP was incapable of supplying it. Roy Wilkins, White's successor, was an uninspiring leader. Wilkins's lukewarm response to the Montgomery bus boycott, jealousy of Martin Luther King, Jr., and bureaucratic assassination of Robert F. Williams (revealed in unpleasant detail in Tim Tyson's recent biography of Williams) betrayed a lamentable combination of arrogance and insecurity. No wonder the NAACP lost its primacy in the civil rights struggle as the Southern Christian Leadership Conference (1957), and then the Student Nonviolent Coordinating Committee (1960), forged a mass movement that encouraged ordinary Southerners to challenge Jim Crow through nonviolent direct action.[13]

Cold War liberalism also profoundly affected the relationship between blacks and world events. Recent books by Brenda Gayle Plummer and Penny Von Eschen have dispelled the notion that black Americans had little interest in foreign affairs with the exception of back-to-Africa movements. Illustrating the liveliness of black discussions of world events and the vigor of black opposition to European colonialism, they also document how the federal government co-opted esrtwhile black critics, ruthlessly pursued stubborn left-wingers such as Paul Robeson, and put recalcitrant organizations such as the Council of African Affairs out of business. The chilling effect was obvious: "many black organizations were completely mute [on foreign affairs] by the mid-1950s," writes Plummer. Even such an innocuous and apolitical figure as Josephine Baker, a cabaret artist long resident in France, became a target of government harassment when, in the early 1950s, she began criticizing American racism during her performing tours of Latin America.[14]

Still, historians writing decades after the death of Stalin should not censure the NAACP too severely for joining the Cold War consensus. The issue of communism was politically and morally complex, and there were always vigorous debates about it inside the association. Walter

White's brand of anticommunism never commanded universal assent, and at various times he was opposed by Charles Houston, Thurgood Marshall, Clarence Mitchell, and Gloster Current. However, the uncompromisingly pro-Soviet stance of the American Communist Party made it very difficult for liberal organizations to resist anticommunism. As George Fredrickson has argued, it is bad history to divorce the domestic policies of Communist parties from either the "international context or Soviet foreign policy." In addition, blacks gained as well as lost from the demise of the Old Left. As Mary Dudziak has stressed, anticommunism became an important factor in persuading the federal government to oppose, on paper at least, racial discrimination; a concern for America's world image informed the *Brown* decision. Blacks also learned the important lesson, according to Bruce Nelson, that "if African Americans were to achieve full citizenship, they could not allow whites to dictate the movement's program, strategy, and timetable."[15]

The commitment of the civil rights movement to the ideal of integration often concealed the extent to which segregated black institutions – churches, colleges, unions, businesses, fraternal societies – furnished the movement with an organizational base. Segregation, of course, was very much a condition forced upon black Southerners by white supremacists. For example, segregation within the federal government, as Desmond King has demonstrated, was designed to discriminate against, and even eliminate, black workers. Yet some forms of segregation, especially in the social and religious spheres, were voluntarily chosen by blacks. Moreover, defensive responses to imposed segregation often took on a life of their own: the National Alliance of Postal Employees, for example, which still exists today, was formed in 1913 because the other postal unions excluded blacks. Traditions of self-help, the ethos of black pride, and mere pragmatism often blurred the distinction between segregation as a necessary evil and segregation as a positive good.[16]

A belated acknowledgment of the strength of black institutions, and a better understanding of the complex relationship between the goal of racial equality and the social reality of racial segregation, has undoubtedly stimulated interest in black separatism, which for many years remained neglected. It is a remarkable fact, for example, that before 1968, despite Amy Jacques-Garvey's indefatigable efforts in donating copies of her late husband's books to libraries throughout the world, the only scholarly study of the United Negro Improvement Association (UNIA), the most popular expression of black nationalism in American history, was the relatively short biography of Marcus Garvey published by E. David Cronon in 1955. To be sure, the UNIA's relatively short lifespan, and the destruction and scattering of its papers, hampered the study of the Garvey phenomenon. But neglect of the UNIA also stemmed from a widespread feeling, among both blacks and whites, that black nationalism was an aberrant, even pathological, ideology, and that Garveyism was an embarrassing episode best forgotten – the dominant image of Garvey was that of *opéra bouffe* hero. The fact that Marcus Garvey was Jamaican, and that he found much of his support among West Indian immigrants, made it easier to relegate the UNIA to the status of historical curiosity, something that stood outside the mainstream of African American history.[17]

Only when Malcolm X and Black Power rekindled interest in black nationalism did historians attempt to reappraise the Garvey movement, a task greatly facilitated after 1981 by the publication of the *Marcus Garvey Papers*, a mammoth research project directed by A. Robert Hill. Thanks to Hill's work and to books by, among others, Theodore Vincent, Tony Martin, Randall Burkett, and Judith Stein, we know much more about the UNIA's social roots, internal politics, religious ideas, gender roles, and international impact. Thanks also to a remarkable study by Winston James, we understand better why Caribbean immigrants were so influential in black nationalist and radical movements in the early decades of the twentieth century. It is nevertheless a revealing comment on how much remains to be done that Cronon's 45-year-old book remains in print, still the only rounded biography of Garvey.[18]

Judged by the decaying fragments of the UNIA, or by religious cults such as the Nation of Islam, Garveyism bequeathed a small legacy. It was in the enduring appeal of racial unity, however, that the basic idea of Garveyism lived on. As Winston James notes, "It is indeed remarkable the way in which, in the 1930s and later, many of Garvey's opponents from the 1920s were to move toward black nationalist positions." Garveyism influenced the Communist Party's strong commitment to racial equality, as well as its specific policy of "self-determination" for Negroes in the Southern Black Belt. DuBois's 1934 *Crisis* editorial, "Segregation," could have been written by Garvey himself. A. Philip Randolph stole a leaf from Garvey's book when he decreed that the March on Washington Movement should be a black-only affair, a decision that not only barred white Communists but also, more importantly, boosted the movement's appeal to blacks. Even Martin Luther King, Jr., an eloquent advocate of integration, built his organization upon the black Church and, while not explicitly excluding whites, ensured that they served in the background as helpers and advisers.[19]

If the civil rights movement derived much of its strength from segregated institutions, should it be regarded as a natural evolution of the Southern black community? Or was it, instead, a drastic intervention, inspired by factors external to the South, that sought deliberately to disrupt that community and replace it with something new? Perhaps we should recognize that it was *both* – the tension between the two forces eventually splitting the Civil Rights Movement over the question of Black Power. We can then modify the notion that an era of accommodation gave way, in the mid-1950s, to an era of protest. Accommodation and protest were not so much opposites, the one denoting passivity and the other resistance, as two sides of the same coin. Both were forms of resistance, each dominant in different times when circumstances favored it.

My premise is not that accommodation necessarily constituted resistance, merely that for the first fifty years of the twentieth century, from disfranchisement to *Brown*, most black Southerners had to work toward racial equality within the boundaries imposed by segregation. Before the 1950s, militant confrontation met overpowering repression: witness the NAACP's collapse in most of the South after 1919, the failure of left-wing farmers' unions in the 1930s, and the overwhelming non-response by black Southerners to A. Philip Randolph's calls for mass nonviolent direct action during World War II. Protest emerged in the shape of the civil rights movement because conditions both internal and external to the South permitted it – the Cold War, the collapse of sharecropping, migration to the cities, the intellectual retreat of racism, the decline of lynching, and the advent of television.

To characterize accommodation as a form of resistance, rather than a mere survival technique, may seem dubious. Yet Eugene D. Genovese's analysis of antebellum paternalism offers a useful parallel. According to Genovese, the slaves accepted planter paternalism but subtly reinterpreted it in order to wrest from their masters the best possible conditions under the circumstances. They emphasized rights, repudiated racism, and expressed through Christianity the hope and expectation of freedom. Paternalism was a survival strategy, a way of humanizing a system of brutal exploitation, and an expression of ideological resistance.[20]

The accommodationism of the Jim Crow era can be analyzed in a similar way. Blacks accepted racial segregation and tried to convert separateness into strength, but they rejected the racist rationale for Jim Crow and never regarded it as a permanent condition. While they appealed to whites' sense of noblesse oblige through supplication and flattery, they continually tried to shift the terms of interracial contact in their favor: from appeasement to cooperation, from cooperation to equality, from equality to integration, from integration to power. Like the slaves' acceptance of paternalism, the strategy of accommodation entailed costs as well as benefits. It achieved incremental gains but gave certain groups a vested interest in segregation; it helped prepare the ideological and institutional groundwork for the Civil Rights Movement, but was incapable of undermining white supremacy by itself.

The distinction between accommodation and protest was never precise. As the sociologist Charles S. Johnson pointed out many years ago, white Southerners failed to construct a true "caste system" because tension and change made racial segregation inherently unstable – in large part because blacks refused to accept that white supremacy was natural and immutable. Hence even the apparently conservative, self-help methods of Booker T. Washington implicitly, and sometimes explicitly, challenged the South's racial order. Thus, blacks could never be sure what whites would or would not tolerate. Indeed, the vagaries and uncertainties of the "color line" were a prominent theme of sociological literature on Southern race relations in the 1930s and 1940s. The significance of actions changed over time, moreover: joining a CIO union in the 1930s, to cite a simple example, implied a direct challenge to racial segregation; in the 1950s it no longer did. On the other hand, Southern whites generally tolerated the growth of the NAACP in the 1940s, but in the late 1950s tried to destroy the organization.

William H. Chafe has recently attempted to resolve such problems of definition by arguing that "even as the parameters for potential activism have shifted, the impulse for community preservation and black advancement has remained a constant." From this perspective, many of the basic themes of accommodation – "the quest for dignity, self-definition, and community improvement" – constituted forms of resistance.[21]

However, the literature on African-American education, an issue of vital concern to blacks during the Age of Segregation, reveals that the relationship between community improvement and resistance to white supremacy was far from straightforward. In the eyes of many scholars, to be sure, the connection between education and the struggle for equality has been crystal clear. According to Gunnar Myrdal (1944), Henry Allen Bullock (1967), and James L. Leloudis (1996) the segregated black schools of the New South uplifted the race and pointed it in the direction of equality. Innumerable histories of black educators, black schools, and black colleges echo this view. Indeed, some historians contend that regardless of curriculum and regardless of disparities between black and white, education had a liberating effect. To quote Diane Ravitch, "Blacks were more often oppressed by the education they did not receive than by the education they did receive."[22]

Yet there is also an extensive scholarship, smaller in quantity but perhaps more powerfully argued, that disputes the education-as-liberation thesis, contending that the schooling secured by black Southerners was too unequal and inadequate decisively to advance the struggle for equality. Louis Harlan's biography of Booker T. Washington, Donald Spivey's critique of "industrial education," John Haley's biography of Charles N. Hunter, Morgan Kousser's analysis of Southern progressivism, and Leon Litwack's book on the Jim Crow South typify this critique of accommodationism. According to Harlan, Washington's racial diplomacy failed, his educational ideas were flawed, and his economic program was based on false premises. Haley believes that accommodationists deluded themselves about whites' sense of justice and fair play. To Kousser, the gains secured through accommodationism were nullified by the widening disparities between black schools and white schools: "In the struggle for jobs, or, more broadly, for increased economic welfare, it is *relative*, not absolute, levels of education that count."[23]

The implication of this critique is that black institution-building along Washingtonian lines did little to promote racial equality because it failed to challenge white supremacy. Idus A. Newby concluded, after studying South Carolina, that black schools and colleges tried to inculcate conservatism and conformity: the civil rights movement took place despite them, not because of them. Historians of the civil rights movement have acknowledged the influence of individual teachers but downplayed the role of teachers in general. As John Dittmer wrote of Mississippi, "As a group, black teachers in the 1950s refused to take a stand, and the movement of the early sixties passed them by."[24]

Glenn Eskew's study of civil rights activism in Birmingham, Alabama, supports the notion of a fundamental discontinuity between institution-building efforts during the Age of Segregation and the *anti*-institutional protests of the Civil Rights Movement. Eskew noted that the indigenous protest movement led by Rev. Fred L. Shuttlesworth between 1956 and 1963 drew its support from a small but loyal following of predominantly working-class black people. When Shuttlesworth and Martin Luther King, Jr. launched the protests that rocked the nation in 1963, they found the bulk of the black middle-class arrayed against them. When SCLC organizer James Bevel urged children at Parker High School to join the demonstrations, principal R. C. Johnson locked the school gates in an effort to stop them. In short, the civil rights movement represented a sharp break from the past – a repudiation of existing black leadership rather than an extension of it.[25]

This clash of interpretations suggests a number of possibilities. One is that the civil rights movement both inspired *and* threatened black Southerners, mobilized *and* antagonized them, because its goals and ideology were actually quite varied. The Montgomery bus boycott, for example, produced astonishing unity because all blacks despised segregated buses and because the goal of integration threatened no vital interest. Schools, however, were a very different matter: integration divided the black community because it threatened the loss of teaching jobs and the demise of valued institutions. Street demonstrations also proved divisive because they disrupted community life, challenged local leaders, and provoked white retaliation that sometimes left black people worse off than they had been before. For the civil rights movement to succeed, therefore, it could not rely solely on the resources of local black communities: it also required outside intervention by the NAACP, other civil rights organizations, and the federal courts.

Another way forward is to explore how accommodationist methods, especially institution-building, contained contradictory tendencies; they were, as Cell suggests, "eclectic and ambiguous, looking forward to collaboration or resistance or both." Again, education provides a good example. Leon Litwack's recent book on the Jim Crow era masterfully illustrates the oppressive environment in which black educators operated, and the compromises and psychic costs that accommodation entailed. Others, however, have stressed the possibilities as well as the constraints, challenging the notion that accommodation necessarily entailed abject surrender to white supremacy. Black educators constantly sought to improve schools, raise academic standards, and develop economic opportunities. They also built alliances with white liberals, influenced the Northern foundations, taught Negro History, and argued the case for democracy. Despite their reputation for conservatism, black teachers helped to initiate the modern Civil Rights Movement by attacking, with the NAACP's support, discriminatory salary scales.[26]

Research on the history of black women, especially the flowering of clubs in the early twentieth century, tells us much about the creative uses of accommodationism. Women's clubs organized neighborhood clean-ups, mounted public health campaigns, and petitioned for better schools. Through such tangible efforts, they pursued the goal of racial equality indirectly. Indeed, much scholarship implies that the political conflict between Washingtonians and DuBoisites was more apparent than real: in their daily engagements with poverty and discrimination, organizations such as the National Association of Colored Women married the ethos of racial uplift with a vision of democracy. Nannie Burroughs, Mary McLeod

Bethune, and Charlotte Hawkins Brown saw no conflict between self-help and civil rights.[27]

Indeed, Glenda Gilmore argues that by the early twentieth century, black women as churchwomen, clubwomen, and teachers were providing the most important leadership in Southern black communities. Disfranchisement abolished black politicians and reduced black men to the same level of political powerlessness as that of black women. Yet because white people regarded black women as less threatening than black men, women became the principal means of communication and cooperation between the two communities. Black women became "spokespeople for and motivators of black citizens," writes Gilmore, and the "deep camouflage of their leadership style – their womanhood – helped them remain invisible as they worked toward political ends." As always, such a role entailed contradictions and ambiguities, hence Gilmore's analogy of the "double agent." Nevertheless, slowly and subtly, black women bent paternalism into cooperation, promoting relationships with whites that implied mutual respect and equality.[28]

Stressing black agency rather than black victimhood offers a new way of interpreting accommodationism and a fresh approach to the Age of Segregation. Yet there are problems with the current celebration of agency. As Chafe notes, but does not sufficiently emphasize, the historian must assess the relationship between the "terror and impenetrability of segregation" and the "strength of black resistance." This raises the question of efficacy. It is easy to get the impression, reading the burgeoning historical literature on the subject, that black women's clubs constituted a powerful grass-roots movement. However, their combined membership never exceeded 50,000 and their ability to effect social change was minimal. Moreover, accommodation, with its associated ethos of racial uplift, accentuated class divisions. By stressing their cultural superiority to the lower classes, blacks who aspired to middle-class status hoped to counteract racist stereotypes that depicted all blacks as ignorant and degraded. But their espousal of bourgeois morality, Kevin Gaines has argued, "implicitly faulted African Americans for their lowly status," thus replicating the "dehumanizing logic of racism."

Their concern for middle-class respectability encouraged black club-women to look down upon the lower classes. They disapproved of gambling, drinking, and sensual dancing; they frowned upon common-law marriages. Their moral intolerance, Deborah Gray White noted, "[drove] a wedge between themselves and the masses of black women." Failing to recruit beyond its middle-class base, the clubwomen's movement lost much of its crusading zeal, and its members frittered away more of their energies on social climbing and internal politics. By 1930, the clubwomen's movement was a spent force. After a modest revival when Mary McLeod Bethune founded the National Council of Negro Women in 1935, it again declined in the 1950s. Nevertheless, the vigor of black women's activism in the early twentieth century – together with women's greater participation in the black Church – had important long-term effects on the struggle for racial equality. A women's club instigated the Montgomery bus boycott and black women supported the civil rights movement in significantly greater numbers than those of black men.[29]

Although Martin Luther King, Jr. continues to attract scholarly attention, many historians of the civil rights movement are now focusing on local communities, lesser known organizations, second-level leaders, and less famous incidents. This large and varied literature emphasizes the importance of state and local context, as well as the "grass-roots" character of a black insurgency that was broadly-based but also loosely-organized, unpredictable, and unstable. If most studies flesh out and stretch the "Montgomery-to-Selma" paradigm, a few explore neglected cultural issues. Brian Ward's study of rhythm and blues, for example, makes fascinating connections between race relations and popular music. The resurgence of black nationalism in the 1960s has received far less attention than the civil rights movement, and the dominant tone of the best studies is highly critical. Bruce Perry's biography of Malcolm X, Gerald Horne's analysis of the 1965 Watts riots, and Hugh Pearson's study of Black Panther leader Huey P. Newton all make a persuasive case that separatist and violent strategies failed. William Van Deburg's celebration of Black Power as a success is less than convincing.[30]

Two emerging themes are of particular interest. The first is that of armed self-defense among black Southerners. Gail O'Brien's study of the 1946 riot in Columbia, Tennessee; Tim Tyson's book on Robert F. Williams, the black leader in Monroe, North Carolina, who mounted armed resistance to the Ku Klux Klan; and Lance Hill's forthcoming book on the Deacons for Defense, an armed group in Louisiana organized in 1964–65, demonstrate that blacks sometimes utilized guns in an organized and effective way.[31] Yet this celebration of guns should not be pushed too far. Armed self-defense could only stabilize the status quo; it could not – unlike nonviolence, which openly confronted white supremacy – fundamentally change it.

The second theme concerns the history and consequences of school integration. There are still accounts of *Brown* that read like heroic narratives, with the victory of integration finally achieved after great trials and tribulations. Many recent studies, however, emphasize widespread disappointment over the results of integration. Often, the public schools integrated only to resegregate. Even when black and white children attend the same schools, the educational benefits have proved elusive. Integration came at a high price, closing thousands of schools that blacks had built at great personal sacrifice. Moreover, some segregated black schools, *pace Brown*, had been excellent. Vanessa Siddle Walker's history of a black high school in North Carolina concluded that teachers had motivated students to learn and even excel, opposing the racist stereotypes that constantly threatened to sap black self-respect. "Something valuable was lost in the process of the great civil rights victory," David Cecelski agrees. The old spirit of "commitment, community, and social mission" declined.[32]

From the vantage point of the twenty-first century, the Jim Crow South of 1900–1950 appears far less stable than it once did, and black resistance far more prominent. Nevertheless, none of the significant movements of that era – accommodationism, racial uplift, separatism, unionism, the radicalism of the Communist Party, the legalism of the NAACP – proved sufficient to topple white supremacy, although they did weaken the foundations. Even World War II, for all the economic and ideological changes it promoted, left racial segregation intact. The conclusion is inescapable that the Montgomery bus boycott really did reveal a decisive shift – from accommodation to confrontation, from racial uplift to collective protest – and that this shift involved a transformation of consciousness, not simply the adaptation of existing ideas to new circumstances. It indeed marked, in the words of Martin Luther King, Jr., the "birth of a new age."[33]

Notes

1. John W. Cell, *The Highest Stage of White Supremacy: The Origins of Segregation in South Africa and the American South* (Cambridge, UK, 1982), pp. 257–62.
2. Taylor Branch, *Parting the Waters: America in the King Years, 1954–63* (New York, 1988); idem, *Pillar of Fire: America in the King Years, 1963–65* (New York, 1997); Robert J. Norrell, *Reaping the Whirlwind: The Civil Rights Movement in Tuskegee* (New York, 1986); Adam Fairclough, *Race and Democracy: The Civil Rights Struggle in Louisiana, 1915–72* (Athens, GA, 1995); Patricia Sullivan, *Days of*

Hope: Race and Democracy in the New Deal Era (Chapel Hill, 1996); John Egerton, *Speak Now Against the Day: The Generation Before the Civil Rights Movement in the South* (New York, 1994).

3. Mark Naison, *Communists in Harlem During the Depression* (Urbana, 1983); Robin D. G. Kelley, *Hammer and Hoe: Alabama Communists during the Great Depression* (Chapel Hill, 1990); Michael K. Honey, *Southern Labor and Black Civil Rights: Organizing Memphis Workers* (Urbana, 1993); Gerald Horne, *Communist Front? The Civil Rights Congress, 1946–1956* (Cranbury, NJ, 1988); Roger Keeran, *The Communist Party and the Auto Workers Union* (Bloomington, 1980); Roger Keeran, "The Communist Influence on American Labor," in Michael E. Brown, Randy Martin, and Frank Rosengarten, eds. *New Studies in the Politics and Culture of U.S. Communism* (New York, 1993), p. 185; Robert Korstad, "Daybreak of Freedom: Tobacco Workers and the CIO, Winston-Salem, North Carolina, 1943–1950," Ph.D. diss., University of North Carolina at Chapel Hill, 1987); Harvey Levenstein, *Communism, Anticommunism, and the CIO* (Westport, CT, 1981); George Fredrickson, *Black Liberation: A Comparative History of Black Ideologies in the United States and South Africa* (New York, 1995); James Goodman, *Stories of Scottsboro: The Rape Case that Shocked 1930s America and Revived the Struggle for Racial Equality* (New York, 1993).

4. Robert Korstad and Nelson Lichtenstein, "Opportunities Found and Lost: Labor, Radicals, and the Early Civil Rights Movement," *Journal of American History*, 75 (1988): 786–811; Rick Halpern, "Organized Labor, Black Workers, and the Twentieth Century South: The Emerging Revision," in Melvyn Stokes and Rick Halpern, eds., *Race and Class in the American South Since 1890* (Oxford, 1994), pp. 73–4; Horace Huntley, "The Red Scare and Black Workers in Alabama: The International Union of Mine, Mill, and Smelter Workers, 1945–1953," in Robert Asher and Charles Stephenson, eds., *Labor Divided: Race and Ethnicity in United States Labor Struggles, 1935–1960* (Albany, 1990), pp. 143–4; Rick Halpern, *Down on the Killing Floor: Black and White Workers in Chicago Packinghouses, 1904–54* (Urbana, 1997), pp. 202–45.

5. Kelley, *Hammer and Hoe*, pp. 228–31; Sullivan, *Days of Hope,* p. 275.

6. Sullivan *Days of Hope*, pp. 273–4; Egerton, *Speak Now Against the Day*, pp. 560–64; Fairclough, *Race and Democracy*, pp. 135–47; Korstad and Lichtenstein, "Opportunities Found and Lost," pp. 801–6; Anthony P. Dunbar, *Against the Grain: Southern Radicals and*

Prophets, 1929–1959 (Charlottesville, 1981), p. 258; Steve Ross-wurm, "Introduction," in Rosswurm, ed., *The CIO's Left-Led Unions* (New Brunswick, 1992).

7. Honey, *Southern Labor and Black Civil Rights,* pp. 202–10, 219, 275–6; Rick Halpern, "Interracial Unionism in the Southwest: Fort Worth's Packinghouse Workers, 1937–1954," in Robert H. Zieger, ed., *Organized Labor in the Twentieth-Century South* (Knoxville, 1991), p. 176; Halpern, "Organized Labor, Black Workers," 73–4; Bruce Nelson, "Organized Labor and the Struggle for Black Equality in Mobile During World War II," *Journal of American History*, 80 (1993): 955, 967–88. See also Herbert Hill, "Black Workers, Organized Labor, and Title VII of the 1964 Civil Rights Act," in Herbert Hill and James E. Jones, ed., *Race in America: The Struggle for Equality* (Madison, 1993), pp. 263–341; Fraser Ottanelli, *The Communist Party of the United States: From the Depression to World War II* (New Brunswick, 1991), pp. 156–7; and Bruce Nelson's important study of longshoremen and steelworkers, *Divided We Stand: American Workers and the Struggle for Black Equality* (Princeton, 2001).

8. Robert J. Norrell, "Caste in Steel: Jim Crow Careers in Birmingham, Alabama," *Journal of Southern History* 73 (1986): 691; Robert J. Norrell, "Labor at the Ballot Box: Alabama Politics from the New Deal to the Dixiecrat Movement," *Journal of Southern History* 57 (1991): 201–34; Thomas J. Sugrue, "Crabgrass-Roots Politics: Race, Rights, and the Reaction Against Liberalism in the Urban North, 1940–1964," *Journal of American History* 82 (1995): 551–78.

9. Allan H. Draper, *Conflict of Interest: Organized Labor and the Civil Rights Movement in the South, 1954–1968* (Ithaca, NY, 1994), pp. 11–13; Egerton, *Speak Now Against the Day,* pp. 515–16; Honey, *Southern Labor and Black Civil Rights,* p. 284; Korstad and Lichtenstein, "Opportunities Found and Lost," p. 811.

10. Richard Kluger, *Simple Justice* (New York, 1975); Genna Rae McNeil, *Groundwork: Charles Hamilton Houston and the Struggle for Civil Rights* (Philadelphia, 1983); Mark V. Tushnet, *The NAACP's Legal Campaign Against Segregated Education, 1925–1950* (Chapel Hill, 1988); idem, *Making Civil Rights Law: Thurgood Marshall and the Supreme Court, 1936–1961* (New York, 1994); Robert L. Zangrando, *The NAACP Crusade Against Lynching, 1909–1950* (Philadelphia, 1980); Richard C. Cortner, *A Mob Intent on Death: The NAACP and the Arkansas Riot Cases* (Middletown, CT, 1988); Kenneth W. Goings, *The NAACP Comes of Age: The Defeat of Judge*

Themes and Periods

John J. Parker (Bloomington, 1990); Michael L. Gillette, "The Rise of the NAACP in Texas, 1937–1957," Ph.D. diss., University of Texas at Austin, 1984; Fairclough, *Race and Democracy*; John Kirk, *Race, Community, and Crisis* (Gainesville, FL, forthcoming); Steven Tuck, *Beyond Atlanta: The Struggle for Racial Equality in Georgia, 1940–1980* (Athens, GA, 2001).

11. Honey, *Southern Labor and Black Civil Rights*, p. 7.
12. Levenstein, *Communism, Anticommunism, and the CIO*, p. 159; Ottanelli, *The Communist Party of the United States*, pp. 198–210; Fredrickson, *Black Liberation*, pp. 218–19; Rosswurm, "Introduction," in Rosswurm, ed., *The CIO's Left-Led Unions*, p. 10. For a contrary view, see Michael Torigian, "National Unity on the Waterfront: Communist Politics and the ILWU During the Second World War," *Labor History*, 30 (Summer 1989): 424–5, 431–2.
13. Timothy B. Tyson, *Radio Free Dixie: Robert F. Williams and the Roots of Black Power* (Chapel Hill, 1999).
14. Brenda Gayle Plummer, *Rising Wind: Black Americans and U.S. Foreign Affairs, 1935–1960* (Chapel Hill, 1996), pp. 167–214; Penny M. Von Eschen, *Race Against Empire: Black Americans and Anticolonialism, 1937–1957* (Ithaca, 1997); Martin B. Duberman, *Paul Robeson* (New York, 1988); Mary L. Dudziak, "Josephine Baker, Racial Protest, and the Cold War," *Journal of American History*, 81 (1994): 543–65; Kenneth R. Janken, "From Colonial Liberation to Cold War Liberalism: Walter White, the NAACP, and Foreign Affairs," *Ethnic and Racial Studies*, 21 (1998): 1074–95.
15. Fredrickson, *Black Liberation*, p. 182; Mary L. Dudziak, "Desegregation as a Cold War Imperative," *Stanford Law Review*, 41 (1988): 61–120; idem, *Cold War Civil Rights: Race and the Image of American Democracy* (Princeton, 2000); Nelson, "Organized Labor and the Struggle for Black Equality in Mobile During World War II," p. 988.
16. Desmond King, *Separate and Unequal: Black Employment in the Federal Government* (Oxford, 1995).
17. E. D. Cronon, *Black Moses: The Story of Marcus Garvey and the Universal Negro Improvement Association* (Madison, 1955).
18. Theodore G. Vincent, *Black Power and the Garvey Movement* (Berkeley, 1971); Tony Martin, *Race First: The Ideological and Organizational Struggles of Marcus Garvey and the Universal Negro Improvement Association* (Westport, 1976); Randall K. Burkett, *Garveyism as a Religious Movement: The Institutionalization of a Black Civil Religion* (Metuchen, NJ, 1978); Judith Stein, *The World*

of Marcus Garvey: Race and Class in Modern Society (Baton Rouge, 1986); Winston James, *Holding Aloft the Banner of Ethiopia: Caribbean Radicalism in Early Twentieth-Century America* (London, 1998).

19. James, *Holding Aloft the Banner of Ethiopia*, p. 187.
20. Eugene D. Genovese, *Roll, Jordan, Roll: The World the Slaves Made* (New York, 1974).
21. William H. Chafe, "'The Gods Bring Threads to Webs Begun,'" *Journal of American History* 86 (2000): 1532.
22. Gunnar Myrdal, *An American Dilemma: The Negro Problem and Modern Democracy*, 2 vols. (New York, 1944), vol. 2, p. 881; Henry Allen Bullock, *A History of Negro Education in the South: From 1619 to the Present* (Cambridge, MA, 1967), pp. vii–ix; James L. Leloudis, *Schooling the New South: Pedagogy, Self, and Society in North Carolina, 1880–1920* (Chapel Hill, 1996), p. 228; Diane Ravitch, *The Revisionists Revised: A Critique of the Radical Attack on the Schools* (New York, 1978), p. 67.
23. Louis R. Harlan, *Booker T. Washington: The Making of a Black Leader, 1856–1901* (New York, 1972); *Booker T. Washington: The Wizard of Tuskegee, 1901–1915* (New York, 1983); Donald Spivey, *Schooling for the Industrial Slavery: Black Industrial Education, 1868–1915* (Westport, 1978); John H. Haley, *Charles N. Hunter and Race Relations in North Carolina* (Chapel Hill, 1987); Leon F. Litwack, *Trouble in Mind: Black Southerners in the Age of Jim Crow* (New York, 1998); J. Morgan Kousser, "Progressivism – For Middle-Class Whites Only: North Carolina Education, 1880–1910," *Journal of Southern History*, 46 (1980): 190.
24. Idus A. Newby, *Black Carolinians: A History of Blacks in South Carolina from 1865 to 1968* (Columbia, SC, 1973), pp. 82–94, 102–11, 258–73; John Dittmer, *Local People: The Struggle for Civil Rights in Mississippi* (Urbana, 1994), p. 75.
25. Glenn T. Eskew, *But for Birmingham: The Local and National Movements in the Civil Rights Struggle* (Chapel Hill, 1997).
26. Litwack, *Trouble in Mind*; Jacqueline Goggin, *Carter G. Woodson: A Life in Black History* (Baton Rouge, 1993); Virginia L. Denton, *Booker T. Washington and the Adult Education Movement* (Gainesville, 1993); Gerald L. Smith, *A Black Educator in the Segregated South: Kentucky's Rufus B. Atwood* (Lexington, 1994); Richard Robbins, *Sidelines Activist: Charles S. Johnson and the Struggle for Civil Rights* (Jackson, MS, 1996); Leroy Davis, *A Clashing of the Soul: John Hope and the Dilemma of African American Leadership*

and Black Higher Education in the Early Twentieth Century (Athens, GA, 1998); Adam Fairclough, *Teaching Equality: Black Schools in the Age of Jim Crow* (Athens, GA, 2000).

27. Jacqueline A. Rouse, *Lugenia Burns Hope: Southern Reformer* (Athens, GA, 1989); Cynthia Neverdon-Morton, *Afro-American Women of the South and the Advancement of the Race, 1895–1925* (Knoxville, 1989); Dorothy Salem, *To Better Our World: Black Women in Organized Reform, 1890–1920* (Brooklyn, 1990); Susan L. Smith, *Sick and Tired of Being Sick and Tired* (Philadelphia, 1995); Evelyn Brooks-Higginbotham; *Righteous Discontent: The Women's Movement in the Black Baptist Church, 1880–1920* (Boston, 1993); Stephanie Shaw, *What a Woman Ought to Be and to Do: Black Professional Women Workers During the Jim Crow Era* (Chicago, 1996); Deborah Gray White, *Too Heavy a Load: Black Women in Defense of Themselves, 1894–1994* (New York, 1999); Charles W. Wadelington and Richard F. Knapp, *Charlotte Hawkins Brown and Palmer Memorial Institute: What One Young African American Woman Could Do* (Chapel Hill, 1999).

28. Glenda E. Gilmore, *Gender and Jim Crow: Women and the Politics of White Supremacy in North Carolina, 1896–1920* (Chapel Hill, 1996).

29. Chafe, "'The Gods Bring Threads to Webs Begun,'" p. 1532, note 2; Kevin K. Gaines, *Uplifting the Race: Black Leadership, Politics, and Culture in the Twentieth Century* (Chapel Hill, 1996), p. 4; White, *Too Heavy a Load*, pp. 70–7, 106–9; Jo Ann Gibson Robinson, *The Montgomery Bus Boycott and the Women Who Started It: The Memoir of Jo Ann Gibson Robinson*, edited by David J. Garrow (Knoxville, 1987); Charles M. Payne, *I've Got the Light of Freedom: The Organizing Tradition and the Mississippi Freedom Struggle* (Berkeley, 1995), pp. 265–83.

30. Clayborne Carson, Ralph E. Luker, Penny A. Russell, eds., *The Papers of Martin Luther King, Jr.* (4 vols., Berkeley, 1992); Keith D. Miller, *Voice of Deliverance: The Language of Martin Luther King, Jr. and its Sources* (New York, 1992); Dittmer, *Local People*; Fairclough, *Race and Democracy*; Payne, *I've Got the Light of Freedom;* Glenda Alice Rabby, *The Pain and the Promise: The Struggle for Civil Rights in Tallahassee, Florida* (Athens, GA, 1999); Andrew M. Manis, *A Fire You Can't Put Out: The Civil Rights Life of Birmingham's Reverend Fred Shuttlesworth* (Tuscaloosa, 1999); Brian Ward, *Just My Soul Responding: Rhythm and Blues, Race Relations, and the Civil Rights Movement* (London, 1998); Timothy J. Minchin, *Hiring*

the Black Worker: The Racial Integration of the Southern Textile Industry, 1960–1980 (Chapel Hill, 1999); Bruce Perry, *Malcolm: The Life of a Man Who Changed Black America* (Barrytown, NY, 1991); Claude Andrew Gregg III, *An Original Man: The Life and Times of Elijah Muhammad* (New York, 1998); Gerald Horne, *Fire This Time: The Watts Uprising and the 1960s* (New York, 1997); Hugh Pearson, *Shadow of the Panther: Huey Newton and the Price of Black Power in America* (Reading, MA, 1994), pp. 314–15; William Van Deburg, *New Day in Babylon: The Black Power Movement and American Culture* (Chicago, 1992).

31. Gail W. O'Brien, *The Color of the Law: Race, Violence, and Justice in the Post-World War II South* (Chapel Hill, 1999); Tyson, *Radio Free Dixie*.

32. Liva Baker, *The Second Battle of New Orleans: The Hundred-Year Struggle to Integrate the Schools* (New York, 1996); William Henry Kellar, *Make Haste Slowly: Moderates, Conservatives, and School Desegregation in Houston* (College Station, TX, 1999); Numan V. Bartley, *The New South, 1945–1980* (Baton Rouge, 1995), pp. 422–3; Vanessa Siddle Walker, *Their Highest Potential: An African American School Community in the Deep South* (Chapel Hill, 1996); David Cecelski, *Along Freedom Road: Hyde County, North Carolina, and the Fate of the Black Schools in the South* (Chapel Hill, 1994), pp. 173–4; Tom Dent, *Southern Journey: A Return to the Civil Rights Movement* (New York, 1997), p. 326.

33. Harvard Sitkoff, "African American Militancy in the World War II South," in *Remaking Dixie: The Impact of World War II on the American South* (Oxford, MS, 1997), pp. 70–95; Barbara Dianne Savage, *Broadcasting Freedom: Radio, War, and the Politics of Race, 1938–1948* (Chapel Hill, 1999); Richard H. King, *Civil Rights and the Idea of Freedom* (New York, 1991).

Part II
Fields

8

Industrial History: The State of the Art
Howell John Harris

It might as well be admitted, right at the outset, that this is the record of a fool's errand. The search for "industrial history" as defined, in particular, by Philip Scranton[1] – an approach to writing the history of industrial societies that ignores the normal academic division of labor and transcends artificial disciplinary boundaries – seems destined at present to result in disappointment. There are few enough book-length monographs reflecting a readiness on the part of historians of business, the economy, labor, and technology to make the effort to read one another's work and dabble in one another's pools; and there is even less evidence of inter- or multi-disciplinarity in the places surveyed here, because this is a review of the *periodical* literature dealing with the history of American industrial society to have been published in the last decade of the twentieth century.[2]

There are five principal reasons why such a review is a potentially worthwhile exercise, contributing to our ability to map this portion of the changing scholarly universe:

1. Periodicals are where we can expect to see the emergent future of the discipline(s) concerned. Newly-minted PhDs and aspiring younger scholars are over-represented, churning out articles to fill the hungry gap until they succeed in producing their first books and gaining a job or tenure. So the surveyor of the journal literature may hope to bring a message back from the frontier of knowledge, reporting on promising leads, dead ends, paths that simply lead around in circles, and other perils.

2. Periodicals, like conferences, are also where much of the public discourse of the specialized academic field is carried on. Accordingly, journals are where one is likely to find speculative work – ruminations on the state and direction of the field – suitable for informing a review such as this.

3. The journal literature, in these as in other research fields, is a neglected scholarly resource. The results of citation surveys often seem to

indicate that most articles in history periodicals cannot be proved to have been read by anybody, apart perhaps from their authors, because they are hardly ever referred to in any subsequent work. This is, perhaps, in some cases, a pity. Journal subscriptions represent a considerable fraction of any academic library's acquisition budget. It may be helpful for readers – it has certainly been useful for this reviewer – to discover what these increasingly expensive periodicals contain.

4. A journal literature survey also offers the possibility of producing a modestly *quantitative* report on content, as well as some qualitative judgment, whereas a review based on published books would inevitably be biased by considerations of local availability and personal familiarity, as well as individual assessments of quality and importance. This is not to claim that the conclusions of the following literature review are in any sense *objective*; but at least they rest on reasonably solid foundations.

5. The basic raw material for such a literature survey is more readily available now than it has ever been, given that one can acquire bibliographic detail so easily from online sources. PC database software permitting its storage and analysis also makes the reviewer's classificatory task more straightforward. However, eventually, one also has to *read* the individual items, both in order to be able to categorize them correctly and to understand their arguments. To make this task manageable, arguable decisions about selection and exclusion had to be made, and the degree of attention devoted to individual articles had to be adjusted in the light of their apparent character and significance, with some read very carefully, many quickly filleted, and others simply skimmed.[3]

What do historians of American industrial society actually write about nowadays? The answers to this question are in some ways surprising, but generally quite predictable.

First of all, on what time-periods do they concentrate their attention?

The procedure employed in producing the chart in Figure 8.1 – and the other figures and tables in this chapter – was straightforward but less than 100 percent reliable. Findings should, therefore, be taken to be indicative rather than definitive. In this case, start and end dates for every article which dealt with an identifiable period of history, rather than a theme which could not conveniently be periodized, were derived from an examination of every item. The unit of measurement in the resulting spreadsheet is the "article-decade," i.e. an article dealing with the period 1890–1914 would turn into a row (record) with values of one in the

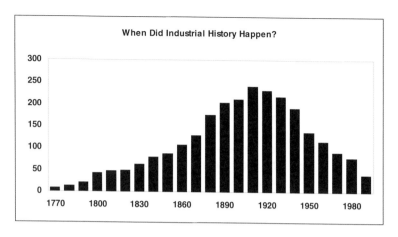

Figure 8.1. When did industrial history happen?

columns (fields) for the 1890s, 1900s, and 1910s. Figure 8.1 summarizes the results, totalling the values column by column (decade by decade).

The picture offered is unsurprising: less than 2 percent of the coverage of the journal literature in industrial history through the 1990s, as defined and surveyed here, has concerned itself with the colonial period, which has accordingly been dropped off the chart. Industrial historians continue to be preoccupied with the classic years of high industrialism, and particularly of the "second industrial revolution."

Labor historians, less than 3 percent of whose outputs concern themselves even marginally with any period before 1800, seem likely to be notably resistant to Christopher Tomlins's recent plea that they should abandon their blinkers and immerse themselves in the study of the colonial and early national periods from a social and cultural-historical perspective. This, according to Tomlins, would be one answer to the intellectual crisis of labor history – a way of reconnecting with the community of academic historians who find it so easy to ignore the hoary old stuff we keep churning out. But most practitioners seem to have concluded, along with David Montgomery, that "The definitive subject of labor history is the making of a social class dependent on wages for its livelihood and the impact exerted by men and women from that class on social and political change" and that, in an American context, one might as well delay the start of one's investigations until the thing one wished to investigate could be said for sure to have existed.[5]

Furthermore, labor history also seems to have been comparatively negligent in its attempts to come to terms with the relatively recent past.

As Daniel Nelson has suggested, the open frontier for historical research in labor and working-class history is the post-World War II period, but few among either the institutional or the more socio-culturally inclined scholars who still profess and call themselves labor historians seem to possess the interest or the conceptual apparatus required to interpret the period.[6] Business and economic historians, and historians of technology, are much better equipped in these respects, and far more attentive to the recent past. They have no disappointments they cannot cope with, not even the collapse of traditional industries in the 1970s and 1980s, which is all grist for their mills, and their main themes – the competitive struggle, entrepreneurship, growth, innovation, state regulation, bureaucratization, and structural change – do not appear to have lost their utility. Business historians, in particular, seem to be in the process of constructing the fragments of a history of the postwar American corporate economy upon which a new synthesis might soon be erected, modifying and extending Alfred Chandler's classic interpretation of the earlier period, which has often been critiqued, but never displaced.[7]

Secondly, where did industrial history happen? There are at least two possible answers to this question. One, the less significant, locates historical experience in *space*. The second attempts to fit the subjects of scholarly production within the confines of the federal government's Standard Industrial Classification (SIC) system, operating at the two-digit level.[8] There are no more surprises when we examine the spatial location of industrial history than there are with its conventional periodization. Industrial history is still, for the most part, given the realities with which it deals and the time-period on which it chooses to concentrate, a study of the old industrial belt.[9] Much of the journal literature has no particular geographical focus – its frame of reference is the nation or the industry. But that minority of journal articles which either does explicitly possess such a focus, or does so implicitly, because of the geographical concentration of its chosen industry, allows us to offer the following description of where industrial history is taken to have happened, using standard census regions.

Much of the journal literature deals with themes having no focus on any particular industry, and some (*c.* 14 percent) of that which actually does so also deals with more than one at a time.[10] In the original dataset, up to three industries rating significant coverage in an article are recorded but, in the interests of speed and simplicity, in Tables 8.2 and 8.3 articles dealing with more than one industry are classified according to the one with the lowest two-digit SIC number among those they include. Most of the second- and third-placed industries concealed by this procedure are, in fact, other examples of frequently-occurring industries shown

Table 8.1 Where Did Industrial History Happen: Regional Location

Region	Proportion
New England	13%
Mid-Atlantic	32%
East North Central	21%
West North Central	3%
South Atlantic	11%
East South Central	5%
West South Central	3%
Mountain	4%
Pacific	8%

elsewhere in the table – e.g. articles on industrial research in the iron and steel industries on behalf of the railroads are classed here under primary metals, SIC code 33, rather than railroad transportation, code 40.[11]

Table 8.2 reflects rather inaccurately the sectoral distribution of employment, investment, and output across the American economy, particularly in those decades of classic industrialism on which historians concentrate. It is, instead, a picture of the patterns of attention and neglect characterizing industrial historiography. The "heavy hitters" are all the usual suspects – the first industrial revolution's old familiars (particularly textiles and railroads); the "Chandler industries" of the second industrial revolution (iron and steel, electrical equipment, food and drink [particularly meat packing], telephones [especially AT&T, a sub-field in its own right], chemicals [particularly DuPont], and, of course, automobiles); and, finally, overlapping with the above, the heavily unionized, sometimes conflict-ridden industries beloved of labor historians – including coal and metal-mining, and the garment trade.

What is ignored is at least as significant as what is included. If we examine summary table 8.3, what is most notable is the stunning neglect of broad swathes of the U.S. labor force and economy.

Financial services owe their semi-respectable ranking primarily to the economic historians, for whom the banking sector represents an important source of conveniently quantitative data and also raises interesting questions to do with the functioning of the monetary system. Business and labor historians, in contrast, have given scant attention either to the institutional functioning of banks, insurance companies, and other intermediaries, or to the social relations of production and consumption within these long-established, large-scale industries. The enormous, amorphous, always dynamic, and now dominant service sector also,

Fields

Table 8.2 Where Did Industrial History Happen: Industrial Location

Industry	SIC Code	% Total	Cumulative
Transportation Equipment (esp. Autos)	37	12.0%	
Primary Metals (esp. Iron & Steel)	33	5.8%	18%
Railroad Transportation	40	5.8%	24%
Electronic & Other Electric Equipment	36	5.5%	29%
Banks (Depository Institutions)	60	5.5%	35%
Textile Mill Products	22	4.6%	39%
Food & Kindred Products (incl. Drink)	20	4.3%	44%
Communications (esp. Telephones)	48	3.6%	47%
Chemicals & Allied Products	28	3.4%	51%
Industrial Machinery & Equipment	35	3.1%	54%
Electricity, Gas, & Sanitary Services (esp. electrical power)	49	2.9%	57%
Coal Mining	12	2.4%	59%
Motion Pictures	78	2.4%	61%
Printing & Publishing	27	2.2%	64%
Instruments & Related Products	38	2.2%	66%
Metal Mining	10	1.9%	68%
Apparel & Other Textile Products	23	1.9%	70%

Table 8.3 Where Did Industrial History Happen: Sectoral Location

Sector	SIC Codes	%
Manufacturing	20–39	51%
Transportation & Public Utilities	40–49	18%
Services	70–89	12%
Financial Services	60–67	9%
Mining	10–14	5%
Construction	15–17	2%
Distribution (Wholesale & Retail Trade)	52–59	2%

surely, offers a huge field for exploration, given that one of the purposes of historical research ought to be the explanation of how we got to here from there. As for the distribution sector – which must always have contributed America's largest number of separate business units (agriculture, perhaps, excepted, depending on whether one classifies it among "industries" for present purposes), and whose importance in understanding the development of both the original "culture of enterprise" and the later "culture of consumption" is vast – there the neglect is near-total.[12] Finally, the construction industry – always one of America's major employers, as well as the enduring core of its labor movement – has suffered a threefold indifference. Its business units are too numerous, small, apparently simple, and ill-recorded to have attracted business historians; its methods too unchanging to interest historians of technology; its workers and their unions too "conservative" and, now, just too male and too pale to draw labor historians, whose oversight, while easy to explain, is hardest to condone.

In sum, what the journal literature seems to show is that, however much some scholars may write about, or appear to be under the influence of, "post-industrialism" when they produce programmatic articles about where we are and where we should be going, the fact is that when they select subjects for research most of them are still firmly beholden to an old agenda. Industrial history remains, for the most part, a study of employers and workers in mid-sized or unusually large firms across an incomplete cross-section of the economy. Its focus is on production, and on traditional primary and secondary, extractive and manufacturing, sectors. Its chronological scope is needlessly limited, its geographical coverage increasingly out of kilter with the postwar distribution of the American population and economic activity. These deficiencies have been recognized for years, but less seems to be being done to redress them than one might have expected.

Finally, who are the industrial historians now? The original dataset attempted to describe authors according to their rank within the academic profession (or the fact of their outsiderness) and their institutional affiliation (if any). However, these prosopographical data were only inconsistently and incompletely recorded in the journals surveyed, so that the only dimension along which all authors could easily be measured was that of gender. But as this is what really counts most in terms of the intellectual politics of industrial history's sub-fields, the difficulty of describing authors in terms of their career stage, and of identifying existing and emerging centers of scholarship, while it remains a potentially interesting project, probably does not result in too serious an omission.

The results of a simple gender analysis are unsurprising: in all four sub-fields, women scholars now make up between 21 and 24 per cent of authors. Analysis in terms of rank as well as gender would probably confirm the general impression that none of these sub-fields will long remain the male domains they used to be, within living memory.

Economic history is the least, and labor history, by a very short head, the most "feminized" discipline. This is no more than one might expect, given that the cliometric revolution of the 1960s and 1970s, among its other baleful consequences, marginalized established women scholars and the kind of economic history they wrote; and that, according to the archivist at the premier research center for labor and working-class history, the Walter Reuther Library at Wayne State, her user population changed its gender balance, if not its complexion, within approximately the last two decades of the twentieth century, from only 10 percent to almost 50 percent female.[13]

As their gender composition, their members' research interests, and the larger world of academic history around them change, most of the journals in all of these sub-fields have felt compelled to confront the "woman question," more often by commissioning notable female scholars to write programmatic articles about the transformative potential of the adoption of a gender agenda, than by printing the results of so doing, which still do not seem to be particularly numerous.[14] But only labor history seems to be being torn apart by increasingly rancorous arguments about this issue, which proceed on several levels at the same time – from the private and somewhat contradictory complaints of male graduate students that "there aren't any jobs in labor history, and they're all going to women," to the more public fights pitting advocates of the ascendant culturalist, gender-race analysis against what Robin Kelley disparages as the "neo-Enlightenment, white boy Left," who complain that issues of class, institution-building, and power are in danger of being marginalized.[15]

Labor history, altogether, presents the sorriest spectacle among industrial history's sub-fields. Ever since the emergence of the "New Labor History" in the 1960s and 1970s, labor historians have been given to navel-gazing about where, if anywhere, their field is going, what it is for and about, and indeed whether it really exists any longer, given its fissiparous tendencies. The rather dispiriting conclusion from reading the work of the 1990s reflected in the principal U.S. journals is that, as the volume of such discussion increased, the amount and quality of new research declined, to a point where the field cannot be said to compare with the rest of industrial history in terms of its intellectual vitality or simple scholarly quality.

How is this to be explained? In part, certainly, it is a reflection of the economics of scholarly production and consumption. The scholars who established the New Labor History are dead, retired, or close to retirement, and there are no signs that they have been, or are going to be, replaced with authors of similar standard. Numbers of subscribers to leading journals, and predictable monograph sales for established publication series, have fallen sharply. Price increases for institutional purchasers can only go some way toward maintaining channels for the declining output, and this market strategy is probably, in the long run, self-defeating. At the same time, among this embattled scholarly "community," which probably deserves the term less than any of the others considered here (given, for example, that participants in the founding meeting of the new Labor and Working-Class History Association were described, by one of them, as "rather grim," and the readiness of labor historians, *still*, to jump at one another's throats over a range of past squabbles, dead for thirty to a hundred years, is remarkable, helping to generate H-LABOR's distinctive tone), notions of what constitutes significant or even acceptable work have dissolved; yet still the journals' pages must be filled.[17] The result has been an increase in the proportion of editorially-generated matter (scholarly controversies, review symposia, review articles, and plain old book reviews) as the number and value of proper research articles have declined. For example, *Labor History* managed to recruit and publish about twice as many articles at the end of the 1980s as a decade later, and the quality declined from the occasionally terrific to the awfully mundane; *ILWCH* has always been more dependent on commissioned material, but its editorial board seems equally hard-pressed to maintain its gatekeeper function.

Labor history's problems are many. At the heart of them may be the contrast between many labor and working-class historians' delusions that their "scholarship" is a form of – or, in the harsh and indifferent American environment, a substitute for – political commitment, and the fact that neither the past, the present, nor the future of the American labor movement and working class (or classes) seem to be graspable within their nets. As Bruce Levine put it, "Those waiting for organized labor to stand up on its hind legs and fight back grow disappointed and disoriented."[18]

We are witnessing the existential crisis of a scholarly community, many of whose members appear to have been drawn towards the job in search of a usable past as a by-product of their alienation from the observable present and attachment to a variety of more or less utopian visions of the future.[19] This is not necessarily a recipe for the production of good history; and yet, as these internal exiles have encountered waves of real-life failure, all they have been left with is the profession of academic history as a point of reference. Attempts continue to reconnect labor and working-class history with activist communities beyond the academy, but the communities which seem to be most available and attractive are often identity-based themselves, not class or occupational, exacerbating the tendencies within labor history to lose touch with its old core concerns. The academic history whose respect many labor historians seem to crave is an identity-based community of its own, in which matters of discourse, gender, race, and culture are where they think the professional action is. Winning what still calls itself labor history an audience within this post-industrial profession, and those allies necessary to ensure a sense of intellectual respectability if not relevance, and victories in the micro-political battles that matter – for jobs, panels at important conferences, favorable book reviews for work which is, charitably, second-rate – seem to be priorities.

Meanwhile, there is an awful lot of good history about work and the working classes in American industrial society that is not getting written. And the prospects of improvement are not bright. For, as Judith Stein recently observed, "The problem of many historiographical responses to the era of Reagan and Thatcher is that as they dispose of the notion of a working class, the capitalist class vanishes with it . . . In an era when there has been a massive reorganization and deployment of capital, historians should take notice . . . The problem of social history may not be its alleged privileging of the working class, but its disinterest in the history of capitalism."[20] Left academics in the United States, a notoriously marginal social group, appear to be dealing with the problems of power and powerlessness – their own and their subjects' – by ignoring them.

It is a relief to turn away from the contemplation of labor history towards disciplines which seem more stable and healthy. Business, economic, and technological history all have a much sounder institutional base and intellectual framework than labor history, with lively and well-attended conferences and well-established scholarly associations enjoying a genuinely international membership.[21] They sustain a range of fine journals which show no sign of any fall-off in volume of submissions, nor any decline in the standards of what is published, nor loss of confidence and direction; indeed, *Business and Economic History* has just been relaunched as *Enterprise and Society*, with Oxford University Press's muscle behind it and more issues per year. They also have one another to read and talk to, though they admit that they do not do this as much as they might. But they all suffer those occasional jitters which are probably endemic in specialized subfields of enquiry which are marginal to the larger community of professional historians which they seem to think exists somewhere they are not.

Historians of technology have weathered their own culture wars in the 1970s and early 1980s, and now enjoy a broad methodological agreement in favor of contextualist over internalist scholarship, but still wonder whether what they do really matters to anybody else.[22] Like most specialists or enthusiasts, they think – even "know" – that it should, particularly because that is one of aims and anticipated benefits of the contextualist approach, which sets out to "integrate a technology's design characteristics with the complexities of its historical ambience." But it appears not to. The indifference of the broader historical profession's flagship journals to the history of technology – as, indeed, to most of industrial history's subfields, labor history partially excepted – is near-total.[23]

Economic historians have absorbed the cliometric revolution of a generation ago, and now take its methods and procedures for granted. They know that economists respect their competence and usefulness – good economic history is even published in the major economics journals. But they worry that garden-variety historians do not read what they write, and they are certain – rightly, in my view – that American historiography is the poorer for this failure of vision.[24]

Business historians also complain that regular historians do not read what they write either.[25] For some, the answer to this problem, and to the perceived failings of the still dominant Chandlerian, institutionalist paradigm,[26] is to incorporate into business history some of the same intellectual apparatus and preoccupations as are to be found among social and cultural historians at large. But there seems little likelihood of as profound a disengagement among business historians, however revisionist, from empirical research and the material past as one can observe among labor and social historians. This is largely because business historians are not simply located in history departments – they come from business schools, economics departments, the world of consultancy, and indeed from business life itself; they remain attentive to a broad range of social science literatures; they are interested in everything from accountancy to technology; and they wish to understand the recent as well as the more remote past. They cannot afford to forget that "businesses are first and foremost economic units that make such decisions as how much of a good to produce, how to make it, and what to charge for it." Few practitioners, even those making the strongest case for the reshaping of the field so as to incorporate historical actors hitherto left out of business history's very male, very pale version of the past, seem to be in danger of so doing. And if they tried, their peers probably would not allow them to get away with it.[27]

Is all well, then, in the more grounded varieties of industrial history? Not entirely. Their common complaints about the lack of a wider audience, the lack of broader resonance, for their sub-field's work, are not entirely justified. Much published scholarship is indeed very narrow. In the history of technology, for example, if what one is contextualizing is the development of wind-power styles, one cannot expect a very broad readership. And much history of technology does appear to have been designed with anorak-appeal in mind. Merritt Roe Smith's success with *Harper's Ferry Armory and the New Technology*, in winning the 1977 Frederick Jackson Turner award of the Organization of American Historians, turns out to have been the swallow that did not make a summer. Business history is still sometimes accused, even by its dissident practitioners, of being too uncritical, even quietly celebratory, of corporate capitalism. Given the ideological and political orientation of so many American historians, their reluctance to hear its message is unsurprising, though still regrettable. It is possible, though not likely, that business history's belated and debated culturalist turn may do something to overcome its isolation. Finally, economic history's continuing neglect, particularly by labor historians, for whom its fervent empiricism might offer a needed antidote to their own growing flakiness, is partly deserved, on a tit-for-tat basis. Economic historians are still capable of producing what Harold C. Livesay memorably termed "quantitative voodoo and cookery" whose results merit, even more than the institutional business history at which he directed the charge, the accusation that their methodology has "acted much like a neutron bomb, wiping out the people while leaving the buildings intact."[28] In some cases, one should even fear for the buildings. For example, as long as economic historians are inclined to suggest, without appearing to have read the enormous institutional labor history literature, that the persistence of the twelve-hour day in steel resulted from the average worker's preferences, they are likely to be ignored, and deservedly so.[29] The thin bibliographies of many economic history articles are among their most striking features.

The weakness of this sort of caricature economic history – what Richard Sutch termed "a finger exercise, a bus driver's holiday, a painless third field for a theorist's vita" – is that, as the canny William Parker wrote, it sacrifices everything else – empirical content, broadly defined, policy and ethical implications – on the altar of a narrow if, to some, intellectually satisfying obsession with theory and method.[30] But this risk is well known, if not always avoided. We can agree with him that "[a] graduate training in academic economics, like instruction in the technique of classical ballet, sets the mind, like the limbs and muscles of the dancer, in the fixed patterns of individual rationality, and makes the effort to flow freely and imaginatively over the social scene always a bit clumsy and predictable." The task of industrial historians who lack the economic historians' narrow but powerful technical skill is to read what they write, to critique it where necessary, to use it where possible, and to encourage collaboration. This way, we might all – labor historians of a certain disposition, perhaps, aside – have a worthwhile future contribution to make to understanding and explaining the historical development of the world's most powerful capitalist society. For "[the] mind has two eyes; the one creates models, the other observes and recalls facts. Used together, they give us the miracle of depth perception." There is no need for us to remain, at best, one-eyed kings in the country of the blind.

Notes

1. Philip Scranton, *Figured Tapestry: Production, Markets, and Power in Philadelphia Textiles, 1885–1941* (New York, 1989), pp. 6–7.
2. For a rare fine example, see Kenneth Lipartito, "When Women Were Switches: Technology, Work, and Gender in the Telephone Industry, 1890–1920," *American Historical Review*, 99 (1993): 1074–1111.
3. Journals covered, 1990–: business history – *Business and Economic History, Business History, Business History Review*; economic history – *Explorations in Economic History, Journal of Economic History*; labor history – *International Labor and Working Class History, International Review of Social History, Labor History*; history of technology – *Technology and Culture*. These are all the premier journals in their respective fields, and certainly contain the greater part of the journal literature, including most that is significant. All except *Labor History* are international in their focus, but only their U.S.-oriented content is dealt with here. Altogether, more than a thousand items (mostly proper articles, but including major review articles, controversies and debates, and substantial notes and documents) have been gathered from these journals – roughly evenly distributed among the major sub-fields, which should minimize composition errors in the following account. There are some other titles – the *Journal of Interdisciplinary History, Journal of Social History*, and *Social Science History* in particular – with a good sprinkling of relevant material; and there are also, less frequently, substantive and review articles in the above fields to be found in mainline U.S. history periodicals. That is before one begins to consider the way in which the boundaries of what is, for example, definable as "labor history" have become so permeable that important articles are

as likely to appear in *Feminist Studies* or the *Journal of Policy History* as they are in labor history journals per se. The weakness of the job market for labor historians also compels aspirants to publish, if at all possible, outside their field, so as not to be typecast. Study of the "Annual Labor History Bibliography," which is one of *Labor History*'s most useful services to its field, indicates the breadth of publication outlets for the genre, and thus the limits of the survey reported here. Nevertheless, what is included is probably more significant than what's not.

4. Tomlins, "Why Wait for Industrialism? Work, Legal Culture, and the Example of Early America – An Historiographical Argument," *Labor History*, 40 (1999): 5–34. Business historians have also been summonsed to pay more attention to colonial and early national history – Edwin J. Perkins, "Banks and Brokers," *Bus. & Ec. His.*, 24:1 (1995): 1–8 at 3; see also his "The Entrepreneurial Spirit in Colonial America: The Foundations of Modern Business History," *Bus. H.R.*, 63 (1989): 160–86.

5. Montgomery, "Commentary and Response," *Labor History*, 40 (1999): 35–9 at 37.

6. Nelson, "Labor and Modern Industry: Better than Ever," *Labor History*, 40 (1999): 39–42.

7. David B. Sicilia, "Distant Proximity: Writing the History of American Business since 1945," *Bus. & Ec. His.*, 26 (1997): 266–81. The best sketch of the postwar period is by Chandler himself – "The Competitive Performance of U.S. Industrial Enterprises since the Second World War," *Bus. H. R.*, 68 (1994): 1–72.

8. See http://www.govtsales.com/sics/sicgroups.htm for a guide. The SIC system has two further levels of precision – codes extend to four digits – but for present purposes the two-digit level is sufficient.

9. See David Meyer, "Emergence of the American Manufacturing Belt: An Interpretation," *Journal of Historical Geography*, 9 (1983): 145–74 and Sukkoo Kim, "Expansion of Markets and the Geographic Distribution of Economic Activities: The Trend in U.S. Regional Manufacturing Structure, 1860–1987," *Quarterly Journal of Economics*, 110 (1995): 883–908.

10. One large industry – for most of the period America's largest – has been excluded from the following account: agriculture (SIC 01, 02, and 07). Together with forestry and fishing (SIC 08 and 09) this has almost as large a share of the journal literature as transportation equipment, because economic and, to a much lesser extent, labor historians pay it considerable attention. Public administration

(Government Services), SIC 91–97, a much smaller scholarly interest, has also been omitted. Inclusion of them would alter the proportions but not the rankings.

11. This procedure differed from that employed to produce the spatial distribution, where multiple counting was allowed for the *c*.16 percent of articles with some geographical focus which spanned two or more census regions.

12. Thomas K. McCraw draws attention to this neglect in "Ideas, Policies, and Outcomes in Business History," *Bus. & Ec. His.*, 19 (1990): 1–9 at 2.

13. Robert Whaples, "A Quantitative History of the Journal of Economic History and the Cliometric Revolution," *J. Ec. His.*, 51 (1991): 289–301 at 295; Margaret Raucher, "Documenting Labor for a New Generation of Scholars," *Labor History*, 38 (1997): 67–75 at 69.

14. Major articles include: Elizabeth Faue, "Gender and the Reconstruction of Labor History, An Introduction," *Labor History*, 34 (1993): 169–77; Leon Fink, "Culture's Last Stand? Gender and the Search for Synthesis in American Labor History," *Labor History*, 34 (1993): 178–89; Wendy Gamber, "Gendered Concerns: Thoughts on the History of Business and the History of Women," *Bus. & Ec. His.*, 23:1 (1994): 129–40 and "A Gendered Enterprise: Placing Nineteenth Century Businesswomen in History," *Bus. H. R*, 72 (1998): 188–218; Alice Kessler-Harris, "Treating the Male as 'Other': Re-defining the Parameters of Labor History," *Labor History*, 34 (1993): 190–204 and "Ideologies and Innovation: Gender Dimensions of Business History," *Bus. & Ec. His.*, 20 (1991): 45–51; Nina E. Lerman, Arwen Palmer Mohun, and Ruth Oldenziel, "'Versatile Tools': Gender Analysis and the History of Technology," *Tech. & Cult.*, 38 (1997): 1–8; Susan Ingalls Lewis, "Beyond Horatia Alger: Breaking through Gendered Assumptions about Business 'Success' in Mid-19th.-Century America," *Bus. & Ec. His.*, 24:1 (1995): 97–105; Kathy Peiss, "'Vital Industry' and Women's Ventures: Conceptualizing Gender in Twentieth Century Business History," *Bus. H. R.*, 72 (1998): 219–41; Sonya O. Rose, "Gender and Labor History: The nineteenth-century Legacy," *Int. Rev. Soc. His.*, 38 [Supp.] (1993): 145–62; and Joan W. Scott, "Conceptualizing Gender in American History," *Bus. H. R.*, 72 (1998): 242–9 (especially rewarding). Even the *Journal of Economic History* has begun to publish articles with a gender agenda, for example Elizabeth Field Hendrey, "The Role of Gender in Biased Technical Change: US Manufacturing, 1850–1919," *J. Ec. His.*, 58 (1998): 1090–1109, which argues (p. 1107)

that, as their occupational spheres were so separate, "men and women must be treated as separate inputs in production functions for manufacturing in the nineteenth and early twentieth centuries."

15. Private email communication (from a woman ABD at an elite Midwestern research university) at conclusion of H-LABOR online discussion, December 1999; Kelley cited in Charles Carlson, "Class in a Multicultural Age: Organization of American Historians Meeting," *ILWCH*, 53 (1998): 188–91 at 189. The lament of the institutionalists kicked off in the debate on Howard Kimeldorf's "Bringing Unions Back In (Or Why We Need a New Old Labor History)," *Labor History*, 32 (1991): 91–103; see, particularly, the responses by Alice Kessler-Harris and Bruce Nelson at 107–10 and 117–25, summarizing the gender, race, etc. cultural critique of neo-institutionalism. Ira Katznelson signalled a call for a different, more state-centered institutionalism, in his contribution to the *ILWCH* Roundtable, "What Next for Labor and Working-Class History?" – "The 'Bourgeois' Dimension: A Provocation About Institutions, Politics, and the Future of Labor History," *ILWCH*, 46 (1994): 7–32, for which he was taken severely to task by, among others, Liz Cohen – "Katznelson's Working Within the System Now": 33–6.

16. See Melvyn Dubofsky's splendidly dismissive discussion of one celebrated bout of introspection, the 1984 DeKalb conference – "Lost In a Fog: Labor Historians' Unrequited Search for a Synthesis," *Labor History*, 32 (1991): 295–300.

17. James R. Barrett, "A National Association for Working-Class History," *ILWCH*, 53 (1998): 191–4 at 194. For an awful indication of what we might have to look forward to, if tendencies toward postmodern playfulness were to be given their head, see the discussion on "The Great (Unwritten) Books in Labor History," reported in Kim Geiger, "1994 Social Science History Association," *ILWCH*, 48 (1995): 160–63.

18. "The History of Politics and the Politics of History," *ILWCH*, 46 (1994): 58–62 at 58.

19. See e.g. Elizabeth Faue, keynote address reported in Richard Skinner and Theresa Ann Case, "Southwest Labor Studies Association Conference," *ILWCH*, 55 (1999): 138–42 at 141–2.

20. Stein, "Where's the Beef?" *ILWCH*, 57 (Spring 2000): 40–7 at 41, 45, responding to Geoff Eley and Keith Nield, "Farewell to the Working Class?": 1–30.

21. The Labor and Working Class History Association, despite having received copious free publicity in scholarly journals and via the H-

LABOR internet discussion list, and despite its avowed openness to activists as well as scholars, has not yet managed to recruit more than half as many members as the Society for the History of Technology, a third as many members as the Business History Conference, or a sixth as many as the Economic History Association – Julie Greene to Andrew H. Lee, "Labor and Working Class History Association Update, July 2000" copied to H-LABOR list, 8 July 2000, archived at http://www2.h-net.msu.edu/; BHC and EHA figures from William J. Hausman, "Business History at the End of the Twentieth Century," unpublished conference address, 1999, notes 4, 5. On the other hand, it is early days for LAWCHA, and, unlike the scholarly associations, its recruitment is almost exclusively American rather than OECD-wide, but with a strong American bias.

22. John M. Staudenmaier, "Recent Trends in the History of Technology," *Am. Hist. Rev.*, 95 (1990): 715–25; Alex Roland, "What Hath Kranzberg Wrought? Or, Does the History of Technology Matter?" *Tech. & Cult.*, 38 (1997): 697–713; Robert Post, "Post Script," *SHOT Newsletter*, 80 (1998): 1.

23. Staudenmaier, "Recent Trends": 716. A search of the *American Historical Review* and *Journal of American History* for the 1990s throws up hardly any articles concerned with business, the economy, management, science, or technology. Labor and working-class history are much more likely, still, to win an audience among non-specialist historians, presumably because their culturalist (gender, ethnicity, and racial) agendas are more in tune with dominant intellectual fashions. The *AHR*'s readiness to print Kenneth Lipartito's "When Women Were Switches," one of the most admired, and boundary-crossing, pieces of industrial history published in the last decade of the twentieth century, and Staudenmaier's review article, was exceptional.

24. Richard Sutch, "All Things Reconsidered: The Life-Cycle Perspective and the Third Task of Economic History," *J. Ec. Hist.*, 51 (1991): 271–88 esp. 277–8. The "third task" in Sutch's title is to get historians to read economic history again. This really should be encouraged. The *Journal*'s editors have made a successful effort to require contributors to write clearly and to explain themselves. There is a wealth of readable, novel work on, for example, invention during the early nineteenth century industrial revolution, labor market behavior in the late nineteenth and early twentieth centuries, racial and other discrimination in urban-industrial labor markets, and the economics of depression and recovery in the 1930s and 1940s, to

which other industrial historians and even regular historians should pay attention.

25. The lament that "nobody loves us" seems to have been a staple of presidential addresses to the Business History Conference – see William Lazonick, "Business History and Economics," *Bus. & Ec. His.*, 20 (1991): 1–14 at 11–12; K. Austin Kerr, "Connections," 22:1 (1993): 1–6 at 2–3; Perkins, "Banks and Brokers": 6–7; William H. Becker, "Managerial Culture and the American Political Economy," 25:1 (1996): 1–7 at 4–5. Of all these, Becker's is the most open to the need for change, for which see also Philip Scranton and Roger Horowitz, "'The Future of Business History': An Introduction," 26:1 (1997): 1–4 (enthusiasts for culturalist approaches) and Ross Thomson, "Directions in Business History: Comments on Dissertations," 19 (1990): 29–34, Thomas J. Misa, "Toward an Historical Sociology of Business Culture," 25:1 (1996): 55–64 at 55–6, and Naomi Lamoreaux, Daniel M.G. Raff, and Peter Temin, "New Economic Approaches to the Study of Business History," 26:1 (1997): 57–79 at 57–61 (doubters advocating a broader variety of social-scientific methodologies alongside Chandler's structural-functionalism).

26. For a splendid review of Chandler's achievements and the limits of institutional business history, see Richard R. John, "Elaborations, Revisions, Dissents: Alfred D. Chandler, Jr.'s *The Visible Hand* after Twenty Years," *Bus. H. R.*, 71 (1997): 151–200.

27. Lamoreaux et al., "New Economic Approaches": 57. The problem for female and other scholars seeking to "incorporate women" into business history (see Angel Kwolek-Folland, *Incorporating Women: A History of Women and Business in the United States* [New York, 1998]) is not just a matter of the comparatively small numbers of female entrepreneurs and managers to be encountered in the past (and particularly in the periods business historians are in the habit of writing about), it is that they have clustered in sectors which business historians neglect in any case – notably retailing and personal services – and that, in terms of size, longevity, innovation, etc., their "firms" scarcely register on business history's normal Richter scale. Therefore, the only way to incorporate women that seems to promise the creation of something bigger than a female scholarly reservation is by altering the canons of significance normally employed. But, as Joan Scott recognized in "Conceptualizing Gender in American History," the effect of doing this might also be to guarantee continuing marginalization while aiming for inclusion. The risk, in other words, would be to define a "women's business history" that ordinary

business historians (including female academics who did not choose to practice it) would simply ignore.

28. "Entrepreneurial Dominance in Business Large and Small, Past and Present," *Bus. H.R.*, 63 (1989): 1–21 at 5.

29. Martha Ellen Shielis, "Collective Choice of Working Conditions: Hours in British and U.S. Iron and Steel, 1890–1923," *J. Ec. Hist.*, 50 (1990): 379–92. See also Kenneth A. Snowden, "Comments on Moehling, Siegler, and Wright," *J. Ec. Hist.*, 58 (1998): 548–52 at 548–9: Carolyn M. Moehling, author of "Work and Family: Inter-generational Support in American Families, 1880–1920," same issue: 535–7, was "a thoroughly modern applied labor economist. This is to say that she likes data – lots of data – and that she knows how to use it." But she was also capable of researching and writing about her topic with little regard for issues of immigration and ethnicity, which might be thought to have some significance for explaining variations in the behaviors in which she was interested.

30. Sutch, "The Third Task of Economic History": 275; William N. Parker, "The Scale and Scope of Alfred D. Chandler, Jr.," *J. Ec. Hist.*, 51 (1991): 958–63 at 961.

31. Parker, "A 'New' Business History? A Commentary on the 1993 Nobel Prize in Economics," *Bus. H.R.*, 67 (1993): 623–36 at 632, 636. (In case anyone has forgotten, the prize was awarded jointly to Douglass C. North and Robert Fogel, signifying the economics profession's seal of approval for a certain kind of econometric history.) It is perhaps indicative of a readiness among economic historians to engage in dialogue with the rest of us that two recent presidential addresses dealt with issues of culture and values – Peter Temin, "Is it Kosher to Talk about Culture?," *J. Ec. His.*, 57 (1997): 267–87 and Deirdre (formerly Donald – another welcome sign of economic historians' newfound flexibility) N. McCloskey, "Bourgeois Virtue and the History of P and S," *J. Ec. His.*, 58 (1998): 297–317.

–9–

Intellectual History, Democracy, and the Culture of Irony

James T. Kloppenberg

In today's world, cultures often rest on conventions. As the fanfare and fireworks announcing the birth of the year 2000 spread around the globe, from Asia to Europe to the Americas, historians could not help but think about an inconvenient fact all the revelers had agreed to overlook. Although there is little reliable evidence about the historical figure Jesus of Nazareth, we do know that he was born during the reign of Herod. Since we also know that Herod died in 4 BC, Jesus must have been born no later than 6 or 5 BC – perhaps the best reason for replacing the customary BC with the designation BCE (before the common era), which acknowledges the conventional rather than historical quality of the dates we have agreed to use. The error seems to have been made by the sixth-century monk Dionysius Exiguus (or, to use the name he preferred, "Dennis the Small"), who gave us the dating system formally adopted by the Synod of Whitby in 664 without knowing much about the history of Judea. As the world breathlessly approached January 1, 2000, I found that knowing we had already entered the twenty-first century five years earlier tended to dampen my enthusiasm about the millennial celebrations, whether they were to occur in 2000 or (as I and others who learned to count with 1 rather than with 0 thought more appropriate) 2001.

But I have changed my mind. What happened as December 31 gave way to January 1 made a lasting impression on me, as I gather it did on many people, although perhaps for rather different reasons depending on the nature of one's celebration. As my wife and I watched television on December 31, we were surprised to see what appeared to be a genuinely global celebration unfolding gradually from East Asia through the Middle East, then spreading from Central to Western Europe, as people from around the world, people from various religious traditions or with no religious affiliation, joined to acknowledge the end of one millennium and the beginning of another – even though in China it was the year 4698, for Zoroastrians 2390, for Muslims 1421, and for Jews 5761.

Why does it matter? The answer to that question relates directly to the theme of this chapter, the relation between intellectual history, democracy, and our contemporary culture of irony. It matters, not only because it is amusing that millions of Westerners actually missed the proper date for their own festivities, and by several years rather than a few days, but also because billions of people around the world, people from various cultural traditions that have little in common, agreed to celebrate a milestone that was perfectly arbitrary. The dating system that we follow is a convention, a construction, something made rather than found. Although no more than a cultural artifact deriving from a miscalculation made centuries ago by an obscure medieval monk, it stands as a symbol of our capacity to reach agreement about when days, years, and centuries should be understood to begin and end. Even though the majority of the world's people do not share the Christian faith that generated the dating system we all now follow, most of those people have decided to agree that, in addition to keeping track of time by their own systems of dating, they will acknowledge and abide by the rules of the conventional Western system simply so that people all over the world can agree on what time it is and what date it is. We take that agreement for granted. We should not: its significance deserves more than casual notice.

Skeptical readers may wonder whether I am claiming that such an obvious manifestation of Western hegemony has anything to with democracy or that such conventions emerge through anything resembling public debate. Of course not. But even if we admit that such conventional arrangements do not embody Truth (with a capital T) or the wisdom or superiority (rather than the historical power) of the West, if we admit that they are arbitrary (and even mistaken, given what we know about the birth of Jesus), we should nevertheless admit that the convention works: it keeps everybody on the same page of the calendar. It enables international commerce, travel, and academic conferences to proceed more or less on schedule. Finally, it contributes to the apparent shrinking of differences that is part of the phenomenon commonly called globalization. Globalization may not alter the culturally variable lived experience of temporality, but nevertheless lays across it a grid of conventional measurement that facilitates transcultural communication and cooperation.

Those preliminary observations about convention bring me to democracy. When the democratic form of government was consolidated for the first time in a modern nation state, when the principle of popular sovereignty became the rationale for the institutions of government and law in the United States in the late eighteenth century, they were justified by invocations of a timeless and universal set of natural laws, laws handed down by God to man and inscribed in reason and conscience. Since we no longer share that confidence, we now talk about popular sovereignty as a fiction, about democracy as a myth, and about the hegemony of an ideology that masks the ability of elites to rule the unwitting masses by waving words in front of their faces. We discuss the invisible workings of an alliance between power and knowledge to sustain disciplinary regimes that command obedience without anyone quite knowing how or why they do. We expose the arbitrariness of signifiers and explore the endless proliferations of meaning in texts. In our day we deal in unmaskings, in disclosure. We busy ourselves rubbing off the glitter that used to elicit reverence, reverence we replace with a hermeneutics of suspicion, a wide-ranging distrust of all claims to authority that culminates in ironic detachment if not cynicism.

In this chapter I want to advance three arguments, all of which depend on the awareness that we now inhabit a world governed by conventions, a culture of irony. First, I will argue that intellectual history is important in that culture of irony because it directs our attention to the questions of meaning that should now be central to our aims as historians. Second, I will argue that the idea of democracy, both as an ideal and as a cultural category, should become central to our thinking about American history, and I will contend that during the last decade it has been dissolving the standard categories of republicanism and liberalism, and those of race, class, and gender, through a more fluid and historically attuned way of understanding the American past. Third, I will briefly suggest that the comparative or transnational study of intellectual history in general and of democracy in particular might provide an especially promising approach that can yield valuable insights unavailable to those who view American history within a narrow national or subnational framework. By necessity, I will discuss these three topics, which move from particular questions of methodology to questions of global history, in decreasing detail. By choice, I will discuss them in expository modes ranging from analytical to hortatory to speculative.

In the first place, I contend, to highjack a phrase from an essay published as early as 1981 by the historian of early modern Europe William Bouwsma, that "we are all intellectual historians now."[1] Bouwsma was not proclaiming the triumph of Wilhelm Dilthey or Bendetto Croce, or of Arthur Lovejoy or Perry Miller (and neither am I). He was merely pointing to the importance that historians of all kinds – social, economic, political, and diplomatic historians; historians of race, regions, religion, gender, ethnicity, and labor – were beginning to place on understanding not only what happened in the past but what it *meant* to those we study and what it means to us. Because we now recognize the role that previously overlooked people have played in shaping their own history, we see them as agents who made choices rather than as pawns who were controlled by others or by a monolithic force called "history." If we want to take seriously the experience of the subaltern, we must pay attention not only to what was done to them but what they did themselves and why they did it. We must see the world as they saw it and understand why they made the choices they made. Our focus on meaning has emerged gradually, and irreversibly, I would argue, after the explosion of information that followed upon the expansion of historical inquiry in the 1960s and 1970s. That expansion has now transformed the study of history by introducing new questions and new approaches. Many of the contributors to this volume have contributed to that expansion and rethinking of historical study, and their chapters reflect that transformation.

But, once we have discovered the worlds we had lost or ignored, we want to understand the experience of those who inhabited those worlds, people formerly unknown or invisible to historians. Achieving that understanding involves interpreting various kinds of evidence, some of which are nonlinguistic, but much of which comes to us through textual records. Those records we try to decipher, decode, and interpret. Those traces of the past we must approach – self-consciously or not – using the standard procedures of intellectual history, the method of hermeneutics. We must move carefully, systematically, from considering the perspective of those we study to our own perspectives and then back again. We must probe meanings by moving constantly, repeatedly, from the part to the whole and back to the part, from the text to the context and back to the text, from the minutely particular to the more general and back to the particular, and from the past to the present and then back again to the past. This is a difficult and painstaking process, and the linguistic turn of recent critical theory and our contemporary sensitivity to multivalence and transgression have made it even more challenging. We must still study authors, texts, genres, contexts, and traditions with the care lavished on them by earlier practitioners of intellectual history inspired by Dilthey's hermeneutics, and we must be equally alert to the complex and changing patterns of reception and response that greeted their texts. Moreover, whereas literary critics or cultural theorists may be able to generate provocative and valuable "strong readings" without necessarily paying any attention whatsoever to the *historical* meanings of texts, the meanings that texts had for their authors and/or readers, historians have a different aim. Historians' imaginations must continue to be disciplined by rigorous analysis of the evidence we find of the meanings individual historical actors understood, whether those actors were central or peripheral, powerful or disinherited, rather than presenting the meanings we can tease out, engender, or impose through the unconstrained exercise of our own creative powers as readers.[2]

The study of meanings has transformed intellectual history as much as it has transformed other historical fields. The long-predicted crisis of intellectual history, a crisis being proclaimed in the direst of terms when I was beginning graduate study in 1974, at the height of enthusiasm for the new social history, has not occurred. Instead, we are witnessing an unprecedented explosion of work in intellectual history, understood broadly as the study of the history of meanings, even if many of those engaged in that work often designate themselves cultural historians rather than intellectual historians. In 1959, when one of the most prominent and widely admired practitioners of intellectual history, Merle Curti, published *The Making of an American Community: A Case Study of Democracy in a Frontier County*, he inaugurated a shift in the focus of intellectual historians that has continued to the present day. Curti probed not only the settlement patterns on the Wisconsin frontier but "the social creed" of its inhabitants, not only the demographics and economic and political institutions but the "shared experiences and shared decisions" of those transgressive men and women who created that liminal, border-land culture of hybridity. After Curti's explicit joining of quantitative and qualitative analysis, of intellectual and social history, neither intellectual history nor social history looked the same. The Organization of American Historians, as a well-deserved but perhaps ill-conceived tribute, began, a generation ago, to award a prize in Curti's name, in even-numbered years to a book in "intellectual history" and in odd-numbered years to a book in "social history." As authors, publishers, and prize-committee members know, it has become increasingly difficult to decide which books fit which category, a problem Curti himself never had to confront because his own work spanned the two artificially divided "fields." The same was true of the work of the many American historians trained by Curti or by Arthur M. Schlesinger, Sr., whose Harvard course "American Social and Intellectual History" provided the model for much of the teaching done in American universities from the 1930s through the 1970s.[3]

Despite common assumptions to the contrary, it is as rare now to find intellectual historians confining their analysis to the narrow explication of a few texts written by intellectuals, or treating the historical meanings of those texts as unproblematical, as it is to find social historians providing quantitative descriptions of the behavior of ordinary people without interpreting its meaning and significance. Intellectual historians now trace the movement of ideas and values across different domains, from religion to popular culture, from race to politics, from gender to the economy, as well as among those who made it their business to write books and scholarly articles. Intellectual history is currently merging with other fields ranging from the history of ethnicity to the history of law, from cultural studies to gender studies. Most scholars who call themselves intellectual historians do not examine disembodied "ideas" in isolation from the people and cultures that produced and disseminated, read and responded to historical texts. They look instead at the intersections between the writings of those who produced books or sermons and those who produced diaries, or spoke at public rallies, or sang songs, or marched in parades, or testified in revivals, or yelled at sporting events, or argued in court-rooms. What did these various activities *mean*? How should we *understand* what they did and what they said?

There is something odd about the disdain that some self-styled hard-nosed empiricists, whether they are social, economic, or political histor-ians, express toward what they think of as intellectual history. For all historians, whether we like it or not, are intellectuals. Taking ideas seriously, our own ideas and the ideas of others whose work we read, teach, criticize, and evaluate, is what we do for a living. What is unsatis-fying or disreputable about such activity? It is what we all do, whether the ideas we take seriously are ideas about the meaning of voting data or geographical mobility, ideas about how authority was exercised in the household, the field, or on the shop floor, or ideas advanced by writers who came before us. As the boundaries between specific fields become ever more permeable in the increasingly interdisciplinary academy of the twenty-first century, we all increasingly depend on each other's work to do our own. Our practice as historians, our own work as intellectuals, shows the folly of reifying distinctions between the fields we occupy.

Let me turn to specific cases to illustrate these general propositions. In 1998 and 1999 I was honored to serve as chair of the Organization of American Historians Curti Prize committee in intellectual history. Like all historians on such committees, I found myself drowning in a flood of books I wanted to read. Committee members read dozens of splendid books, and the dynamic I have been describing made our decision especially difficult. That experience convinced me Bouwsma was right: we are all intellectual historians now.

After lengthy debate, we awarded the prize to Rogers Smith, a scholar located in a Department of Political Science, who considers himself a specialist in constitutional law and political theory rather than intellectual history. Smith's splendid book *Civic Ideals: Conflicting Visions of Citizenship in U.S. History* uses the idea of "ascriptive Americanism" to explain our nation's recurrent reinscriptions of exclusionary hierarchies even after their repeated repudiation during the periods of the Revolution and Confederation, the Civil War and Reconstruction, and the Civil Rights Movement and the Great Society. Not only does *Civic Ideals* cross conventional boundaries between and within the disciplines of history, political science, and law, almost all the books our committee considered finalists were later awarded prizes by other committees of the OAH or the American Historical Association that were *not* supposed to be looking at intellectual history. I will mention only five of these books from many possibilities: Christine Heyrman's study of antebellum Southern evangelical religion, *Southern Cross*; Daniel Rodgers's study of European influences on American progressives, *Atlantic Crossings*; Amy Dru Stanley's study of the relation between contract theory, race, gender, and law in late nineteenth-century America, *From Bondage to Contract*; Matthew Jacobson's study of immigration and race, *Whiteness of a Different Color*; and Linda Kerber's study of the relation between rights and obligations in the circuitous journey American women have taken toward full citizenship, a fine book with the odd title *No Constitutional Right to Be Ladies*. Kerber's book, like the others I named, has won multiple prizes from different groups, including the Littleton-Griswold Prize in legal history from the American Historical Association, another committee I served on in 1998 and 1999. That committee, too, faced the daunting challenge of deciding what constitutes legal history now that the lines between law and culture have grown so faint, and several of the same books mentioned above were among the finalists for the award.[4]

In sum, my experiences on the Curti and Littleton-Griswold prize committees confirm my conviction that, even if we are not all intellectual historians now, many of us historians – including many of those who are writing histories winning prizes in the fields we somewhat arbitrarily designate social, political, and legal history – are doing work that falls as easily within the increasingly capacious boundaries of intellectual history as it does within other categories of historical scholarship.

Consider several recent studies of early American culture that demonstrate this tendency to blend various kinds of evidence into persuasive historical arguments. Stephen Innes's *Creating the Commonwealth: The Economic Culture of Puritan New England* is a careful analysis of

socio-economic history that demonstrates how inseparable the Puritans'
religious faith was from their attitudes toward productivity and profit.
Innes recovers but sharpens Max Weber's insights by combining astute
treatments of Puritan religious and ethical ideas with an equally incisive
and detailed treatment of the economic activity that brought unexpected
prosperity to New England. His analysis amplifies and confirms arguments
advanced by Christine Heyrman in her first book, *Commerce and Culture:
The Maritime Communities of Colonial Massachusetts, 1690–1750*,
another study that marries the close analysis of economic activity to an
equally careful rendering of the thought worlds of those early settlers
who managed to derive unexpected profits from the sea. Only by paying
close attention to the Puritans' thought and their behavior can we see the
futility of asking when or whether they should be understood as "precapitalist" or participants in the "market revolution," wooden categories that
blind us to their own complicated experience rather than illuminating it
for us.[5]

The study of American religion has likewise been transformed by
generations of scholars well-grounded in Puritan theology but more
interested than Perry Miller in connecting philosophical treatises and
sermons with lived religion. David D. Hall, whose book *Worlds of Wonder,
Days of Judgment: Popular Religious Belief in Early New England*
exemplifies this approach by combining intellectual and social history,
has recently argued that Puritanism should be seen as a "middle way," a
practice of negotiating conflicts on central issues in which there were
ambiguities in doctrine and persistent disagreements about practice. In
contrast to Miller, who sought to delineate precisely the doctrine of
Puritanism and then to demonstrate why the Puritans suffered from guilt
because of their failure to live up to their ideals, and in contrast to social
historians of the 1960s and 1970s, who judged Puritanism irrelevant
because of the gap between social life and Puritan ideals, Hall portrays
Puritanism as the unending process of negotiating the meaning in practical
terms of doctrines that might have been unchanging in principle but whose
application was often ambiguous. They were consequently, from the
beginning, "contested," "multilayered," and "fluid" – key words in this
new form of intellectual history. "This fluidity [in the play of meanings],"
Hall observes, "had much to do with the structures and differences in
everyday life, be these the difference between clergy and laity, men and
women, young and old, center and periphery. In acknowledging that
religious practices were socially mediated, we move from an essentialist
understanding of Puritanism to one that regards it as manifested in
practices that themselves were variously appropriated."[6]

Heyrman's study of antebellum Southern religion points, in much the same way, to the interplay between ideas and practice and the impossibility of understanding either dimension of life without the other. Among the pressing issues confronting students of early American culture are the following, none of which can be answered without a rigorous (and difficult) hermeneutical search for historical meanings: why did some Indians respond enthusiastically to the appeals of missionaries, whose complicity in the imperial projects of European powers seems to us transparent? Why did evangelical Christianity spread so rapidly across the American landscape from the mid-eighteenth to the mid-nineteenth century? What role did Christianization play in shaping the diverse cultures of African Americans, whether enslaved or free? Did blacks imagine freedom coming through revolt against slave masters, through the abolition of slavery, or through divine intervention? How did they envision their futures after slavery?[7]

The study of race and ethnicity has likewise moved beyond separate studies of theory and practice. Scholars such as Rogers Smith and Matthew Jacobson illuminate the constructed nature of racial and ethnic concepts, categories, and languages and also the very concrete work such social constructions have done in shaping and constricting the life experiences of those so artificially compartmentalized. Such topics might seem to lend themselves most easily to Foucaultian or Gramscian treatments focusing on the consequences of discursive or hegemonic power. Yet a growing number of scholars seems inclined to take seriously what Dirk Hoerder, himself a veteran quantifier concerned with explaining global migration systems, calls the "emotional/intellectual/spiritual life of the actors and interest groups" involved.[8]

One of the oldest and most distinguished fields of inquiry in intellectual history concerns the relation between social and political ideas and reform movements, a tradition to which Rodgers's *Atlantic Crossings*, like his earlier books *The Work Ethic in Industrial America* and *Contested Truths: Keywords in American History*, is a valuable addition. Given contemporary critical consensus about the ubiquity and invisibility of power and the desirability of transgressive eruptions, such once-familiar studies of political thought now require tortured accounts of the "political imaginary" to explain how those who were supposedly captured within all-encompassing discursive regimes managed to envision alternatives. Earlier historians and theorists, respecting the capacity of individuals to imagine worlds other than those they inhabited, took for granted this human capacity. Today, historians who respect their own capacity to subvert or denaturalize reigning paradigms can approach such inquiries with less difficulty than can some critical theorists. But given what we know about American politics, as well as political thought, earlier assumptions about an uncomplicated transmission of ideas from theorists to the political process now seem untenable. Once again, our analytical sophistication complicates the challenge facing historians of American public life. In a recent essay, Rodgers argues that we must understand both the visionary's imagination and the shrewdness of party bosses. He deploys an argument developed by the feminist theorist Nancy Fraser: "The successful meeting of social need and imaginable public solution is the intellectual precursor to legislation, and it has dynamics as critical to the political process as the end games of interest and party manoeuvre. As in the study of religion and economic behavior in early America, or the study of immigrants' aspirations and categories of ethnicity, we must integrate the analysis of political ideas with political activity in order to understand American history.

The final category I will briefly discuss is law and gender. Both Stanley's and Kerber's books range across the social history of gender roles, the transformative effects of economic developments, the force of diverse new liberatory ideologies, and the power of the law to maintain – and eventually to change – patterns of authority. Just as both of these books use insights from contemporary critical theory to broaden and deepen the study of legal history, so influential legal theorists, especially Cass Sunstein, Akhil Amar, and Joan Williams, are increasingly relying on historical insights and evidence to propel their reformist analyses of contemporary American law and society.[10] Intellectual history, as I have argued elsewhere, has become an increasingly important voice in contemporary critical debates, and Stanley's and Kerber's books promise to make equally valuable contributions.[11]

My second argument concerns the value of the idea of democracy for our study of history. It is an argument in two parts. The first concerns the appropriateness of democracy as a conceptual framework and as a normative standard in our contemporary culture. Democracy is uniquely suited to our particular cultural moment because we inhabit a culture of irony. Contemporary intellectuals, like many people in our self-consciously hip fin de siècle/nouveau siècle culture, adopt an ironic stance toward all values, traditions, and attributions of responsibility. Like Nicholas Cage's character in the film *Leaving Las Vegas* or Matt Damon's in *Good Will Hunting*, to cite just two of countless potential examples from the 1990s, we keep our distance from any commitments or explanations. Many of us pretend that we cannot quite remember or even understand exactly why we are doing what we are doing – whether what we are doing is drinking ourselves to death, drifting aimlessly, or making other antiheroic gestures such as writing or reading historical scholarship. In this culture of irony, everything is unstable and up for grabs. All of our activities are subject to critique or exposure as masks shielding ulterior motives – or perhaps shielding the meaninglessness of our lives – so we had better maintain a distance from what we are doing.

That currently fashionable pose is a surface manifestation of a deeper and more significant set of developments in philosophy and critical theory. A thorough-going historicism can be traced to various sources, including the work of Thomas Kuhn in the history of science, Clifford Geertz in cultural anthropology, and Richard Rorty in philosophy. Thanks to their work, and the work of other thinkers in other disciplines, many intellectuals now proclaim that all our commitments are contingent, and that the attempt to escape history is futile. This tendency toward historicism has gathered increasing momentum since 1989. Because no social scientist in Europe or the United States predicted the end of communism in Eastern Europe and the Soviet Union, some social scientists have admitted, often grudgingly, that universal laws of social and political behavior now seem impossible. The historicity of all ideas and institutions, together with the unpredictability of human affairs, is now fairly widely accepted. In a sense, all intellectuals are historians now. There are, of course, plenty of social scientists who inhabit a never-never land where they engage in a practice they call "rational choice theory," but as a historian I find it hard to take them seriously. The evidence – martyrs, suicides, lottery ticket buyers, and fans of the Boston Red Sox – against their central premise is simply too compelling. This triumph of historical thinking is good news, especially for us historians, since thinking historically is what we do for a living.[12]

But there is a problem implicit in this postmodern culture of irony: a tendency toward distrust and polarization: We have given up on older ideals, older standards, but what at first looked like new horizons now look more and more like dead ends. We have traded in the aspiration to universality for the embrace of difference – for example, the appreciation of otherness. We have given up on the notion of necessity and accept the contingency of our cultural values. Having come to see the oppression masked by claims to wholeness and objectivity, we now prefer the disarray of fragmentation, the particularity of an admittedly subjective perspective. All claims to authority are now immediately suspect, whether those claims come from dictators or popularly elected representatives, from self-appointed seers or apparently selfless idealists.

Studying democracy is especially important today because the idea of democracy is uniquely well suited to this culture of irony. In place of older claims to objectivity with a capital "O" and reason with a capital "R," democracy as an ideal and as a practice offers all individuals the chance to participate in shaping the goals and the procedures that will govern our way of life. Whatever our community – from the local to the global – or our community of discourse – from the informal to the professional – democracy offers the ideals of autonomy, equality, and participation against those of dependency, hierarchy, and exclusion.

These ideals are attractive to many today not because they are grounded in the Enlightenment principles of reason, order, and God-given rights – which was, of course, the rationale offered for them in the eighteenth century. Such ideals appeal today because they are open-ended, because their meanings are subject to negotiation, and because they can accommodate the pluralism of contemporary life. Democracy in the culture of irony can rest on two simple assumptions. First, it is not possible to specify once and for all, or to impose on all persons, a narrow or fixed conception of the good life; for that reason, such decisions should be made according to democratic procedures. Democratic cultures allow different individuals to pursue different objectives by inviting them to participate in the process of shaping the rules of the game and determining its purpose.

The second assumption is equally straightforward: the assumption of uncertainty necessitates deliberation. We cannot know, or impose on all persons, a fixed and unitary conception of the truth. In a democracy, particular, provisional truths must emerge from the process of free inquiry, from the verification of truth claims in experience, and from democratic deliberation understood as the means of resolving – at least provisionally – whatever disputes remain in discursive communities of various kinds. Only when all members of a democracy broaden their perspectives sufficiently to "weigh well" – the original meaning of the Latin "deliberare" – and consider seriously the views of others who disagree with them, is democratic deliberation possible.

An alternative conception of democracy as the mere tallying of individual desires, the elevation of unexamined and indefensible personal preferences to the level of privileged rights or insights, although currently fashionable, is of relatively recent vintage. It dates only from the 1950s. The ideal of democratic deliberation, by contrast, is of ancient lineage. Despite its roots in classical, Christian, and Enlightenment thought, however, it need not be understood as imposing a certain form of reasoning or conversation to the exclusion of others – the logic of educated white males, for example, as against alternative forms of deliberation preferred by members of other groups. Instead the question of what constitutes democratic deliberation must itself be subject to debate. The expansion of the relevant community is part of the democratic dynamic that has been developing since the re-evaluations of human capacity beginning with the Renaissance and continuing up to the present. Challenges to the forms of argument preferred by those in power is a long-standing tradition that women and minorities today continue by questioning established notions of logic and evidence.[13]

Historians can show how specific debates and struggles developed over the meaning of democracy, how the actual battles fought in American history complicate not only the older, discredited ideals that lacked sensitivity to those marginalized and excluded, but how the too rigid application of new norms can likewise tend to obscure important parts of the dynamic story of democracy. The ideas of difference, contingency, fragmentation, and subjectivity are important reminders that the standards of universality, necessity, wholeness, and objectivity can be oppressive. But without a commitment to democracy as deliberation, such values can prove more corrosive than constructive. Democracy conceived as deliberation can provide a standard of judgment as well as a procedure in our culture of irony. A focus on democracy need not celebrate America; it can provide, instead, merely a way of framing inquiries into America's failure to reach its own democratic ideals.

If democracy is uniquely well suited to the needs of those who embrace a culture of irony in our postmodern moment, democracy also remains attractive – although for different reasons – to those who embrace older ideals derived from the Enlightenment or from religious traditions. Intellectuals who emphasize the importance of democracy on such grounds include thinkers as different as John Rawls and Jürgen Habermas, Alasdair MacIntyre and Charles Taylor – and some American historians. To such thinkers, some of whom write in the spirit of John Dewey, democracy is not now, nor has it ever been, a question merely of political institutions. Instead, it is an ethical ideal that rests on a conception of what it is to be human.[14]

Historians can make an important contribution to this contemporary discourse by demonstrating in detail how Americans' theory and practice of democracy have developed over several centuries. This means rejecting the standard dichotomies that have dominated our analysis in recent years, since these frameworks are too wooden to accommodate the multitude of individuals in America's past and the complexity of those individuals' aspirations and activities. Rather than arguing about when and how Americans outside the South departed from a precapitalist world of harmonious community, for example, we should see instead, as Stephen Innes, Christine Heyrman, Robert Shalhope, and others have done, that Americans in the middle colonies and New England in the seventeenth and eighteenth centuries worked to balance a prudent desire to prosper with equally fervent commitments to various religious ideals.[15] In place of the sterile juxtaposition of liberalism and republicanism, to take another example, we should see how eighteenth- and nineteenth-century Americans worked to balance their commitments to individual rights against their equally firm commitments to personal and civic virtue. Willi Paul Adams, in particular, has demonstrated how the early state constitutions used the language of liberalism in their proclamation of rights, the language of republicanism in their invocations of the common good, and the language of democracy in their commitment to the idea of popular sovereignty. This use of democratic ideas might strike Edmund Morgan, Pauline Maier, and other late twentieth-century commentators as a fiction or a myth, but it was as real to Americans of the 1780s as the churches and courthouses in which they gathered to argue and hammer out the rules they adopted as their fundamental law.[16]

It is true that many eighteenth-century Americans feared democracy for the same reason that Tocqueville and Mill later devoted so much attention to it: they realized that it is a broadly cultural ideal rather than a narrow set of institutional arrangements. The principle of democracy is equality, as Aristotle understood well before Tocqueville or Mill or Dewey, and that principle challenges the legitimacy of all forms of hierarchy without turning subversion and transgression themselves into absolute values. If we so uncritically privilege difference as to make it a new, unassailable standard, we merely replace one non-democratic norm with another. As Tocqueville and Mill both saw, the elevation of individuality threatened to submerge reasoned debate beneath a tide of romantic self-assertion. We will have to balance our academic culture's current understandable inclination to heed the voices that would speak on behalf of the disinherited against the need to adjudicate among competing claims and diverse standards of judgment.

The difference between democracy and anarchy has been just as important as the difference between democracy and hierarchy. The principle of popular sovereignty was of such enormous importance in America, as Bernard Bailyn, Gordon Wood, and Hendrik Hartog have shown in different ways, because it provided legitimacy for the new nation's Constitutional framework and for the authority of those who elected to serve in government. That set in motion a democratic dynamic that developed in ways no one in eighteenth-century America could have predicted. In Linda Kerber's *Women of the Republic*, John Brooke's *The Heart of the Commonwealth*, Gordon Wood's *Radicalism of the American Revolution*, Robert Shalhope's *The Roots of Democracy*, and Saul Cornell's *The Other Founders*, we can see how new generations of Americans took advantage of the unprecedented opportunities presented to them in a democratizing culture to establish new forms of community, new forms of communication, and new forms of enterprise, not out of devotion to a theory of possessive individualism, but simply because they had an unprecedented degree of freedom to make choices for themselves and their families.[17] If we wish to make sense of these choices as they saw them, we must trade in our conceptual categories and adopt their ways of looking at the world instead of ours.

I do not mean to suggest by this recommendation that, as a norm or an analytical category, democracy should simply supplant ideas about rights or the common good. Democracy by itself has never been enough, because, without a commitment to the principle of autonomy, any group of three can yield a majority of two committed to enslaving the other one. Rights matter, which is why African Americans, women, and other marginalized groups have used rights talk in their quest for inclusion in American democracy.

If the principle of democracy is equality, the method of democracy is deliberation, which requires an ethical commitment to the importance of the autonomy of each individual and requires each individual to be willing to advance reasons for his or her preferences. This idea of a republic of reasons stands in sharp contrast to our contemporary culture of irony. The deliberative ideal is apparent in the local and state declarations of independence that preceded Jefferson's draft, in Jefferson's commitment to the vitality of local government, in Madison's characterizations of the debates among delegates to the Constitutional Convention, and in the framers' justification of the provision for Amendment in that Constitution. Unlike the sons of the Enlightenment who made the French Revolution, those who wrote the U.S. Constitution doubted that reason could disclose timeless principles beyond the need for change. Establishing the centrality of that insight is perhaps the greatest achievement of Lance Banning's monumental study of Madison, *The Sacred Fire of Liberty*.[18]

The commitment to deliberation failed to resolve the problem of slavery, although that did not discourage those committed to the abolitionist cause, whose antislavery sentiment developed not from their desire to legitimate a market economy, as David Brion Davis has argued, but because they were devoted to ideals of benevolence derived from religious and political commitments (as Elizabeth Clark and Paul Goodman have made clear).[19] The commitment to deliberation is likewise apparent in the contrast between Lincoln's caution and the dogmatic certainties of the slaveholders and abolitionists who reviled him.[20] It is apparent in the insistence of Jane Addams and John Dewey, Florence Kelley and Louis Brandeis, Ida Tarbell and Upton Sinclair, that the scale of economic organization is as important as its shape, since only through participation on a daily basis can workers, like citizens, learn to understand and appreciate multiple perspectives and develop the capacity to shape the institutions that envelop them.[21]

Such deliberation, even when premised on ideals alien to the culture of irony, does not in practice promise the resolution of differences, an end to conflict, or a snug consensus. But unless we understand that democratic culture requires a commitment to deliberation as an ethical principle, we cannot explain when and why democracy has failed to work, nor can we begin to move toward understanding or resolving those differences that can be resolved. As Tocqueville pointed out, the commitment to this ethic of reciprocity, to the importance of seeing things from different perspectives and reaching provisional agreement through dialogue and compromise, is at the heart of democracy in America.[22]

The logic of democracy encourages the endless spawning of new ambitions and new expectations that challenge any provisional agreements that have been reached in American history. If historians can make clear that rhythm of frustration and aspiration, they can help complicate the simplistic sloganeering that dominates our politics and feeds the cynicism of the culture of irony. For over a decade studies have been piling up evidence that the politics of "false choices" presented by the two parties has little to do with the American public's perception of the issues and what needs to be done. Other studies show the public's increasing dissatisfaction with the simplifications purveyed by newspaper and television reporters utterly uninterested in policy and obsessed with the "spin" of politics conceived as a game played by cynics.[23]

Because historians have a commitment to the particular, to the specific, and to the hard evidence of the American past, the historical study of democracy can help provide antidotes to the mindless reductionism of so much contemporary political and cultural debate by showing the origins of our difficulties and the reasons why complex, historically-rooted problems resist simple solutions. Historians who write for a broad audience, instead of merely for each other, can help illuminate the origin of problems that politicians and journalists often evade or distort, and thereby help foster the spirit of deliberation that democracy requires. Historians can show how and why the principles of autonomy and equality have replaced those of dependency and hierarchy. Even more important, they can show how and why that transformation has been partial and complicated by demonstrating the tenacious hold of competing values.

Authority, for example, appealed not only to patricians but to early American feminists such as Judith Sargent Murray, who considered it a fundamental fact of nature and absolutely necessary for stability. When a contemporary critic such as Nina Baym reads Murray as a proto-postmodernist whose work subverts her commitment to authority, historians can help explain the reasons why Murray's feminism took the shape it did rather than the shape contemporary critics might prefer.[24] Religion, to cite a second example, seems to many contemporary commentators to represent tradition and hierarchy against the challenges of democracy. But historians should point out as well the crucial role of religion in the American Revolution, in antislavery agitation, in the parts of progressivism allied with the social gospel, and especially in the Civil Rights movement and the antiwar movement of the 1960s and 1970s. The dichotomy offered by today's pundits between progressives and people of faith cannot be sustained by the historical record.[25]

Finally, historians can help to demonstrate that racism, whether directed toward African Americans or toward Asians or Hispanics, has unfortunately been as American as apple pie. It cannot be made to disappear simply by demonizing all whites or lionizing all nonwhites. Historians who study those excluded from the mainstream of American democracy illuminate the problematical nature of attempts to incorporate diversity within any culture premised on assumptions about the fundamental commonality – most notably, the willingness to abide by the will of the majority – that must underlie democratic institutions. The scope of democratic citizenship expanded during the eighteenth, nineteenth, and twentieth centuries largely as a result of changing conceptions of the criteria appropriate for determining who should participate in the decision-making process. The ideas that supplanted older versions of racial supremacy required acceptance of something like the African American thinker W.E.B. DuBois's notion of "double consciousness," the effort to keep in balance – because it is not possible fully to reconcile – the competing demands of the self and the other. Such a democratic self is constituted by the tension between one's own awareness of membership in a particular community – a community defined by race, class, gender, or ethnicity – and one's aspiration to membership in the larger, more cosmopolitan and transracial human community, and one's awareness that the "other" is always multiple rather than singular. These contradictory demands alert individuals – especially, DuBois argued, but not exclusively members of racial minorities – to the necessity of working to legitimate a cultural ideal beyond the summing up of purely individual preferences.[26]

Only when the preferences of members of a majority are formed through interaction with, and recognition of, the different desires of members of minorities can the latter hope to escape oppression. Only if it is possible to persuade all members of democratic cultures that their ideal must incorporate this sort of "double consciousness," a sensibility to which some members of racial minorities come naturally (albeit painfully), and to which other people come by embracing ethical imperatives such as the Christian law of love or political ideas such as the ethic of reciprocity, will it be possible to move toward the ideal of a "postethnic America" that David Hollinger persuasively laid out in his book of that title.[27] If historians shift their focus from questions of capitalism, or republicanism, or race, class, and gender to the concept of democracy, they will have to be tough-minded about it, demonstrating that merely preaching the values of being reasonable and learning to get along with each other has never been sufficient to destabilize power, end injustice, or secure democracy. Historians can help to reawaken, and to sharpen, the sense of democracy as an unfinished project, to show how earlier battles for democracy have been fought, and to make clear that contemporary American culture is a product of those battles.

In this brief final section I will suggest a third topic: comparative or transnational historical inquiry. Readers familiar with *The Journal of American History* will know that interest is growing in comparative history and transnational history, or simply in perceptions of the United States from other national or cultural perspectives. That development dovetails with both of the arguments I have advanced in this chapter. First, the conception of history as hermeneutics requires interpreting the meaning of American experience with the benefit of critical distance as well as close attention to the historical meanings of texts, and such interpretation can be done more fruitfully when the inquiry proceeds from a variety of different vantage points. Approaching American history in relation to different national histories or from different national and cultural perspectives places the inquiry in a broader framework. If we recognize that all of our frameworks – from our very notion of what date it is to our conception of what history is and what we historians ought to do – are conventions, or constructions, then we are more likely to approach them critically rather than seeing them as emerging from the very nature of things. Second, since the ideal of democracy now commands nearly universal approbation, examining democracy in a comparative or transnational framework can reveal what is distinctive, not simply about the United States, but about the different experiences of every nation, as well as indicating what, if anything, runs across national borders.

Historians approaching the study of American history from different national backgrounds, and placing that study within different comparative perspectives or transnational analytical frameworks, are as ideally suited to illuminate American democracy as were earlier European commentators from Tocqueville to Marx to Weber. There is something bracing about assessments coming from scholars of America history who are free of the national passions that Americans cannot help sharing, and those assessments are perhaps especially valuable to those Americans who consider themselves critics of the United States. Finally, to bring us back where we started, it becomes especially clear to Americans who venture away from home – as comparativists or transnationalists – that there is something myopic as well as artificial about the cultural self-centeredness that plagues us in the United States. Things are different elsewhere, and the experience of difference can alert Americans, and American historians, to the fact that our own way of looking at our world inevitably prevents us from seeing ourselves as others do. Like the insights hermeneutics provides when pursued with sufficient rigor, that insight can help historians acquire the critical distance they need, particularly in our imperfectly democratic culture of irony.[28]

Notes

1. William Bouwsma, "From History of Ideas to History of Meaning," *Journal of Interdisciplinary History*, 12 (1981): 279–91. A more recent overview of developments in American intellectual history is Thomas Bender, "Intellectual and Cultural History," in Eric Foner, ed., *The New American History*, 2nd edition (Philadelphia, 1997).
2. On these issues see Mark Bevir, *The Logic of the History of Ideas* (Cambridge, UK, 1999); James T. Kloppenberg, "Deconstruction and Hermeneutics as Strategies for Intellectual History," *Intellectual History Newsletter*, 9 (1987): 3–22; and James T. Kloppenberg, "Studying Ideas Historically," *History and Theory*, forthcoming.
3. Merle Curti, *"The Making of an American Community: A Case Study of Democracy in a Frontier County* (Stanford, 1959); John Pettegrew,

"The Present-Minded Professor: Merle Curti's Work as an Intellectual Historian," a paper delivered at the 1997 annual meeting of the Organization of American Historians; John Pettegrew, "A Tribute: Merle Curti, Pragmatist Historian," *Intellectual History Newsletter*, 18 (1996): 70–5; John Higham, *History: Professional Scholarship in America* (Princeton, 1965); John Higham, *Writing American History: Essays on Modern Scholarship* (Bloomington, 1970).

4. Rogers Smith, *Civic Ideals: Conflicting Visions of Citizenship in U.S. History* (New Haven, 1997); Christine Heyrman, *Southern Cross: The Beginnings of the Bible Belt* (New York, 1997); Daniel Rodgers, *Atlantic Crossings: Social Politics in a Progressive Age* (Cambridge, MA, 1998); Amy Dru Stanley, *From Bondage to Contract: Wage Labor, Marriage, and the Market in the Age of Slave Emancipation* (New York, 1998); Matthew F. Jacobson, *Whiteness of a Different Color: European Immigrants and the Alchemy of Race* (Cambridge, MA, 1998); Linda Kerber, *No Constitutional Right to Be Ladies: Women and the Obligations of Citizenship* (New York, 1998).

5. Stephen Innes, *Creating the Commonwealth: The Economic Culture of Puritan New England* (New York, 1995); Christine Heyrman, *Commerce and Culture: The Maritime Communities of Colonial Massachusetts, 1690–1750* (New York, 1984). On the unhelpfulness of the concept of a market revolution for understanding later eras in American history, see Daniel Feller's Chapter Three of this volume.

6. David D. Hall, "Narrating Puritanism," in *New Directions in American Religious History*, ed. Harry Stout and D. G. Hart (New York, 1997), pp. 51–83; and David D. Hall, *Worlds of Wonder, Days of Judgment: Popular Religious Belief in Early New England* (Cambridge, MA, 1990). Other recent examples on this tendency in Puritan studies include Jane Kamensky, *Governing the Tongue: The Politics of Speech in Early New England* (New York, 1997); Mark Peterson, *The Price of Redemption: The Spiritual Economy of Puritan New England* (Stanford, 1997); and, with a somewhat different focus on the sociology of intellectuals, Darren Staloff, *The Making of an American Thinking Class: Intellectuals and Intelligentsia in Puritan Massachusetts* (New York, 1998). For broader discussion of the focus on the interplay between doctrine and practice in American religion, see Mark Noll's Chapter Four in this volume.

7. This emphasis on agency runs through many of the chapters in this volume, especially those by Simon Newman, Peter Parish, David Turley, and Christopher Clark.

8. Dirk Hoerder, "From Euro- and Afro-Atlantic to Pacific Migration System: A Comparative Approach to North American History," in Thomas Bender, ed., *Rethinking American History in a Global Age*, forthcoming; Hoerder, "Segmented Macrosystems and Networking Individuals: The Balancing Functions of Migration Processes," in Jan Lucassen and Leo Lucassen, eds., *Migrations, Migration History, History: Old Paradigms and New Perspectives* (Bern, 1997); Hoerder, *Cultures in Contact: European and World Migration, 11th Century to 1990s* (Durham, 2001). An exemplary exploration of the intermingling of immigrants' thought worlds and their experience is Wolfgang Helbich, "Different, But Not Out of this World: German Images of the United States between Two Wars, 1871–1914," in David Barclay and Elisabeth Glaser-Schmidt, eds., *Transatlantic Images and Perceptions: Germany and America since 1776* (Cambridge, UK, 1997).

9. Daniel T. Rodgers, "The Age of Social Politics," in Bender, ed., *Rethinking American History in a Global Age*; idem, *The Work Ethic in Industrial America, 1850–1920* (Chicago, 1978); idem, *Contested Truths: Keywords in American Politics Since Independence* (New York, 1987).

10. Cass Sunstein, *The Partial Constitution* (Cambridge, MA, 1993); Akhil Reed Amar, *The Bill of Rights: Creation and Reconstruction* (New Haven, 1998); Joan Williams, *Unbending Gender: Why Family and Work Conflict and What to Do About It* (New York, 2000).

11. On intellectual history and legal history, see James T. Kloppenberg, "The Theory and Practice of Legal History," *Harvard Law Review*, 106 (1993): 1332–51; and Kloppenberg, "Deliberative Democracy and Judicial Supremacy," *Law and History Review*, 13 (1995): 393–412.

12. For more detailed discussion of these developments, see James T. Kloppenberg, "Why History Matters to Political Theory," in Kloppenberg, *The Virtues of Liberalism* (New York, 1998), pp. 155–78; and Kloppenberg, "Pragmatism: An Old Name for some New Ways of Thinking?" *The Journal of American History*, 83 (1996): 100–38. On rational choice theory considered from diverse perspectives, see Jeffrey Freedman, ed., *The Rational Choice Controversy: Economic Models of Politics Reconsidered* (New Haven, 1996), a volume generated in response to Donald P. Green and Ian Shapiro, *Pathologies of Rational Choice Theory: A Critique of Applications in Political Science* (New Haven, 1994).

13. Two fine overviews are John Dunn, ed., *Democracy: The Unfinished Journey, 508 BC to AD 1993* (Oxford, 1992); and David Copp, Jean Hampton, and John E. Roemer, eds., *The Idea of Democracy* (Cambridge, UK, 1993). For an especially insightful discussion of these issues from a self-consciously feminist perspective indebted to Habermas, see Seyla Benhabib, *Situating the Self: Gender, Community, and Postmodernism in Contemporary Ethics* (New York, 1992), and the lively debate in Seyla Benhabib, Judith Butler, Drucilla Cornell, and Nancy Fraser, *Feminist Contentions: A Philosophical Exchange* (New York, 1995).
14. On Dewey see Steven C. Rockefeller, *John Dewey: Religious Faith and Democratic Humanism* (New York, 1991); Alan Ryan, *John Dewey and the High Tide of American Liberalism* (New York, 1995); and especially Robert B. Westbrook, *John Dewey and American Democracy* (Ithaca, 1991). I discuss Dewey's concept of democracy in greater detail in James T. Kloppenberg, *Uncertain Victory: Social Democracy and Progressivism in European and American Thought, 1870–1920* (New York, 1986), and Kloppenberg, "Democracy and Disenchantment: From Weber and Dewey to Habermas and Rorty," in *The Virtues of Liberalism*, pp. 82–99.
15. See Innes, *Creating the Commonwealth*; Heyrman, *Commerce and Culture*; Robert Shalhope, *Bennington and the Green Mountain Boys: The Emergence of Liberal Democracy in Vermont, 1760–1850* (Baltimore, 1996); and Robert Shalhope, "Man-Child in a Changing Time: Hiram Harwood of Bennington, Vermont," a paper based on Harwood's extraordinary diary that Shalhope is developing into a full-scale biography of a man on the frontier who kept a detailed record not only of the way his world was changing but also of his changing aspirations and consolations.
16. Willi Paul Adams, *First American Constitutions: Republican Ideology and the Making of the State Constitutions in the Revolutionary Era*, trans. Rita and Robert Kimber (Chapel Hill, 1980); Edmund S. Morgan, *Inventing the People: The Rise of Popular Sovereignty in England and America* (New York, 1988); Pauline Maier, *American Scripture: Making the Declaration of Independence* (New York, 1997). I discuss these issues in James T. Kloppenberg, "The Virtues of Liberalism: Christianity, Republicanism, and Ethics in Early American Political Discourse," in *The Virtues of Liberalism*, pp. 21–37.
17. Bernard Bailyn, "The Ideological Fulfillment of the American Revolution," in Bailyn *Faces of Revolution: Personalities and Themes*

in the Struggle for American Independence (New York, 1990), pp. 225–68; Gordon Wood, *The Creation of the American Republic, 1776–1787* (New York, 1969); Hendrik Hartog, "The Constitution of Aspiration and 'The Rights That Belong to Us All,'" *The Journal of American History*, 74 (1987): 1013–34; Linda K. Kerber, *Women of the Republic: Intellect and Ideology in Revolutionary America* (Chapel Hill, 1980); John L. Brooke, *The Heart of the Commonwealth: Society and Political Culture in Worcester County, Massachusetts, 1713–1861* (New York, 1989); Gordon Wood, *The Radicalism of the American Revolution* (New York, 1992); Robert E. Shalhope, *The Roots of Democracy: American Thought and Culture, 1760–1800* (Boston, 1990); Saul Cornell, *The Other Founders: Anti-Federalism and the Dissenting Tradition in America, 1788–1828* (Chapel Hill, 1999).

18. Lance Banning, *The Sacred Fire of Liberty: James Madison and the Founding of the Federal Republic* (Ithaca, 1995); and on Jefferson, Peter S. Onuf, ed., *Jeffersonian Legacies* (Charlottesville, 1993); and Peter S. Onuf, *Jefferson's Empire: The Language of American Nationhood* (Charlottesville, 2000).

19. For competing perspectives on antislavery see Thomas Bender, ed., *The Antislavery Debate: Capitalism and Abolitionism as a Problem in Historical Interpretation* (Berkeley, 1992); and Elizabeth B. Clark, "'The Sacred Rights of the Weak': Pain, Sympathy, and the Culture of Individual Rights in Antebellum America," *The Journal of American History*, 82 (1995): 463–93.

20. Among the multitude of studies of Lincoln and the political culture of Civil War America, see especially Eric Foner, *Free Soil, Free Labor, Free Men* (New York, 1970); Garry Wills, *Lincoln at Gettysburg: The Words That Remade America* (New York, 1992); J. David Greenstone, *The Lincoln Persuasion: Remaking American Liberalism* (Princeton, 1993); Daniel Walker Howe, *Making the American Self: Jonathan Edwards to Abraham Lincoln* (Cambridge, MA, 1997).

21. On progressivism, especially valuable among recent studies, in addition to Rodgers, *Atlantic Crossings*, and Westbrook, *John Dewey and American Democracy*, are Eldon J. Eisenach, *The Lost Promise of Progressivism* (Lawrence, 1994); Ellen Fitzpatrick, *Endless Crusade: Women Social Scientists and Progressive Reform* (New York, 1990); Kathryn Kish Sklar, *Florence Kelley and the Nation's Work: The Rise of Women's Political Culture, 1830–1900* (New Haven, 1995); James J. Connolly, *The Triumph of Ethnic Progressivism: Urban Political Culture in Boston, 1900–1925* (Cambridge,

MA,1998); and Axel R. Schäfer, *American Progressives and German Social Reform, 1875–1920: Social Ethics, Moral Control, and the Regulatory State in a Transatlantic Context* (Stuttgart, 2000).

22. On the ethic of reciprocity and its importance in Tocqueville's analysis, see James T. Kloppenberg, "Life Everlasting: Tocqueville in America," in Kloppenberg, *The Virtues of Liberalism*, pp. 71–81.

23. See especially E. J. Dionne, *Why Americans Hate Politics* (New York, 1991); Kathleen Hall Jamieson, *Packaging the Presidency: A History and Criticism of Presidential Campaign Advertising*, 2nd edn. (New York, 1994); Judith Lichtenberg, ed., *Democracy and the Mass Media* (Cambridge, UK, 1990); and, more generally, James T. Kloppenberg, "Political Ideas in Twentieth-Century America," in Kloppenberg, *The Virtues of Liberalism*, pp. 124–54.

24. Compare Nina Baym's Introductory Essay to Judith Sargent Murray, *The Gleaner* (Schenectady, 1992) with Sheila L. Skemp, ed., *Judith Sargent Murray: A Brief Biography with Documents* (Boston, 1998).

25. See Mark A. Noll, ed., *Religion and American Politics from the Colonial Period to the 1980s* (New York, 1990); James T. Kloppenberg, "Knowledge and Belief in American Public Life," in Kloppenberg, *The Virtues of Liberalism*, pp. 38–58; Richard H. King, *Civil Rights and the Idea of Freedom* (New York, 1992); and Noll's Chapter Four in this volume.

26. A fine introduction to DuBois's thought and the uses to which it has been put is Thomas C. Holt's essay in *A Companion to American Thought*, ed. Richard Wightman Fox and James T. Kloppenberg (Oxford, 1995), pp. 187–90.

27. David A. Hollinger, *Postethnic America*, 2nd edn. (New York, 2000).

28. There is a long tradition of comparative or transnational work in intellectual history, and a thorough discussion of such work would require another chapter as long as this one. Fortunately, the contributors to the volume *Rethinking American History in A Global Age*, ed. Thomas Bender (forthcoming), examine these questions in detail and exemplify as well as explore the potential costs and benefits of such studies.

–10–

Women's History and Gender
S. Jay Kleinberg

Despite the proliferation of scholarship on women during the last hundred years, their place in historical studies remains unsettled and open to debate. This chapter considers how or whether inserting women into the historical canon changes the nature of history itself.[1] It begins with the development of women's history and gender history and the contested theoretical ground between them. It then investigates how the inclusion of women alters our understanding of history. Women's history and gender history have distinctive theoretical and philosophical underpinnings and offer different insights into the study of women in the past. Gender history augments rather than substitutes for women's history.

The debates between women's history and gender history are the combined result of the way women's history began, the use of postmodern theories, and, possibly, a backlash against woman-centered history. The proliferation of studies of women, and their growing inclusiveness in terms of race, region, and class, has led some historians to worry that the balance has tipped too far in favor of fashionable considerations of difference, even though a few branches of history still seem relatively immune to the inclusion of women as a significant area of study.[2] For others, post-structuralist linguistic exercises have obscured the process of doing history and turned it into some sort of historical or semantic relativism. Over-lapping this group are those who fear that gender history opens the door for ignoring women or re-marginalizing their experiences. Thus, the debates surrounding the place of women in the historiographical literature remain lively and crucial to our formulation of how we do history in the new millennium.[3]

Writing women back into the past has taken various forms. It can be a correction of the historical narrative to make it more comprehensive (women's history), a matter of equitable treatment of the sexes (feminist history), or an attempt to explore how social interpretations of biological categories influence men's and women's activities (gender history). In women's history, women are the subject matter, while in gender history women or men can take center stage and the emphasis shifts more towards the cultural dynamics of roles.[4] Women's history first examined the lives of notable women and their contributions to momentous events, then moved on to a delineation of women's struggle for political, economic, and social rights, the complexities of their daily lives and life cycles, and the underlying experiences which encouraged female activism.[5]

The initial approach to women's history, contribution history, began within the conventional historical canon. Mary Beard, an 1897 graduate of DePauw University, lamented that the history taught in schools in the early decades of the twentieth century was "the history of men – of men's minds and manners," but that nowhere was there "any comprehensive treatment of women's contributions to civilization and culture."[6] Early historical studies of women owed much to the Progressive Era acceptance of women's place in politics and public life but did not challenge the belief propounded by E. H. Carr that history is "concerned with those who, whether victorious or defeated, achieved something," a definition which excludes social processes, and forces one down the byways of political history.[7] If, like English historian Edward Freeman, one assumes that "history is past politics and politics present history," then as long as women did not vote or belong to political parties, they might seem historically irrelevant.[8] To give women back their history was to recount their political and civic activities, as Mary Beard did in *Women's Work in Municipalities* (1915).[9]

Between the Progressive Era and the revival of interest in women's history in the 1960s, a number of women outside the academy published studies that rejected Freeman's narrow definition of history. Julia Cherry Spruill's *Women's Life and Work in the Southern Colonies* (1938) and Eleanor Flexner's *Century of Struggle: The Woman's Rights Movement in the United States* (1959) inserted women into the historical record. Spruill's pioneering account of Southern women's daily lives drew heavily upon manuscript sources to produce a social history that concentrated on elite plantation ladies and townswomen rather than small farmers or agricultural laborers. She occasionally mentioned African Americans, but only in connection with their service to whites. Spruill also considered the employments open to (white) women, together with their education and political views, but neglected slave women's work in the fields and their place as historical agents. This restricted vision of women's history established an approach to the past that privileged genteel white women even as it expanded historical coverage by discussing housewifery and family life.

Flexner's work had a more clearly political focus and widened the historical vision in other ways. *Century of Struggle* reached across race, class, and region in its effort to understand "what women had achieved in the century between, roughly, 1820 and 1920."[10] Her description of the struggle for women's rights embraced slavery and anti-slavery, female reform movements (black as well as white), education, female trade unionists, and the battle for suffrage. It emphasized women's contributions to and conflicts with the institutional structures that oppressed them, extending the female presence into most aspects of society rather than confining them to the home. While sticking closely to the history of female accomplishments, *Century of Struggle* ranged widely across issues of class and race, setting the stage for new avenues of inquiry into women's place in American society. Written in the chilly political climate of the 1950s, Flexner's work counteracted the pernicious notion of pundits such as Marynia Farnham and Frederick Lundberg that women's lives were eternally and solely linked to home and family.[11]

A new wave of women's history analyzed female activism and political movements and explored women's domestic and homosocial worlds. The timing of these works was no historical coincidence; the women's liberation movement of the 1960s and 1970s sparked curiosity about women in the past and led scholars to question their omission from the historical record. It also prompted many more women to undertake postgraduate study and make women the subject of their doctoral dissertations.[12] Such histories as *The Ideas of the Woman Suffrage Movement* by Aileen Kraditor (1965), Gerda Lerner's *The Grimké Sisters of South Carolina* (1967), and William O'Neill's *Everyone Was Brave* (1969) focused on women even if they did not challenge the political orientation of historical study.

Feminist history has been seen by some as a second stage in the process of inserting women into the historical past, following on from contribution history. It takes a distinctive approach through its subject selection, going beyond the histories of suffrage and reform to reconstruct women's world "on their own terms."[13] In so doing, feminist history puts women's concerns at the center of investigation. Women are not necessarily compared to men; instead their world has an intrinsic importance and interest. Yet feminist history is not the same as the history of feminism. William O'Neill's study of the suffrage movement, *Everyone Was Brave*, consciously did not take a stand on whether women should be equal to men. This contrasts sharply with Nancy Cott's *The Grounding of Modern Feminism,* which explores women's "outlooks in order to suggest what was possible and likely among a larger generality of women."[14]

The new social history, which gave impetus to women's history, has been accused of devaluing the narrative (telling a story) and wandering from the grand synthesis. Thomas Bender expressed concern over the proliferation of histories devoted to "the private or *gemeinschaftlich* worlds of trades, occupations, and professions; locality; sisterhood; race and ethnicity and family" which do not contribute to the meta-narrative of "the making of public culture," the proper business of historians.[15] The fragmentation of social – and especially women's – history challenged the patriarchal view of the past that privileged elite white men's story and disrupted the master narrative of American exceptionalism.[16]

Historical studies have become more than some truth "out there" to be discovered. They are, according to Joan Scott, "what we know about the past" as "constructed by historians." Incorporating women potentially creates a "plurality of stories," a genuinely democratic history that includes the experiences of all people, not just selected elites.[17] It also destabilizes, or at least calls into question, historians' traditional periodizations. When Joan Kelly asked whether the Renaissance was a Renaissance for women she pointed to the inadequacy of historical chronologies divided by wars, revolutions, and artistic/social movements. Women participated in these events in such a distinctive fashion that they had, arguably, a different meaning for them, or, perhaps, no meaning at all.[18]

My own study of *Women in the United States, 1830–1945* utilizes a periodization which begins with the Industrial, rather than the American, Revolution, and regards women's suffrage and some – but not all – wars, as crucial dividing points. World War I was, for the United States, a short engagement with relatively few casualties and arguably little direct impact on women.[19] By contrast, the Civil War was a watershed. Female participation in the abolitionist movement and war effort, the emancipation of slave women and men, and the war itself fomented a crisis in gender relations, economic systems, and political structures.[20]

Winning the vote, rather than World War I, had a lasting influence on women's lives, making 1920 a key dividing point in the female chronology of the twentieth century. While, as Nancy Cott observes, there were notable continuities in women's organizations before and after the Nineteenth Amendment, suffrage was a significant, albeit not uncontested, division in women's experiences.[21] The importance of the Nineteenth Amendment was hotly debated at the time and continues to shape the study of women, even though acquiring the vote affected some groups more than others. It took another four decades before African American women in the South could vote in any number, some western states barred

Native Americans from voting until the 1940s, and women born in Asia were also deprived of their civic rights during this era.[22]

The women's liberation movement radically redefined politics to include sexual politics, linking the domestic and more conventionally construed historical and political worlds.[23] Barbara Welter's "Cult of True Womanhood" (1966) formulated the ideology of separate spheres, reclaiming women's domestic and emotional work as historically important.[24] A few years later, Anne Firor Scott's *The Southern Lady* (1970) brought Spruill into the nineteenth and twentieth centuries, discussing female domestic and political experiences from the perspective of genteel white women.[25] In a similar vein, Carroll Smith-Rosenberg's landmark study of same-sex friendships enlarged the legitimate field of inquiry for historians from politics to relationships, but was restricted by its sources to a largely middle-class white view of the world.[26]

One formidable task women's history encountered was that of writing inclusive history. Ellen Carol DuBois and Vicki L. Ruiz state that "most of the early work in U.S. women's history paid little attention to race and assumed instead a universal women's experience, defined in contrast to 'man's history." They believe that concentrating on the differences between the male and female past helped to legitimize women's history, but a uni-racial model emerged which replaced the universal man of American history with a universal (white, middle-class) woman.[27]

The dominant paradigm in women's history, that of separate spheres, marginalized women of color, working-class women, and immigrants because the didactic literature of the mid-nineteenth century from which Barbara Welter derived her portrait of the pious, pure, submissive, and domestic female, was aimed at middle-class white women. Historians needed to transcend both these sources and the models built upon them in order to understand the variety of women's lives. Women had multiple identities across class, race, region, religion, and ethnic group so that a single model did not and could not do justice to the complexities of their experiences.[28] The category "woman" had to be broken into its constituent elements, so that the intersecting hierarchies of class/race/sex/ethnicity could be examined and understood. As bell hooks has argued, heeding these interlocking systems of domination acknowledges the diversity and complexity of the female experience.[29]

Critics of separate spheres and women's history as the study of white women have pioneered the innovative use of historical sources to uncover women's hidden past. Plantation records, female slave narratives, Native American legends, material culture, civil court cases, the manuscript

Census, and other biostatistical sources add a new dimension to the organizational papers found in the backs of cupboards and library storerooms, diaries, and institutional records and open fresh areas of research and documentation for those interested in women's lives.[30]

While DuBois and Ruiz are right to highlight the need to write inclusive history, their statement that the early women's history was uni-racial or uni-class overlooks important areas of inquiry in social and economic history. Studies of women broke new ground in their analysis of everyday life, moving beyond the high politics that had previously been understood as the main business of history. Following on from pathbreaking Progressive Era investigations such as Edith Abbott's *Women in Industry* (1910), Gerda Lerner scrutinized women's status in the early years of the Industrial Revolution in her important article, "The Lady and the Mill Girl."[31] Quantitative and qualitative analyses of women workers followed, including Tamara Hareven's studies of textile mill workers in Amoskeag, S. J. Kleinberg's investigation of women in steel mill cities, Thomas Dublin, Lisa Vogel, and Mary Blewett on textile and shoe workers, Virginia Yans-McLaughlin and Miriam Cohen on Italian women in Buffalo and New York City, and Alice Kessler-Harris, Elizabeth Jameson, Robin Miller Jacoby, and Nancy Schrom Dye on women and trade unions.[32]

These historians discussed working-class women of various racial, religious, and ethnic backgrounds, although they tended to concentrate on white working women in northeastern cities. The scholarship of the early 1970s expanded historical discourse by asserting that ethnic women had their own history to be written, that women's work inside and outside the home was relevant to our understanding of historical processes, and that it was possible to recover the past outside an institutional framework. Other works, including those by Claudia Goldin, Sharon Harley, and Elizabeth Pleck, specifically focused on the African American women's employment patterns and their need to combine work and motherhood.[33]

When associated with the growing interest in social history, women's history called into question the hierarchical understandings which made some aspects of the past worthy of study and others deserving of obscurity.[34] Using qualitative and quantitative techniques, women's historians have considered both the central tendencies and the variations between groups of women. As Jeffrey Cox and Shelton Stromquist observe, social history challenges previous narrative strategies through its "focus on the multiplicity and diversity of past experience, which provides a source for alternative narratives."[35] This accords well with the transition within women's history itself toward a more complex and nuanced understanding of the divisions as well as the commonalities of women's experiences across time and place. Nancy Hewitt, Jean O'Brien, and Nancy Rosebaugh argue that the category "woman" has been shattered by its variations between classes, races, and places. They view scholarship as returning to the "personal and engaged style of early feminist writing in which the subjectivity of the author openly informs analysis."[36] Such openness to the complexities of experience and identity decenters the prevailing master narratives of American history.[37]

The call to reorder historical priorities has far-reaching consequences. As Darlene Clark Hine commented, "a re-construction of American history that does not challenge our assumptions – about the people, power, places, and politics of importance – has failed." For Hine this meant overcoming the view prevalent in the 1960s that "Black history included race but not gender."[38] Most treatments of slavery written before the 1980s focused on issues of masculinity and militancy, either excluding women altogether or regarding them as objects to be protected or abused. Angela Davis wrote, in her 1971 article on the role of female slaves, one of the first challenges to this tendency to subsume or ignore African American women's experience, while *The Woman in American History* (1971) and *Black Women in White America* (1972) by Gerda Lerner contributed to an integrated women's history. It took another decade before monographs delved into African American women's experiences in slavery and after emancipation, with such works as Deborah Gray White's *Ar'n't I a Woman* and Jacqueline Jones's *Labor of Love, Labor of Sorrow* serving as a correction to the notion that "all the women are white and all the blacks are men."[39]

Historical practice was less well developed with regard to other women of color and slow to incorporate the experiences of Native, Asian, or Hispanic women. Early texts either ignored them altogether or mentioned them only in passing.[40] This partially reflects the East Coast orientation of many of these works, but even histories of the West omitted women of color.[41] Works such as Joan Jensen's sensitive treatment of women's agricultural experiences reversed this neglect by presenting accounts of Native American, African American, Hispanic women, and native- and foreign-born white women.[42]

Julie Roy Jeffrey's *Frontier Women* confirms the growing importance of multicultural women's studies, a rejection of the East Coast domination of American historiography in general, and a much more nuanced treatment of Western women. The first edition of this work, published in 1979, challenged the then-prevalent view of the westward movement as a male movement. According to Jeffrey, she "organized the book around the ways in which new standards for middle-class female behavior affected white women's experiences in the West." By the second edition, the frontier had become a place of cultural contact and the emphasis shifted to "what the emigration of white women might have meant for the other women – Native American, Hispanic, Chinese, and African American (in small numbers) – who were also participants in western life." The emphasis moved away from pioneering to the displacement and marginalization of women of color and poor white women.[43] The new Western women's history, as exemplified by Jeffrey, Jameson, Armitage, and Jensen, is a much more inclusive narrative which encompasses all women's lives, not just those of a privileged class/race/ethnic group.[44] The success of this history rests in its recovery of a diverse past that does not duck behind the excuse that the sources do not exist to research a particular group's experiences.

At the same time that narrative, empirical histories of women were being written and women's history itself was becoming more inclusive, new trends in history and new linguistic forms began to disrupt the field. The issues raised by the dialogue between women's historians and gender historians contribute to the category of historical analysis termed the "Theory Wars" by Lisa Duggan, a search for theoretical frameworks similar to those used in the social sciences or, increasingly, in linguistic, cultural, and media studies.[45] From the mid-1980s onwards, historians debated whether the use of post-structuralist theory impeded or promoted the acceptance of women's place in history and the academy.[46]

Most women's and gender historians lay claim to doing feminist history, that is, favoring equality of the sexes. They accomplish this in distinctive ways: women's history does it by focusing on women's quest for equality, while gender historians link politics "inextricably to analyses of gender as the production of knowledge about sexual difference."[47] Feminist historians, according to Judith Bennett's analysis of feminism and history, have two tasks: to eliminate the misogynistic traditions within the academy and to contribute to the understanding and therefore the eradication of women's oppression. This model of scholarship assumes that the truth (however defined) will set women free. Since post-structuralists regard the truth as subjective, they substitute linguistic analysis for "retrievable historical reality," which makes the discovery of patterns of change over time more difficult.[48]

For Bennett, the study of gender, dedicated to understanding the social constructions of female- and male-ness, integrates both sexes into the subject studied. This will overcome the "deeply rooted prejudices" she finds present in much contemporary history in which the insertion of "race/class/gender" is a politically correct camouflage for deeply-rooted prejudice. She finds an increasingly sophisticated history emerging which contains more complex categories of analysis. Bennett calls for the integration of gender into all subjects studied. Women should not be treated "as a separate, peculiar subject (i.e., instead of always implicitly asking 'how were women's lives different from the (male) norm?') we can seek, by focusing on gender, to understand the social constructions of both femaleness and maleness."[49] Yet women do need to be treated as a separate subject *as well as* social constructions precisely because their lives varied so much from men's. Women's experiences had their own integrity and frequently must be investigated through distinctive sources and techniques.[50]

When the history of women began as a field, gender had only a linguistic definition referring to whether words were masculine, feminine, or neuter.[51] Increasingly, "gender" has been substituted for sex as the category denoting male/female-ness, within both the academy and society, as a means of accommodating the concept of socially-constructed roles. The new meaning of the word "gender" encapsulates "the social organization of the relationship between the sexes" based upon "perceived differences between the sexes . . . and is a primary way of signifying relationships of power."[52] In other words, gender is not sex but the relationship between the sexes and manifests the fundamental power relationships between the sexes and inequality.[53]

Instead of regarding sex as a biological category and the history of women as the history of that biological group, "many who participated in the early compensatory phase of women's history are now bringing a similar energy and excitement to challenging wider areas of study." This statement by the Editorial Collective of *Gender and History* in 1989 framed the debate between women's history and gender history.[54] By the 1980s, gender had become, in Gisela Bock's analysis, an "intellectual construct, a way of perceiving and studying people, an analytical tool that helps us to discover neglected areas of history. It is a conceptual form of sociocultural inquiry that challenges the sex-blindness of traditional historiography."[55]

Joan Scott led the rejection of the history of women in favor of gender history. Concerned to change historical practice, Scott criticized what she called the "positivism" of women's historians who seemingly believed that, if they could but document women's presence in the past, they would be able to change the established definitions of historical categories. Instead, she feared that the "separate treatment of women could serve to confirm their marginal and particularized relationship to those (male) subjects already established as dominant and universal."[56] Penelope

Fields

Corfield agreed with this stance when she described the history of women as mutating into a broader gender history that considers the societal implications of the roles imputed to both sexes across a broad range of issues.[57]

At its most basic level, gender history, like the post-structural movement from which it derived, is about the use of language to describe/inscribe meaning. As Mary Poovey put it, the conditions which produce both texts and individual subjects are elusive "precisely because the material and economic relations of production can only make themselves known through representations."[58] Language and representation have an independent existence in which the control of the meaning takes primacy.[59] To many women's historians this seems to devalue the documentation of women's experiences and reduces history to linguistic relativism.[60] History is about more than the study of language; it needs to take into account people's social, economic, and political conditions and their sex. Poovey may believe that "woman' is only a social construct that has no basis in nature," but, outside the post-structuralist community, it has a perceived biological meaning which has shaped women's (and men's) daily experiences.[61] These experiences change over time, are influenced by race, class, region, and a host of other attributes, and are socially inflected. They cannot be dismissed by historians merely as some sort of linguistic turn.[62]

In practice, the growing use of the terms gender/gender history has altered the subjects of historical discourse by questioning how linguistic and sociocultural perceptions affect roles and relationships. Making gender visible has led some male historians to reconceptualize their own intellectual persona. Michael S. Kimmel describes his intellectual odyssey from seeing himself, if he ever thought about it at all, as the generic person to realizing that he was a middle-class white man. For him, masculinity (the fear that others "will get something on you") has become the motivating force of much historical action.[63]

Gender history has the power to provide a much more complex understanding of the past and the ways in which the social designation of sexual roles shaped society, politics, and economics. Works such as E. Anthony Rotundo's *American Manhood* (1993) and Mark E. Kann's *A Republic of Men* (1998) consider masculinity and its impact upon politics and culture.[64] These studies make explicit much that was implicit in historical writing by exploring expressions of masculinity and its reification in economics, politics, social structure, culture, and personal relationships. They contribute to our understanding of the assumptions behind American social, political, and economic systems rather than accepting the gendered dynamics as either given or immutable.

– 232 –

Linda Kerber delineated the political uses of motherhood in *The Women of the Republic: Intellect and Ideology in Revolutionary America* (1980). She articulated the concept of republican mothers using women's role as domestic educators to inculcate republican virtues into their sons.[65] Kann builds upon this in his explorations of how the founding fathers created and sustained "a republic based on male governance and female subordination."[66] This places gender at the heart of colonial and early U.S. history. It leads us to question the very basis on which the American Republic was founded. As Kerber observes, "a few of the shrewdest members of the founding generation understood that the status of married women gave the lie to claims of government by the consent of the governed."[67]

When Abigail Adams wrote to her husband John (later second President of the United States) to "please remember the ladies. All men would be tyrants if they could," she stated a self-evident truth which her husband and his colleagues dismissed by saying "we know better than to repeal our Masculinist systems."[68] But, as with the Constitutional acceptance of slavery, the founding fathers deliberately structured a republic based upon hierarchies of race and gender which took centuries to undermine. The reconstruction of history to account for women's and men's (or the races') relative places requires a thorough reappraisal of our interpretation of the past. It also results in a gendered interpretation because it forces us to take account of the masculinist state of mind and actions of a given period or society.

Theda Perdue makes this point strongly in *Cherokee Women* (1998), an analysis of gender relations and cultural contact in colonial North Carolina and Georgia. Perdue's inquiry situates Native women as "major players in the great historical drama that is the American past," putting the construction of gender roles at the heart of the conflict between Native and European Americans. Cherokee women derived their position in society from their strong roles within a matrilineal family system and from a view of motherhood which "evoked power rather than sentimentality," while Europeans feared an egalitarian society in which women had sexual autonomy and controlled property.[69] Contact with Europeans shifted the sources of power within the Cherokee community: trade in animal skins replaced agriculture as a significant source of sustenance, individualism replaced communalism, and women's influence declined. Since military matters dominated intercultural contacts, the colonial authorities dealt only with warriors and ignored women's role within Cherokee political systems.

In Perdue's work, understanding how and why gender roles were constructed is crucial to understanding Cherokee society, its contact with

Europeans, and the shaping of early American political culture. This is both gender and women's history. There is an awareness of the specific circumstances which differently shaped women's and men's roles in two distinctive societies, while power relations are set in their specific socio-historical context. Women are the primary subject matter, with cultural contact and conflict seen through their changing status. The incorporation of gendered models of behavior and causal relationships alters how history is done and, more arguably, becomes central to the process/task of investigating the past.

Economic history, no less than social history, can be re-visioned through the inclusion of women and an examination of the gendered dynamics of economic institutions. Explorations of economic development can only be complete if they analyze the changing nature of women's contributions, the shift to employment outside the home, the overwhelming impact of race, ethnicity, and marital status on the kind of work undertaken, and the strains between employment inside and outside the home. They must also look at the gendered dynamics of men's work, for these altered in industrial America as much as women's did, albeit responding to a distinct family dynamic and set of assumptions. Labor history has gone from being a consideration of strikes, labor relations, and "the brains under the workingman's cap," to a much more inclusive analysis of who works, at what jobs, and under what circumstances.[70]

Let me give two additional examples of how writing women into the center of the story fundamentally alters our knowledge of the past. *The Shadow of the Mills: Working Class Families in Pittsburgh, 1870–1907* (1989) examined the family dynamics of the labor force, how the bosses could assume men would be able to work a 12-hour day under brutal conditions and still be fed and clothed, and the impact of such working conditions on home life. Earlier histories of the steel industry had examined labor relations and the Bessemer process, but none had questioned the gendered assumptions which made the steel industry possible or the role of the family in the larger economy.[71] This work demonstrated that women's work in the home had economic value and was as much a part of the history of labor as strikes and industrial processes.

The second example concerns the ways in which racism interacted with sexism to warp the lives of women of color. Particularly in the South, African Americans were second-class citizens, poorly served by government and prevented from participating in public life through intimidation. Native Americans endured the loss of their land and relegation to economically marginal land. Mexican-, Chinese-, and Japanese-American women also encountered prejudices which limited the jobs they could get, their ability to vote, and land ownership. Racial and gender politics inflected significant New Deal legislation. The Social Security Act (1935) shaped the federal government's role in welfare for generations, to the detriment of women, especially those clustered in domestic service and agriculture who came, not coincidentally, disproportionately from racial-ethnic groups. Alice Kessler-Harris's study of the racist/sexist dynamics of the Social Security Act makes the situation of women, especially African American women, central to the construction of the Social Security Act.[72]

The gendered assumptions about who should work and who should look after the family resulted in a legislation that privileged white men's occupations, discriminated against working women, and penalized families that did not conform to the family wage ideology. We learn so much more about the Great Depression and New Deal once we incorporate women and the gendered basis of legislation into our scrutiny of the interstices of political, economic, and social behavior. Unfortunately, some historians still write about this era without considering women. A gender-neutral history can still easily become a woman-free history; a recent history of the welfare state in the South managed to omit African American women's role in agricultural and domestic labor from its consideration of "Southern paternalism."[73] As a result, it represents an incomplete analysis of Southern society and politics.

One of the key tensions between women's and gender historians is the fear that women's experiences will be ignored or made to disappear through some linguistic device. When Scott writes that "identity is not an objectively determined sense of self defined by needs and interests," it seemingly negates the study of women as self-defined and reduces them to being seen *only* through a gendered lens.[74] The danger in this approach is that it denies women agency and it removes them from their specific social, economic, cultural, and political contexts.

A number of scholars have protested against subsuming the history of women under the study of gender because they object to the way that "post-structuralists deconstruct gender relations in a socioeconomic void," as Joan Hoff described the process.[75] June Purvis and Amanda Weatherill believe that "gender history is yet another variation of men's history, peppered with frequent references to 'gender' but with little reference to women's lives."[76] These historians of women fear that gender historians will place greater "emphasis on men than women and more emphasis on difference or diversity among women rather than on commonalities they may share" and so re-marginalize women.[77]

They are concerned that the new gender history will supplant women's history.[78] Judith P. Zinsser observes that "scholars have sometimes substituted 'gender' for 'women' as more neutral and more acceptable, and with a resulting loss of feminist perspective."[79] Hoff worries that not only will we lose the feminist perspective, but also that women will be omitted altogether if gender history replaces women's history. She observes that women's historians paid careful attention to matters of gender some time before it became a fashionable phrase imported from France.[80]

As historians we can position these debates in terms of the development of studies of the past which included women and which have de-essentialized men as the basic category of historical analysis. The outpouring of scholarship on women's activities and on women and men as gendered categories illuminate the profound changes that have occurred in the study of the past. These include a concern for the diversity of experiences, the typical and ordinary, and the impact of grand events upon everyday folk as well as elites.

The incorporation of women into the historical narrative destabilizes the process of doing history from a male point of view. It expands the subject matter, asserts that women's interests and activities, however much they varied from one group to another, are historically relevant, and redefines the important questions. The inclusion of women, until recently defined implicitly as the other, entails reconceptualizing the discipline which gave legitimacy to male activities and ignored female ones as trivial and not worth recording. Adding women's stories and activities to the written record fundamentally alters how we study the past and what we consider history to be. This does not mean that we necessarily accept Scott's notion of a "relativized concept of gender," or that it becomes a new grand narrative, even as we seek a history which focuses on women and makes their concerns central to our study.[81]

Yet the question remains whether gender will permeate contemporary and future historical practice and on what basis. Post-structuralist gender studies are a linguistic dead-end which dehistoricize women's past and reduce reality to a constructed concept. If the gendered paradigm becomes the way that the study of masculinity replaces the history of women, then history will be narrower and less interesting for it. Gender history (as the study of sex roles in the past) and women's history are two distinct, but overlapping, research areas. The consideration of women's experiences is separate from the study of power relationships, although informed by that study. It is essential that the investigation of women's past permeates all aspects of history. There is so much we still do not know about women's lives and the commonalities and differences between the classes, races, and regions that the only way forward is to write multifaceted history that integrates women into all branches of our study of change over time.

Notes

1. Bonnie Smith, *The Gender of History: Men, Women, and Historical Practice* (Cambridge, MA, 1998) discusses the historical profession's relegation of women to the sidelines as "amateurs." Gerda Lerner, *The Creation of Feminist Consciousness From the Middle Ages to 1870* (Oxford, 1993), p. 249, observes that by the time people started to write history (a self-conscious record of the past), women's lesser education hampered their efforts. On women's experiences in the academy see Eileen Boris and Nupur Chaudhuri, *Voices of Women Historians: The Personal, the Political, the Professional* (Bloomington, 1999).

2. See for example Peter Novick, *That Noble Dream: The "Objectivity Question" and the American Historical Profession* (Cambridge, UK, 1988). Alison Mackinnon, "Were Women Present at the Demographic Transition? Questions from a Feminist Historian to Historical Demographers," *Gender and History*, 7 (1995): 222–40. Lee J. Alston and Joseph P. Ferrie, *Southern Paternalism and the American Welfare State* (Cambridge, UK, 1999) write about welfare policy without mentioning women.

3. In addition to the texts cited elsewhere in the notes, readers are referred to *Gender and History, Journal of Women's History, Signs, Women's Studies International Forum*, and *Women's History Review* for coverage of the main debates.

4. June Purvis, "From 'Women Worthies' to Post-structuralism? Debate and Controversy in Women's History in Britain" in June Purvis, ed., *Women's History in Britain, 1850–1945* (London, 1995), p. 6.

5. There are notable exceptions to the political orientation of the early histories. See especially Edith Abbott, *Women in Industry* (New York, 1910) and Alice Clark, *The Working Life of Women in the Seventeenth Century* (1919).

6. Mary Beard, 1935, quoted by Nancy Cott, *A Woman Making History: Mary Ritter Beard Through Her Letters* (New Haven, 1991), p. 15.

Fields

7. Edward Hallett Carr, *What is History?* (New York, 1963), p. 168.
8. Cited in Joan Wallach Scott, "History in Crisis? The Others' Side of the Story," *American Historical Review*, 94 (1989): 680.
9. Mary Ritter Beard, *Women's Work in Municipalities* (New York, 1915). Also see Arthur Meier Schlesinger, Sr., *Rise of the City* (New York, 1933).
10. Eleanor Flexner, *Century of Struggle: The Woman's Rights Movement in the United States* (New York, 1974 [orig., 1959]), p. xi.
11. Ferdinand Lundberg and Marynia F. Farnham, *Modern Woman: The Lost Sex* (New York, 1947). Ellen C. DuBois, "Foremothers I: Eleanor Flexner and the History of American Feminism," *Gender and History*, 3 (1991): 81–90.
12. Judith P. Zinsser, *History and Feminism: A Glass Half Full* (New York, 1993), p. 161, n. 30. Between 1930 and 1959, 13 percent of PhDs were women, falling to 10 percent in the 1960s. The proportion of new history PhDs who were women rose from 14 percent in 1977 to 38 percent in 1999.
13. Gerda Lerner, *The Majority Finds Its Past* (New York, 1979), p. 148.
14. William O'Neill, *Everyone Was Brave* (Chicago, 1969), p. viii: Nancy Cott, *The Grounding of Modern Feminism* (New Haven, 1987), p. 9.
15. Thomas Bender, "The Need for Synthesis in American History," *Journal of American History*, 73 (1986): 127. Joyce Appleby, Lynn Hunt, and Margaret Jacob in *Telling the Truth about History* (New York, 1994), pp. 232–5 employ the term metanarrative to mean an over-arching grand theme.
16. Charles and Mary R. Beard, *The Rise of American Civilization* (New York, 1933).
17. Scott, "History in Crisis": 680–81, 691–2.
18. Joan Kelly, *Women, History, and Ideas: the Essays of Joan Kelly* (Chicago, 1984), p. 15.
19. S. J. Kleinberg, *Women in the United States, 1830–1945* (New Brunswick, NJ, 1999), p. 5. Maurine Weiner Greenwald, *Women, War, and Work: The Impact of World War I on Women Workers in the United States* (Westport, CT, 1980); Rhodri Jeffreys-Jones, *Changing Differences: Women and the Shaping of American Foreign Policy, 1917–1994* (New Brunswick, NJ, 1995), p. 28. For the sake of brevity, I am omitting the debate about whether WWI was crucial in women obtaining suffrage.
20. LeeAnn Whites, *The Civil War as a Crisis in Gender: Augusta, Georgia, 1860–1890* (Athens, GA, 1995).

21. Nancy Cott, "Across the Great Divide: Women in Politics Before and After 1920," in Louise A. Tilly and Patricia Gurin, eds., *Women, Politics, and Change* (New York, 1990), pp. 153–76.

22. Kristi Andersen, *After Suffrage: Women in Partisan and Electoral Politics before the New Deal* (Chicago, 1996).

23. Kate Millett, *Sexual Politics* (Garden City, NY, 1970).

24. Barbara Welter, "Cult of True Womanhood," *American Quarterly*, 18 (1966): 151–74.

25. Anne Firor Scott, *The Southern Lady* (Chicago, 1970).

26. Carroll Smith-Rosenberg, "The Female World of Love and Ritual: Relations between Women in Nineteenth-Century America," *Signs*, 1 (1975): 1–29.

27. Ellen Carol DuBois and Vicki L. Ruiz, eds., *Unequal Sisters: A Multi-Cultural Reader in U.S. Women's History* (New York, 1990), p. xi.

28. Evelyn Brooks Higginbotham, "African-American Women's History and the Metalanguage of Race," *Signs*, 17 (1992): 251–74.

29. bell hooks, "Feminism: A Tranformational Politic," in Deborah L. Rhodes, ed., *Theoretical Perspectives on Sexual Differences* (New Haven, CT, 1990), p. 187.

30. For discussion of sources see Deborah Gray White, *Ar'n't I a Woman? Female Slaves in the Plantation South* (New York, 1985), pp. 15–24 and S.J. Kleinberg, "The Systematic Study of Urban Women," in Milton Cantor and Bruce Laurie, eds., *Class, Sex and the Woman Worker* (Westport, CT, 1977), pp. 20–42.

31. Abbott, *Women in Industry*; Gerda Lerner, "The Lady and the Mill Girl: Changes in the Status of Women in the Age of Jackson," *Mid-Continent American Studies Journal*, 10 (1969): 5–15.

32. Tamara Hareven, *Family Time and Industrial Time* (Cambridge, MA, 1982) examines women in New England factories and families. Cantor and Laurie, *Class, Sex and the Woman Worker* reprinted the essays by these authors presented at the Women's History Conference at the State University of New York, Brockport (1974) or the second Berkshire Conference on the History of Women (Radcliffe College, 1974).

33. Claudia Goldin, "Female Labor Force Participation: The Origin of Black and White Differences," *Journal of Economic History*, 37 (1977): 87–112; Sharon Harley, "Northern Black Female Workers: Jacksonian Era," in Sharon Harley and Rosalyn Terborg-Penn, ed., *The Afro-American Woman: Struggles and Images* (1978); Elizabeth H. Pleck, "A Mother's Wage: Income Earning Among Married Black and Italian Women, 1896–1911," in Michael Gordon, ed., *The*

American Family in Social Historical Perspective (New York, 2nd edn., 1978).

34. Gisela Bock, "Women's History and Gender History: Aspects of an International Debate," *Gender and History*, 1 (1989): 6.
35. Jeffrey Cox and Shelton Stromquist, eds., *Contesting the Master Narrative: Essays in Social History* (Iowa City, 1998), p. 9.
36. Nancy Hewitt, Jean O'Barr, and Nancy Rosebaugh, eds., *Talking Gender: Public Images, Personal Journeys, and Political Critiques* (Chapel Hill, 1996), p. 4.
37. Dorothy Ross, "Grand Narrative in American Historical Writing: From Romance to Uncertainty," *American Historical Review*, 100 (1995): 651–77.
38. Darlene Clark Hine, *Black Women and the Re-Construction of American History* (Bloomington, 1994), pp. xxiii, xvii.
39. Angela Davis, "Reflections on the Black Woman's Role in the Community of Slaves," *Black Scholar*, 3 (1971): 3–15; Gerda Lerner, *The Woman in American History* (Menlo Park, CA, 1971) and *Black Women in White America: A Documentary History* (New York, 1972) (also see Lerner's early article, "Early Community Work of Black Club Women," *Journal of Negro History*, 59 (1959): 158–67); Deborah Gray White, pp. 17–22; Jacqueline Jones, *Labor of Love, Labor of Sorrow: Black Women, Work, and the Family from Slavery to the Present (*New York, 1985). The phrase is taken from the title of Gloria T. Hull, Patricia Bell Scott, and Barbara Smith, eds., *All the Women are White, All the Blacks are Men, But Some of Us Are Brave: Black Women's Studies* (Old Westbury, NY, 1982).
40. Lerner's *The Woman in American History* does not include Native Americans. Neither do Lois W. Banner, *Women in Modern America: A Brief History* (New York, 1974) or Mary Ryan, *Womanhood in America: From Colonial Times to the Present* (New York, 1975).
41. Dee Brown, *The Gentle Tamers: Women of the Old Wild West* (Lincoln, 1969 [orig., 1959], p. 21 discusses Native Americans in terms of their abusing white women.
42. Joan Jensen, *With These Hands: Women Working on the Land* (New York, 1981); Patricia Albers and Bea Medicine, *The Hidden Half: Studies of Plains Indian Women* (Washington, DC, 1983); Gretchen M. Bataille and Kathleen M. Sands, *American Indian Women: Telling Their Lives* (Lincoln, 1984). Also see Carol Ruth Berkin and Mary Beth Norton, *Women of America: A History* (Boston, 1979) and Catherine Clinton, *The Other Civil War: American Women in the Nineteenth Century* (New York, 1984).

43. Julie Roy Jeffrey, *Frontier Women: "Civilizing" the West? 1840–1880* (New York, rev. edn., 1998), pp. 5–7.
44. The essays collected in Susan Armitage and Elizabeth Jameson, eds., *The Women's West* (Norman, 1987) and Lillian Schlissel, Vicki L. Ruiz, and Janice Monk eds., *Western Women: Their Land, Their Lives* (Albuquerque, 1987) exemplify this inclusionary approach.
45. Penelope J. Corfield, "History and the Challenge of Gender History," *Rethinking History*, 1 (1997): 241–58; June Purvis and Amanda Weatherill, "Playing the Gender History Game: A Reply to Penelope J. Corfield," *Rethinking History*, 3 (1999): 333–38; Penelope J. Corfield, "From Women's History to Gender History: A Reply to 'Playing the Gender History Game,'" *Rethinking History*, 3 (1999): 339–41; Joan Wallach Scott, *Gender and the Politics of History* (New York, 1988); Joan Hoff, "Gender as a Postmodern Category of Paralysis," *Women's History Review*, 3 (1994): 149–68; Lisa Duggan, "The Theory Wars, or, Who's Afraid of Judith Butler?" *Journal of Women's History*, 10 (1998): 9.
46. Tania Modelski, *Feminism without Women: Culture and Criticism in a "Postfeminist" Age* (New York, 1991).
47. Scott, *Gender and the Politics of History*, p. 6.
48. Hoff, "Gender as a Postmodern Category," p. 149.
49. Judith Bennett, "Feminism and History," *Gender and History*, 1 (1989): 256–8.
50. Margaret Strobel, "Getting to the Source: Becoming a Historian, Being an Activist, and Thinking Archivally," *Journal of Women's History*, 11 (1999): 181–92.
51. *Webster's Third Unabridged Dictionary* (Springfield, MA, 1965), p. 944.
52. Scott, *Gender and the Politics of History*, pp. 28, 42.
53. Gerda Lerner, *The Creation of Patriarchy* (New York, 1986).
54. The Editorial Collective, "Why Gender and History," *Gender and History*, 1 (1989): 1.
55. Gisela Bock, "Women's History and Gender History," p. 11.
56. Scott, *Gender and the Politics of History*, pp. 3–4.
57. Corfield, "Women's History to Gender History," p. 342.
58. Mary Poovey, *Uneven Developments: The Ideological Work in Gender in Mid-Victorian England* (Chicago, 1988), p. 18.
59. Scott, *Gender and the Politics of History*, p. 5.
60. This point is discussed by Louise M. Newman, "Critical Theory and the History of Women: What's At Stake in Deconstructing Women's History," *Journal of Women's History*, 2 (1991): 58–68.

61. Mary Poovey, "Feminism and Deconstruction, *Feminist Studies*, 14 (1988): 52.
62. Kathleen Canning, "Feminist History After the Linguistic Turn: Historicizing Discourse and Experience," in Sharlene Hesse-Biber, Christina Gilmartin, and Robin Lydenberg, eds., *Feminist Approaches to Theory and Methodology: An Interdisciplinary Reader* (New York, 1999), p. 46, defines the linguistic turn as the "historical analysis of representation as opposed to the pursuit of a discernible, retrievable historical 'reality.'"
63. Michael S. Kimmel, "Men and Women's Studies," in Hewitt, O'Barr, and Rosebaugh, *Talking Gender*, pp. 155, 162.
64. E. Anthony Rotundo, *American Manhood: Transformations in Masculinity from the Revolution to the Modern Era* (New York, 1993); Mark E. Kann, *A Republic of Men: The American Founders, Gendered Language, and Patriarchal Politics* (New York, 1998).
65. Linda Kerber, *The Women of the Republic: Intellect and Ideology in Revolutionary America* (Chapel Hill, 1980).
66. Kann, *A Republic of Men*, p. 1.
67. Linda Kerber, *Toward an Intellectual History of Women* (Charlotte, 1997), p. 15.
68. L. H. Butterfield, Marc Friedlaender and Mary-Jo Kline, eds., *The Book of Abigail and John: Selected Letters of the Adams Family, 1762–1784* (Cambridge, MA, 1975), pp. 121, 123.
69. Theda Perdue, *Cherokee Women: Gender and Culture Change, 1700–1835* (Lincoln, 1998), pp. 11, 101.
70. Joan Acker, "Rewriting Class, Race, and Gender: Problems in Feminist Rethinking," in Myra Marx Ferree, Judith Lorber, and Beth B. Hess, eds., *Revisioning Gender* (Thousand Oaks, CA, 1999), pp. 44–69, points to the continued importance of keeping economic relations to the fore in gender analysis. For examples of the new labor history see Elizabeth Faue, *Community of Suffering and Struggle: Women, Men, and the Labor Movement in Minneapolis, 1915–1945* (Chapel Hill, 1991); Nancy Gabin, *Feminism in the Labor Movement: Women and the United Auto Workers, 1935–1975* (Ithaca, NY, 1990); Vicki L. Ruiz, *Cannery Women, Cannery Lives: Mexican Women, Unionization, and the California Food Processing Industry, 1930–1950* (Albuquerque, 1987).
71. S. J. Kleinberg, *The Shadow of the Mills: Working Class Families in Pittsburgh, 1870–1907* (Pittsburgh, 1989); David Brody, *Steelworkers in America: The Nonunion Era* (Cambridge, MA, 1960); Peter Temin, *Iron and Steel in Nineteenth Century America: An Economic Inquiry*

(Cambridge, MA, 1964). Studies which analyzed a family economy (and thus examined gender) include Hareven, *Family Time and Industrial Time*, John Bodnar, *Worker's World: Kinship, Community and Protest in an Industrial Society, 1900–1940* (Baltimore, 1982), and Elizabeth H. Pleck, *Black Migration and Poverty: Boston, 1865–1900* (New York, 1979).

72. Alice Kessler-Harris, "Designing Women and Old Fools: The Construction of the Social Security Amendments of 1939," in Kerber, Kessler-Harris, and Sklar, *US History as Women's History: New Feminist Essays* (Chapel Hill, 1995) gives an insightful reading into the gendered politics of the Social Security Act and its amendments.

73. Alston and Ferrie, *Southern Paternalism*.

74. Scott, *Gender and the Politics of History*, p. 5

75. Hoff, "Gender as a Postmodern Category," p. 154.

76. Purvis and Weatherill, "Playing the Gender History Game," p. 334.

77. Kathleen L. Barry, "Tootsie Syndrome, Or 'We Have Met the Enemy and They are Us,'" *Women's Studies International Forum*, 12 (1989): 487–93.

78. Sara Evans to Anne Firor Scott, Susan K. Cahn, and Elizabeth Faue, "Women's History in the New Millennium: A Conversation across Three 'Generations': Part 2," *Journal of Women's History*, 11 (1999): 213.

79. Zinsser, *History and Feminism*, p. 116.

80. Hoff, "Gender as a Postmodern Category": 158–60.

81. Scott, *Gender and the Politics of History*, p. 10. Allan Megill, "Recounting the Past: 'Description,' Explanation, and Narrative in Historiography," *American Historical Review*, 94 (1989): 627–53, explores the meaning of narrative in history.

–11–

Print and the Public Sphere in Early America

Robert A. Gross

Who can resist the impulse to decry the politics of democracy in the media age? With the relentless reduction of elections to advertising, sound bites, and staged events, all orchestrated by political consultants for broadcast to passive television viewers, the temptation is well-nigh irresistible. Yearning for a time when politics was at once participatory and educational, critics inside and outside the academy look back to shining episodes in the past – the Lincoln-Douglas debates, the Constitutional convention, the publication of the *Federalist* essays – and treat them as emblems of a lost golden age. That nostalgia is understandable, and it affects more than Americans. Ever since the fall of the Berlin Wall and the collapse of Communism, talk about "civil society" and "the public sphere" has driven scholarship in numerous fields and inspired a multinational effort to identify the essential ingredients of democracy for the common good.

The signal event in this search was the publication in 1989 of Jürgen Habermas's *Structural Transformation of the Public Sphere*, the first appearance in English of a work originally issued in 1962 and emanating from debates in German Marxist circles, notably the Frankfurt School of cultural criticism. Though little known to most American academics for a quarter-century, Habermas was taken up quickly by political scientists and sociologists and eventually by cultural historians of early America, especially of the eighteenth century. In that era, as Habermas saw it, modern politics was born with the first emergence onto the historical stage of a "public" critically engaged in rational discussion of public affairs. In Habermas's formulation, it was through the institutions of a new print culture – not just books and periodicals but the clubs, coffee-houses, salons, reading rooms, and libraries in which they were read and discussed – that the "bourgeois public sphere" took shape in England and France.

This argument found a receptive audience in the United States, and it was amplified two years later when Benedict Anderson's *Imagined Communities*, first published in 1983, was reissued by Verso Books. Though written in apparent unawareness of Habermas, *Imagined Communities* underscored the centrality of print media to the constitution of the modern world. Under the aegis of "print-capitalism" seeking out markets for readers around the globe, Anderson argued, "rapidly growing numbers of people" in Europe and the Americas came "to think about themselves, and to relate themselves to others, in profoundly new ways." No longer were they content to be subjects of "polyglot" empires and "universal" Churches. Now, out of the experience of reading the ascendant genre of the newspaper, they identified as members of those "imagined communities" we call nations, bound together as speakers and readers of a common language and embracing the same political destiny by virtue of that fact. The "public sphere" and the "nation" were thus twins, born of the same historical process. Together, they provide organizing themes not only for contemporary critics of "the media" but also for practitioners in the expansive interdisciplinary field known as the history of the book. The German social philosopher and the British political anthropologist are in fact inescapable presences, their names invoked as frequently as Foucault's in the 1980s, their key concepts employed as self-evident terms. Like the phenomena they study, Habermas and Anderson are fixtures in the history of print.[1]

"Print and the Public Sphere" thus comes readily to mind as the lens through which to survey the contributions of book history to scholarship on the early republic. The theme is not merely a recent fashion. It is nearly as antique as the printing press, whose champions in the Protestant Reformation hailed "the divine art" as a providential agent of human emancipation. "The art of Printing," declared one English dissenter, "will so spread knowledge that the common people, knowing their own rights and liberties[,] will not be governed by way of oppression and so, little by little, all kingdoms will be like to Macaria." That progressive view has leaped across the centuries and found a congenial home in Paris, where *histoire du livre* arguably began with Lucien Febvre and Henri-Jean Martin's *The Coming of the Book* (1956). In the writings of Roger Chartier, the current *doyen* of the field, the printed word constitutes an arena of contending forces. "The book always aims at installing an order," Chartier maintains, but its claims are always opposed. Resisting the presumptions of the book, "the reader's liberty" is ever-ready to "distort and reformulate," circumvent and subvert the "significations" deployed to constrain it. "This dialectic between imposition and appropriation" forms the dynamic of book history. With that assertion, Chartier highlights the agency of individuals in a challenge to the bleak determinism of Foucault and thereby aligns himself with Habermas in Continental debates during the last two decades of the twentieth century. Liberty versus order: that whiggish theme is built into the intellectual foundations of the public sphere. It requires no grand tour of Europe, past or present, to discern the attraction of Habermas's framework for historians of the early American republic. What themes more suited to the conventional narrative of the Revolutionary era than the spread of enlightenment, the challenge to deference, and the rise of an informed citizenry, confident of its capacity for self-government in an independent republic?[2]

With its long lineage in European and American thought, the idea of public sphere carries impressive credentials, and it speaks to central themes in the eighteenth-century Atlantic world. I thus approached the subject, "Print and the Public Sphere," with the serenity of Benjamin Franklin, fully expecting to demonstrate the power of the press in the new republic. I should have imitated the skepticism of Samuel Johnson, who knew that life upsets one's most cherished assumptions. True, Habermas has set the agenda for recent research. With his emphasis on the discursive practices of reading and writing, he enhances the significance of literature in early American culture – a point of considerable importance to departments of English. For historians of print culture, he lends a grandeur to the business of tracking book sales, reconstructing library collections, compiling databases of the "reading experience." Nonetheless, as so often in research, the inquiry has taken surprising turns. The more closely we scrutinize Habermas's theory, the more limitations we find. It took no time for feminists to discern the gendered character of the public sphere. At the center of the historical stage, in Habermas's analysis, is the white, male middle class, the advance agent of progress. Rejecting that view, scholars of women's history have reconfigured the social landscape. Alongside the male terrain of coffeehouses, taverns, and clubs, they locate a heterosocial space of salons and parlors, where women joined with men in writing and talking about books, ideas, and affairs of state. Such revisions enlarge the scope of the public sphere. Other studies attenuate its connections to print. The republic of letters was riddled with contradictions. Even as they professed a new ideal of citizenship, marked by selfless service to the common good, most people declined to abide by its impersonal terms, either in print or in life. Americans in the early republic still inhabited a small-scale, face-to-face society, even in port cities such as Philadelphia and New York, and they were faithful to personalized norms. Print, like all institutions, adapted to the dominant ethos. Far from acting as an agent in its own right, ushering in a brave new world, it was integrated into a largely verbal culture. Well into the nineteenth century, the media age remained a distant future.[3]

At first glance, eighteenth-century America looks to be an ideal setting for the public sphere. Had Habermas glanced across the Atlantic to the thirteen continental colonies, he would have discerned a society remarkably close to his model, where "private people came together as a public." In the port cities, presided over by merchants, professionals, and gentlemen, there arose a vigorous print culture. Seventeenth-century Puritans had kept a tight control over the press, and Virginians had kept it out entirely; in the following century, Anglo-Americans proved more receptive. Parliament abandoned licensing in 1695, and though the Crown tried to continue controls over colonial printers, it was to no avail. Censorship by prior restraint gave way to prosecution for libel as the main method of regulation. The press quickened with new life in the freer environment. Boston got America's first newspaper in 1704, when a royal postmaster named John Campbell hired a printer and began publishing the *Boston News-Letter*. It was only the fourth newspaper in the Anglo-American world to be established outside of London. Though it is credited by the historian Charles Clark as "an early and crucial agent in the transformation, by depersonalization and enlargement, of the public sphere," the *News-Letter* was little different, in substance or subscribers, from the handwritten newsletters that had been circulating for some years among the local elite. Close to the royal government, Campbell boasted that his paper was "published by Authority" and filled its columns with the comings and goings of ships and with reprints from the *London Gazette*. With 250 subscribers, he had the market to himself for fifteen years. The coming of competition stirred things up. Boston's newspapers began to air local controversies, criticizing ministers and magistrates, and serving as vehicles for factional fights in provincial politics. Six papers were rivals for readers by 1763. By then, the typical weekly had 600 subscribers; it reached many more through coffeehouses and taverns, which were well-stocked not only with rum but also with reading matter. It was good business, as one tavern-keeper advertised, to be "supplied with the newspapers."[4]

The same story can be told for Philadelphia, New York, and other major ports. But in the Southern colonies, printing developed more fitfully. Proscribed by Virginia authorities as a nursery of sedition, the press did not find a welcome in the Chesapeake colony until 1730, when the new occupant of the Governor's Palace in Williamsburg recruited the colony's first printer. A newspaper, the *Virginia Gazette*, was soon circulating throughout the province. It had to suffice for the rapidly growing population for three decades. "We had but one press," recalled Thomas Jefferson, "and that having the whole business of the government, and no competition for public favor, nothing disagreeable to the governor could be got into it." Only after Joseph Royle declined to publish the "Virginia Resolves," passed by the House of Burgesses to protest the Stamp Act in 1765, did opponents of the governor take steps to find a more congenial printer. By 1774, three newspapers, all called the *Virginia Gazette*, were competing with news and opinion about the growing Revolutionary movement. Resistance to British imperial policy had transformed the press. On the eve of independence, the colonies had forty-two newspapers and eighty-two presses, Loyalist as well as Patriot, with some reaching as many as 3,000 readers.[5]

Colonial observers congratulated themselves on this expansion of the press, in both numbers and vigor, in language that could have come from Habermas. In his 1765 *Dissertation on the Feudal and Canon Law*, a series of newspaper essays composed in response to the Stamp Act, John Adams proclaimed New Englanders an enlightened people. "A native of America," he wrote, in a conflation of region and nation, "who cannot read and write is as rare an appearance as a Jacobite or a Roman Catholic, that is, as rare as a comet or an earthquake." Thanks to broad-based literacy and an educated elite, New Englanders could take advantage of a free press and defend their rights. "None of the means of information are more sacred, and have been cherished with more tenderness and care by the settlers of America than the press." Knowledge was power, ignorance slavery. A decade of debate over the British threat entrenched that faith. "They are a well-informed, reasoning commonality . . . perhaps the most of any on earth," one colonist explained to an English correspondent, "because of the free intercourse between man and man that prevails in America." Crucial to this "intercourse" were "the freedom and general circulation of newspapers, and the eagerness and leisure of the people to read them, or to listen to those who do." Devotion to the press surged in the wake of the Revolution. The United States had ninety-six newspapers at the start of the new national government in 1790, including eight dailies; twenty years later, Isaiah Thomas was able to count around 350. For another three decades, the number of newspapers would grow faster than the burgeoning population.[6]

These developments, set forth by Arthur M. Schlesinger in the late 1950s, are not news to students of colonial America, though they have been rediscovered in the recent wave of scholarship on the history of the book. I rehearse them because of the centrality of the press to the public sphere, as depicted by Habermas and explicated by Michael D. Warner, whose *Letters of the Republic: Publication and the Public Sphere in Eighteenth-Century America* first introduced the German social theorist to early American studies. Coming out in 1990, just one year after the first American edition of *Structural Transformation of the Public Sphere*, Warner is as responsible as anybody for the Habermas vogue of the 1990s. Yet he was no epigone. Warner creatively drew upon Habermas to develop his own account of the changing meanings of print in eighteenth-century America. To the evangelical Christians who aspired to build a New Israel in the American wilderness, the Bible, "the book above all books," represented the ideal text. It was the pure, unmediated communication of the Holy Spirit. In its pages, hungry souls sought union with Christ. Whether preached from the pulpit, written down in manuscript, or set in type, the gospel was always the living Word. On that model, Warner maintained, Puritans read words in print as embodiments of an author. The Reverend Cotton Mather, New England's most assiduous writer, delighted in giving away copies of his books, and as he did so, he reminded the recipients, "Remember, that I am speaking to you, all the while you have the Book before you!" As originating spirit, the author was one with the text, animating its every word.[7]

This "ethic of personal presence," as Warner calls it, was supplanted in the eighteenth century by its opposite. Advanced by newspapers from the 1720s on, the new ideal of discourse recast the meaning of print in impersonal terms. No longer did it radiate a living spirit, human or divine; cold type carried abstract truth. Detached from specific persons, the press was identified with a general public – more precisely, "a reading public." In the pages of newspapers, citizens followed the rule of reason. They discussed principles, not personalities; they forswore self-interest for the common good. The voice of the press was anonymous. Speaking for everyone in general and nobody in particular, it could claim to represent a new force – public opinion – that was constituted in its columns of type. It thus embodied the sovereignty of the people. The republic was born in print.[8]

Such was the vision, according to Warner, held by the Patriot elite that led the American Revolution and established the new republic. According to its prescriptions, the cultural practice of literacy was remade. In pamphlets and newspapers, critics of the mother country assumed the *persona* of virtuous statesmen from Greece and Rome – Aristides, Cato, Cicero, Demosthenes – and studded their essays with learned references to antiquity. Their duty, as they saw it, was to expose the danger of imperial measures, to set forth the causes and consequences of the crisis, and to lay out a reasoned plan of resistance. The responsibility of the public was to read and reflect – and ultimately to support the gentlemen who spoke in their name. Though this perspective advanced the interests of a specific class, it held sway in the struggle for independence and achieved its greatest triumph in the Constitution. In the opening words of that document, "We the People," the framers assumed the authority of "the public" and designed a nation. With ratification, that subterfuge became a universal faith. To read the national charter, Warner suggests, is to be subject to its discourse, with no escape from the verbal embrace. "With the Constitution, consent is to sovereignty as readership is to authorship." In that crucible of print, a national consciousness was forged. "The nation [was] . . . imagined through the public sphere."[9]

In that formulation, Warner traced the path from Habermas to Anderson that is now a familiar route. But he did not stop there. The classic public sphere, he discerned, was undone in its turn by a new rendition of print culture. In the capitalist world of Anglo-America, books were marketed as commodities to satisfy individual wants. Reading could serve as a means of "distinction," a way to display status and parade "politeness." Dropping the cloak of divinity in one gesture and spurning civic duty in another, print was harnessed to selfish ends. "It is the self-interested individual, not the polity, that profits from the cultivation of politeness through the consumption of books." A special sort of book was valued above all: the "polite" genre of belles lettres, which came to include the novel. The more Americans cultivated such reading, the further they drifted from the republican realm. In this pursuit of private advantage, they were fulfilling the logic of the marketplace. As Habermas had proposed, the capitalist dynamic culminated in a liberal public sphere.[10]

In this succession of moves – from Puritanism to republicanism and thence to liberalism – Warner charts a familiar course through America's "long eighteenth century." At the time he wrote, historians were still deep in the debate over the relative claims of republicanism and liberalism in our political culture. By now, that subject has been exhausted. If Habermas serves only to illustrate what we already know, there would be little point to grappling with his or Warner's dense prose. Actually, Warner's central contribution was to the field of literary studies. Through his exposition of the changing meanings of print, he recovers a lost world of thought and feeling in eighteenth-century writing. Whatever their aesthetic limitations, the "letters of the republic" performed the crucial cultural work of forming citizens. By that act of retrieval, a literature that has often seemed remote to later generations gains new vitality. No wonder so many students of early American literature have followed in Warner's wake. The problem is that an incisive account of ideology has been taken for a description of social fact. Print culture constituted the public sphere: that is now the conventional wisdom. Unwittingly, this conviction produces its own distortions. It dispatches other meanings of print, such as the piety of the Puritans, into obscurity, and it sunders the links between text and life. Cut off from the coffeehouses, clubs, and other face-to-face settings in which it once circulated, print now occupies an abstract, autonomous realm unto itself. Such isolationism has generated a backlash. One school of thought, led by Jay Fliegelman and Christopher Looby, insists on the continuing power of speech as cultural performance. ". . . Eighteenth-century print culture [was] unable to stand apart from the politics of sincerity and authenticity . . . ," argues Fliegelman. "Americans continued to be invested in the affective and personal power of voice," Looby agrees. The point is well taken, though it can produce its own exaggerations, with the defenders of speech and print squaring off in opposite corners. The fundamental question is, as Fliegelman recognizes, more subtle: the "dialectical relation" between the two modes.[11]

The challenge, then, is to situate print, along with writing, speech, and other forms of expression, in its social milieu. From this perspective, we can interrogate the theory of the public sphere. Habermas links together four elements: (1) a style of political conversation (critical reason); (2) a mode of discourse (impartiality and anonymity); (3) a set of institutions (newspapers, bookstores, coffeehouses, clubs, taverns, salons, and other voluntary associations); and (4) a distinct social category (white men of the commercial and professional middle class). In his telling, the bourgeoisie carved out, for a brief but critical historical moment, an autonomous realm, independent of State and Church and separate from family and work, where people could read and reason about public affairs. How rational was that discourse? How impartial? How open that forum? How free-ranging its deliberations? To these questions I now turn, in an historian's exercise of critical reason.

Let us start with the ideal of impartiality, which gave rise to the use of pseudonyms to disguise the identity of authors. That practice originated in the literary culture of gentlemen, who pursued letters for all sorts of reasons – curiosity, sociability, public service, status display – but never for money. A man of honor stood above such mean concerns. Should he deign to offer a piece of writing to the press, he did so anonymously or under a pseudonym, lest the dignity of his name be tainted by being vulgarly hawked in trade. But in the public sphere of the eighteenth century, the aristocratic pseudonym acquired a republican rationale. "It is of no importance whether or not an author gives his name," one writer, with the *nom de plume* "Philadelphiensis," told readers. All that matters are "the illustrations and arguments he affords us and not . . . his name." Yet, in a small-scale society, where people knew one another, by reputation if not in person, it proved impossible to maintain this line. A sixteen-year-old apprentice in his brother's shop, Benjamin Franklin learned that lesson at the start of his writing career. He penned a series of essays in the persona of "Silence Dogood," a moralizing Boston widow, and submitted them to his brother's paper, *The New-England Courant*, secretly, for fear of rejection. The series gained a following, and soon the widow was the talk of the town. After eavesdropping on the streets, Franklin parodied the gossip in "Silence's" voice. One woman claimed, "I was a Person of an ill Character, and kept a criminal Correspondence with a Gentleman who assisted me in Writing. One of the Gallants clear'd me of this random Charge, by saying, That tho' I wrote in the Character of a Woman, he knew me to be a Man." A half-century later, the Connecticut wit John Trumbull stumbled into a wasp's nest of criticism after satirizing his countrymen in the *Connecticut Courant*. In a display of republican principle, he took on the character of a "universal Correspondent" and published his pieces "without the name of the writer to defend it, or of any great man to patronize it." He would trust to "the mercy of the public" for "a fair and unprejudiced perusal." That was not how it turned out. Some readers took the jibes personally, certain that for all his pretenses of impartiality, the Correspondent meant to shame them in public. How dare he assail personal characters, while remaining unknown! The Correspondent had the duty to reveal his name. Trumbull refused that call, only to drop the disinterested pose and exchange tit for tat. He demanded that two critics "throw off the mask" of anonymity and denounced another as a hypocrite for praising the Correspondent essays "in private conversation, where you thought I should hear of it" and then condemning them in public. In the heat of argument, with reputations at stake, civic virtue dissolved.[12]

Impartiality, it appears, was a political weapon, to be used as need be. In the pre-Revolutionary debate over British imperial policy, there was a division of labor between genres: pamphlets took the high road of reason and principle; newspapers descended into personal abuse. It was central to Whig strategy to expose the ministerial conspirators against American liberty, whether in Whitehall or in Boston, and to dramatize, through vivid examples, the "corruption" and "luxury" of royal officials. To that end, the billingsgate of eighteenth-century journalism was well adapted. Peter

Fields

Oliver, the Loyalist magistrate and brother-in-law of Massachusetts Governor Thomas Hutchinson, who smarted under the attacks of the *Boston Gazette* and *Massachusetts Spy*, grasped the essential technique: a public figure could be hopelessly discredited through humiliation in the press:

> [the Faction] used every low & dirty Art, from Mouth to Press, to stigmatize those who would not coincide with their Measures; such Arts as an Oyster Wench disdains to lower her Reputation to . . . . If a Man, in publick Office, was advanced in Life; he was an old wizzled Face Dog. If he had met with a Misfortune, by breaking a leg, he was a limping Dog, and so on.

Not only top officials came under the censorious eye of the press; lesser fry also got their just deserts. Newspapers did not hesitate to expose by name violators of the various nonimportation agreements. Conversely, printers risked their safety and their businesses when they actually tried to protect the anonymity of unpopular correspondents. For refusing to name an author, William Goddard, printer of the *Pennsylvania Chronicle*, got a beating at the British Coffeehouse. Loyalists played the same game. The tenor of politics was no more elevated in the factional fights of the new republic. In the campaign to ratify the Constitution, Federalists liked to present themselves as gentlemen of reason and principle, but they exploited the politics of personality to carry their cause. No matter that the Anti-federalist opposition clung to the ideal of impersonal print. To block the message, it was essential to discredit the messengers. Hence, Federalists insisted that critics of the Constitution identify themselves publicly, in hopes of exposing their rivals as mere mechanics and common farmers, utterly unqualified to discourse about government. At the same time, they played up "the splendor of names," notably, George Washington and Benjamin Franklin, on their side. In the process, Federalists repudiated the faith in impartial discourse at the heart of the public sphere. Anonymity became a despicable cover for irrational, self-seeking claims. The true gentleman spoke in his own person, offering a cultivated model of civic virtue for popular emulation. In the figure of George Washington, Federalists found their man, whose impersonal "personality" – the conscious construction of a lifetime – was invoked time and again to legitimate the new nation.[13]

Ultimately, the ideology of impartial print ran aground on the shoals of self-interest. It was a rare author who could withstand the temptation to divulge his name in the face of popular enthusiasm for his work. Thomas Paine was not one. When *Common Sense* was issued in January

1776, it carried no name, not even a pseudonym, on the title page. That was a deliberate statement of principle. "Who the Author of this Production is, is wholly unnecessary to the Public, as the Object for Attention is the *Doctrine itself*, not the *Man*." Paine had second thoughts on the matter after the pamphlet proved wildly successful. Though he never sought profit from the work – so he claimed – he did try to control its distribution, and that bid brought him into an embarrassing controversy with the original publisher Robert Bell. Who is this "Mr. ANONYMOUS," Bell asked in the Philadelphia press, this "author without a name," who uttered "absolute falsehoods" in print without fear of detection, in a "cunning" scheme of "catch-penny author-craft" to monopolize the profits of *Common Sense* to himself? To prove Paine's hypocrisy, Bell pointed to the common report. "You say you wanted to remain unknown ... but, in practice, yourself telling it in every beer-house, gives the direct LIE to the assertor of such a falsehood." Such disputes were perhaps inevitable, when authors lacked legal protection for their rights. For all the appeal of selflessness, anonymity made a person easy prey to the machinations of others. John Trumbull realized that early on and, a decade after the Correspondent series, sent a new letter to the *Connecticut Courant*: a plea for the state legislature to enact a copyright law. Having learned from hard experience that there was no safety in anonymity, Trumbull cast aside republicanism and embraced the market. "A work of Genius," he observed, "is a work of time, the effect of long labor, study, and application." Its fruits rightfully belonged to the author who had brought it forth. This was "a principle of natural justice." Well before the development of an active literary marketplace, Trumbull had discovered the fatal flaw in the bourgeois public sphere. Without a name to which copyright can be attached, an author is public property, vulnerable to one and all. Trumbull had made the odyssey from republicanism to liberalism that Warner discerns as the trajectory of the age. But as Christopher Grasso, the student of Trumbull on whose perceptive account I have drawn, advises, that had been an option from the start. "Traditional, republican, and liberal constructions of public writing – along with a conception of literary practice drawn from the sociable community of polite letters – should be considered less as successive stages or distinct epochs than as overlapping and even concurrent possibilities," to be called forth when the "local cultural and socioeconomic circumstances of print production and public speech are right."[14]

One alternative to Trumbull's dilemma was simply to stay out of print. That was the choice made by men and women of privilege, who joined in the face-to-face activities of the public sphere – the coffeehouses, clubs, tea tables, and salons – and entered into literary exercises and civil conversation. When the leading merchants, lawyers, and gentlemen of Annapolis, Maryland, gathered together for a meeting of the Homony Club in the tense years before the Revolution, they set aside their political differences and devoted themselves to the pleasures of food, drink, and wit. An evening's entertainment included numerous toasts and odes, performed in a boisterous atmosphere behind closed doors. These pastimes, carefully preserved in the club records, carried on a long, genteel tradition of manuscript culture. Salons, in turn, provided a setting for female sociability and politeness, in company with men. Adopting neoclassical nicknames, the participants shared their poems, letters, and journals, nearly all in manuscript. In an intimate coterie, women could cultivate their talents, without fear of ridicule by strangers. That concern was well grounded. Misogyny, at times, permeated the press. Consider the case of Hudson, New York, in the early republic, reported by the historian John Brooke. In its newspapers, female readers were obliged to see themselves through the male gaze. In fiction and news items, they were portrayed either as victims of violence and abuse or as careless disturbers of domestic peace. Either way, they were defined by male power, the limits to their lives prescribed in print. As the editors made plain, the public forum of the press was no place for a lady. Nor was it congenial to enthusiasts of such religious sects as the Shakers, who followed Mother Ann Lee out of "the world" and built a separate society. To keep out dangerous influences, the Shakers were as inquisitorial as the pope, tightly patrolling the letters and books that arrived from outside. Under the "Millennial Laws" imposed in 1821, "the Brethren and Sisters [were] not allowed to purchase nor borrow books nor pamphlets of the world not of Believers . . . without permission of the Elders." To the faithful, the spoken word was the most reliable source of truth. Shakers bonded in song and dance, sharing the divine spirit in collective rituals. If print was too vulgar for the gentlemen of the Homony Club, too hostile for the ladies of the salon, it was too profane for the Shakers.[15]

As this brief survey suggests, the eighteenth-century press does not fulfil key requirements of Habermas's model. Its impartiality was inconsistent, its rationality debatable, its openness to subordinate classes limited. Not surprisingly, it also fails the test of independent, free-ranging debate. Both political and economic constraints restricted what could be said. That was due, in part, to the force of law. Colonial authorities intermittently punished seditious libel, and their Revolutionary successors continued the practice, though the Federalists' campaign to suppress dissent with a national law was a political debacle. The more important source of constraint was the printers and publishers themselves. In Habermas's theory, the bourgeois public sphere maintains a critical distance from the private household, the center of family and work. When people "come together as a public" and enter into rational deliberation, they suspend their personal advantage to consider the common good. Not so for the printers, who made a living as the functionaries of the public sphere. They could not forget about the household; it was the very site of their labor. Ideally, principle and interest went hand in hand. But a man with hungry mouths to feed could not afford too many scruples. Prudent printers strove to steer their way amid the several constituencies on whom they depended. Royal government and local assembly, commonly at odds with one another, awarded printing contracts, placed official advertising, handed out appointments, and distributed other forms of patronage. But such revenue was seldom sufficient. Local merchants and lawyers were thus necessary sources of income from advertising, subscriptions, and job printing. Consequently, though some printers, such as William Bradford of New York, took pride in being a "Servant of Government," it was good business to follow a neutral course, placating everybody and offending none. Taking self-abnegating vows of blandness, printers cultivated images of themselves as neutral tradesmen, "mere mechanics" with no independent views of their own, smudged with ink merely for the sake of pay. In the businesslike simile of Benjamin Franklin, "a Newspaper was like a Stage Coach in which any one who would pay had a Right to a Place . . . ." Liberty of the press was a commercial strategy, not a political principle.[16]

Notwithstanding these pressures, newspapers became more aggressive organs of political opinion during the course of the eighteenth century. Embracing a libertarian ideology, many printers projected themselves as "men of independent intellect and principle." Their vocation was to be watchmen on the towers of liberty and "scourges of tyranny." In the Revolutionary movement, Patriot editors performed that role for an expanding market of middling readers. Principle could be profitable, as Isaiah Thomas, who built a circulation of 3,000 for his militant *Massachusetts Spy*, proved. John Holt, printer to New York's Sons of Liberty, deemed "the great Use of News papers" to be "that they form the best opportunities of Intelligence, that could be devised, of every publick matter that concerns us . . . . It was by the Means of News papers that we receiv'd & spread the Notice of the tyrannical Designs formed against America, and kindl'd a Spirit that has been sufficient to repel them." But, as we have seen, there were clear limits to that "intelligence." Nobody merited the freedom to advocate at the community's expense. Only a handful of editors, most of them Loyalists, ever tried to publish both sides of the imperial dispute, and they were mobbed for that effort. It was, in the words of historian John Nerone, a republican "commonwealth of ideas" that Patriot printers promoted, not a liberal "marketplace of ideas" open to any and all views.[17]

On these terms, printers entered the lists in the political battles of the early republic. Few maintained an independence of party, owing to a familiar combination of principle and interest. In the new nation, public subsidies were more important than ever to a printer's well-being, and such patronage was awarded mainly to the party faithful. As newspapers were integrated into the partisan machinery, workingmen of the press gained a new stature, especially among the Republicans. They were ideologues by profession, dedicated to the elaboration of the party line. Promoting candidates, attacking rivals, rallying voters, they emerged as the crucial links between politicians and the rank-and-file. There was no dispassionate consideration of issues in their pages, no pretense of impartiality. Editors played up personalities, advertising the virtues of party leaders, exposing the vices of the other side.

The task of the party press was to fashion, through "common rhetoric and common ideas," an imagined community of party, rather than nation. More precisely, as David Waldstreicher has recently shown, it was through party, as represented in the press, that vast numbers of white males – and a good many women as well – came to identify with nation. In local communities all over the republic, party loyalists gathered together to commemorate national events – the Fourth of July, Washington's birthday, the inauguration of Jefferson – by drinking toasts, singing, orating, and parading in affirmation of their common bonds. Such occasions were faithfully reported in the press. Republicans in Richmond could read the speeches and toasts of compatriots in Baltimore and Philadelphia and determine to outdo them in celebration of the cause. Indeed, local festivities were conducted with two audiences in mind: the stalwarts who participated in the events and the strangers who read about them. By this means, newspapers became central to the popular political culture of nineteenth-century America. Immersed in the round of rallies, speeches, and torch-light parades, editors brought together "rationality" and "ritual" in their work. If not the arena of critical reason envisioned by Habermas, the public sphere they brought into print was a livelier place, pulsating with the energy of speeches and marches, the personalities of leaders, and the slogans of the moment. Converting new supporters was not on the agenda. In the Jacksonian "politics of affiliation," the party press preached to the choir.[18]

Yet, newspapers were not indispensable to public life. Out on the expanding frontier and in many rural areas, the printing press was an uncommon sight. The South, in particular, lagged well behind the North in access to print, with fewer papers, lower circulation, and higher rates of illiteracy among the free population. As in the colonial period, the Southern press stayed close to centers of power – port towns, state capitals – and to the interests of the gentry. That did not stop party activists from getting out the vote in the hotly contested elections of 1828 and 1840. They relied on the familiar methods of a largely oral culture – stump speeches at barbecues, court days, and rallies – with great success. Turnout in many parts of the South reached or exceed that in the North. The age of Jackson was not always or everywhere "an age of print."[19]

By this route, we return to the problem with which we started: print and the public sphere. Was this vision of "private people coming together as a public" and engaging, through conversation and reading, in critical-rational discourse ever more than a utopian dream in Habermas's mind? An earlier generation of American historians once thought so. As Henry Steele Commager saw it, the enlightened genius of the founding fathers produced an "empire of reason." There are few advocates of that view today. The public sphere, as Warner suggests, is better seen as an ideology that informed political discourse and shaped literary forms. Therein lay its power. It was the animating vision of the eighteenth-century Republic of Letters, the cosmopolitan community of learned men dedicated to inaugurating the rule of reason. Imbued with that ideal, Enlightenment moderates pursued free discussion of public affairs, only to set in motion a far-ranging assault on the *ancien régime*. Thomas Paine's *Common Sense* electrified Americans with its ridicule of British monarchy as funda-mentally irrational, at odds with nature, reason, and the heart. In a republic, the anonymous author proclaimed, "THE LAW IS KING." So, too, did such writers as Mercy Otis Warren and Judith Sargent Murray seize upon the instrument of reason to enter the public sphere and challenge tradi-tional prejudices against their sex.

But one man's reason is another's passion. Custodians of the public sphere held the power to define those terms. Printers and politicians in the early republic lived up to their professions of impartiality about as faithfully as today's presidential candidates to their pledges to avoid negative campaigning. Federalists stigmatized their opponents not merely as ill-informed but as foolish, impulsive, and irrational, altogether unworthy of a public voice. In the magazines of the early republic, the ideal male citizen was admired less for himself than for what he was *not*:

a wastrel farmer, a fickle woman, an animalistic black slave. Dismissed in simile and metaphor, subordinate groups had a long struggle to declare themselves subjects in print. The public sphere could close the very doors to popular discussion of politics it opened up.[20]

It is not surprising that the ideal of the public sphere was chiefly honored in the breach. In a small-scale, interdependent community, where people kept a close eye on their neighbors, print was limited in its effects on daily life; it could not perform the specialized role of constituting an independent public forum. It inhabited a hierarchical and personalized world, and it reflected that ethos. Dissenters could grumble that the country press was typically "under the influence of the little lord of the village" and dream up schemes to circumvent that power, such as Massachusetts farmer William Manning's plan to organize little societies of workingmen in every town to subscribe to a monthly magazine devoted to their interests. But there was no escaping the condescension of the squire or the gossip of the neighbors, in print or in life. Pseudonyms hinted what they purported to conceal; anonymity could be a path to notoriety. Ironically, it may be this preoccupation with personality that constitutes the early republic's true legacy to our print media today. Raised in a religious culture to seek out the "personal presence" in a text, eighteenth-century fans of the other new genre of the age – the novel – perpetuated that impulse and identified with authors and characters alike. They lionized Rousseau, wept with Werther, and flocked to Charlotte Temple's grave. A culture of celebrity, fusing fact and fiction, was at hand, soliciting the hopes and dreams of ordinary folk. On the commercial exploitation of those possibilities, the media age has been built, with technologies of communication nobody could have imagined two hundred years ago. But for its cultural bases, we owe a substantial debt to the writers, readers, and printers of the new republic.[21]

Notes

1. Michael Schudson, "Was There Ever a Public Sphere? If So, When? Reflections on the American Case," in Craig Calhoun, ed., *Habermas and the Public Sphere* (Cambridge, MA, 1992), pp. 143–63; Jurgen Habermas, *The Structural Transformation of the Public Sphere: An Inquiry into a Category of Bourgeois Society*, trans. Thomas Burger

(Cambridge, MA, 1989); Benedict Anderson, *Imagined Communities: Reflections on the Origins and Spread of Nationalism*, rev. edn. (London and New York, 1991; orig. pub. 1983), p. 36.

2. Elizabeth Eisenstein, *The Printing Press as an Agent of Change: Communications and Cultural Transformations in Early-Modern Europe* (Cambridge, UK, 1980), pp. 305, 317; Lucien Febvre and Henri-Jean Martin, *The Coming of the Book: The Impact of Printing 1450–1800* (London, 1976); Roger Chartier, *The Order of Books: Readers, Authors, and Libraries in Europe between the Fourteenth and Eighteenth Centuries*, trans. Lydia G. Cochrane (Stanford, CA, 1994), p. 9.

3. E. J. Clery, "Women, Publicity and the Coffee-House Myth," *Women: A Cultural Review*, 2 (1991): 168–77; Mary Ryan, *Women in Public: Between Banners and Ballotts, 1825–1880* (Baltimore and London, 1990), pp. 11–14; Ryan, "Gender and Public Access: Women's Politics in Nineteenth-Century America," in Calhoun, ed., *Habermas and the Public Sphere*, pp. 259–88; Fredrika J. Teute, "Roman Matron on the Banks of Tiber Creek: Margaret Bayard Smith and the Politicization of Spheres in the Nation's Capital," and Jan Lewis, "Politics and the Ambivalence of the Private Sphere: Women in Early Washington, D.C.," both in Donald R. Kennon, ed., *A Republic for the Ages: The United States Capitol and the Political Culture of the Early Republic* (Charlottesville and London, 1999), pp. 89–121 and 122–54.

4. Habermas, *Structural Transformation*, 27; Richard D. Brown, "The Shifting Freedoms of the Press in the Eighteenth Century," in Hugh Amory and David D. Hall, eds., *A History of the Book in America. Volume One: The Colonial Book in the Atlantic World* (Cambridge, UK, 2000), p. 366 [hereafter cited as *HBA*]; Charles E. Clark, *The Public Prints: The Newspaper in Anglo-American Culture, 1665–1740* (New York, 1994), pp. 77–102 at 79, 92.; Sheila McIntyre, "'I Heare It So Variously Reported': News-Letters, Newspapers, and the Ministerial Network of New England, 1670–1730," *New England Quarterly* 71 (1998): 593–614; Charles E. Clark, "Early American Journalism: News and Opinion in the Popular Press," in Amory and Hall, eds., *HBA*, pp. 347–65; David W. Conroy, *In Public Houses: Drink and the Revolution of Authority in Colonial Massachusetts* (Chapel Hill, 1995), p. 234.

5. David D. Hall, "The Chesapeake in the Seventeenth Century," and Calhoun Winton, "The Southern Book Trade in the Eighteenth Century," in Amory and Hall, eds., *HBA*, pp. 56, 238–39; Stephen Botein, "Printers and the American Revolution," in John B. Hench and Bernard

Bailyn, eds., *The Press and the American Revolution* (Worcester, MA, 1980), pp. 23–45; Arthur M. Schlesinger, *Prelude to Independence: The Newspaper War on Britain 1764–1776* (New York, 1957), p. 68.

6. John Adams, "Dissertation on the Feudal and Canon Law," in Charles Francis Adams, ed., *The Works of John Adams . . .* (Boston, 1851), 3: 447–64; Hugh Amory and David D. Hall, "Afterword," in Amory and Hall, eds., *HBA*, p. 483.

7. David D. Hall, *Worlds of Wonder, Days of Judgment: Popular Religious Belief in Early New England* (New York, 1989), pp. 21–31; Warner, *Letters of the Republic* (Cambridge, MA, 1990), pp. 20–2.

8. Warner, *Letters*, pp. 22, 34–72 at 39. The social outlook that underlay the rhetoric of the Revolutionary elite was first set forth in Gordon S. Wood, "The Democratization of Mind in the American Revolution," in *Leadership in the American Revolution* (Washington, DC, 1974), pp. 63–88.

9. Warner, *Letters*, pp. 42–3, 73–117 at 110, 120.

10. Warner, *Letters*, pp. 132–42 at 132.

11. Jay Fliegelman, *Declaring Independence: Jefferson, Natural Language, and the Culture of Performance* (Stanford, 1993), 128–9; Christopher Looby, *Voicing America: Language, Literary Form, and the Origins of the United States* (Chicago, 1996), p. 44, n. 84.

12. Louis B. Wright, *The First Gentlemen of Virginia: Intellectual Qualities of the Early Colonial Ruling Class* (San Marino, CA, 1940); William Charvat, *The Profession of Authorship in America, 1800–1870*, ed. Matthew J. Bruccoli (Columbus, OH, 1968), pp. 5–12; Wood, "Democratization of Mind"; Saul Cornell, *The Other Founders: Anti-Federalism and the Dissenting Tradition in America, 1788–1828* (Chapel Hill, NC, 1999), p. 105; Warner, *Letters*, pp. 82–86; Christopher Grasso, *A Speaking Aristocracy: Transforming Public Discourse in Eighteenth-Century Connecticut* (Chapel Hill, NC, 1999), pp. 301–11.

13. Peter Oliver, *Origin and Progress of the American Revolution: A Tory View*, eds. Douglass Adair and John A. Schutz (San Marino, CA, 1961), pp. 96–7; Thomas C. Leonard, "News for a Revolution: The Exposé in America, 1768–1773," *Journal of American History*, 67 (1980): 26–40; Jerome Nerone, *Violence against the Press: Policing the Public Sphere in U.S. History* (New York, 1994), pp. 26–33; Cornell, *Other Founders*, pp. 99–106.

14. Thomas Paine, "Common Sense" in Merrill Jensen, ed., *Tracts of the American Revolution 1763–1776* (Indianapolis, 1967), p. 402;

Richard Gimbel, *Thomas Paine: A Bibliographical Check List of COMMON SENSE with an Account of Its Publication* (New Haven, 1956), pp. 17–57 at 25, 28–29; Grasso, *A Speaking Aristocracy*, pp. 318–24.

15. David S. Shields, *Civil Tongues and Polite Letters in British America* (Chapel Hill, 1997), pp. 198–208; Shields, "Eighteenth-Century Literary Culture," in Amory and Hall, eds., *HBA*, pp. 434–76; John L. Brooke, "'Not to Purchase nor Borrow Books nor Pamphlets of the World': Women, Religion, and Print Culture in the Hudson Valley, 1785–1825," paper presented at the conference on "Microhistory: Advantages and Limitations for the Study of Early American History," sponsored by the Omohundro Institute of Early American History and Culture, Storrs, Connecticut, October 15–17, 1999.

16. Stephen Botein, "'Mere Mechanics' and an Open Press: The Business and Political Strategies of the Colonial American Printer," *Perspectives in American History*, 9 (1975): 127–35; Benjamin Franklin, *Autobiography*, Leonard W. Labaree *et al.* eds., (New Haven and London, 1964), p. 165.

17. Stephen Botein, "Printers and the American Revolution," p. 45; Brown, "Shifting Freedoms of the Press;" Jeffery A. Smith, *Printers and Press Freedom: The Ideology of Early American Journalism* (New York, 1988); Nerone, *Violence against the Press*, p. 51.

18. Jeffrey L. Pasley, *"The Tyranny of Printers": The Rise of Newspaper Politics in the Early American Republic* (Charlottesville, 2001), p. 12; David Waldstreicher, *In the Midst of Perpetual Fetes: The Making of American Nationalism, 1776–1820* (Chapel Hill, 1997), pp. 202, 217–19; Robert A. Gross, *Printing, Politics, and the People* (Worcester, 1989); Michael Schudson, *The Good Citizen: A History of American Civic Life* (Cambridge, MA, 1999).

19. John L. Brooke, "'To Be Read by the Whole People': Press, Party, and the Public Sphere in the United States, 1790–1840," forthcoming in *Proceedings of the American Antiquarian Society*, 110 (2000).

20. Henry Steele Commager, *The Empire of Reason: How Europe Imagined and America Realized the Enlightenment* (Garden City, NY, 1977); David D. Hall, "Learned Culture in the Eighteenth Century," in Amory and Hall, eds., *HBA*, pp. 414–16; Paine, "Common Sense," p. 434; Carroll Smith-Rosenberg, "Dis-Covering the Subject of the 'Great Constitutional Discussion,' 1786–1789," *Journal of American History*, 79 (1992): 841–73.

21. Amory and Hall, "Introduction," *HBA*, pp. 10–11; Grasso, *A Speaking Aristocracy*, p. 452; Michael Merrill and Sean Wilentz, eds., *The Key*

of Liberty: The Life and Democratic Writings of William Manning, "A Laborer," 1747–1814 (Cambridge, MA, 1993); Robert Darnton, *The Great Cat Massacre and Other Episodes in French Cultural History* (New York, 1984), pp. 215–56; Cathy Davidson, "The Life and Times of Charlotte Temple: The Biography of a Book," in Davidson, ed., *Reading in America: Literature and Social History* (Baltimore and London, 1989) pp. 157–79.

–12–

The Rise of Film History
Melvyn Stokes

Moving pictures first appeared, as a form of popular entertainment, in the 1890s. Within less than a generation, going to the "movies" had become a well-established part of American social and cultural life. By 1922, around 40 million admissions were being recorded each week; by 1928, that figure had expanded to 65 million; in 1946, it reached an all-time peak of 82 million.[1] Thereafter, for a complex of reasons, numbers declined. By the 1950s, television was challenging motion pictures – and beginning to replace them – as the dominant form of American popular entertainment. Yet, if actual movie-going became a minority pastime in the second half of the twentieth century,[2] Hollywood's characteristic output, the feature film, increased enormously in both popularity and accessibility during the 1980s and 1990s. The key to this paradox was the emergence of the VCR, cable and satellite TV, laser discs, and DVDs. Under the influence of these technological changes, the main site of movie-watching shifted from the cinema to the home. Films could be viewed by anyone surfing the vast number of television channels (some dedicated exclusively to movies) made possible by cable, satellite, and digital television. They could be rented from a range of outlets or bought in music shops and supermarkets.[3]

The movie business has been a major American industry since the 1910s. With the decline of many other national cinemas during World War I, it swiftly attained hegemonic status in the world. Since then, it has probably done more to shape the way the United States has been viewed by non-Americans than any other single influence. It has also affected the way Americans and others perceive American history itself. Despite the millions of words written about the Civil War and the television programs made about it, for example, it seems likely that most Americans' view of the Civil War and Reconstruction is still mainly shaped by *Gone With the Wind* (1939).[4] Some films actually appear to have made history as well as representing it: *The Birth of a Nation* (1915), a virulently racist film, provoked a campaign against it by the National Association for the Advancement of Colored People that generated considerable publicity and, noted a black correspondent of W.E.B. DuBois, helped strengthen the NAACP itself by placing "the name of the Association before a great many persons who do not know that there is such an organization at work for the good of the race."[5] Films may also have influenced the actions of presidents. Many of the programs and tactics of the New Deal (including "fireside chats," the Civilian Conservation Corps, and the Works Progress Administration) were first outlined in *Gabriel Over the White House* (1933), previewed shortly before Franklin D. Roosevelt's inauguration and apparently seen several times by the new president;[6] Richard Nixon watched *Patton* (1970) a number of times before ordering the invasion of Cambodia (his secretary of state described him as a "walking ad for that movie");[7] and Ronald Reagan (the first movie actor to become president) often seemed unable to distinguish between the real and reel worlds.

Movies have also profoundly influenced American society and culture. From the 1910s, aided by promotional publicity (later fan clubs and fan magazines), the movie-going public was encouraged to identify with screen "stars." As women, in particular, tried to imitate screen goddesses, the movies encouraged the use of certain kinds of cosmetics and the wearing of certain kinds of clothes: for example, Macy's sold half a million copies of the dress worn by Joan Crawford in *Letty Lynton* (1932).[8] As well as helping to create universal standards of beauty and desirability, movies affected courtship rituals and, in all probability, other aspects of sexual relationships too. Exploring "Middletown" (Muncie, Indiana) in 1935, Robert and Helen Lynd found everywhere a "sense of sharp, free behavior between the sexes (patterned on the movies)."[9] Films have also affected styles of speech: many phrases from movies have entered the language, from Al Jolson's "you ain't heard nothing yet" and Mae West's "come up and see me sometime" to Clint Eastwood's "go ahead, make my day" and Arnold Schwarzenegger's "hasta la vista, baby." American film, moreover, has had wider (though more indescribable) effects. For, hidden deep in the memory of most of us – American and non-American alike, so great has been the power of Hollywood – is a world in which Rick and Ilsa will always have Paris, Rhett, frankly, doesn't give a damn, Scarlett is waiting for that tomorrow which is another day, the Joads are struggling towards California on Route 66, Charles Foster Kane is losing everything (Rosebud included) – and Donald Lockwood is forever singin' and dancing in the rain.

In addition to *influencing* American society and culture, of course, film has also *reflected* them. It offers visual evidence on the way people looked, the clothes they wore, the cars they drove, and the appearance of their homes and workplaces. More importantly, perhaps, it echoes – in a complex and always mediated way – changes in political, economic, sexual, and social relationships, patterns of human behavior, and attitudes to racial and ethnic groups. Films themselves are made by groups of people. They are also products of a particular industry at a specific time. They are released into a society with certain parameters of acceptability, some of them set by law, some by mechanisms of censorship or industry self-regulation (such as the Production Code Administration), some by pressure groups (for example, the Legion of Decency), and some by popular attitudes. They are viewed by critics and, if they are to be commercially successful, by mass audiences. The films themselves and their reception can provide much evidence on social and cultural history, even if the task of analyzing that evidence is itself rarely simple and unproblematic.

Despite the importance of American film, comparatively little effort was made before the 1960s and 1970s to write serious film history (as opposed to anecdotal "biographies" of stars and movie moguls), and most of what did appear was not by professional historians. The first two major "histories" of American film were published by Terry Ramsaye in 1926 and Benjamin B. Hampton in 1931.[10] Both were produced by men who had worked in the film industry. Ramsaye had been an engineer before turning to journalism in 1906. For the next eight years, he wrote for a variety of Midwestern newspapers before becoming an editor/producer of motion pictures. In 1920, James R. Quirk, the publisher of *Photoplay Magazine*, commissioned him to write a series of twelve articles on the rise of the motion picture industry. Severing his formal connections with the film industry, Ramsaye set to work and soon found that there was material for considerably more than twelve articles. His series was finally published in thirty-six instalments over three years and republished, in 1926, as a two-volume work entitled *A Million And One Nights*.[11] The book itself reflected both Ramsaye's background in the motion picture industry and his experience as a journalist. Highly impressionistic and anecdotal, it focused on the film industry's business and technological giants (especially Thomas A. Edison) to the exclusion of other aesthetic, social, and economic factors.

Unlike Ramsaye, who carved out a successful niche for himself within the film industry,[12] the next man to tackle a history of the movies did so from a considerably more critical perspective. Like Ramsaye, Benjamin B. Hampton had a background in journalism. He had edited and published newspapers in Illinois for several years before moving to New York. In

1907, he acquired an old periodical and turned it into a highly successful monthly magazine. Like many other "monthlies" of the time, *Hampton's* was a crusading magazine. It "muckraked" the sugar trust, exploiters of child labor, and New York's wealthy Trinity church. In 1909–10 it helped ruin the Taft Administration in the Ballinger-Pinchot affair. Shortly thereafter, when the magazine turned its attention to the railroads, Hampton found his credit sources drying up and was forced to sell it.[13] For five years, he was employed by the American Tobacco Company before, in 1916, becoming a producer of motion pictures. Unfortunately for him, Hampton proved no more successful in the movie business than he had with his magazine: he found it impossible, as an independent producer, to compete with larger conglomerates. Returning from Los Angeles to New York, however, he was encouraged by old reformist friends, including Amos Pinchot and John Dewey, to write a book focusing on his concerns over the implications of corporatization in the film business both for Hollywood itself and the entire democratic process. His *A History of the Movies* (1931) was primarily a business history of Hollywood. It largely ignored films themselves, save as commodities, in order to focus on such matters as the defeat of the Edison Trust and the emergence of chains of movie theaters.[14]

The next writer to attempt a general history of motion pictures shared Hampton's anxieties over tendencies within the movie industry itself, though his views both of how to produce a history of the movies and the purposes of movies themselves were very different. Lewis Jacobs, a writer and film-maker, believed that film could be socially useful. One of the quartet of people who founded *Experimental Cinema*, a socialist film journal, in 1930, he continued writing about cinema from a very left-wing perspective when the journal succumbed in mid-decade to a range of aesthetic and political disputes. Yet while his *The Rise of the American Film* (1939) defended the right of movies to address social questions (and to be made without excessive interference), the attempt to examine the main elements of the movie industry in each of what Jacobs saw as the six stages of its growth often became little more than a description of the "significant" films released in each stage. When it came to answering some of the major questions relating to American movies – such as who made them and why – Jacobs, like Ramsaye, emphasized the crucial role played by individual pioneers.[15]

After the publication of Jacobs's book, there were no major attempts to produce a comprehensive history of American film for almost twenty years. Two new surveys, however, were both produced in 1957: Arthur Knight's *The Liveliest Art* and Richard Griffith and Arthur Mayer's *The*

Movies.[16] Neither was a scholarly work; Mayer, indeed, was a former theater manager and studio publicist whose memoirs give an entertaining, if unreliable, insider's picture of the movie industry of the 1930s and 1940s.[17] In fact, the first serious film histories by academics did not appear until the following decade: Albert R. Fulton's *Motion Pictures: The Development of an Art* (1960) and Kenneth Macgowan's *Behind the Screen* (1965).[18]

While a few other examples of what can be identified as film history appeared in the late 1960s and early 1970s, a revised version of the *Harvard Guide to American History*, published in 1974, listed only thirty-eight books on the history of motion pictures.[19] The decade of the 1970s as a whole, however, witnessed the beginnings of a change. Film history started to emerge as a serious academic subject. While this happened for a number of reasons, two, in particular, are worth emphasizing. First, there was a veritable explosion in cinema studies as a subject. In 1967, only 200 colleges offered film-related courses; by 1977, the number exceeded 1,000.[20] This vast expansion created a huge demand for introductory texts – including scholarly surveys that would provide an overview of the history of American cinema. Not only were there no such surveys in film history, there was almost no basic research on which to base such texts. Predictably, therefore, the books written between the 1920s and the 1950s by Ramsaye, Hampton, Jacobs, and Knight were reissued in paperback form and used to provide many thousands of film students with their first knowledge of film history.

The first of a new generation of general histories was published in 1971: Gerald Mast's *A Short History of the Movies*. In common with both its predecessors and its immediate successors, however, Mast's book depended crucially on anecdotal evidence, presenting an account of movie history focusing on the activity of great (or at least famous) men. Before the 1970s, almost no one seemed aware that there were conventional archival materials available for writing the history of film. A second factor in the beginnings of serious film history, therefore, was the discovery that there were such materials. A major break-through in this respect was the publication in 1975 of Tino Balio's history of United Artists (the studio founded by Charlie Chaplin, Douglas Fairbanks, Mary Pickford, and D. W. Griffith). Balio's study was pioneering in two principal ways: it eschewed the conventional approach to the social history of the movies ("great men") in order to concentrate attention on UA as an economic institution and it was also based on thorough research in the studio archives.[21] Douglas Gomery also did extensive work in the Warner Bros. Archives for his (unaccountably unpublished) Ph.D. thesis.[22] It was not only studio archives, however, that started to become available. The Production Code Administration files at the Academy of Motion Picture Arts and Sciences Library encouraged work on the administration of the Hays Code. Later, scholars would examine the records of pro-censorship organizations, such as the Legion of Decency. In *Film: The Democratic Art* (1976), Garth Jowett demonstrated the existence of a wealth of material showing that cinema did have a social history, and that history was recorded in a variety of places, including, for instance, the Payne Fund studies published in the 1930s into the effects of movies.[23]

In 1982, Gerald Mast edited an extensive collection of documents on film history that included many primary as well as secondary materials.[24] The fact that Mast was a professor of English rather than a historian, however, underscores the rather eccentric manner in which film history evolved. For, like Mast, most of those involved in the great expansion of film teaching in the 1970s and 1980s came not from history departments but from departments of English, literature, history of art, theater, speech, communication studies, or philosophy. Even those who taught film history were usually located in other departments. Much of the trajectory of film history from the 1970s to the present day, therefore, can be explained by the fact that it developed, as a sub-discipline, within the field of film studies rather than that of history proper.

The fact that most film history was initially written by non-historians confronting archival material, in some cases for the first time, is a curiosity. But it also poses the question of the attitude of professionally-trained historians to film history in its early years. There was, for example, the journal *Film and History* that commenced publication in the mid-1970s, and was mainly edited by and for professional historians. In many ways, this praiseworthy endeavor failed: it had almost no influence on the development of film history within film studies and also did not really impinge on the consciousness of many "card-carrying" historians. The latter, it often seems, were (and to a significant extent still are) intent mainly on holding fiction films to some standard of historical verisimilitude, and, without themselves having undergone training in how to discuss films as texts, find it very awkward to say much more than "it is/is not accurate."[25] Indeed, engaging with films historically as cultural artifacts appears to have come much more easily to practitioners of American Studies, with its interdisciplinary orientation, than it does to historians.[26]

A high proportion of the film history that was written and published in the 1970s and early 1980s was politically and ideologically committed: it dealt with the ways in which Hollywood protected existing inequalities and institutions. There were, perhaps, two principal reasons for this. The first, growing out of the scholarship of the *Annales* school in France and the work of British cultural and social historians (notably Raymond Williams and E. P. Thompson), was the attempt of the "new social history" to construct a past in which ordinary people fought for control over their own lives and circumstances.

Consequently, Robert Sklar, writing a cultural history of the movies, interpreted that history – from early struggles over censorship to the later Hollywood blacklist – as one of continual struggle between a dominant native middle-class culture and working-class and/or immigrant ideas and behavior.[27] Allied to this were a number of attempts to interpret aspects of film history from a Marxist viewpoint. Richard S. Dyer, for example, analyzing stardom, presented it as having an ideological function: through the medium of their own, polysemic images, stars reconciled conflicts and contradictions in society at large. They consequently aided the maintenance of the status quo and helped uphold the dominance of the capitalist ideology. Dyer recognized, however, that not every star image was able to reconcile such contradictions and, in exceptional cases, such images could be seen as subversive.[28]

The second reason was the impact of social movements, especially the growing strength of feminism and the aftermath of the civil rights movement. Thus, for example, Molly Haskell argued that the narrative of most films required even the most intelligent and capable of female characters in the end to submit themselves to men. She saw such screen images as not only an accurate reflection of male attitudes to women in American society generally but as helping to perpetuate stereotypes of women's inferiority.[29] Thomas Cripps interpreted the ways in which blacks were depicted on screen between 1900 and 1942 in a more complex manner, seeing such images as the result of a mediation between society itself, the almost entirely non-black film industry, and pressure from particular social groups. After 1942, he believed, Hollywood – influenced by pressure from civil rights groups rather than as a result of any change in public sentiment – had begun to improve the image of blacks on film.[30]

Two other forms of film history were effectively pioneered in the 1970s. Attempts were made to investigate and explain the technological advances that had underpinned the growth of the industry. A group of scholars, including Harry M. Geldud, Douglas Gomery, Gorham A. Kindem, Dudley Andrew, R. T. Ryan, and Patrick Ogle, explored issues such as the introduction of sound, the innovation of color, and the birth of deep-focus cinematography.[31] The decade also saw the beginning of local studies in film exhibition and reception. In 1977, Richard Alan

Nelson and Burnes St. Patrick Hollyman explored early cinema in Florida and Austin, Texas, respectively.[32] In 1979, Douglas Gomery published articles on the arrival of the movies in Milwaukee and cinematic business practices in Chicago.[33] Two articles by other film historians, however, would be of especial significance for the future. Each challenged the prevailing view that saw the audiences for the nickelodeons as primarily drawn from the working class. Russell Merritt, using Boston as a test case, argued that exhibitors soon became intent on attracting middle-class movie-goers. The successful strategy they employed to do this was to offer special concessions to women and children, to show certain kinds of film only, and to locate nickelodeons in commercial districts, where they might better attract middle-class patrons, instead of in working-class residential areas.[34] Robert C. Allen, in a survey of New York nickelodeons, found that a number of primarily working-class districts had relatively few nickelodeons, while large numbers were to be found located in increasingly middle-class areas. Allen also drew attention to the growing number of legitimate theaters that were trying to appeal to a predominantly middle-class clientele with a mixture of film and vaudeville.[35]

Many of the publications of the 1970s were pioneering and created future possibilities – especially the work of Merritt and Allen, which provoked a much later critical response from Sklar and (in the mid-1990s) a major debate on the social origins of early New York cinema audiences in the *Cinema Journal*.[36] But film history itself occupied only a small area of the vast and growing field of American film studies. Most film studies practitioners were primarily interested in analyzing films as *texts* in order to establish how textual mechanisms operated in order to produce meaning and pleasure. To help in this endeavor, they appropriated a variety of theoretical tools, including the structuralism of Ferdinand de Saussure, Claude Lévi-Strauss, and the early Roland Barthes, Althusserian Marxism, the ciné-semiology of Christian Metz, and the Lacanian psychoanalysis of the later Metz, Raymond Bellour, and Jean-Louis Baudry. Meanwhile, from a different perspective, a number of feminist writers began to address theoretical concerns, notably the relationship between film texts and their female spectatorship. Probably the most important of these early writings was Laura Mulvey's path-breaking essay on "Visual and Other Pleasures," published in 1975 in the British journal *Screen*.[37]

For at least a decade after 1975, film studies was convulsed by debates on theoretical issues, fought out in the pages of the growing number of film journals. In effect, during this time, film history was peripheral to the main directions in which the field was developing. Attempts to show how signifying practices determined the meaning of film texts or how psychoanalysis could shed light on the experience of the (theoretical) spectator were essentially ahistorical. Thus, in the first book to set out possible methodologies for studying film history, and to record publications in film history over the previous years, while there was a discussion of both semiotics and Lacanian psychoanalysis, that discussion was relatively brief.[38] The book itself, written by Robert C. Allen and Douglas Gomery, suggested various strategies for writing differing kinds of film history: aesthetic, technological, economic, and social. Its publication (in 1985) was exceptionally well-timed, since it coincided with (and contributed to) the beginning of a period in which film history would rise to occupy a far more significant place within the field of film studies as a whole.

From the mid-1980s onward, a number of film scholars were making a case for the contextual analysis of texts. The narrative and style of those texts, they contended, could often only be understood through an examination of the circumstances of their production. Therefore, in *The Classical Hollywood Cinema: Film Style and Mode of Production to 1960* (1985), David Bordwell, Kristin Thompson, and Janet Staiger investigated the link between texts and methods of production. Thomas Schatz discussed the effect of the different studios' house style on the movies they produced in *The Genius of the System* (1988).[39] It also became increasingly clear that the narrative content of films was often greatly influenced by Hollywood's system of self-censorship. In *The Wages of Sin* (1991), Lea Jacobs, who had examined the files of the Hays office on the "fallen woman" type of film, found that what could be shown in these films was the consequence of a process of constant negotiation. After the establishment of the Production Code Administration in 1934, however, the moral imperatives of the Breen office resulted in a considerably more integrated narrative form.[40] Films themselves came from an intertextual environment that often had important effects on their narrative strategies. William Uricchio and Roberta Pearson, for example, have analyzed some of the intertextual influences – including Shakespearean plays – on early silent film.[41]

Other historians have explored such factors as the law, politics, and economics on the style and narrative form of motion pictures. The law of obscenity, for example, underpinned the prohibitions of the Hays Code in establishing boundaries over what could or could not be shown in films – at least until both the Hays code and the law itself began to change in the aftermath of the *Burstyn v. Wilson* (often known as the *Miracle*) case of 1952.[42] One example of political influence on the production of films was the successful pressure applied by the United States government on

Hollywood during World War II to make films supporting such officially-sanctioned ideals as national unity and equality.[43] The investigations into Hollywood launched by the House Committee on Un-American Activities in 1947 and 1951–52 afforded another illustration of attempted political interference with film-making.[44] There were continuous pressures from private organizations, notably the Roman Catholic Church and its Legion of Decency, to moderate and control the content of motion pictures.[45] In terms of economics, as Thomas Schatz noted, the growth of transnational corporations during the 1960s had a major effect in creating the "block-buster" syndrome adopted by Hollywood in the following decade.[46]

This new scholarship encouraged the notion that texts could be better understood through analysis of the circumstances of their production. One of the most exciting developments in film history in recent years, however, has been the movement toward studying not so much how films are produced, but how they are received. This was influenced, to some extent, by the growing importance of reception in literary studies following the work of German reception theorists such as Hans Robert Jauss.[47] It paralleled the turn in literary studies to the "new" historicism and a growing interest in reading and the history of reading.

Several factors, of course, can be seen at work in determining the reception of films. One is exhibition: Douglas Gomery demonstrated how the distribution tactics of the "Big Five" studios during the classical era (insisting on strictly-controlled exhibition patterns allowing films "first," "second" or "clearance" runs according to the type and location of the cinema) influenced the attitude of movie-goers towards the films they saw.[48] Another is stardom and the manner in which the discursive apparatus surrounding it may be interpreted by film-goers. Richard Dyer, for example, showed how star personalities signify different things to different groups in different historical circumstances, examining the manner in which Marilyn Monroe signified white female sexuality, Paul Robeson symbolized blackness, and Judy Garland was appropriated as a gay icon.[49]

As reception studies have begun to take off, however, they have marked out two principal areas of interest. The first, that of "Historical Reception Studies," has been particularly associated with the work of Janet Staiger. Advocates of this approach explore the interpretative strategies pursued in response to films. Much of the evidence for these strategies comes from review journalism. In analyzing the reviews of D. W. Griffith's *The Birth of a Nation* (1915), for example, Staiger found general agreement on the part of contemporary reviewers to separate out the "narrational procedures" of the film (which most praised) from its subject matter and the potential effects of the latter on spectators (issues that prompted much controversy and debate). But the synchronic reaction to the film, Staiger pointed out, was only part of the story. There was a diachronic response as well, as successive generations with their own political agendas and cultural competences confronted the film. Starting in December 1939, for example, David Platt published a series of articles in the communist newspaper, *The Daily Worker*, in which he argued that *The Birth of a Nation* had been part of a conscious effort on the part of Hollywood – in collusion with capitalist interests – to rule both working-class blacks and whites by dividing them. This attempt by Platt to demonstrate a link between racism and class exploitation was challenged in the *New Leader* by Seymour Stern. Probably motivated mainly by anti-Stalinism (after the revelations of the purges, the failures in the Spanish Civil War, and the signing of the Hitler-Stalin pact), Stern challenged this interpretation of the film, arguing that Griffith had been neither reactionary nor racist in making it, and attacking critics such as Platt as "totalitarians."[50]

The second major approach to investigating reception is the study of how audiences have responded to movies. The fact, as Robert C. Allen pointed out in a 1990 article, that the "direct study of contemporary audiences" was "already fraught with enormous theoretical and methodo-logical problems" inevitably meant such problems would be "multiplied greatly when questions of audience are cast in the past tense."[51] Certainly the history of the audience remains perhaps the most elusive aspect of film history, since audiences form only the most temporary of communi-ties and leave few traces of their presence. In the late 1980s and the 1990s, however, encouraged by a variety of factors – the turn to reception in literary studies, the rise of cultural studies, investigations into television audiences, feminist efforts to identify a more "active" female spectator-ship, and the impact of the *Cinema Journal* debate over the social com-position of early New York movie-going – more and more scholars began to write about movie audiences. One approach that came to be known as "ethnography" involved using techniques of oral history plus question-naires to investigate the attitudes of a specific sub-set of movie-goers: the fans of particular films or stars.[52] One thing this approach made clear was that fandom was often an enduring phenomenon, with fans retaining a sense of loyalty that served as a source of both individual and group identity over extended periods of time.

In the beginning, it seemed that work on audiences would be hampered by the restricted amount of primary material available to the academic researcher. This was perhaps the principal anxiety I had in organizing a conference in 1998 on the subject of "Hollywood and Its Spectators."

The paper-givers at that conference, however, it rapidly became clear, were a deeply resourceful and imaginative group. Among other sources they exploited to construct insights into audiences were the foreign-language and African American press, local newspapers, labor, socialist, and radical journals, correspondence among exhibitors, exhibitors' trade journals, the records of reform, censorship, and labor organizations, city archives, surveys by social scientists, the work of polling organizations, poster collections, Sears catalogs, and oral history collections. It appeared to me, on the evidence of that conference and the response to it, that sometime in the 1990s film history had begun to move away from a prevailing paradigm based on production to one focusing on reception.[53] As a historian, that seemed to me very much an advance. For the historical significance of film (as of most popular culture) is to be found more in its reception than in its production – is to be found, in fact, in the meanings, sometimes not clearly articulated, that audiences read into it and the many uses they make of it.

More and more film history has been published in recent years. One recognition of the growing maturity of the field as a whole is the appearance of the "History of the American Cinema" series dedicated to synthesizing (as well as adding new research findings to) our knowledge of film history in various periods.[54] While it is still the case that most of this history is written by scholars who are not historians, at least in terms of their formal institutional affiliation, some of it now is.[55] Moreover, during the last decade and a half of the twentieth century, American historians in general demonstrated growing interest in film. In December 1986, the *Journal of American History* began to publish film reviews. In December 1988, the *American Historical Review* featured a forum on history and film.[56] Film topics also started to receive more attention in other historical journals. To a considerable extent, of course, this reflected the increasing fascination of historians with cultural (and especially popular cultural) themes. Since this fascination currently shows little sign of ending, it is very likely that historians' engagement with (and contribution to) film history will only continue to increase in the first years of the twenty-first century.

Acknowledgement

I would like to thank Robert C. Allen and Richard Maltby for their very helpful comments on an earlier version of this chapter.

Notes

1. Richard Koszarski, *An Evening's Entertainment: The Age of the Silent Feature Picture 1915–1928* (Berkeley, 1990), p. 26; Joel W. Finler, *The Hollywood Story* (New York, 1988), p. 288.

2. Total attendance at the movies declined after 1960 to around 20 million a week, at which point it stabilized for more than two decades. With the advent of multiplex cinemas in the late 1980s, attendance began to rise again.

3. In 1998, around half of all U.S. consumers rented a video at least once a month. Sixty percent of all households own feature films on video, with the average number of feature film titles per household standing at forty-one. Robert C. Allen, "Home Alone Together: Hollywood and the 'family film,'" in Melvyn Stokes and Richard Maltby, eds., *Identifying Hollywood's Audiences: Cultural Identity and the Movies* (London, 1999), p. 118.

4. When *Gone With the Wind* was premiered on network television over two nights in 1976, NBC claimed a total audience of 162 million. Ninety percent of the U.S. population are believed to have seen the movie at least once. By comparison, around 40 million Americans watched one or more of the programs in Ken Burns's documentary series on the Civil War, first broadcast in 1990. David Thomson, *Showman: The Life of David O. Selznick* (London, 1993), p. 676; Jim Cullen, *The Civil War in Popular Culture: A Reusable Past* (Washington, DC, 1975), p. 67; Robert Brent Toplin, ed., *Ken Burns's The Civil War: Historians Respond* (New York, 1996), p. xv.

5. Chas A. Gird to W. E. B. DuBois, August 20, 1915, NAACP Papers, Library of Congress. The high profile of the NAACP fight against the film helped the organization effectively to double in size: its 5,000 membership in January 1915 had increased to "nearly 10,000" by December 1915. See Minutes of the Meeting of the NAACP Board of Directors, January 5, 1915 and December 13, 1915, both in NAACP Papers.

6. Terry Christiansen, *Reel Politics: American Political Movies from "Birth of a Nation" to "Platoon"* (Oxford, 1992), p. 34; Robert L. McConnell, "The Genesis and Ideology of *Gabriel Over the White House*," *Cinema Journal*, 15:2 (1976): 15.

7. William Shawcross, *Sideshow: Kissinger, Nixon and the Destruction of Cambodia* (New York, 1979), pp. 135, 144.

8. Charlotte Hertzog and Jane Marie Gaines, "'Puffed sleeves before tea time': Joan Crawford, Adrian and women audiences," *Wide Angle*, 6:4

(1985): 25. While "merchandising" of products associated with the movies (sometimes in stores associated with particularly studios) is often perceived as a modern innovation, it was pioneered in the late 1920s and the 1930s. See Charles Eckert, "The Carole Lombard in Macy's Window," *Quarterly Review of Film Studies*, 3:1 (1978): 1–21.

9. Robert S. Lynd and Helen Merrell Lynd, *Middletown in Transition: A Study in Cultural Conflicts* (New York, 1937), p. 170.
10. The very first years of the movies were also covered in Robert Grau, *The Theatre of Science: A Volume of Progress and Achievement in the Motion Picture Industry* (New York, 1914).
11. Terry Ramsaye, *A Million and One Nights: A History of the Motion Picture*, 2 vols. (New York, 1926), I, p. v.
12. Ramsaye edited the *Pathé News* and *Pathé Review* in 1928–30, before becoming the editor of the *Motion Picture Herald* and other trade periodicals in the 1930s. In the last years of his life, he was a consulting editor for Quigley Publications.
13. Louis Filler, *Crusaders for American Liberalism* (Yellow Springs, OH, 1950), pp. 271–2, 300, 332, 366–7. Also see C. C. Regier, *The Era of the Muckrakers* (Chapel Hill, 1932), pp. 175–7.
14. Benjamin B. Hampton, *A History of the Movies* (New York, 1931).
15. Lewis Jacobs, *The Rise of the American Film* (New York, 1939).
16. Arthur Knight, *The Liveliest Art* (New York, 1957); Richard Griffith and Arthur Mayer, *The Movies: The Sixty-Year Story of the World of Hollywood and Its Effect on America. From Pre-Nickelodeon Days to the Present* (New York, 1957).
17. Arthur Mayer, *Merely Colossal: The Story of the Movies from the Long Chaise to the Chaise Longue* (New York, 1953).
18. Albert R. Fulton, *Motion Pictures: The Development of an Art from Silent Films to the Age of Television* (Norman, OK, 1960); Kenneth Macgowan, *Behind the Screen: The History and Techniques of the Motion Picture* (New York, 1965).
19. Frank Freidel with Richard K. Showman, ed., *Harvard Guide to American History* (Cambridge, MA, 1974), pp. 582–3.
20. Robert C. Allen and Douglas Gomery, *Film History: Theory and Practice* (New York, 1985), p. 27.
21. Tino Balio, *United Artists: The Studio Built by the Stars* (Madison, WI, 1975). For a later study of this type, see Richard B. Jewell, *The RKO Story* (New York, 1982).

22. J. Douglas Gomery, "The Coming of Sound to the American Cinema: A History of the Transformation of an Industry," Ph.D. dissertation, University of Wisconsin-Madison, 1975.

23. Garth Jowett, *Film: The Democratic Art* (Boston, 1976).

24. Gerald Mast, *The Movies in Our Midst: Documents in the Cultural History of Film in America* (Chicago, 1982).

25. See, for example, Robert Brent Toplin, ed., *History by Hollywood: The Use and Abuse of the American Past* (Urbana, IL, 1996) and Ted Mico, John Miller-Monzon, and David Rubel, eds., *Past Imperfect: History According to the Movies* (London, 1996).

26. For examples of this approach, see Andrew Bergman, *We're in the Money: Depression America and Its Films* (New York, 1971) and Lary May, *Screening Out the Past: The Birth of Mass Culture and the Motion Picture Industry* (New York, 1980).

27. Robert Sklar, *Movie-Made America: A Cultural History of American Movies* (New York, 1975). Also see Jowett, *Film: The Democratic Art*.

28. Richard S. Dyer, *Stars* (London, 1979).

29. Molly Haskell, *From Reverence to Rape: The Treatment of Women in the Movies* (New York, 1974); cf. Marjorie Rosen, *Popcorn Venus* (New York, 1973).

30. Thomas Cripps, *Slow Fade to Black: The Negro in American Film, 1900–1942* (New York, 1977). Also see Donald Bogle, *Toms, Coons, Mulattoes, Mammies and Bucks: An Interpretive History of Blacks in American Films* (New York, 1973); Daniel J. Leab, *From Sambo to Superspade: The Black Experience in Motion Pictures* (Boston, 1976).

31. Harry M. Geldud, *The Birth of the Talkies: From Edison to Jolson* (Bloomington, IN, 1975); Douglas Gomery, "Problems in Film History: How Fox Innovated Sound," *Quarterly Review of Film Studies*, 1:3 (August 1976): 315–30; Gorham A. Kindem, "Hollywood's Conversion to Color: The Technological, Economic and Aesthetic Factors," *Journal of the University Film Association*, 31:2 (Spring 1979): 29–36; Dudley Andrew, "The Postwar Struggle for Color," *Cinema Journal*, 18:2 (Spring 1979): 41–52; R. T. Ryan, *A History of Motion Picture Color* (New York, 1978); Patrick Ogle, "Technological and Aesthetic Influences Upon the Development of Deep Focus Cinematography in the United States," *Screen*, 13:1 (Spring 1972): 45–72.

32. Richard Alan Nelson, "Florida: The Forgotten Film Capital," *Journal of the University Film Association*, 29:3 (Summer 1977): 9–21;

Burnes St. Patrick Hollyman, "The First Picture Shows: Austin, Texas, 1894–1913," *Journal of the University Film Asssociation*, 29:3 (Summer 1977): 3–8.

33. Douglas Gomery, "Saxe Amusement Enterprises: The Movies Come to Milwaukee," *Milwaukee History*, 2:2 (Spring 1979): 18–28; Douglas Gomery, "The Growth of Movie Monopolies: The Case of Balaban and Katz," *Wide Angle*, 3:1 (1979): 54–63.

34. Russell Merritt, "Nickelodeon Theaters, 1905–1914: Building An Audience for the Movies," in Tino Balio, ed., *The American Film Industry* (Madison, WI., 1976), pp. 59–79.

35. Robert C. Allen "Motion Picture Exhibition in Manhattan, 1906–1912: Beyond the Nickelodeon," *Cinema Journal*, 19:2 (Spring 1979), reprinted in John Fell, ed., *Film Before Griffith* (Berkeley, CA, 1983), pp. 162–75.

36. Robert Sklar, "Oh! Althusser: Historiography and the Rise of Cinema Studies," *Radical History Review*, 41 (Spring 1988), reprinted in Robert Sklar and Charles Musser, eds., *Resisting Images: Essays in Cinema and History* (Philadelphia, 1990), pp. 12–35; Ben Singer, "Manhattan Nickelodeons: New Data on Audiences and Exhibitors," *Cinema Journal*, 35:3 (Spring 1996): 3–35; Sumio Higashi, "Dialogue: Manhattan's Nickelodeons," ibid.: 72–73; Robert C. Allen, "Manhattan Myopia: or, Oh! Iowa!," ibid.: 75–103; Ben Singer, "New York, Just Like I Pictured It . . . ," ibid.: 104–28; William Uricchio and Roberta Pearson, "Dialogue: Manhattan's Nickelodeons New York! New York!," ibid., 36:4 (Summer 1996): 98–102; Judith Thissen, "Oy, Myopia! A Reaction from Judith Thissen on the Singer-Allen Controversy," ibid.: 102–7; Ben Singer, "Manhattan Melodrama – A Response from Ben Singer," ibid.: 107–12.

37. Laura Mulvey, "Visual and Other Pleasures," reprinted in Mulvey, *Visual and Other Pleasures* (London, 1989), pp. 14–26.

38. Allen and Gomery, *Film History*, pp. 76–8, 167–9.

39. David Bordwell, Kristin Thompson, and Janet Staiger, *The Classical Hollywood Cinema: Film Style and Mode of Production to 1960* (New York, 1985); Thomas Schatz, *The Genius of the System: Hollywood Filmmaking in the Studio Era* (New York, 1988).

40. Lea Jacobs, *The Wages of Sin: Censorship and the Fallen Woman Film, 1928–1942* (Madison, WI, 1991).

41. William Uricchio and Roberta Pearson, *Reframing Culture: The Case of the Vitagraph Quality Films* (Princeton, NJ, 1993).

42. See Richard S. Randall, "Censorship: From *The Miracle* to *Deep Throat*," in Balio, *American Film Industry*, pp. 432–57; Stephen

Vaughan, "Morality and Entertainment: The Origins of the Motion Picture Production Code," *Journal of American History*, 77 (1990): 39–65.

43. Clayton R. Koppes and Gregory D. Black, *Hollywood Goes to War: How Politics, Profits and Propaganda Shaped World War II* (Berkeley, CA, 1987); Dana Polan, *Power and Paranoia: History, Narrative, and the American Cinema, 1940–1950* (New York, 1986). For a much broader (and very revisionist) study of Hollywood's impact on politics and American culture, see Lary May, *The Big Tomorrow: Hollywood and the Politics of the American Way* (Chicago, 2000).

44. See Larry Ceplair and Steven Englund, *The Inquisition in Hollywood: Politics in the Film Community, 1930–1960* (New York, 1980); Polan, *Power and Paranoia;* Lary May, "Movie Star Politics: The Screen Actors' Guild, Cultural Conversion, and the Hollywood Red Scare," in May, ed., *Recasting America: Culture and Politics in the Age of the Cold War* (Chicago, 1989), chapter 7; Bernard F. Dick, *Radical Innocence: A Critical Study of the Hollywood Ten* (Lexington, KY, 1989).

45. Gregory D. Black, *Hollywood Censored: Morality Codes, Catholics, and the Movies* (Cambridge, UK, 1994); idem, *The Catholic Crusade Against the Movies, 1940–1975* (Cambridge, UK, 1998); James M. Skinner, *The Cross and the Cinema: The Legion of Decency and the National Catholic Office for Motion Pictures, 1933–1970* (Westport, CT, 1993); Frank Walsh, *Sin and Censorship: The Catholic Church and the Motion Picture Industry* (New Haven, CT, 1996).

46. Thomas Schatz, "The New Hollywood," in Jim Collins, Hilary Radner, and Ava Preacher Collins, eds., *Film Theory Goes to the Movies* (New York, 1993), pp. 8–36.

47. Hans Robert Jauss, *Toward an Aesthetic of Reception*, trans. Timothy Bahti (Minneapolis, MN, 1982).

48. Douglas Gomery, *Shared Pleasures: A History of Movie Presentation in the United States* (Madison, WI, 1992), especially pp. 66–9.

49. Richard Dyer, *Heavenly Bodies: Film Stars and Society* (New York, 1986).

50. Janet Staiger, *Interpreting Films: Studies in the Historical Reception of American Cinema* (Princeton, NJ, 1992), especially pp. 139, 146–8.

51. Robert C. Allen, "From exhibition to reception: reflections on the audience in film history," *Screen*, 31:4 (1990): 351.

52. See Helen Taylor, *Scarlett's Women: "Gone With the Wind" and Its Female Fans* (London, 1989); Jackie Stacey, *Star-gazing: Hollywood*

Cinema and Female Spectatorship (London, 1994); Annette Kuhn, "'That day did last me all my life': Cinema memory and enduring fandom," in Stokes and Maltby, eds., *Identifying Hollywood's Audiences*, pp. 135–46.

53. Three volumes of revised papers from the conference – with some additional contributions – have so far been published: Melvyn Stokes and Richard Maltby, eds. *American Movie Audiences: From the Turn of the Century to the Early Sound Era* (London, 1999); idem, *Identifying Hollywood's Audiences*; and idem, *Hollywood Spectatorship: Changing Perceptions of Cinema Audiences* (London, 2001).

54. Charles Musser, *The Emergence of Cinema: The American Screen to 1907* (Berkeley, CA, 1990); Eileen Bowser, *The Transformation of Cinema: 1907–1915* (New York, 1990); Richard Koszarski, *An Evening's Entertainment*; Donald Crafton, *The Talkies: American Cinema's Transition to Sound, 1926–1931* (New York, 1997); Tino Balio, *Grand Design: Hollywood as a Modern Business Enterprise, 1930–1939* (New York, 1993); Thomas Schatz, *Boom and Bust: Hollywood in the 1940s* (Berkeley, CA, 1999).

55. See for example Kathryn H. Fuller, *At the Picture Show: Small-town Audiences and the Growth of Movie Fan Culture* (Washington, DC, 1996); Steven J. Ross, *Working-class Hollywood: Silent Film and the Shaping of Class in America* (Princeton, NJ, 1998).

56. Robert Brent Toplin, "Introduction," *Journal of American History*, 76, part II (1989–90): 1003.

Part III
Regional History

–13–

The American West: From Exceptionalism to Internationalism
Patricia Nelson Limerick

In the late 1970s and the early 1980s, historians – often quite distinguished ones – pronounced obituaries and conducted memorial services for the field of Western American history. The field was in demographic decline; the meetings of the Western History Association had a dwindling attendance; the assumption seemed to be that Western historians spent their time fretfully restating and revising the Turner Thesis. Here, to serve as one example of this enthusiasm for sending Western history off to the graveyard, is the comment of a distinguished American colonial historian at a conference in 1984:

> Yet how important is the "West" (minus California and urban population clusters in the Pacific Northwest) in the twentieth century or even in the nineteenth century? . . . For in our role as scholars, we must recognize that the subject of westward expansion itself no longer engages the attention of many, perhaps most, historians of the United States. Surveys of college and university curricula indicate a steady decline in courses dealing with "history of the west"; significant numbers of graduate students no longer write dissertations on this subject; and few of the leading members of our profession have achieved their scholarly reputations in this field.[1]

And then matters took quite a turn. There are different ways we could summarize this change. One way of putting it would be to say that "race, class, and gender" finally "went West," and rendered the old Turnerian interpretative squabbles blessedly irrelevant. To some degree, the revitalization of regional history involved building alliances with fields of history already in their own eras of reinvigoration. Thus, the whole transformation hinged on some acts of surprisingly quick redefinition: to use one example, casting the history of Mexicans and Mexican Americans as central, not peripheral, to Western American history was one source of great revitalization. Apart from alliances with fields of history already in the midst of their own renaissances, another way of explaining the change might be to say that young historians, looking for their areas of specialization, began to sense opportunity. Even if the promise of frontier opportunity had not worked out for many homesteaders, the Trans-Mississippi West's promise of fresh, unexplored research topics, rich in untapped meaning, began to draw flocks of the ambitious. Perhaps just as consequentially, the change in the field of Western American history may well have been part of a much bigger change in regional self-perception. In retrospect, it is now clear that the transformation of the writing of Western history ran parallel to a very comparable transformation, very similar in spirit, in Western creative writing – in poetry, novels, memoirs, and essays, as well as in Western landscape painting and photography.

In other words, regional writers, intellectuals, and artists – though they were not part of a coordinated movement – were all responding to unmistakable changes in their spatial and temporal surroundings. In the 1970s and early 1980s, the interior West underwent another resource boom, this time in energy – oil and coal. That boom came to quite a sudden end in 1983 and 1984. This bust was followed, equally suddenly, by a boom in recreation, tourism, second-home settlement, and scenic-amenity consumption that continues to this day, making the interior West the fastest-growing section of the country. Traditional rural enterprises – ranching, farming, logging – have, at the same time, been in pretty steep decline. With all these rapid changes to attend to, writers of every kind had a *new set of outcomes to explain*.[2] The "punchline" of Western history was changing every day, and old plots and narratives for explaining how the present evolved from the past were breaking under the strain. Changed conditions called for a new kind of relevance.

It is also my guess that observers in the future will see the end of the Cold War as an important aspect of the context of these changes. Celebrating the triumph of white pioneers was a historiographic activity particularly well-suited to the ideological imperatives of the United States's stance of innocence and virtue in the contest with the Soviet Union. Consider the timing of the revival of Frederick Jackson Turner's frontier thesis. After very intensive critiques in the 1930s, the Turner Thesis got its second lease on life with the publication of Ray Allen Billington's textbook, *Westward Expansion*, in 1949.[3] A version of Western history as flattering to American vanity as Billington's certainly made a nice fit with the ideological needs of the early Cold War. In truth, the project of characterizing a critical interpretation of Western American history as subversive, anti-American, and even Communist-influenced played a part in the field's debates in the late 1980s and early 1990s.

My own memories of this whole transformation may be more and more shaped by the classic distortions of nostalgia and other varieties of sentimentality, but here, briefly, is my personal view of the shift in Western history. In 1987, I published a book called *The Legacy of Conquest*. The world seemed strikingly untransformed and unshaken by this event. Then, in 1989, we held a conference in Santa Fe, called "Trails: Toward a New Western History." At that conference, several people – Richard White, Donald Worster, and I – made various proclamations about our having left the sterile debates of the past behind, and arrived at the practice of a *new* Western history.

Whether any of us intended to capitalize those words and then put them forward as the title of a historiographic movement, I truly do not know. It really did not matter very much what we intended, since the transformation of Western American history was about to become a case study in the power of the media. First, the *Washington Post* did a story on the New Western History, with the reporter telling me that he was very happy to have the chance to do this story, since it was the kind of story the *New York Times* usually got first. Then the *New York Times* followed the *Post*, with the reporter verifying the *Post* writer's hypothesis, and expressing his irritation that the *Post* writer had gotten there first. Then a series of newspapers and newsmagazines followed these pace-setters, and we had a prime opportunity to learn, as Richard White observed, that the press follows the press. And before anyone could decide whether this was a desirable outcome or not, we found ourselves custodians of a movement called the New Western History.

Curiously, the emergence of the New Western History had an unexpectedly revitalizing effect on, literally, the fortunes of the Old Western History. As of 1989, there was one collection of the essays of Frederick Jackson Turner in print, and that volume had very limited sales. After the stories in the *Post* and the *Times*, Turner's sales climbed. Attacking Turner, even just declaring him to be irrelevant, turned out to stimulate a desire to *read* Turner. While it was not exactly my intention to enhance the value of Turner's intellectual estate, it certainly seems a situation preferable to those old days of lamentations and obituaries for the field.

Attendance at the Western History Association, down to two or three hundred in the early 1980s, is now regularly near or over a thousand. Textbook writers have been making some significant changes, and additions, to their treatment of the Trans-Mississippi West. Editors from publishing houses such as W. W. Norton and Oxford University Press, never seen before at the Western History Association, are regular presences. Obituaries for the field seem, themselves, to have died away. And, in a process which *might* be called revitalization, or something else entirely, yesterday's spirited young rebels have become, alas, the Establishment.

What was the central content of this movement now wearing the label of the New Western History? For an interview that appeared in *People Magazine*, I boiled the project down to four words beginning with "c": continuity; convergence; conquest; and complexity. It was an occasion of mixed satisfaction and sorrow when several friends told me that they thought that the interview in *People* was the best statement of my position they had seen.[4]

First, a few words about *Continuity*. Twenty years ago, right at the heart of the dominant version of Western history, stood a big discontinuity between the nineteenth-century West and the twentieth-century West. As Frederick Jackson Turner had declared, the frontier closed in 1890. Frontier stories came to a halt; in the end of the Indian wars and the creation of National Forests and Parks, frontier issues reached resolution; the West lost its distinctiveness. These assumptions remained orthodoxy in college history textbooks into the 1990s.[5] Nearly all of the textbooks stopped indexing any usages of the word "West" after 1890 because, to their authors, the frontier was the West, the West was the frontier, and both had departed as significant subjects of study before the twentieth century started. Most unhappily, this "closing" of the frontier and the West, at a stroke, declared the work of Western historians irrelevant to any understanding of the West today. To study the frontier was to study an era that had definitively and solidly *ended*, with no narrative or causal ties connecting the past to the present.

Nearer the ground, Western life told quite a different story. There was more homesteading *after* 1890 than before. A number of extractive industries – timber, oil, coal, uranium – went through their principal booms and busts *after* 1890. If one went solely by the numbers, the nineteenth-century westward movement was the tiny, quiet prelude to the much more sizable movement of people into the West in the twentieth century. Even more important, any number of conflicts and dilemmas, stirred up in the nineteenth century, remained to haunt Westerners in the twentieth century. Conflicts over water use, public lands, boom/bust economies, local authority versus federal authority, relations between Mexico and the United States (as well as between Mexican Americans and Anglos), Indian land and water claims, as well as freedom of religious practice: most of the issues that had agitated the nineteenth-century West continued to stir things up a century later. The assertion of continuity in Western history, along with the discounting of the belief in "the end of the frontier," reunited the pieces of a fragmented story, and promised to help Westerners steer their way through dilemmas which seemed to come from nowhere, but which actually came with long pedigrees.[6]

Then we turn to *Convergence*. In earlier versions of Western history, the doings of white people, especially white men, controlled center stage. With attention fixed on the westward movement of white Americans, the older Western history could only recognize Indian people as obstacles or barriers to the big process of frontier expansion, while Chinese and Mexican workers could find relevance only as they contributed to the building of railroads and the developing of agriculture. White Americans were the leading men (and, much more rarely, women) of Western history.

In practice, the American West looked dramatically different. The West was, in truth, a place of extraordinary convergence, one of the great meeting zones of the planet. In the Trans-Mississippi West, Indian America, Latin America, Anglo America, Asia America, and Afro America all met, and their representatives jockeyed for position with each other and tried to figure each other out. The westward movement of white Americans was unquestionably important, but so was the westward movement of African Americans, the northward movement from Mexico, the eastward movement from Asia, and the prior presence of Indian people.[7]

Next comes the theme of *Conquest*. The word "frontier" was the essential term for Western historians in earlier generations. In 1893, Turner wisely passed up the opportunity to define the term; the word, he said, "is an elastic one, and for our purposes does not need sharp definition."[8] The term was, in fact, quite sharp in its meaning if historians were willing to merge their point of view with that of English-speaking white people, heading into the interior from the Atlantic Coast. From that angle of vision, the frontier *was* the edge of civilization, the area where white domination had not yet been consummated. Saturated with nationalistic pride, the emotional and ideological associations of the frontier had the curious effect of exempting United States history from world history. In popular understanding, places such as South Africa, the Belgian Congo, Algeria, New Zealand, and Australia had unmistakably undergone invasions and conquests, and the United States, meanwhile, had a frontier, an ever-expanding zone of freedom, opportunity, and democracy.

As Western historians grew more uncomfortable with the problems built into the term "frontier," a number of enterprising souls set forth to salvage it, trying to redeem it for continued use by reducing its ethno-centricity and increasing its inclusivity. My own preference was to give up on these time-consuming exercises in redefinition and, instead, to place Western American history back into global history with an explicit and honest use of the word "conquest." In the last five hundred years, the biggest story on the planet has been the movement of Europeans from Europe into every other continent. Like many other parts of the planet, the American West had been transformed by this story, as the seizure of resources and the imposition of colonial dominance, along with often more benign processes of collaboration, intermarriage, and syncretism, have reshaped the lives of native people. Calling this process "conquest" cleared away the fog.[9]

And then, finally, to the notion of *Complexity*. The desire for a telling of Western American history in which good guys are easily distinguished from bad guys is deep and persistent. Myth-makers have shaped thinking all over the planet; residents of other nations, as well as many Americans, want the Old West to be the place in the past where we are permitted to escape complexity. Black hats should mark the heads of villains and white hats the heads of heroes, and yet the moral reality of Westerners makes gray hats the appropriate headgear. Human behavior in the American West, both past and present, has shown the same level of moral complexity as human behavior in any other part of the planet. Thus, a major project of the New Western History had to be the assertion that benefits often came packaged with injuries, good intentions could lead to regrettable outcomes, and the "negative" aspects of life wove themselves into a permanent knot with the "positive" aspects. If the New Western Historians had a slogan, it was the ritual declaration "It's more complicated than that," and, perhaps by virtue of that complication, as I will argue, more worthy of the attention of historians in seemingly unrelated fields. Taking up a thoroughly unlicensed prophetic mode, we told the press in 1989 that a new era of vitality in Western American history was about to dawn. I was able to say this with some confidence, because I knew of quite a number of works in progress that embodied this fresh start for the field. It seemed to me almost certain that the next years would see the publication of quite a number of studies, set in the Trans-Mississippi West and bringing fresh understandings to both regional and national history. I hoped that was true; I *believed* it was true; but it still seemed a very kind act of providence when it actually *proved* to be true.

It is my personal belief that the renaissance in Western American history has been good news for general U.S. history in several ways. Paying greater attention to Western history offers several benefits to American historians in any field. Quite a number of scholars have made the case for the recognition that the "black/white binary" (or the practice of defining race relations as, primarily, the interactions of whites and African Americans) requires remodeling, in order to reckon with the national and continental history of relations between and among Indian people, Hispanics, Asian Americans, African Americans, and whites. In this cause, attention to the West is a curative in itself.

Every now and then, in Western history, situations of inter-ethnic encounter came down to a clearly defined meeting of two groups. More often, situations involved encounters of people from three or four or more ethnic identities. Consider, as one painful example, the Camp Grant Massacre in 1871 in Arizona. At that massacre, an informal army of Arizona civilians descended on a peaceful camp and killed over one hundred Apaches, mostly women and children. This certainly seems to be an episode in interracial conflict, but on the other side, it was also an episode in interracial collaboration. The attackers at Camp Grant were a consortium of Hispanics, Anglo-Americans, and Papago – or Tohono O'odham – Indian people. However much in conflict those three groups might have been on other matters, they could agree on their appraisal of Apaches.[10]

In the wars for conquest, it was a rare situation to have a clear arrangement of "Indians" versus "whites." Crow Indian scouts were, of course, on Custer's side at Little Big Horn. For the Army, taking advantage of earlier antipathies and hostilities to use one tribe as auxiliaries in fighting another tribe was more the rule than the exception.[11] And complicating that picture was, of course, the post-Civil War use of African American troops – the Ninth and Tenth Cavalry and the Twenty-Fourth and Twenty-Fifth Infantry – in the Indian wars and *other* engagements. Describing the use of Black troops to control an uprising of Mexican Americans, the 1877 El Paso Salt War, historian Quintard Taylor sums up this complicated Western scenario: "In an era when black men themselves increasingly became the victims of violence, the African American troops of the Ninth Cavalry stood between white and brown men in one of the worst ethnic and political feuds in nineteenth-century Texas."[12] When Black soldiers fought Latinos or Indians, or, for that matter, when African Americans ransacked Korean stores in the Rodney King uprising of 1992 in Los Angeles, the usual black/white binary of the conventional approach to American race relations is not of much use. When an Oregon newspaper editor in 1865 argued against the Reconstruction amendments, he pointed out the complexity of the West's interethnic encounter: "If we make the African a citizen, we cannot deny the same right to the Indian or the Mongolian. Then how long would we have peace and prosperity when four races, separate, distinct, and antagonistic should be at the polls and contend for the control of government?"[13]

Along with dramatic demonstrations of the need for a much more complicated model of national race relations, the West offers the essential case studies for tracking that now much-studied phenomenon of race as a social and cultural construction, subject to shifts and transformations in meaning. The history of anti-miscegenation laws in the American West, as well as the patterns of *de jure* and *de facto* segregation in schools and public facilities, add a crucial dimension to the study of those practices in the United States, since such laws and practices applied to a range of ethnic groups beyond African Americans and often involved quite extraordinary and intricate attempts to categorize and classify racial groups, and to figure out a hierarchy in which to place those groups.[14]

The defining of Indian identity would be sufficient in itself to make the case for Western American history as an essential subject of study in the construction of race and ethnicity. The current use of the blood quantum – by which the federal government and many tribes measure an individual's status as an Indian by the percentage of a particular tribe's "blood" the individual has – is an extraordinary product of history. Treaties and the federal relationship to tribal government make the question of "who is an Indian" a matter of political and economic consequence. A 1991 study reported the variation of tribal definitions of the blood quantum: 19 tribes required a ½ quantum to qualify for tribal membership; while 145 tribes demanded a ¼ quantum. This widespread solution – of defining Indian identity on the basis of a claim to a certain fraction [using terms like one-quarter Arapaho; one-half Navajo; full-blood Lakota] – gives the notion of "blood" as the source of identity an extraordinary political and cultural weight.[15]

While the blood quantum sets a curious standard for verifiable "purity" in the certification of Indian identity, on the other side, mainstream American society often shows an equally striking credulity and "will to believe" in these matters, a will to believe with little concern at all with evidence. The famous 1970s public affairs advertisement, showing an Indian weeping over pollution and ecological destruction, took up a permanent place in the memories of millions of Americans and many international observers of the United States as well. The actor who played the ecologically disheartened Indian, Iron Eyes Cody, told the story of the filming of this advertisement, in his autobiography, and that story in itself is fairly instructive. Cody did *not* swim, and, for the opening scene showing him padding in a canoe, was so fearful of upsetting the canoe that he insisted that a helicopter hover overhead while he paddled, with a rescue force ready to descend instantly if he capsized. Moreover, for the scene with the tear, Cody's own ability to cry on demand worked for a while, but finally had to be supplemented with eye drops.[16]

So the scene of the Indian at home in nature rested on a certain technological support system behind it. But what Cody did not tell his readers was an interesting fact about his own origins. A film historian, Angela Aleiss, has recently looked closely at the background of this archetypal Indian actor. It turns out that Cody was born and raised in Louisiana, and his parents were two Italian immigrants. When he relocated to Hollywood, Cody relocated his identity, from Italian to Indian.[17] While there are probably many descendants of European immigrants in the United States who care deeply about pollution and environmental degradation, a public service advertisement showing an Italian American in tears, grieving over the state of the earth, would probably have left viewers more puzzled than moved. The grieving Indian, by contrast, met expectation and made perfect sense.

The Iron Eyes Cody story, finally, puts the spotlight back on our will to believe, and the well-established understandings that placed Cody's constructed identity and his sorrow over the injuries done to nature so entirely beyond the realm of our doubt and skepticism. The UCLA historian Melissa Meyer has recently offered this forceful appraisal: "The Indians who populate the American popular imagination bear absolutely no relationship to real native people either in the past or in the present."[18] The gap, between the clarity and recognizability of the imagined Indian and the actual complexity and complication of contemporary Indian identities, is dizzying in its scale. It is hard to know where one could go for a better demonstration of the proposition that race and ethnicity are matters of social construction, and not simply pre-existing conditions into which individuals are born.[19]

In a similar way, Western American history invites historians of the United States in general to pay greater attention to the human relationship to nature and place. In the mid- to late 1980s, when I was writing *The Legacy of Conquest*, this issue seemed very compelling because the practice of environmental history presented a solution to the fragmentation of historical studies by ethnicity, race, class, and gender. The work of Richard White, especially, made it clear that the study of the transforma- tion of a place, landscape, and ecosystem required the scholar to pay attention to all the people who had an impact on that site.[20] So I began as, and still remain, a believer in the faith that place-centered history made exclusiveness unworkable. Employers and workers; women and men; farmers, ranchers, and urban-based tourists and consumers of agricultural products; whites, Indians, Mexicans, Asian Americans, African Americans: tracking change in human impacts on a physical landscape made it impossible to "play favorites" in allocating attention. Everyone who was there had to figure in the story of the transformation of natural environments, if that story was going to make any sense.

But making the case for environmental history as a bedrock force for inclusiveness in historical writing was not, for a time, a particularly easy or convincing argument to make. For perfectly understandable reasons, much of what was initially called environmental history was focused on the rise of the conservation movement, on the appreciation of forests and open spaces, and on the management of the West's public lands – national parks, national forests, Bureau of Land Management holdings. There were some significant challenges to this model: William Cronon's *Nature's Metropolis* was a major step toward placing cities centrally in environmental history and Robert Gottlieb's *Forcing the Spring* made a persuasive case for recognizing the public health movement as a line of origin for contemporary environmentalism, a point of origin of equal significance to the rise of public lands conservation.[21] And yet, the most visible school of environmental scholarship, probably best symbolized by Roderick Nash's *Wilderness and the American Mind*, remained resolutely focused on the writings, thought, and actions of white American men, from Henry David Thoreau to George Perkins Marsh to John Muir and Gifford Pinchot to Aldo Leopold and Bob Marshall, and so on, with Indian people serving purely as ephemeral, mythical presences in the virgin wilderness, and other ethnic groups remaining entirely invisible. Anyone intent on making the claim that environmental history mandated a full commitment to ethnic inclusiveness would not wish to draw his or her audience's attention to Roderick Nash and other founders of the field.[22]

And yet, over the last few years of the twentieth century, environmental history went through its own transformation, from its origins as a study of white American attitudes toward "untouched" nature to a much more complicated exploration of human relationships with resources, landscapes, and material settings.[23] In fact, connecting ethnic history to environmental history is one of the most promising enterprises in the field of Western history, with implications for the entire planet. It has been stimulated by books such as David Montejano's *Anglos and Mexicans in the Making of Texas* and Neil Foley's *The White Scourge*. Although neither author, I believe, set out deliberately to establish a connection between ethnic history and the history of the environment, inequities in land and its control are so central to both books that they truly hover on the brink of crossing over into environmental history.[24]

Take two topics that seemed to be placed on two entirely separate tracks of Western American history: the creation of National Parks, and the removal and displacement of Indian people. In fact, those two stories *had* to remain separate, if anyone was going to believe in the vision and dream of national parks as zones of nature without significant human impact. The conquest of Indians was the sad and regrettable aspect of Western history, and the creation of National Parks was the happy and progressive aspect of Western history, and keeping those two aspects separate was an important part of the project of postponing a serious reckoning with the complexity of the region's past.

In a publishing event that, in itself, stands for both the revitalization of the field of Western history and the joining of environmental and ethnic history, several recent books set forward the proposition that the creation of the U.S. National Parks *required* the removal of native people, a precedent full of consequence for the cause of nature preservation globally, as preservation has come into conflict with the livelihoods and cultural practices of local residents.[25]

All the areas that are now national parks had a significant Indian presence before the conquest. Thus, a process of dispossession took place in Yellowstone and Yosemite, Glacier, and the Olympic Peninsula, and the other celebrated parks in the system. Even when Indian people had been forced from their camps and villages within the parks, traditional practices of fishing and hunting remained sources of friction and some-times violence. The prohibition of hunting in National Parks reclassified long-running Indian subsistence practices as poaching, and park officials worked strenuously to restrict those practices. In the case of Glacier National Park in Montana, the scenario may present its greatest irony. In the early years of the Park, officials lamented the fact that the elk sometimes strayed over the park boundary, into the Blackfeet Reservation. Park Service personnel were quite agitated over the fact that the Blackfeet continued to use some of those elk for purposes of subsistence. And then, with the elimination of wolves and other predators, along with the prohibition on human hunting, the Park's elk population skyrocketed, exceeding the available grazing resources. By this point, Park officials were actually trying to haze the elk and drive them over the border into the Blackfeet Reservation, in hopes that the Indians would kill them and thus reduce the grazing pressure!

At Yosemite National Park, some Indian people were permitted to remain as residents in a village within the park's boundaries – because they provided an important, if subordinate part of the labor force in the tourist economy. But the cruelty and autocracy of Park Service policy were quite extraordinary here. Park officials could dismiss or evict individuals at will; if an Indian head of household lost his job, or retired, the whole family had to leave the Park. This process of attrition reduced the size of the Yosemite Indian community until, in 1996, the last Yosemite Indian to reside in the national park retired from his job as a forester, and left the Park.

As Mark Spence puts it, "wilderness preservation went hand in hand with native dispossession."[26] The process of conquest turns out to lie at the foundation of those islands of imagined, natural innocence, the national parks. When the national park idea was exported to Africa, many American conservationists seemed surprised when it turned out that nature preservation meant *lots* of friction with indigenous people. And yet the removal of Indian people from American parks had made this consequence perfectly predictable. And it is to the full implications of the process of invasion and conquest, dispossession, and removal that I will now turn.

Back in the late 1980s, one dimension of the transformation of the field of Western history yielded a particularly rich harvest of confusion and misunderstanding. As I have mentioned, several of us concluded that the word "frontier" offered an array of disadvantages: it was vague and foggy in definition; when it was clear in definition, it was usually ethnocentric, favoring the point of view of white Americans; and, perhaps most important, over-use of the word "frontier" obscured the similarities between the settlement of the American West and the global processes of European expansion elsewhere. Reliance on the word "frontier," we thought, ratified and even enshrined an unproductive form of American exceptionalism. By this formulation, South Africa, for instance, underwent a process of invasion, conquest, displacement, and domination, while the United States, the older terminology suggested, enjoyed an expanding frontier of democracy, equality, and opportunity.

So we proposed dropping the word "frontier," which had now acquired the label "the f-word," and substituting the word "conquest." And then, at that point, I lost spin control entirely. Several scholars in frontier history responded to this proposal by declaring that the New Western Historians had prohibited a study of process on behalf of a study of region; we had, they said, dropped the study of the westward-moving frontier in order to redirect all attention to the study of the Trans-Mississippi West. Of course, that *was not* what we had said: we still wanted to study process, but we wanted to use a clearer, more honest word to *characterize* that process.

Before I could regain my bearings and make that clarification, however, a pointless argument over the virtues of "process versus place" depleted everyone's energies.[27] Again, to quote my quotable colleague Richard White, this was one of the few historical debates to die purely of its own boredom. Once the process/place debate crawled off to its corner to fade quietly away, we could remember that the point had never been to discount the study of process; the point was to give the process a clearer name in order to study it more effectively, and to reposition Western American history in a bigger context of colonialism and imperialism.

Fortunately, despite the time wasted in that debate, circumstances finally allowed me to regain my footing on this subject. The University of Colorado History Department offers capstone courses for its graduating seniors, and the capstone courses are team-taught exercises in comparative history. In the Fall of 1998 and the Fall of 1999, two colleagues – James Jankowski, a historian of the Middle East, and Chidi Nwaubani, a historian of West Africa – and I collaborated in teaching a course comparing colonialism and imperialism in the American West, West Africa, and parts of the Middle East, particularly Egypt.

The first time we taught this course, we tried to cover everything under the sun and thereby drove ourselves and the students batty, trying to deliver on a far too ambitious agenda of topics. The second time, we deliberated and chose what seemed to be the six most fruitful topics for comparison: first, the rationales and justifications of the imperialists; second, the inclusion, or perhaps co-optation, of indigenous people in structures of governance; third, the change in religious practices in response to Christianity; fourth, the transformation of gender roles for indigenous women; fifth, the reconstructing of identities in response to colonialism; and sixth, the advocacy of anti-colonial agendas by nationalists. When it came to this sixth item, we were extraordinarily lucky. We had the students read Vine Deloria, Jr.'s *Custer Died for Your Sins: An Indian Manifesto*, and this was surely the first time that that crucial declaration of Indian nationalism had been read along with declarations of Egyptian, Arabic, Islamic, Nigerian, and Pan-African nationalism.[28] But our luck reached its peak with the fact that Vine Deloria, Jr. is our colleague at the University of Colorado, and he came to our class and talked very frankly about the "behind the scenes" story of 1960s American Indian nationalism.

In all six categories, we were struck by many similarities. Take, for instance, the insistence on the part of colonial authorities in many parts of the world that western-style education was essential to the civilizing process, an insistence followed quite rapidly by the authorities' anxiety and even alarm over the intractability of the educated elite, especially alarm over their capacity to use print – articles, books, and newspapers – to challenge the colonial power. The educated native, in the judgment of one British administrator in West Africa, was "a worse evil than the primitive savage."[29] To move from studies of the challenge that educated Africans posed to the colonial power structure to Peter Iverson's biography of Carlos Montezuma is to inhabit a world in which it does appear that historians in different fields have a lot to say to each other. Passages from Fred Hoxie's study of the Crow people also make a perfect fit. In a meeting where federal representatives pushed for a land cession, the Crow elders:

> Brought forward a group of young men who have recently returned to the reservation from extended terms in government schools. "Here gathered near me you see the boys we sent to school," Spotted Horse pointed out; "they are young men now and can read and write;" . . . One of the returned students . . . went on to read an itemized list of promises broken, payments missed and annuities delayed. The commissioners were stunned. Said one, "This is the first time I have dealt with Indians that they ever gave me anything on a piece of paper!"[30]

Along with alarm over the unexpected powers of education, colonial thinking about the uplifting of native women offered an exact match, too. The curriculum of boarding schools in Africa matched the curriculum of boarding schools in the American West, with indigenous women's aspirations channeled into and confined by that multi-national human misery called "domestic science." Equally striking was the declaration, made with almost exactly similar phrasing in these very different venues, that one major mission of the colonizers was to uplift the degraded status of native women (and "degradation" was indeed their noun of global preference), with that declaration often being made by men who opposed white women's rights in their own home countries. Since writing *The Legacy of Conquest*, I hope I have come to appreciate gender issues more. I have, in particular, benefited tremendously from two extraordinary books: Leila Ahmed's *Women and Gender in Islam: Historical Roots of a Modern Debate*, especially her chapter on the "Discourse of the Veil," and Oyeronke Oweumi's *The Invention of Women: Making an African Sense of Western Gender Discourse*. An informative Western American counterpart to these books, Laura Klein and Lillian Ackerman's collection, *Women and Power in Native North America*, made a fine fit with this African and Middle Eastern reading.[31]

On the other side of the process, the ways in which the colonized people responded to Christianity bore a striking resemblance to each other. We all became temporarily expert in Islamic Modernism, and became fascinated by Mohammed Abduh's declaration that true Islam had the jump on Christianity: if purified of wrongheaded customs and habits accumulated over the centuries, the *original* Islam was Christianity's superior in reason and efficiency. The familiar characterization of Islamic Modernism – as a process of "marching backward into the future" – became an unexpected and even unsettling match to movements such as the Ghost Dance and the Native American Church in the American West, movements in which Indian people returned to the past in order to come out ahead in the future. All of this also fitted very closely to the pattern of movements such as the Aladura Churches in West Africa, and their Africanization of Christian beliefs and practices. The whole exercise of comparison offered an extremely useful reminder, for Western American historians, that the familiar polarity between tradition and assimilation is not a very useful framework for thought. The responses of colonized people to the introduction of Christianity showed us the *normality* of the story of Nicholas Black Elk, as explored by Michael Steltencamp.[32] In the writings of John G. Neihardt, Black Elk was enshrined as the archetype of traditional Lakota religious belief; outside those writings, Black Elk himself converted to Catholicism and, moreover, interpreted Catholicism as a logical extension of Lakota belief. In the context of world history, the comparable practices of Wovoka, prophet of the Ghost Dance (rejecting white presence and even dreaming of the disappearance of whites, while at the same time incorporating many elements of Christian belief and practice), came to seem more the predictable norm of human behavior, rather than a puzzling and inexplicable contradiction.

Meanwhile, in the two opening sections of the course, on the rationales of the imperialists and on the use of "indirect rule," or the incorporation of indigenous people into the structures of colonial governance, the patterns often seemed to be peas in a pod. In countless cases having to do with the process we have called "westward expansion" or "the frontier" or even "conquest," the devices, techniques, strategies, and justifications used by the United States bear an unsettling resemblance to the practices used by European countries as they wielded power around the planet. And yet American commissioners of Indian affairs did seem to have one habit of mind rarely seen among, for example, British colonial officials. American bureaucrats were often full of regret, generous with statements about how sad the early history of the displacement of Indians made them feel. They were, in other words, quick to condemn their predecessors, eager to lament the cruelties and brutalities of those who had preceded them in the project of mastering the natives, and quick to declare that *they* would be a great deal more enlightened in their own practices.

The question left hanging by our deliberations in the course was this: did this U.S. willingness to express regret and sorrow add up to any difference in practice? Was this ritual expression of regret purely a matter of rhetoric and idle sentiment? Was it a concession to the United States's mounting enthusiasm for a portrait of itself as the nation of innocence and virtue? Did this rhetoric have any moderating impact on the exercise of power? Leaving the plane of rhetoric, the reality encapsulated in the 1903 Supreme Court decision *Lone Wolf v. Hitchcock*, declaring the plenary power of Congress to follow its own will in Indian affairs regardless of treaty obligations, seemed to be an important disclosure of the *actual* practice of American colonialism and imperialism, rendering the expressions of sentiment and sorrow something of a literary exercise.

There are indeed differences that ask for a reckoning but, in general, the similarities in colonial practices in our varying locales – American West, Egypt, West Africa – are very striking. But where should we turn for our explanations of the similarities in the workings of colonial powers in such different settings? Ascribing the similarities to coincidence seems an unsatisfactory line of approach. My own conviction is that two different lines of explanation actually supplement each other: first, colonizing powers were very much aware of each other, and attuned to each other's example; some of the similarities in their operations thus disclose direct influence and imitation, especially given the simultaneity of the post-Civil-War burst of U.S. westward expansion, the scramble for Africa, and the formalization of the British presence in Egypt. Second, it may well be that there are only a limited number of strategies and techniques by which one group of people can establish and maintain dominance over another and, similarly, a limited number of strategies and techniques for the colonized people to turn to in response. For instance, whatever the locale of the area undergoing conquest and whatever the colonizing nation, wielding power by the constant and vigilant exercise of force proved to be expensive and draining, and sometimes morally troubling to politicians and public audiences in the home country. Thus, it was the path of wisdom (and economy) to figure out a way to get the colonized to participate in their own governance and subordination: hence the similar strategies of British officials such as Lord Cromer maintaining Egyptians in office; colonial administrators such as Frederick Lugard delegating authority to paramount chiefs in Northern Nigeria; and Office of Indian Affairs bureaucrats appointing Indian chiefs and councils, as well as Indian judges and policemen.

In all this territory, when it comes to the actual, material operations of colonialism – processes of dispossession, assertions of legitimacy, appropriation of land and labor – in all these matters, the international similarities are abundant, and the claim for American exceptionalism is very thin. In fact, the claim to exceptionalism might well be a much later retrospective development. In the nineteenth century, white Americans frequently used the word "empire" to describe their enterprise in westward expansion, and they were indefatigable quoters of Bishop Berkeley, "Westward the course of empire takes its way." And yet, when it comes to the historical *memory* of these North American practices in colonialism, then the case for American exceptionalism becomes much stronger, as many white Americans (including a number of our students) continue to practice a cheerful, optimistic denial (or perhaps amnesia) over the whole subject.

To use the most available example, a small but decidedly audible percentage of our students began convinced and remain convinced that the United States should never have been included in this course. They phrased their discomfort in some curious ways. "The United States does not belong in this course," one of them put it, "because it was conquering itself" – which is probably not the way the Sioux or Navajo or Utes or Comanches saw the situation. Other students asserted that the expansion of the United States deserved an entirely different framework because of the innocent intentions of settlers: this was not colonialism because the settlers were pursuing land, opportunity, and fresh starts – even though the same thing might be said of European settlers in Kenya, or in South Africa, or in Algeria. But these student assertions of innocence rarely operated on behalf of the United Kingdom. None of the students has seemed at all inclined to claim a comparable innocence and virtue for British colonial officials or settlers. In fact, at times in class, I have found myself entirely alone in asserting that folks such as Lord Cromer and Lord Lugard deserve some consideration as complicated human beings who should not be reduced to stereotypes.

In part, when some students try to assert an exemption for the United States, they are guided by the common understanding offered in the standard American history textbooks: that the United States became an imperial power with the Spanish-American War or, more precisely, with the suppression of the Philippines insurrection. In other words, in a judgment ratified by many writers of American history textbooks, a nation needs to send an army across an ocean before its assertion of dominance will meet the standards for imperialism; asserting dominance over contiguous land just does not pass the test. In finding grounds for exceptionalism, the students are also evidently responding to the fact that the area acquired by the United States in wars with Indians and with Mexico became incorporated into the nation state, and that is obviously quite different from the fate undergone by Nigeria or Egypt. But that is a difference of outcome and hindsight, and not necessarily a difference in the process by which dominance was asserted.

In fact, some patterns that at first struck me as significant differences, setting the example of the United States off from the case studies of Egypt and Nigeria, lost that status when we looked more closely at them. It would be easy to say that imperialism in many parts of Africa and the Middle East hinged on the use of indigenous people as a labor force. At first glance, common understanding would say that the situation in the American West differed considerably on this count. But books such as Albert Hurtado's *Indian Survival on the California Frontier* and a collection of essays, *Native Americans and Wage Labor*, edited by Alice Littlefield and Martha Knack reduce that perception of difference considerably.[33] Areas of recent white settlement were often areas of heavy labor demand, and Indian people were, far more often than we have usually recognized, incorporated into developing economies as workers – as laborers in the fur trade, in mining, in roadbuilding, in railroad construction, in livestock herding, in the building of irrigation systems, in farmwork, in domestic service, in laundry, and in cutting the wood to build and heat homes in new settlements. While the scale, and certainly the visibility, of the use of native labor may have been quite a bit smaller in the American West, it was undeniably far more significant than we have realized.

Indeed, the whole subject of demographic proportions is another case where difference at first seems great, and then contracts. Europeans were greatly outnumbered in West Africa and in most parts of the Middle East, except in Algeria. At first, that sense of a small population of colonizers, dwarfed by much greater numbers of indigenous people, seems to make quite a contrast with the situation in the American West, where the Indian population had not been particularly dense to start with, in most areas, and then had been devastated by European-introduced diseases. But I gradually woke up to the fact that the lived reality of a late nineteenth- or early twentieth-century Indian reservation really was not all that different from the demographic arrangements in the Middle East and Africa. An Indian reservation meant a handful of whites clustered in what were often remote locations – an agent, a teacher, a blacksmith, a demonstration farmer, perhaps a doctor, a few of these men with wives and children, surrounded by several hundred Indian people. Chicago and New York and their sizable white population might be on the same continent, but that made little difference in day-to-day life. So, curiously, regardless of the proportions of Euro-Americans to Indians on the North American continent, the demographic encounters of the ground-level, face-to-face workings of colonialism were not all that different from the population proportions presented by the Middle East and Africa.

As this course has certainly demonstrated to me, and as I hope our future co-authored book will demonstrate to a wide readership, the exploration of Western American history in the context of global history proves to be the most instructive and valuable aspect of the field's renaissance. Placing the Euro-American conquest of the Trans-Mississippi West in the global context of the history of colonialism and imperialism, Western historians now have a glorious opportunity to explore both what was distinctive and particular about the United States's methods of territorial acquisition, and what were shared practices, methods, and goals in international imperial operations. Once the territory claimed for the most determined defense of American exceptionalism, the history of the American West now offers an abundance of demonstrations in support of the proposition that promises to energize the work of historians in the twenty-first century – the recognition that the same historical case study can be revealing, thought-provoking, and instructive at regional, national, and global levels of meaning.

Notes

1. James Henretta, quoted in Patricia Nelson Limerick, *Legacy of Conquest* (New York, 1987), p. 20.
2. For an overview of these changes, see William Riebsame, ed., *The Atlas of the New West* (New York, 1997).
3. Ray Allen Billington, *Westward Expansion* (New York, 1949).
4. This section on the "Four C's" appears not only in *People Magazine* but also in the introduction to Patricia Nelson Limerick, *Something in the Soil: Legacies and Reckonings in the New West* (New York, 2000).
5. See Patricia Nelson Limerick, "The Case of the Premature Departure: The Trans-Mississippi West and American History Textbooks," *The Journal of American History*, 78, no. 4 (March 1992): 1380–94.
6. For an example of this approach in action, see Richard White, *"It's Your Misfortune and None of My Own": A New History of the American West* (Norman, OK, 1991).
7. See for example David Gutiérrez, *Walls and Mirrors: Mexican Americans, Mexican Immigrants, and the Politics of Ethnicity* (Berkeley,

CA, 1995); Shirley Ann Wilson Moore, *"To Place Our Deeds": The African American Community in Richmond, California, 1910–1963* (Berkeley, CA, 2000); George J. Sanchez, *Becoming Mexican American: Ethnicity, Culture, and Identity in Chicano Los Angeles, 1900–1945* (New York, 1993); Ronald Takaki, *Strangers from a Different Shore: A History of Asian Americans* (New York, 1989); Quintard Taylor, Jr., *In Search of the Racial Frontier* (New York, 1998).

8. Frederick Jackson Turner, *The Frontier in American History* (1920; rpt. Tucson, 1986), p. 2.

9. For explorations of the processes of conquest, see books such as David Wallace Adams, *Education for Extinction: American Indians and the Boarding School Experience, 1875–1928* (Lawrence, KA, 1995); Lisbeth Haas, *Conquests and Historical Identities in California, 1769–1936* (Berkeley, CA, 1995); Frederick Hoxie, *Parading Through History: The Making of the Crow Nation in America, 1805–1935* (New York, 1995); David Rich Lewis, *Neither Wolf Nor Dog: American Indians, Environment, and Agrarian Change* (New York, 1994).

10. Don Schellie, *Vast Domain of Blood: The Story of the Camp Grant Massacre* (Los Angeles, 1968).

11. Thomas Dunlay, *Wolves for the Blue Soldiers: Indian Scouts and Auxiliaries with the United States Army, 1860–1890* (Lincoln, 1982).

12. Quintard Taylor, *In Search of the Racial Frontier*, p. 173.

13. Quoted in Limerick, *The Legacy of Conquest*, p. 279.

14. On anti-miscegenation laws, see the forthcoming book by Peggy Pascoe.

15. Melissa L. Meyer, "Blood Is Thicker than Family," in Valerie Matsumoto and Blake Allmendinger, ed., *Over the Edge: Remapping the American West* (Berkeley, CA, 1999).

16. Iron Eyes Cody, as told to Collin Perry, *Iron Eyes: My Life as a Hollywood Indian* (New York, 1982), pp. 268–70.

17. Ron Russell, "Make-Believe Indian," *New Times: Los Angeles* 4, No. 14 (April 8–14, 1999): 14–21.

18. Meyer, "Blood Is Thicker than Family," p. 241.

19. For one of the most illuminating explorations of Indian identity, see Alexandra Harmon, *Indians in the Making: Ethnic Relations and Indian Identities around Puget Sound* (Berkeley, CA, 1998).

20. Richard White, *Land Use, Environment, and Social Change: The Shaping of Island County, Washington* (Seattle, 1980), and idem, *The Roots of Dependency: Subsistence, Environment, and Social Change among the Choctaws, Pawnees, and Navajos* (Lincoln, 1983).

21. William Cronon, *Nature's Metropolis* (New York, 1991); Robert Gottlieb, *Forcing the Spring: The Transformation of the American Environmental Movement* (Washington, DC, 1993).
22. Roderick Nash, *Wilderness and the American Mind*, 3rd edn. (New Haven, 1982).
23. See for example the work of Donald E. Worster, including Worster, *Nature's Economy: A History of Ecological Ideas* (Cambridge, UK, 1985); idem, *Rivers of Empire: Water, Aridity, and the Growth of the American West* (New York, 1985); idem, ed., *The Ends of the Earth: Perspectives on Modern Environmental History* (Cambridge, UK, 1988); idem, *Under Western Skies: Nature and History in the American West* (New York, 1992); idem, *The Wealth of Nature: Environmental History and the Ecological Imagination* (New York, 1993).
24. David Montejano, *Anglos and Mexicans in the Making of Texas, 1836–1986* (Austin, TX, 1987); Neil Foley, *The White Scourge: Mexicans, Blacks, and Poor Whites in Texas Cotton Culture* (Berkeley, CA, 1997).
25. Theodore Catton, *Inhabited Wilderness: Indians, Eskimos, and National Parks in Alaska* (Albuquerque, 1997); Robert H. Keller and Michael F. Turek, *American Indians and National Parks* (Tucson, 1998); Mark David Spence, *Dispossessing the Wilderness: Indian Removal and the Making of the National Parks* (New York, 1999); Louis Warren, *The Hunter's Game: Poachers and Conservationists in Twentieth Century America* (New Haven, 1997). For further information (and a comparative dimension), see Krishna B. Ghimire and Michael P. Pimbert, eds., *Social Change and Conservation* (London, 1997); Stan Stevens, ed., *Conservation Through Cultural Survival: Indigenous People and Protected Areas* (Washington, DC, 1997); Patrick C. West and Steven R. Brechin, eds., *Resident Peoples and National Parks* (Tucson, 1991); Charles Zerner, ed., *People, Plants, and Justice: The Politics of Nature Conservation* (New York, 2000).
26. Spence, *Dispossessing the Wilderness*, p. 3.
27. For useful coverage of the process/place debate from a standpoint sympathetic to the location of the frontier story/history of the American West within the wider historical process of imperial expansion, see Kerwin Lee Klein, "Reclaiming the 'F' Word, Or Being and Becoming Postwestern," *Pacific Historical Review*, 65, no. 2 (May 1996): 179–215. For a debate on the issue that foregrounds environmental issues, see Susan Rhoades Neel, "A Place of

Extremes: Nature, History, and the American West" and Dan Flores, "Place versus Region in Western Environmental History" in Clyde A. Milner, II, *A New Significance: Re-envisioning the History of the American West* (New York, 1996), pp. 105–24, 130–4. The case for studying "frontier" and "region/place" as part of the same historical process (frontiers becoming regions/places) is advanced by William Cronon, George Miles, and Jay Gitlin in "Becoming West: Toward a New Meaning for Western History," in Cronon, Miles, and Gitlin, eds., *Under an Open Sky: Rethinking America's Western Past* (New York, 1992), pp. 2–27. Also on this theme, see Stephen Aron, "Lessons in Conquest: Towards a Greater Western History," *Pacific Historical Review*, 63 (1994): 125–48.

28. Vine Deloria, Jr., *Custer Died for Your Sins: An Indian Manifesto* (New York, 1969).

29. Quoted in Michael Crowder, *West Africa under Colonial Rule* (Evanston, IL, 1968), p. 199.

30. Hoxie, *Parading Through History*, pp. 233–4.

31. Leila Ahmed, *Women and Gender in Islam: Historical Roots of a Modern Debate* (New Haven, 1992); Oyeronke Oyewumi, *The Invention of Women: Making an African Sense of Western Gender Discourse* (Minneapolis, 1997); Laura F. Klein and Lillian A. Ackerman, eds., *Women and Power in Native North America* (Norman, OK, 1995).

32. Michael Steltencamp, *Black Elk: Holy Man of the Oglala* (Norman, OK., 1993).

33. Albert Hurtado, *Indian Survival on the California Frontier* (New Haven, 1988); Alice Littlefield and Martha C. Knack, eds., *Native Americans and Wage Labor: Ethnohistorical Perspectives* (Norman, OK, 1996).

Orpheus Turning: The Present State of Southern History

Michael O'Brien

> So much for the past and present. The future is called "perhaps," which is the only possible thing to call the future. And the important thing is not to allow that to scare you.
>
> Tennessee Williams, preface to *Orpheus Descending*[1]

The present state of Southern history can be considered on various levels: its place in the American historical profession, its relationship to disciplines and methodologies, and the shifting of its philosophical rationale and narrative shape. Such a consideration is not usual. Recent Southern history has been little given to the synoptic view and to asking itself or others where the subject stands. While it used to be a grim and dispiriting ritual of the Southern Historical Association that its presidential address would define the South and offer a shape for its history, this habit has much abated.[2] The *Journal of Southern History* has a preference for microcosmic studies and (unlike the *Journal of American History*) an aversion to commissioning synthetic review-essays or special issues. And it is uncommon for general symposia on American history to include an essay on the South, since they tend to be organized by period (the American Revolution or the New Deal), methodology (economic history), or groups of national scope (immigrants, women).[3] Region tends to fall away, except when it is pertinent to these other matters, to the Civil War or labor relations or the non-ratification of the Equal Rights Amendment. In general, then, the Southern historian possesses fewer roadmaps than is usual within the American historical tradition.

First, the professional landscape. The writing of Southern history is moderately healthy, if numbers mean health. In 1936, when the Southern Historical Association first met in Birmingham, Alabama, it had 109 attendants. In Louisville in 1970, which was the first one I attended, there were 1744 people registered and the association had 2948 members. In Birmingham in 1998, the figures were 1453 and 3402, respectively.[4] So, in the last thirty years of the twentieth century, the SHA acquired a few hundred more members, who wanted to see each other somewhat less than they used to. This relative stability is fairly impressive, given a proliferation of subdisciplines, conferences, and organizations, many of them Southern in focus.[5] In short, Southern history is one of the larger intellectual constituencies of American history, but perhaps about to shrink. It happened that the expansion of Southern history and literature in the American imagination in the 1950s and 1960s coincided with the sharp expansion of American higher education; that generation drawn to Southern history and subsequently employed begins to retire. It is very doubtful that these historians would be replaced, man or woman for man; hence it is probable that the number of Southern historians will have shrunk by a half in the first decade or two of the twenty-first century, though much will be written under different rubrics that might once have been called Southern history.[6]

However, for the moment, there seems to be little slackening in the production of Southern narratives. Young historians seem still to be drawn. The American Historical Association's database of dissertations-in-progress shows perhaps 300 registered on Southern history, either on topics of regional scope, in state or local history, or in African American history of Southern emphasis.[7] The center of gravity for advanced graduate study has moved, however. In 1963, that center was arguably in New Haven, when C. Vann Woodward and David Potter were in their heyday. This was, in fact, a traditional pattern, when one recalls the earlier influence of William Archibald Dunning at Columbia, of Ulrich Phillips at Yale, of William Dodd at Chicago. Today it is hard to think of a Northern university with a comparable influence, though individual Ivy League universities have single figures of great note. Rather, the subject is decentralized, but is most studied in various Southern locations – Chapel Hill, Charlottesville, Atlanta, Oxford (Mississippi) – which sometimes have institutes specifically dedicated to Southern studies. It seems probable that the recent initiative of the National Endowment for the Humanities, whose head is a Mississippian, to fund regional study centers will accelerate this trend. Such a pattern is cause for concern, for it threatens that Southern history should become only a thing Southerners do in the South, but the worry may be less pressing than a comparable situation two generations ago might have elicited. Partly offsetting a decline in Northern is a rise in international interest.[8] And Southern universities are more cosmopolitan than they used to be, even if nativism is scarcely extinct and there is a tendency for colleges to demonstrate a progress into worldliness by expunging the South from their curricula. It has been a while since any of us had any reason to remember the physical location of the *South Atlantic Quarterly* in the South.

One professional change is especially significant. The future of Southern history looks coequally female. Although men may still slightly outnumber women in new doctorates, the former are disproportionately crowded in subdisciplines, such as political and military history, of diminished influence. Southern history seems to be a subject that women find attractive, unlike diplomatic or (oddly) Native American history. With this process of recruitment going on since around 1980, a number of the senior positions in Southern history are now occupied by women, who tend to attract graduate students mostly female, sometimes male, but both much drawn to the history of gender. Usually the best attended session at the Southern Historical Association each year, except for the presidential address, is the annual session of the Southern Association for Women Historians. So a fascinating process of transformation and adaptation is in process, in which female Southern historians are not merely creating new topics, previously oblivious to the male tradition, but reconfiguring topics once thought distant from gender. Drew Faust's *Mothers of Invention* has made inroads on traditional understandings of the Civil War, for example.[9] In this process, several things are notable. First, as one might expect, new women have meant new men. The definitive Southern males are no longer the ugly but potent figures who sought and found mastery, such as James Henry Hammond.[10] Rather, we are being given a series of ambivalent characters who commit suicide, have affairs with their chauffeurs, get murdered by their slaves, seem never to get the hang of patriarchy, and inveterately are plunged into crises of manhood.[11] Thomas Jefferson becomes, not a Founding Father, but the common-law husband of Sally Hemings, a man surreptitious and confused.[12] Even Pitchfork Ben Tillman now has masculine angst.[13] Secondly, the old cultural warfare between Southern intellectuals and the American "mainstream," in which the former complained of being marginalized, is being duplicated in the relationship between Southern and American women's history.[14] Thirdly, there is an imminent crisis of purpose and evidence, since women historians have mostly gone in search of a usable liberal tradition – what Jacquelyn Hall has called "a female anti-racist tradition"[15] – but very often encounter Southern conservative women defending slavery, sewing KKK sheets, nurturing Confederate veterans, refusing the suffrage, spitting at Civil Rights protesters.[16] Lastly, whether the female historians who are assuming the responsibility for the direction of Southern history and falling heir to its legacy will choose to address the full range of that history – economics, battles, county politics, ecology, intellectual culture, and much else – will determine whether the history of the South will become or remain more than an episode in the history of gender.

What of interdisciplinary relationships? These have mutated. A few generations ago, economics and sociology were potent influences, while psychology was of some moment, literature was preeminent, and anthropology persistently irrelevant. The history of slavery from as far back as Ulrich Phillips and as late as Robert Fogel had first been an economic problem, and the history of the New South in the hands of that Beardian, C. Vann Woodward, had been understood as largely a matter of colonial, economic dependency.[17] Southern historians were supposed then to know their statistics. A few know them still (Stanley Engerman, Gavin Wright, Peter Coclanis), but the band is much diminished.[18] Social history is a softer methodology, which has lost touch with the founding disciplines for which it once formed a convergence. Sociology, too, is a lost influence: John Shelton Reed is the last of the line of sociologists, commencing with Howard Odum and Rupert Vance in the 1920s, who insisted that studying the South first required a notion of social structure, and Reed is an empirical sociologist, not an interpreter of grand theory drawn from Marx, Durkheim, or Weber.[19] As to psychology, its status is peculiar. Southern history is often a Gothic genre, anxious and neurotic, so it has naturally been drawn to psychology. Occasionally, this has eventuated in historians who have drawn formally on psychological theory, notably Stanley Elkins and Richard King.[20] But usually it has led to historians who offer psychological readings of people or events, but without any specific allegiance to a Freud or Jung, but who use the common language that the psychological tradition has transmitted to the lay intellectual. Nonetheless, the implicit influence of psychology is great. The South is persistently regarded as a patient stretched on a couch, repressing or confessing to incest, rape, murder, or to trouble about lovers, fathers, and mothers.

One great change lies in the linkage of history to fiction and poetry, and secondarily to literary criticism. There is no modern Southern novelist who means as much to this time as William Faulkner did to 1950, and no literary critic as influential as Allen Tate once was. Eudora Welty and the late Walker Percy have been important, but the younger generation of, for example, Lee Smith and Clyde Edgerton have not had as marked an impact. The reasons for this are complex, but one may be that the postmodernist moment has been around in Southern literature for a generation and longer, and Southern historians seem to be very reluctant postmodernists.[21] On the other hand, paradoxically, the relationship between historians and literary critics is much healthier. In the 1950s, the idea that the critic should read history (beyond the odd volume of Woodward) was only intermittently entertained, however much talk there was of the importance and burden of history. The South's recent literary critics are immeasurably better read in historical literature.[22] Concomitantly, as intellectual history is now more significant as a subdiscipline, some Southern historians are more conversant with literary theory and practice, and have themselves often been literary critics.[23]

What is new as an influence is popular culture. The Center for the Study of Southern Culture at the University of Mississippi has peculiarly fostered studies of country music, the blues, sports, and material culture, all embodied in a great *Encyclopedia of Southern Culture*.[24] The Center for the Study of the American South in Chapel Hill has likewise sponsored a semi-academic, semi-popular periodical called *Southern Cultures*, where one habitually finds (amid more solemn topics lightly narrated) essays on sororities, cooking, and basketball.[25] Woodward's generation, though it defended the integrity of the populist tradition, was mandarin by instinct, and so less likely to write about Hank Williams and Goo Goo Clusters. If Allen Tate and Donald Davidson defined the elite and vernacular polarities of the Southern Agrarian tradition, it is not Tate the follower of T. S. Eliot, but Davidson the librettist of a hillbilly opera who better presaged the modern Southern sensibility, at least among men. Academic women seem more resistant to these democratic allures.

Lastly, there is the matter of how Southern and African American history relate. Once Negro history was largely a subset of Southern history, especially when it was written by white Southerners such as Ulrich Phillips. In time, largely following the demographic patterns of outmigration, writing about the experience of black Americans outside the orbit of the South came to be as important as that within; the former is now, almost certainly, more important. The African American experience is too large a topic with too weighty a moral authority to be contained within a narrative of Southern history. Indeed it has sought a partial release from the confines even of American history. African American intellectual life, at least as it is embodied in what has become its headquarters at the DuBois Institute at Harvard, has been imaginatively reaching out to an international experience.[26] Henry Louis Gates makes television documentaries about Africa, but not about Alabama. The South appears very little in his work.[27] He once summarized his purpose as the attempt to comprehend "a late twentieth-century world profoundly fissured by nationality, ethnicity, race, class, and gender."[28] In that list, the word "region" does not occur. On the surface, this is a casual, unthinking omission, but I suspect it has a deep structure. Gates has been interested in what can take and has taken black Americans away from what has imprisoned them, physically by acts of expatriation as narrated in slave narratives, intellectually by deftly deconstructing the crude atavisms of race. Whatever else this may mean, it seems to mean looking away from what was the experience of most black Americans for most of American history – that is, the South. There is unfinished business here, something not confronted and, in the case of Gates's memoir *Colored People*, even sentimentalized.

This pattern is broader than the DuBois Institute. African American history in the last two generations has been an expansive field, while Southern history has been fairly static, changing but not appreciably having more impact on the American imagination, indeed probably declining. Black history drives a Mercedes, Southern history the family Buick. So, if anything, the old relationship is beginning to reverse itself. Black history is no longer a subset of Southern history, but Southern history begins to be a subset of black history, at least as it is understood and taught outside the South. This is a practical question: all departments have to have a black historian, but a Southern historian is a luxury, so increasingly and only sometimes Southern history is given to the African American scholar to do. For the moment, this is a promising development, even if it will tend to make much of Southern history (the part remote from the black experience) marginal and unintelligible, but that is an old story, denoting little change. If you are a backcountry Southerner, it does not much matter if Southern history is narrated by the descendant of a slaveholder or by that of a slave; neither will be much bothered with you. The promise resides in the sophisticated debate about identity and multiculturalism, to be found especially in the work of Anthony Appiah, which ought to affect the debate about Southern culture and identity.[29] The South is going from being single to being multiple and stands (as usual) in peril of dissipating. But this was true of black identity in the last generation, too, as integration was ambivalently attempted. Black Americans and Ghanaians, among others, have hazarded ways to salvage what is usable in the idea of race out of the bitter authoritarianism of racism. By their logic and desire, identity becomes a cultural role. But we have many identities and roles.[30]

The Southern/African American equation is the sharpest instance of a wider phenomenon. For what grew more opaque during the last generation is the scope of "Southern." Logically, to write Southern history, one needs to know who the Southerners are. As far as historical narrative went, this used to be simple. Southerners were the descendants of the Europeans who colonized the southeastern corner of what is now the United States and was briefly the Confederacy, the people who owned or consented to the ownership of slaves, those who ordered the system of Jim Crow. There were prettier ways of describing them, which they themselves preferred, and the community encompassed many anguished dissidents, mostly ineffective. But, to count as a Southerner, it helped to be a man, white, born in the South or (if expatriate) publicly troubled by the exile, preferably in a work of fiction. In general, one could be a woman and Southern, if only in an ancillary way, but (with rare exceptions) one could not be black and Southern, nor Native American and Southern. To be thought Southern after 1865 usually required two qualifications: to have social power within the region, but to be marginal in the nation; the injustice of the latter was used to justify the necessity of the former.

The last few generations in the twentieth century have left this standpoint in hopeless confusion. Once the South was understood to have made Southerners, by whatever mechanism the historian or sociologist preferred to describe, whether it was by the land or poverty or shared experience. In practice, of course, it only made certain people Southerners, though regionalism was in theory an inclusive premise.[31] But the experiences of the post-World War II economic transformation and the Civil Rights movement upset this reasoning. Urbanization killed off the Agrarian definition of the Southern way of life, by making modernity too ubiquitous to be excluded from the formation of identity. Then, around 1965, for the first time, polling data showed a significant number of blacks in the South being willing to describe themselves as Southern. This did for Ulrich Phillips's presumption that Southernness was white supremacy. Further, outmigration and immigration scrambled the argument that "Southern" was occasioned by descent and residence. Was a black Mississippian migrant in Detroit a Southerner? Were his or her children, if they stayed in the North or chose to move to Texas? Was someone from Minnesota who moved to North Carolina a Southerner? What of the Mississippi Chinese and the Melungeons? In our time, diversity is not supposed to preclude sharing. But such reasoning does vitiate the arguments of C. Vann Woodward. For, if you arrived late to Southern culture, if you did not share the old experiences of war and poverty, did not Woodward imply that you could not be Southern? Were not mid-western migrants to North Carolina among those driving the machinery of the "Bulldozer Revolution?"[32]

These confusions will be familiar to students of migration and the nation state in the modern world, whose burgeoning literature ought to influence how we understand the South, since they offer dizzyingly and clumsily an "appreciation of the practices of identity-formation in a world (modern, late-capitalist, postmodern, *fin-de-siècle*, supermodern) where processes of globalization (creolization, compression, hybridity, synchronicity) have made traditional conceptions of individuals as members of fixed and separate societies and cultures redundant."[33] Yet the question of whether the child of a Turkish migrant in Heidelberg is a German is, whatever else it is, first a legal question. Though Southern identity is an outgrowth of the discourses of nationalism, the South is not a nation state, has no fixed boundaries, issues no passports, collects no taxes. The South is a willingness of the heart. Or so the last generation of the twentieth century was disposed to think. In the collapse of the essentialist presumptions of the old intellectual order, there was a turn in the 1970s toward self-consciousness as the workable premise for constructing Southern history, toward understanding "culture [as] a form of narrative or discourse."[34] A Southerner possessed an identity; of late he is often understood to be someone nurtured by patterns of social memory.[35] This was, in its day, an elegant solution to the problem. It was the solution to be offered elsewhere, a little later, which has given us so many books on nationalism and inventing tradition, and has now worked its way back even to that most un-Hegelian of discourses, British history.[36] The European version of deconstructing the project of Romantic nationalism arose from the crisis of citizenship occasioned by the collapse of eastern Europe and the coalescence of the European Union, the successive challenges to nationality caused by fragmentation, integration, and migration. The Southern version arose from the crisis of citizenship that the American racial crisis occasioned, plus migration. When the world is a kaleidoscope of shifting forms, modern people tend to fall back on what they know or can imagine they have, a self. The Civil Rights movement itself, by initiating or reiterating the premise that the personal is political and transmitting it to feminism, doubtless helped to make this step plausible.

In retrospect, it was an impractical solution. Two kinds of Southern scholars had offered it. John Shelton Reed deployed the techniques of polling and the presumptions of social psychology to map the psychic configuration of the region, and thereby to offer a geography of feeling.[37] Various intellectual and literary historians explored how individual Southerners had fashioned their sense of Southern identity.[38] The former was a technique for a mass society, in which individuals matter little, while the latter could only cope with individuals. But the centreground of historical narrative has worked in a rougher, readier manner, especially in an era in which social history has been dominant. It requires workable generalizations for narratives of any scope; individuals who can be used to explain patterns, patterns which can be used to explain individuals. Idiosyncrasy is kept at arm's length. But the aggregate is suspect, too, since social history has of late abjured the homogeneous, mistrusted the idea of continuity, and favored the premise of conflict.[39] So, while in theory narratives about the South ought to confine themselves to those who have accepted the identity of Southern, this would exclude probably a majority of the people who have lived in the southeastern United States. Most importantly, it would exclude almost all African Americans before 1965, which is not a morally or politically acceptable hypothesis in our time. So a middle ground has had to be found, which is the Hegelian premise that self-perception is dialectically created by the self-perception of others, so even the un-Southern resident of the South forms part of Southern culture. The net effect, however, is disappointingly unrigorous. The South has become a space in time, on which anyone who has crowded is accounted part of the narrative, whether or not they knowingly chose to belong to that story. However much we praise discourse, we cannot afford to ground our history in it, because it is too quicksilver.

What of the subject matters of Southern history? The shape has changed markedly. Much arises from the familiar, wider shifts in historical methodologies: the rise of social history, the decline of political history, the emergence of feminism, the premise of multiculturalism, the significance of theory. Southern history, with small variations, followed and occasionally led the broader patterns of American historical literature in the last generation, if conservatively. In general, the South has had more social history, less theory, a more cautious feminism, and a more tentative multiculturalism.

As a subdiscipline, Southern history does not much predate the 1880s; history written before the Civil War concerned itself with the history of individual states, almost never the region. For much of the early days of the enterprise, the necessary preoccupation was with the period from Jamestown to 1877, when 1877 was only yesterday. Two moments merited intense scrutiny, the Revolutionary, Virginian moment centering on Washington, Madison, Jefferson, and Marshall, and then the origins and course of the Civil War. The colonial experience was thought to explain the antebellum one, with the latter (if you were a Southern liberal) being thought to be a defection from the civic virtues laid down in the seventeenth and eighteenth centuries or (if you were a conservative) a flowering. It is in the late nineteenth century that the anachronism of the colonial South is invented.

From the early 1950s to the early 1970s, from C. Vann Woodward's *Origins of the New South* to Eugene Genovese's *Roll, Jordan, Roll*, which was the high water mark of Southern historical literature, perhaps the most significant development was that the colonial South began to drift away from the rest of the Southern narrative; this tendency has drastically accelerated.[40] In 1967, when essays in historiography were offered to Fletcher Green under the title of *Writing Southern History*, the two editors (neither of them colonialists) gave three chapters to the period before 1800.[41] When the effort was renewed in 1987 for Sanford Higginbotham as *Interpreting Southern History*, a single chapter was thought to be sufficient for everything before 1800.[42] The recent Norton anthology of Southern literature offers precisely three items from Southern culture before Jefferson, 16 pages out of 1155.[43] This is unusually drastic, but symptomatic.

Why this falling away? No doubt, much arises from a foreshortening of historical memory, the falling away of classical and medieval history, the growing antiquity and remoteness of the early modern for many who think that they are expansive to think earlier than 1900. Our having passed the year 2000 is unlikely to help; soon, it will begin to seem that three centuries intercede between us and 1750. Moreover, what drove this yoking of colonial and antebellum was the sense that colonization mattered as the prelude to nation-making. Southern historians are less preoccupied now with the region's relationship to the nation, as the idea of the nation has lost its privileged status.[44] But some causes of this dissevering are institutional. Colonial history has become peculiarly the domain of the Institute for Early American History in Williamsburg, which has firm opinions about the chronological boundaries of its *imperium*. While in one sense the Institute has strengthened understanding of what could loosely be called Southern history by fostering so many studies of the Chesapeake and colonies southward, in another it did not, ironically by being so successful. Southern colonial history has become almost the narrative of American colonial history and succeeded, to a large extent, in displacing the premise of the Puritan origins of the American self. But in succeeding in becoming American, or even more in being transatlantic, Afro-Caribbean, and imperial, that history has ceased to be significantly Southern, except as an aside. So the best articles on colonial Georgia now go to the *William and Mary Quarterly*, not the *Journal of Southern History*, and the annual convention of the Southern Historical Association usually has thin submissions on topics before 1800. Jack Greene's work, for example, though it has rich implications for the antebellum South, is little used for these purposes by later historians and he himself seems indifferent to the possibility.[45] Only studies of slavery seem to be a partial exception, though a large one, to this unhealthy disjunction.[46]

This has left the history of the Old South more firmly defined as antebellum, as something that matters because it looks towards and explains the Civil War, which is a specialized function to explain a large, diffuse, and complicated society or set of societies. Here we encounter an oddity. The dominant figure for the last generation and more has been Eugene Genovese. In theory, Genovese's work ought to have encouraged a sense of continuity with the colonial South, since he commenced with the premise that the Old South was premodern. In practice, he has been relatively indifferent to the colonial experience and, in effect, encouraged a tendency to isolate the Old South and make it self-contained and exceptionalist, though a sort of moral intensification of the problem of Western culture. For, like Woodward, Genovese has believed in the discontinuity of Southern history. But, whereas Genovese thought that everything changed in 1865, mostly for the worse, but was not very interested in what the postbellum South turned into, Woodward believed that everything changed in 1865, eventually for the better, but was not very interested in what had been before. The twin effect of these dominant influences was to slice Southern history down the middle. While there have been persistent efforts to establish a continuity between 1830 and 1900, these struggled against the tide. I think this is about to change. Woodward is now dead and it seems probable that his synthesis, which was eerily extended beyond a normal lifespan by his own longevity and iron will, will be abruptly reconsidered.

One reason is that the Civil Rights movement begins to displace the Civil War as the moral centerpiece of Southern history. Not that the writing of Civil War history is going to go away. But I suspect its constituency will be, more and more, the public that retains a puzzling fascination with the conflict, and so it will be as much an annex of public history as a scholarly venture in dialogue with the rest of Southern or American historiography. The urgent business of Southern history will be, rather, to reconfigure the period from the 1870s to the present day. This will mean that antebellum historians will face a choice: to be the last act in an early modern drama not much interested in them, or to make a case for the late antebellum South as the first act of the modern South, or at least as the crossing of the ways, to use Allen Tate's phrase. Even Genovese, now transformed into a Roman Catholic intellectual, has begun to respond to this pressure, by trying to annex the modern South to a conservative tradition commenced in the Old South, but I see little evidence that many beyond the small community of conservative historians are persuaded by this move.[47] Rather, precisely the interpretation that Genovese abominates is likely to happen. The Old South will be seen as fluid, multiple, contingent. The evidence already exists to make a decent case for this, in work like that of James Oakes, and it is a trend in works by younger scholars.[48] Nonetheless, inventing a semi-Old South as the prelude to the New South will be an optional extra for many. I doubt that the real excitement will be there, but later.[49]

We do not yet know what this new history of the New South will look like. For the moment, Woodward's understanding of the period from 1877 to 1913 remains unexpectedly canonical. Edward Ayers's *The Promise of the New South* hinted at possibilities, suggested vitalities, but did not supplant Woodward.[50] Indeed, Ayers has explained that synthesis is no longer a historian's responsibility in a postmodern world.[51] Feminist scholars have offered intriguing work, but they too mistrust synthesis, at least beyond matters of gender.[52] Work on the period from 1913 to the late 1940s is episodic, while the historians of the Civil Rights movement are still struggling free of the perspectives generated by the movement itself. The celebratory barely begins to make way for the critical. Insofar as there is a clear direction, it seems to lie in making the Civil Rights Movement less of a dramatic transformation, making the segregated South look more contested and less bleak, making the world partly fashioned by Martin Luther King Jr. less of an improvement. The question of continuity, which once centered on 1865, increasingly centers on 1965. But there is much confusion and more guilt here, as yet unresolved, perhaps irresolvable. It is precisely this moral complexity, the tension between hope and realism, which will give the subject vitality. Yet this sense of social contestation wavers around a mean. As Laura Edwards has put it, "Recent scholarship uses the analytical lenses of gender, sexuality, and race to highlight fissures in southern society and the ability of ordinary southerners to disrupt the social order."[53] That is, the Gemeinschaft to Gesellschaft theme, once so popular, has been much battered. But there is a lingering sense that there has been a stable order somewhere to be disrupted, even as it becomes hard to locate.

As long as that sense lingers, the project of Southern history is likely to continue. When the South was invented in the early nineteenth century, it was conjectured as one instance of the patterns that human beings inherited in God's natural order and sustained by their imaginative free will: these shapes included societies, races, classes, and sexes. Like those other orders, the South's rationale was that it stood between man and chaos, whether that was threatened by Nat Turner, the Seminoles, Charles Sumner, Sarah Grimké, malaria, or David Hume. The project of the South has, therefore, flourished on the idea of peril, on the sense that the South stands always on the brink of dissipation. Each generation has redefined the order by identifying different perils. Postmodernism is as good a bogeyman as any, if too amiable in tone to justify dread. But racial crisis is persistent, the genders are at odds, ethnicity is making a comeback, and religion is divisive, so on the whole, things are looking bad enough for the discourse to keep going. It will persist as long as a respectable number of the people in the southeastern United States find the South to be a useful category of analysis. I suspect the proportion begins to decline, but for the moment it seems enough.

Notes

1. Tennessee Williams, "The Past, the Present, and the Perhaps," in *The Rose Tattoo: Camino Real: Orpheus Descending* (Harmondsworth, 1976), p. 241.
2. A partial exception is Paul K. Conkin, "Hot, Humid, and Sad," *Journal of Southern History*, 64 (1998): 3–22.
3. See, for example, Eric Foner, ed., *The New American History* (Philadelphia, 1990), which has seven chapters divided by chronology, and six more on social history, women's history, African American history, labor history, ethnicity and immigration, and diplomatic history.
4. Bennett H. Wall, "Annual Report of the Secretary-Treasurer," *Journal of Southern History*, 37 (1971): 248, 249; William F. Holmes, "Annual Report of the Secretary-Treasurer," *Journal of Southern History*, 65 (1999): 367, 371. However, not everyone who attends the annual convention is a member of the SHA and the convention serves a few hundred European and Latin American historians, who are allocated a portion of the program. A formal purpose of the association is, to foster not only Southern history but also the practise of history in the South.
5. The calendar of regular Southern conferences has grown very crowded; for example, the Porter Fortune Symposium at the University of Mississippi, the Southern Intellectual History Circle, the Saint George Tucker Society, the Southern Association of Women Historians, and the Society for the Study of Southern Literature.
6. I infer this from the statistics in Carl Abbott, "Tracing the Trends in U.S. Regional History," *Perspectives*, 28 (1990): 4–8. In 1988, 63

percent of those who taught courses in Southern history were aged between 40 and 55.

7. See http://www.theaha.org/pubs/dissertations/.

8. On this, see Michael O'Brien, ed., "The South in the World," *Southern Cultures*, 4 (Winter 1998): 1–83.

9. Drew Gilpin Faust, *Mothers of Invention: Women of the Slaveholding South in the American Civil War* (Chapel Hill, 1996). She is, however, the only woman historian among the fourteen contributors to James M. McPherson and William J. Cooper, Jr., eds., *Writing the Civil War: The Quest to Understand* (Columbia, SC, 1998).

10. Drew Gilpin Faust, *James Henry Hammond and the Old South: A Design for Mastery* (Baton Rouge, 1982).

11. Bertram Wyatt-Brown, *The House of Percy: Honor, Melancholy, and Imagination in a Southern Family* (New York, 1994); Melton A. McLaurin, *Celia: A Slave* (Athens, GA, 1991); William A. Link, "The Jordan Hatcher Case: Politics and 'a Spirit of Insubordination' in Antebellum Virginia," *Journal of Southern History*, 64 (November 1998): 615–48; John Howard, *Men Like That: A Southern Queer History* (Chicago, 1999); Anne Goodwyn Jones, "The Work of Gender in the Southern Renaissance," in *Southern Writers and Their Worlds*, edited by Christopher Morris and Steven G. Reinhardt (College Station, TX, 1996), pp. 41–56; Ted Ownby, *Subduing Satan: Religion, Recreation, and Manhood in the Rural South, 1865–1920* (Chapel Hill, 1990).

12. Jan Ellen Lewis, and Peter S. Onuf, eds., *Sally Hemings and Thomas Jefferson: History, Memory, and Civic Culture* (Charlottesville, 1999).

13. Stephen Kantrowitz, *Ben Tillman and the Reconstruction of White Supremacy* (Chapel Hill, 2000).

14. See, especially, Catherine Clinton, ed., *Half Sisters of History: Southern Women and the American Past* (Durham, NC, 1994), but also Jacquelyn Dowd Hall, "Open Secrets: Memory, Imagination, and the Refashioning of Southern Identity," *American Quarterly* 50 (1998): 109–24.

15. Hall, "Open Secrets": 122.

16. Younger women seem more disposed to grapple with this phenomenon. For example, Elna C. Green, "From Antisuffragism to Anti-Communism: The Conservative Career of Ida M. Darden," *Journal of Southern History*, 65 (1999): 287–316, which speaks of "a growing body of literature on conservative women and female antifeminism" (287).

17. Ulrich Bonnell Phillips, *American Negro Slavery: A Survey of the Supply, Employment and Control of Negro Labor as Determined by the Plantation Regime*, with a foreword by Eugene D. Genovese, reprint, 1918 (Baton Rouge, 1966); Robert William Fogel and Stanley L. Engerman, *Time on the Cross: The Economics of American Negro Slavery* (Boston, 1974); C. Vann Woodward, *Origins of the New South, 1877–1913* (Baton Rouge, 1951).

18. Stanley L. Engerman, ed., *The Terms of Labor: Slavery, Serfdom, and Free Labor* (Stanford, 1999); Gavin Wright, *Old South, New South: Revolutions in the Southern Economy Since the Civil War* (New York, 1986); Peter A. Coclanis, *The Shadow of a Dream: Economic Life and Death in the South Carolina Low Country, 1670-1920* (New York, 1989).

19. For Reed on Vance, see John Shelton Reed and Daniel Joseph Singal, eds., *Regionalism and the South: Selected Papers of Rupert Vance* (Chapel Hill, 1982).

20. Stanley M. Elkins, *Slavery: A Problem in American Institutional and Intellectual Life*, with an introduction by Nathan Glazer, reprint, 1959 (New York, 1963); Richard H. King, *A Southern Renaissance: The Cultural Awakening of the American South, 1930–1955* (New York, 1980).

21. Fred Hobson, *The Southern Writer in the Postmodern World*. Mercer University Lamar Memorial Lectures, no. 33 (Athens, GA, 1991).

22. An excellent example is Michael Kreyling, *Inventing Southern Literature* (Jackson, MS, 1998).

23. On this, see Fred Hobson, "Of Canons and Cultural Wars: Southern Literature and Literary Scholarship After Midcentury," in *The Future of Southern Letters*, edited by Jefferson Humphries and John Lowe (New York, 1996), pp. 72–86. It is now common for volumes of essays to contain historians and literary critics coequally: see for example Morris and Reinhardt, *Southern Writers and Their Worlds* and Anne Goodwyn Jones and Susan V. Donaldson, eds., *Haunted Bodies: Gender and Southern Texts* (Charlottesville, 1998).

24. Charles Reagan Wilson and William Ferris, eds., *Encyclopedia of Southern Culture* (Chapel Hill, 1989).

25. For historians who are interested in popular culture, see Charles Reagan Wilson, *Judgment and Grace in Dixie: Southern Faiths from Faulkner to Elvis* (Athens, GA, 1995), and James C. Cobb, *Redefining Southern Culture: Mind and Identity in the Modern South* (Athens, GA, 1999).

26. Anthony Appiah, Henry Louis Gates, Jr., and Michael Colin Vazquez, eds., *The Dictionary of Global Culture* (New York, 1997).
27. Surprisingly, this is true even of his West Virginian memoir: Henry Louis Gates, Jr., *Colored People: A Memoir* (New York, 1994). But there is an anecdote about a basketball game in North Carolina, in which Gates reproves a white racist fan and Gates's father mockingly stops him by saying, "Nigger, is you *crazy*? We am in de Souf." Henry Louis Gates, Jr., *Loose Canons: Notes on the Culture Wars* (New York, 1992), p. 148.
28. Gates, *Loose Canons*, p. xv.
29. See especially Kwame Anthony Appiah, *In My Father's House: Africa in the Philosophy of Culture* (New York, 1992), and Kwame Anthony Appiah and Amy Gutmann, *Color Conscious: The Political Morality of Race* (Princeton, NJ, 1996).
30. This parallels the argument for a lightly-held ethnicity in David A. Hollinger, *Postethnic America: Beyond Multiculturalism* (New York, 1995).
31. Valuable is David L. Carlton and Peter A. Coclanis, "Another 'Great Migration': From Region to Race in Southern Liberalism," *Southern Cultures*, 3 (Winter 1997): 37–62, which argues that region is a weaker analytical premise now than in the 1930s, but race a more powerful one.
32. C. Vann Woodward, *The Burden of Southern History*, rev. edn., reprint, 1960 (Baton Rouge, 1968).
33. Nigel Rapport and Andrew Dawson, eds., *Migrants of Identity: Perceptions of Home in a World of Movement* (Oxford, 1998), p. 3. Useful is Saskia Sassen, *Globalization and Its Discontents: Essays on the New Mobility of People and Money* (New York, 1998).
34. Jefferson Humphries, "The Discourse of Southernness: Or How We Can Know There Will Still Be Such a Thing as the South and Southern Literary Culture in the Twenty-First Century," in Humphries and Lowe, *The Future of Southern Letters*, p. 120.
35. On this, see Edward L. Ayers, "Memory and the South," *Southern Cultures*, 2 (1995): 5–8, and Scot A. French, "What is Social Memory?" *Southern Cultures*, 2 (1995): 9–18. For a feminist version, see Hall, "Open Secrets."
36. Most important have been Eric Hobsbawm and Terence Ranger, eds., *The Invention of Tradition* (Cambridge, UK, 1983) and Benedict Anderson, *Imagined Communities: Reflections on the Origin and Spread of Nationalism*, revised and enlarged edn., reprint, 1983 (London, 1991). On British history, see Colin Kidd, *British Identities*

Before Nationalism: Ethnicity and Nationhood in the Atlantic World, 1600-1800 (Cambridge, UK, 1999).

37. First in John Shelton Reed, *The Enduring South: Subcultural Persistence in Mass Society*, with a foreword by Edwin M. Yoder, Jr., reprint, 1972 (Chapel Hill, 1974), and then somewhat more systematically in idem., *Southerners: The Social Psychology of Sectionalism* (Chapel Hill, 1983).

38. For example, Michael O'Brien, *The Idea of the American South, 1920–1941* (Baltimore, MD, 1979); King, *A Southern Renaissance*; Daniel J. Singal, *The War Within: From Victorian to Modernist Thought in the South, 1919–1945* (Chapel Hill, 1982); Richard Gray, *Writing the South: Ideas of an American Region* (Cambridge, UK, 1986).

39. The hostile reaction to the work of David Hackett Fischer is evidence for this: see David Hackett Fischer, *Albion's Seed: Four British Folkways in America* (New York, 1989).

40. In this, I differ from the view expressed in John B. Boles, "The New Southern History," *Mississippi Quarterly*, 45 (Fall 1992): 369–83.

41. Arthur S. Link and Rembert W. Patrick, eds., *Writing Southern History: Essays in Historiography in Honor of Fletcher M. Green* (Baton Rouge, 1965).

42. John B. Boles and Evelyn Thomas Nolen, eds., *Interpreting Southern History: Historiographical Essays in Honor of Sanford W. Higginbotham* (Baton Rouge, 1987).

43. William L. Andrews, Minrose C. Gwin, Trudier Harris, and Fred Hobson, eds., *The Literature of the American South: A Norton Anthology* (New York, 1998).

44. Among the last of the books with this concern, in a series of volumes peculiarly defined by the issue of nationalism, is Dewey W. Grantham, *The South in Modern America: A Region at Odds*. New American Nation Series (New York, 1994).

45. See, especially, Jack P. Greene, *Pursuits of Happiness: The Social Development of Early Modern British Colonies and the Formation of American Culture* (Chapel Hill, 1988). A rare exception is Joyce E. Chaplin, *An Anxious Pursuit: Agricultural Innovation and Modernity in the Lower South, 1730–1815* (Chapel Hill, 1993).

46. Notably Ira Berlin, *Many Thousands Gone: The First Two Centuries of Slavery in North America* (Cambridge, MA, 1998), and, on a more specialized topic, Sylvia R. Frey and Betty Wood, *Come Shouting to Zion: African-American Protestantism in American South and British Caribbean to 1830* (Chapel Hill, 1998).

47. Eugene D. Genovese, *The Southern Tradition: The Achievement and Limitations of an American Conservatism*. The William E. Massey Sr. Lectures in the History of American Civilization 1993 (Cambridge, MA., 1994). See also Elizabeth Fox-Genovese, "The Anxiety of History: The Southern Confrontation with Modernity," *Southern Cultures*, Inaugural issue 1993: 65–82.

48. James Oakes, *Slavery and Freedom: An Interpretation of the Old South* (New York, 1990). See Jonathan Daniel Wells, *The Origins of the Southern Middle Class: Literature, Politics, and Economy, 1820–1880*, dissertation, University of Michigan (1998), and Beth Barton Schweiger, *The Gospel Working up: Progress and the Pulpit in Nineteenth Century America* (New York, 1999).

49. The AHA database suggests that dissertations are being written in a rough proportion of one colonial study for every two on the antebellum period, and every five on the years after 1877.

50. Edward L. Ayers, *The Promise of the New South: Life After Reconstruction* (New York, 1992).

51. Edward L. Ayers, "Narrating the New South," *Journal of Southern History*, 61 (1995): 555–66.

52. Glenda Elizabeth Gilmore, *Gender and Jim Crow: Women and the Politics of White Supremacy in North Carolina, 1896–1920* (Chapel Hill, 1996), and Jane Dailey, "Deference and Violence in the Postbellum Urban South: Manners and Massacres in Danville, Virginia," *Journal of Southern History*, 63 (1997): 552–90. For a later period, see Grace Elizabeth Hale, *Making Whiteness: The Culture of Segregation in the South, 1890–1940* (New York, 1998).

53. Laura F. Edwards, "Law, Domestic Violence, and the Limits of Patriarchal Authority in the Antebellum South," *Journal of Southern History*, 65 (1999): 735.

Part IV
Perspectives and Problems

–15–

Class and the Construction of "Race": White Racism in the American South

Michael Tadman

Academic attitudes to "race" changed profoundly over the twentieth century. Ulrich B. Phillips, that great pioneering historian of slavery, was by any sensible definition a racist, and "race" for him was a biological fact. His project as a historian was to use his assumptions about inherent black "inferiority" to construct and reinforce a tradition with which Southern whites could be comfortable.[1] Nowadays, however, almost all academics see "race" as being socially (not biologically) constructed, and they recognize the lack of significance in notions of genetic differences between color groups. There is, today, a healthy academic interest in unpacking the processes by which whites, to suit their own purposes, have historically constructed and reconstructed black people (that is, stereotyped them and allocated to them supposedly inbuilt character-istics).[2] Recent years have also seen much research into "whiteness," and into the ways in which various ethnic groups of European or part-European ancestry have sought to set themselves apart from blacks in order to gain the "wages of whiteness."[3] Important work is also being done on how black people have imagined and constructed whites.[4]

This chapter is concerned with the broad agenda of antebellum slavery and the construction of "race." In particular, I am concerned with debates on connections between white class interests and the construction of "blackness." Three main issues will be addressed. The first is the question of whether explicitly racialized slavery predated or was a product of the antebellum period. The second arises from Eugene Genovese's thesis of antebellum paternalism, a thesis which builds explicitly on a particular interpretation of connections between "race" and class. The third concern, inspired in part by George Fredrickson's "herrenvolk democracy" thesis, is the question of whether shared ideas of being members of the "master race" led yeoman and poor whites to support planters and to support the system of slavery.

We turn first to the antebellum period and the question of "racial" slavery. When exploring white attitudes to "blackness" during the centuries of American slavery, scholars have often written of change over time, but the suggested chronologies have shown a good deal of variety. For some, because of their reading of English cultural prejudices, American racism dated from the arrival of the first black people in the English colonies in the seventeenth century. For others, slavery only became consciously based on a "racial" ideology in the Revolutionary era. Others, making connections between intensive Abolitionist pressure against slavery from the 1830s onward and an apparent increase in defensive slaveholder references to black "biological inferiority," see explicit racialized slavery as a phenomenon of the antebellum period.

Theoretical and ideological assumptions – psycho-cultural, socio-economic, Marxist, and Weberian – have been of great importance for historians who have sought to date the racialization of American slavery. Winthrop Jordan took what might be called a psycho-cultural approach in his research. He argued that English culture had for centuries been predisposed to weight "blackness" with negative associations – dirty, evil, sinister, fearful, deadly – and he felt that this cultural tradition, together with the "shock" of contact with Africans, led English colonists to see black people as natural slaves. This meant that, from the very beginning, American slavery was based on an idea of "race."[5]

In contrast to Jordan, Edmund S. Morgan took what might be called a broad socio-economic approach. He saw the fixing of slavery as an institution based on "race" and on "blackness" taking place as a deliberate class reaction by the Virginia elite following Bacon's Rebellion of 1676. The rebellion had exposed dangerous divisions between the elite and white laborers, and, as a result, the elite adopted the strategy of emphasizing the privileges of freedom for the white laboring class, while fixing enslaved black people as the core of the propertyless laboring class.[6]

Ira Berlin's *Many Thousands Gone: The First Two Centuries of Slavery in North America* also takes a socio-economic approach. More specifically, Berlin tackles slavery from the perspective of a historian of labor. He sees "race" as being not just socially constructed in a one-off process, but as being "historically constructed" and reconstructed in the changing circumstances of labor struggle during centuries of slavery. For Berlin, the antebellum cotton revolution represented a major phase in the ratcheting up of pressure on slaves, and he suggests that Southern whites hardened their images of blacks in these years. Slaveholders, he suggests, had in some earlier periods "readily accepted a common humanity with slaves," but "nineteenth-century white Americans redefined blackness by endowing it with a hard edge and confining people of African descent to a place of permanent inferiority."[7]

Marxist writers such as Barbara J. Fields have much in common with the broad socio-economic school but, because of their very explicit interest in theorizing class and the interconnections between "race" and class, they have been particularly important in forcing greater theoretical precision in writing about "race" and slavery. Fields suggests that psycho-cultural writers tend mistakenly to slip into seeing racism not as being socially constructed but as being a primordial "transhistorical" force which is inherent in society. She is explicit that racism arises out of class interests, is a historical product, and has a dateable beginning. She sees class as being grounded in material fact, while "race," she maintains, is an ideology which develops to legitimize patterns of class interests. For her, "race" grew out of the special bourgeois relationships and interests which unfolded in the Revolutionary era.[8]

George Fredrickson notes that left-liberals have been slower to theorize than have Marxists, but adds that pressure from Marxist work encouraged him to become explicit about theory and to "come out of the closet" as a Weberian.[9] He expresses reservations about Marxist determinism and about a "monistic class analysis," and feels that class alone cannot always explain racism (or nationalism). Instead, following Max Weber, he combines class with the concept of a sense of "ethnic status," the latter representing group traditions and identities which, although produced by particular historical experiences, do not necessarily reflect current economic class interests.[10]

Fredrickson suggests that, in exploring the connections between American slavery and racism, we should distinguish between "societal" (or implicit) racism and "explicit and rationalized" (or biological) racism. Unlike psycho-cultural historians, he does not suggest that, in the first years of the colonial era, whites immediately responded to blacks with ideas of inbuilt white superiority. Instead, he argues that while societal racism developed from the late seventeenth century, it was only from the 1830s that explicit biological racism emerged – with the special circum-stances of the abolitionist attack on slavery, with pseudo-scientific researches into "race," and with class-conscious elite initiatives. Slave-holders consciously exploited new biological ideas in order to appeal to white "tribalism." The "new" racism formed the basis for a highly aggressive white world view, with planter interests promoting the notion of the "master race" and the idea that black slavery served the interests of all whites by protecting them from drudgery and servitude. Supposedly, then, slavery joined all whites together in a sense of being members of a "herrenvolk democracy" (democracy for the "master race").[11]

Historians, consequently, have paid a good deal of attention to questions concerning the timing of the onset of biological racism and the nature of racialization in the antebellum period. Psycho-cultural historians imply a basic continuity in biological racism, while others see various discontinuities. Opponents of psycho-cultural historians, because they generally want to see racism as arising through the rationalization of a period of exploitation, suggest a delay in the onset of biological racism. It might be, however, that what actually happened did not fit either with primordialism or with a notion of delayed racism. It might be that for socio-economic rather than for psycho-cultural reasons there was – from the earliest colonial times and over the centuries of slavery – a continuous pattern of biological racism among slaveowners and would-be slave-owners. It might also be that, again for socio-economic reasons, there was from the beginning a pattern of nonslaveholders seeing black people in a range of differing ways.

From the start, in the early seventeenth century, slaveowners and would-be slaveowners knew that blacks could be bought from the West Indies or from Africa as slaves, but they also knew that whites could not be bought as slaves for life. The owner's interest was always to recruit labor and to exploit it as intensively as possible. This meant that owners and intending-owners had strong reasons of self-interest to regard blacks as being biologically different and, thus, suitable for enslavement from the beginning. (At the same time, nevertheless, labor scarcity or the shortage of white female partners for owners and would-be owners might mean that a few blacks had enough bargaining power to achieve favored economic or quasi-familial positions, even to achieve freedom.) It is probable, in consequence, that slaveholding society adopted biological racism from the start, but that many *non*slaveholders of the seventeenth century had no pressing reason to see blacks as inherently inferior (and might occasionally have developed close relationships with them). To a limited extent, the pattern of some variety among nonslaveholders seems to have continued over the long run of slavery, although most Southern whites probably came to see white supremacy (if not slavery) as in their interests, and came to resist any externally-imposed reordering of white-black relations.

If what has just been said is valid, it would seem that the 1830s shift towards biological racism perceived by George Frederickson under-emphasizes basic patterns of continuity. It is possible that the perspectives of intellectual history and the focus on antebellum sectional and propaganda sources tend to give an exaggerated sense of discontinuity. Antebellum intellectual trends would make available an elaborate vocabulary of biological racism, but basic biological arguments seem to have been present from the first published proslavery works. The antebellum decision to give special emphasis to the biological argument depended, in fact, on the particular propaganda situation of the period.

From the beginning, and certainly in the 1780s (with the rise of British abolitionism), the biological argument had always been fundamental in the British West Indian defense of slavery. Proslavery writers everywhere were opportunistic and chose the arguments that gave them the most advantage. In the Caribbean, planter propaganda was pitched so as to appeal to the British Parliament. Planters gave primary stress to the idea that slavery was unavoidable since blacks, biologically, were suited only to servile labor. They sought to impress Parliament with the economic importance of slavery to Britain and her empire, and then deployed arguments about the protective role of slavery for blacks. Finally, they asserted colonial rights to self-rule and to the protection of property.[12] Biological arguments and assumptions would have been equally familiar in Britain's mainland American colonies. Indeed, Larry Tise, in his study of the proslavery argument from 1701 to 1840, found not only that the biological argument was prominent in the British Caribbean, but also that it was a constant in most of North America throughout his 140-year survey.[13]

Just as the British Caribbean planters selected their arguments and emphases to suit their special circumstances, so did the slaveholding interests of North America. In the Revolutionary era and shortly after, it was the Northern states of the U.S. which produced most of the carefully articulated defenses of slavery because, at that time, it was in those states where slavery was most threatened.[14] The biological argument was mixed, as it was in later years, with arguments about economics and about the threats posed by a freed black population. By the 1830s, however, there were in the South very good tactical reasons to increase the prominence given to the biological argument. Of fundamental importance was the fact that slavery was now a phenomenon of the Southern states, rather than being any longer a feature of the nation as a whole. It therefore now made tactical sense to emphasize the idea that the South was special, and this led to persistent stress on two central ideas – black "racial inferiority" and the "familial" nature of slavery. The "racial" argument allowed the South the *defensive* claim that its population problem was unique in America, and that slavery therefore had to stay. At the same time, the familial argument allowed it to claim that it had turned its "problem" into a positive virtue and had discovered the basis of the good society. While Southern propagandists prophesied that the growth of cities and factories would bring class war in the North, they argued that social harmony was assured in the special circumstances of the South, with the slave system both protecting black labor from abuse and preempting the growth of a potentially dangerous white proletariat.[15] Perhaps, then, the propaganda evidence analyzed by intellectual historians gives an impression of significantly greater discontinuity on the biological question than was really felt by the many generations of Southern slaveholders. In certain circumstances, biological arguments offered special propaganda opportunities, but in practice owners had always thought in biological terms when making their basic rationalizations of why they owned black people.

Our next discussion is on slavery, "race," and class as reflected in Eugene Genovese's "web of paternalism" thesis, which for many years has remained the central reference point for those concerned with the nature of relationships between masters and slaves.[16] His theory of antebellum racialized relations has been founded upon a class-based model, with that model building outwards from an interpretation of the world view of the master class. In the following paragraphs I want to outline Genovese's formulation of the interconnections between "race" and class in antebellum slavery, but I also want to outline an alternative to his model. I want to propose that the idea of a web of paternalism was indeed important for masters, but that it was important in a far narrower way than Genovese argues. I suggest that the slaveowner's commitment to an idea of reciprocal duties between master and slave was far shallower and far more selective than Genovese argues, and that the great mass of slaves saw slavery much more as a system of arbitrary power than of reciprocal duties and agreements about minimum standards.

Central to my argument is a concept that I call "key slaves."[17] By key slaves I mean a small percentage of relatively favored slaves with whom the master thought that he had close mutual emotional ties. Typically key slaves might be the driver (that is, the black supervisor of field workers), the butler or body servant, or the mammy. The owner's concept of key slaves was, I think, vital in allowing him a positive self-image as a benevolent master. It allowed him to see himself as treating his "worthy" (i.e. key) slaves generously, while at the same time treating his supposedly coarse, unsophisticated, and otherwise "unworthy" slaves with indifference. Key slaves, then, were crucially important in the mind of the master class.

According to Genovese, the special circumstances of the antebellum South – with the African slave trade ended, with masters taking increased interest in the health and expansion of their slave population, and with owners generally living close to their slaves – fostered an intricate web of paternalistic links between masters and slaves. Because masters (unlike in the wage system) owned their labor, Genovese suggests that a special non-bourgeois set of economic and social relationships developed. The system was based on class exploitation and class struggle, but was centered on a process by which owners gave their slaves certain privileges – certain limitations in work demands, certain protections of family. The slaves, he argues, reinterpreted these privileges as rights. A process of struggle took place, but for slaves it was a defensive struggle – a struggle not to remove the system of slavery but instead to protect "rights" within the system. Slaves were not docile "Samboes," and they did not accept slavery as a legitimate system. But, still, face-to-face paternalism linked them to their individual master. As Genovese maintained, "Wherever paternalism exists it undermines solidarity among the oppressed by linking them as individuals to their oppressor."[18]

Genovese emphasized that slavery was cruel, and that it rested ultimately on the power of the gun. But, at the same time, he repeatedly insisted that the mutual obligations of paternalism meant something in practice. In *Roll, Jordan, Roll*, he wrote: "Perceived cruelty seems to have been intolerable to society as a whole primarily because it threatened a delicate fabric of implicit reciprocal duties, the acceptance of which by both masters and slaves alone could keep the regime intact."[19] Genovese emphasized that the slaveholders' insistence on having a "black family" must be taken with deadly seriousness. Paternalism, he argued, meant that the slaves had a concept of minimum standards, and this meant that "A master who used the whip too often or with too much vigor risked their [the slaves'] hatred. Masters who failed to respect family sensibilities or who separated husbands from wives could be sure of it."[20] Paternalism, he insisted, was not an empty concept. While it did not prevent great cruelty, it did bring elements of genuine mutual affection between masters and slaves.

There is a great deal to be said for Genovese's fundamental assumption – that racism arises out of class-based exploitation, and that particular class relationships produce particular patterns of racism. But problems arise with the ways in which he applies his particular class model of white society. First, it might be that he takes slaveholders too literally when they (and especially their planter leaders and propagandists) argued that antebellum slavery was based on the notion of a "household," of a "family, white and black." Second, he uses his model of the slaveholders' world view, not just to interpret white attitudes, but also to infer how slaves would have thought. It is doubtful, however, whether most slaveholders took the conventions of paternalism anywhere near as seriously as Genovese does. It is also doubtful whether a model of the *planters'* view is a sufficient basis for inferring what slaves themselves thought.

One guide to the very distinct worlds of masters and slaves is what actually happened to the slave members of the "family, white and black." My own work suggests that one in five marriages of Upper-South slaves were forcibly wrecked by sale to traders, and a third of all children under fourteen years of age were parted from their parent or parents by long-distance sale. Moreover, these sales were inspired by profit, not by pressing necessity. Owners routinely transgressed the minimum standards that Genovese suggests slaves set for them, and slaves knew that the culture of owners was one, not of respect for black family sensibilities, but of disregard for nearly all black families. Such a situation would have meant widespread hatred of masters, a situation which suggests that the mass of slaves had little sense of working within an organic relationship of paternalistic understandings.[21]

There is an important paradox in the patterns just set out. Why were there such repeated slaveholder references to "my family, white and black," and yet, in practice, such disregard for black members of this extended family? The "key slave" concept seems to help resolve this problem. For ideological and psychological reasons, a great many owners needed key slaves. Such owners could feel that they had genuine affection for their key slaves and that slavery was truly a family institution. With few exceptions, key slaves are, in fact, the only slaves to appear in the letters, diaries, and published reminiscences of owners, rank-and-file slaves being almost completely invisible in these sources. Key slaves represented only a tiny fraction of all slaves. They included the servant who played with the young master when both were boys, who carried the master's books to school and later to college, and who attended him when he went off to fight the Yankees. Or perhaps the servant stayed at home during the war, hid the family silver from the invading Yankees, and was eventually buried in the white graveyard.

Key slaves were important in the minds of a substantial proportion of slaveowners. These owners, believing that they had intimate links to such slaves, could regard themselves as benefactors while ignoring or exploiting the great mass of other slaves. Both in the antebellum period and for later rationalizers of the South, therefore, key slaves were essential for all who thought seriously about the ownership of people. Not only, however, did they form a small minority of all slaves, but some owners who did not reflect very much on these matters could bypass the ideological and psychological need for key slaves. All of this suggests an extremely selective and incomplete commitment to Genovese's web of paternalism. The idea of the "family, white and black" had a great role in the South's opportunistic proslavery arguments, but it seems likely that the great mass of rank-and-file slaves had no sense of living within a web of paternalistic relationships. The mass of slaves had good reason to emphasize conflict and distrust rather than ideas of mutual responsibilities. A paternalistic model, relying heavily on building outwards from the slaveowners' world view, seems in practice to miss much that was essential in the behavior of owners and in the perception of slaves.

Our final main theme is a discussion of white society and the "herrenvolk democracy" thesis as touching planters, yeomen farmers, and poor whites. Having said something about relationships between masters and slaves, we can now turn to white inter-class relationships and the idea of "race." Here I am concerned with a series of interlinked questions: Why did nonslaveholders seem to support the planter elite over slavery, and why did they stand with the planters in the Civil War? Was racism the vital factor which bound the white South together? In particular, I am concerned with the "herrenvolk democracy" thesis proposed by George Fredrickson, a thesis which argues that the planter class, despite its strong aristocratic-elitist tendencies, made a deliberate and successful appeal for nonslaveholder support on the basis that the continuance of slavery guaranteed democracy and equal rights for all white people – for those they called the "master race." In exploring the significance of this thesis, I shall first note the contrasting arguments of Fredrickson and Eugene Genovese. I will then review a series of excellent case studies of yeoman farmers and poor whites, and take note of a recent flourishing of work on economic, religious, sexual, and other contacts between slaves and nonslaveholders.

Fredrickson developed the "herrenvolk" thesis in *Black Image in the White Mind* (1971), used it as an organizing device in *White Supremacy* (1981), and explored it further in a 1983 essay reproduced in *The Arrogance of Race* (1988).[22] Spelling out a Weberian approach in *The Arrogance of Race*, he saw the planter elite as pursuing its class interests of domination by tapping into "white tribalism" and a "folk tradition" of racism. Fredrickson had no doubt that the "herrenvolk" appeal was successful, writing that "The *herrenvolk* ideology, as well as the racial fears that sustained it, had enabled the planter elite to line up most of the nonslaveholding whites behind a system of black servitude that offered them no economic benefits."[23]

Genovese, in his reflections on the paradox of yeoman resentment of planters but failure to challenge their dominance, rejected as "elitist cant unworthy of attention" the traditional idea that yeomen did not know their own class interests and deferred to their planter betters.[24] He also wrote dismissively of the idea, "recently repackaged . . . so nicely [by Fredrickson] as 'Herrenvolk Democracy,'" that racism was the essential cement of white society.[25] Genovese saw racism as part of the process of class collaboration, but rejected racist "false consciousness" arguments. Instead, he saw at work a combination of the elite's achievement of cultural hegemony and the logical calculation of class interests by non-elite whites. In the non-plantation (mainly upcountry) areas, he argued, yeomen dominated local politics. They hated the gentry's pretensions, but their insular culture and "states rights" attitudes led them to take the view that, as long as slaveholders made few demands on them and their region, they were content to have them defend Southern freedom against Northern meddlers. In the plantation belt, he noted, yeomen did surrender political power to the planters. He suggested, though, that their support for planters came, not from "racial panics," but from family links, and from planter assistance in ginning cotton, loaning slaves, and buying surplus produce. Besides, he argued, the yeomen of the plantation belt generally aspired to join the ranks of the planters, or at least found them convenient guarantors of the only world they knew.[26]

A limitation on both Fredrickson's and Genovese's important discussions of nonplanter attitudes was the shortage of supporting primary evidence, but from 1983 onward the innovative work of several scholars has added much new material and insight. Stephen Hahn (1983), J. William Harris (1985), Lacy K. Ford (1988), and Stephanie McCurry (1995) have all produced fine case studies of yeoman farmers in particular locations, and all have maintained that yeomen supported slavery, their motivation being essentially a combination of fierce localism, attachment to small property-owning values, and racism.[27] Two further local case studies, Bill Cecil-Fronsman's (1992) analysis of "common whites" (yeomen and poor whites), and Charles C. Bolton's 1994 book on poor whites, suggest more ambivalence in support for planters, and have much to say about non-planter contacts between blacks and whites.[28]

Steven Hahn, in his work on yeomen in upcountry Georgia, found strong class tensions between yeomen and planters, especially as yeomen tried to hold to their small-producerist values and resented the planters' "haughty pretensions." But, at the same time, he argued, their values as small property-owners led them into support for the planters. As small property-holders, "they saw blacks as symbols of a condition they most feared – abject and perpetual dependency – and as a group whose strict subordination provided essential safeguards for their way of life. Whatever . . . the force of racism in its own right, the attitudes of the yeomanry toward Afro-Americans must be understood, historically, as attitudes of petty property owners toward the propertyless poor."[29] J. William Harris's study focused on the rural sections of Georgia and South Carolina that encircle Augusta. Like Hahn, he pointed to class tensions, but also to yeoman-planter agreement on certain essentials. The two groups shared a deep racism, an attachment to property ownership, and a belief in the South as a near-ideal society in which slavery guaranteed republican liberty for whites.

Lacy Ford's study of upcountry South Carolina again emphasized the values of small property-owners. In the North, yeomen might have been associated with "Free Soil," but in the South, he argued, slavery increasingly came to be seen as essential for guaranteeing the rights of small property-holders and preventing them from being thrown into the hands of capitalists. Planter and yeoman shared the "country-republican" ideal of personal independence, and slavery came to be regarded as essential for its continuation. "Herrenvolk" racism was part of these values, and he argued: "The presence of blacks allowed an entire race of would-be masters without slaves to enjoy certain caste privileges and to flaunt a certain instinctive sense of natural mastery."[30] Ford added a brief note on poor whites, suggesting that "White skin was ordinarily enough to entitle the small minority of propertyless and economically marginal whites to recognition as independent citizens."[31] But his focus was on yeomen, whose sharing of values with planters led them enthusiastically to follow the route of secessionist radicalism.

In Stephanie McCurry's study, the focus switched to the Low Country of South Carolina. She emphasized strong class tensions between yeomen and planters in a highly class-conscious Low Country society, and argued that an appeal to "herrenvolk democracy" was not viable because class inequalities were so real in this region. Nevertheless, she saw yeomen and planters as being firmly linked through their sharing of certain fundamental values. For McCurry, racism was part of the picture, but what was crucial in her gender-conscious analysis was the combination of property values and patriarchy. Yeomen supported slavery because the basis of their social values was the struggle to hold on to their position as property-holders and because of the notion, shared with planters, that the male head of household was patriarch over his dependants. The slaveowner was the patriarch who commanded dependants both black and white – his slaves and his white family. Similarly, the yeoman farmer commanded his own dependants – his wife and his children. Both yeoman and planter subscribed to conservative Christian republicanism. The planter was master of his great household, white and black, and yeomen themselves were "masters of small worlds."[32]

Bill Cecil-Fronsman broke important new ground, bringing much more detailed attention to grass-roots black-white contact than previous studies had done. His focus was on North Carolina and its common whites – a group defined as comprising nonslaveholders together with small slave-holders who saw themselves as non-elite. Planters, he argued, achieved a limited hegemony: they did not always convince common whites that the social order was fair, but hegemony was maintained in the sense that class conflicts were not such as to threaten planter dominance. Cecil-Fronsman saw slavery as exaggerating white inequalities, swallowing the best land, and preventing the growth of industrial job opportunities, but, he added: "The great paradox of the antebellum South was that although slavery was not in the common whites' interests, neither was emancipa-tion."[33] Common whites came to believe that their place in society depended on the maintenance of a degraded place for blacks: the idea of competing for jobs with a liberated black population appeared unthinkable.

Cecil-Fronsman argued, however, that the attitudes of common whites were complicated. Despite a thoroughly racist culture, "some common whites rejected and others significantly modified the racism that was so pervasive."[34] Some, especially among the poorest of whites, made links with slaves – trading with them, collaborating with them in stealing and selling the planter's property, gambling and socializing at taverns, sharing religious meetings, helping runaways, forming friendships, and enjoying casual or caring sexual relationships. Although it is hard to know how often such direct black-white associations occurred, Cecil-Fronsman suggested that "As long as blacks stayed in their places, *most* [my italics] common whites did little to abuse blacks and did not spend a good deal of time dwelling on their alleged shortcomings of character."[35] Common whites often saw slaves as being very harshly treated and knew slavery to be wrong, but, he argued, because of racism, self-interest, localism, and sometimes kinship links, they were willing to defend slavery, especially against a threat to the Southern community from outsiders.

Charles Bolton's study, like Cecil-Fronsman's, is of great importance because it attempts the difficult task of exploring grass-roots white contact with blacks. Indeed, Bolton's exclusive focus on poor whites (landless and slaveless) made work with primary sources particularly challenging.

His study of large poor white populations in sections of North Carolina and Mississippi argued that the idea of "herrenvolk democracy" had limited resonance with poor whites because they were acutely aware of the real and profound class inequalities in white society and they knew that slavery contributed to their poverty. They knew, too, that slavery failed to protect a substantial class of whites from hard physical labor. In some cases, these people worked in the fields as hired labor alongside slaves and thereby directly felt the power of the planter over white and black. Like Cecil-Fronsman, Bolton provided important evidence of social, sexual, and trading contacts with slaves, connections which raise questions about poor white commitment to slavery. The complicated picture of interactions with blacks did not, Bolton suggested, fit neatly with hegemony, "herrenvolk," or country republican theories. Even so, black-white alliances were limited, and "poor whites, in their dealings with blacks, were just as likely to display racial hatred and violence as they were to engage in acts of mutual understanding and cooperation."[36] Moreover, however strong their resentments of planters and however alarmingly they linked with slaves, still Bolton concluded that in the end poor whites did not pose a significant threat to the planter elite. Racism, kinship, and religion spread links through white society, and the potential for non-elite conflict with planters was also reduced by poor white differences with yeomen and the safety valve of geographic mobility for poor whites.

As well as the perspectives derived from the remarkable series of recent books on yeoman and poor whites, the last few years have seen major contributions from an exciting crop of books, articles, and theses on particular overlaps between black and white experiences – especially trading, sexual, and religious connections. These studies share some ground with aspects of Cecil-Fronsman's and Bolton's work, and sometimes suggest serious breaks in white supremacist solidarity. Because the nature of available primary sources makes it difficult to break decisively into areas of intimate contact between black and white, and because the studies just mentioned tend to work not by sampling techniques but by building up individual examples, they are suggestive, therefore, rather than conclusive investigations.

Philip Morgan's 1980s work on illicit economic activity between slaves and nonslaveholders stimulated in the 1990s a great deal of research on this important area of black-white connections.[37] Researchers on independent economic activity by slaves – variously called the "peasant breach," the "internal economy," the "slaves' economy" – found many slaves gaining income by earning cash bonuses for extra productivity;

working for cash on Sundays; selling eggs, cotton, logs, moss, barrels, or other goods produced in the slaves' own time; stealing planters' goods and selling them to other whites; or hiring their own time and retaining some of the value of their labor. The goods might be sold to planters, in local towns, or to itinerant traders, storeholders, or other whites. And with the income, slaves might buy little extras, or might drink, socialize, and gamble in taverns or stores, quite often it seems with nonslaveholding whites. Slaveholders would sometimes be happy to buy goods from slaves, and would sometimes have goods ready to sell in exchange, but many slaveowners worried about the subversive social contacts (including white ones) that the money might lead to.

Research on independent economic activity has brought exciting new insights into the lives of slaves, and such activity was surely of profound importance for slaves themselves. It is less clear, as yet, how deeply this activity impacted on black-white relations. When the buying and selling was with the slaveowner, it might influence the owner's perceptions of the slaves concerned, but bring only very limited contacts with other whites. Trading opportunities with outsiders would generally have been greatest for urban slaves, for those living near towns, and for elite skilled slaves. Trading with whites other than ones' owner naturally blurred the color line, but it is not yet clear to what extent.[38]

Several studies have recently suggested more widespread sexual contact between blacks and nonslaveholding whites than has previously been assumed. Rationalizations of slavery traditionally played on the "Buck" stereotype (the black man as sexual beast) as well as on the stereotype of the docile "Sambo."[39] Nevertheless, Diane Miller Sommerville's recent work has suggested that panic about "the black man as rapist" was a post-slavery phenomenon.[40] Martha Hodes, too, has suggested surprising flexibility in sexual areas, and has rejected the idea that sex between white women and black men has always been met in the South with violence and disbelief. She suggests that it was only from the 1850s, and especially after the Civil War, that such relationships came to be seen as a challenge to white men's social control – a challenge to be confronted with violence.[41] Timothy Lockley has found further surprising evidence for Savannah, Georgia, suggesting that sex between non-elite white men and black women was quite common there, and was common enough to alarm elite whites.[42] Studies such as those mentioned above suggest that while "Buck" was always essential for rationalizing and theorizing the slave system, on a practical day-to-day level there might have been significantly more flexibility over black-white sexual issues than is usually assumed.

Scholars have also paid increasing attention to the South's (mostly evangelical) "biracial" Churches, but levels of black membership are still not established, nor do we know whether slave membership was skewed towards "key slaves."[43] Work by Betty Wood shows, however, that there were places where slaves had some authority over whites (as deacons or as church leaders), and she also found situations where white members were forced to think about the violence done to slaves, and where black women (with the assistance of an influential white male backer) protected themselves from abuse.[44]

Recent studies in such areas as the slaves' economy, sexual relations, and Church membership have already opened up exciting routes into the overlaps between the worlds of slaves and of non-elite whites, and research of this sort promises to produce further important results. Another important entry point – a sample of direct non-elite statements and reported opinions – has been successfully explored in recent work by David Brown.[45] Brown's sample comes from the travel writings of Frederick Law Olmsted, who reported numerous conversations with yeomen and poor whites, and who stated that the intention of his eight-year period of research on the antebellum South was faithfully to report the ordinary condition of the laborers of the South.

Generally Olmsted did not find solid support for slavery so much as ambivalence. In the mountain districts, although he saw no great friendliness towards blacks, he did not encounter an acceptance of slavery's benefits for nonslaveholders, nor did he find an acceptance of the "racial" defence of slavery. In the plantation belt, in at least a dozen reported conversations with yeomen (and in other non-reported soundings), he found what he took to be the overwhelming opinion of this group: slavery was a curse for nonslaveholders, but blacks, if freed, would have to be moved out of the region or they would steal all the yeomen had. The yeomen, it seems, tolerated slavery, but did not accept proslavery rhetoric unquestioningly. And as long as most blacks were slaves (and posed no threat), the yeomen felt no need to develop a fixed biological ideology about blacks. Olmsted was contemptuous of the "debased" and "ignorant" state of poor whites. He found much hatred of blacks, but he also found much poor-white trading and mixing with slaves.

Overall, Brown, reflecting on the Olmsted material and on much other evidence, gives at best only strictly qualified support for the "herrenvolk" thesis. He suggests that "nonslaveholders had a common perception of difference in relation to blacks, but it was not one exclusively viewed in terms of race, nor was it one which automatically generated a unifying sense of whiteness. Their outlook stood in contrast to the fully developed biological racism of Southern slaveholders."[46] There does, indeed, seem to have been considerable ambiguity in non-elite attitudes towards slavery and "race." A great many yeomen and poor whites resented planters and probably saw slavery as a curse. Still, however, they feared abolition, and they therefore favored a system of black subordination. At the same time, the fact that slavery provided security for non-elite whites, and that it removed most black-white job competition, probably meant that many poor whites and yeomen did not feel the need to think in terms of a biological version of white supremacy.

The overall patterns of attitudes and ideology across the centuries of American slavery seem to stem from class interests and perceived class interests, and these patterns seem to combine centuries of basic continuity in biological racism by slaveholders with a somewhat more varied pattern by nonslaveholders. The experience and interests of yeomen and poor whites (and urban laboring whites) varied significantly according to time and circumstance, and such variations would have influenced attitudes. Recent evidence does suggest some significant antebellum blurring of the "race" line by nonslaveholder whites, and possibly in some situations of the colonial and Revolutionary eras the blurring would have been even greater. The "herrenvolk democracy" thesis in its fullest definition may apply more to the postbellum period of black-white labor competition than to the years of slavery. Perhaps, during slavery, societal racism was rather more common among non-elite whites than was biological racism. Slaveholder racism has sometimes been seen as having been "softened" by "paternalism," and, over the century and more following the ending of slavery, there was much white myth-making about the "Sunny South." But the slaveholders' romantic, "soft" racism was probably restricted to key slaves, and the role of "soft" or "romantic" racism was in any case to buttress and rationalize the grand system of crude exploitation that was slavery in America.

Notes

1. Quotation from Ulrich B. Phillips, "The Central Theme of Southern History," *American Historical Review*, 24 (1928): 30–43.

2. See for example Michael Omi and Howard Winant, *Racial Formation in the United States from the 1960s to the 1990s* (New York, 2nd edn., 1994).
3. See for example David Roediger, *The Wages of Whiteness: Race and the Making of the American Working Class* (London, 1991).
4. See Mia Bay, *The White Image in the Black Mind: African-American Ideas about White People, 1830–1925* (New York, 2000).
5. Winthrop D. Jordan, *White over Black: American Attitudes Towards the Negro, 1550–1812* (Baltimore, 1968). Theodore W. Allen divides historians who deal with the origins of American slavery into psycho-cultural and socio-economic. See Allen, *The Invention of the White Race* (London, 1994), vol. 1, pp. 1–24.
6. Edmund S. Morgan, *American Slavery, American Freedom: The Ordeal of Colonial Virginia* (New York, 1975).
7. Ira Berlin, *Many Thousands Gone: The First Two Centuries of Slavery in North America* (Cambridge, MA, 1998), pp. 364, 358.
8. Barbara J. Fields, "Ideology and Race in American History," pp. 143–77 in J. Morgan Kousser and James M. McPherson, eds., *Religion, Race, and Reconstruction: Essays in Honor of C. Vann Woodward* (New York, 1982).
9. George M. Fredrickson, *The Arrogance of Race: Historical Perspectives on Slavery, Racism, and Social Inequality* (Middletown, CT, 1988), pp. 158–9.
10. Ibid., pp. 3–7, 159, 109–11, 125–41, 216–8, 252.
11. See Fredrickson, *Arrogance of Race*, and Fredrickson, *The Black Image in the White Mind: The Debate on Afro-American Character and Destiny, 1817–1914* (New York, 1971).
12. M. J. Steele, "Power, Prejudice and Profit: The World View of the Jamaican Slaveowning Elite, 1788–1834," unpublished PhD thesis, University of Liverpool, 1988, esp. pp. 159–71.
13. Larry E. Tise, *Proslavery: A History of the Defense of Slavery in America, 1701–1840* (Athens, GA, 1987), p. 122.
14. Ibid., pp. 183–203.
15. On the opportunist pattern of proslavery arguments, see also Peter Kolchin, *American Slavery* (London, 1993), p. 196.
16. See Eugene D. Genovese's, *Roll, Jordan, Roll: The World the Slaves Made* (New York, 1974) and his numerous other studies. The profound influence of Genovese's work on the South is shown not just by those who have been fully convinced by his major theses but by the fact that all scholars in the field have been obliged to grapple with his ideas. James Oakes, in *The Ruling Race: A History of*

American Slaveholders (London and New York, 1982), was one of his most explicit critics. Oakes argued that the paternalistic relationships which Genovese talked about might have existed in the colonial period, and might have lingered in some old seaboard districts, but he felt that generally such patterns were overwhelmed by what he saw as the surging commercialism of the antebellum period. Most antebellum slaveowners – especially those below the old elite – were, he argued, aggressive capitalist entrepreneurs. Oakes's more recent book, *Slavery and Freedom: An Interpretation of the Old South* (New York, 1990) gives a more complex view of slavery's relationship with capitalism. Clarence E. Walker's *Deromanticizing Black History: Critical Essays and Reappraisals* (Knoxville, 1991) includes a chapter which vigorously criticizes Genovese's use of hegemony and paternalism. He sees these concepts as being stretched too far, and argues that Genovese's formulation underplays the coercive nature of slavery and deemphasizes the role of racism. William Dusinberre's *Them Dark Days: Slavery in the American Rice Swamps* (New York, 1996) depicts the elite rice planters not as paternalists but as callous gentlemen capitalists. Instead of Genovese's steady framework of master-slave accommodation, based on negotiations over rights and privileges, he sees owners as frequently withdrawing privileges. Further, so as to maximize the owner's powers of manipulation, Dusinberre believes, privileges tended to be given to individuals, not to slaves as a group.

17. My "key slave" argument is outlined in the introduction to the 1996 edition of Tadman, *Speculators and Slaves: Masters, Traders, and Slaves in the Old South* (Madison, WI, 1989; enlarged 1996), and will be the organizing device for Tadman, *Worlds of Masters and Slaves* (forthcoming).
18. Genovese, *Roll*, pp. 5–6.
19. Ibid., p. 73.
20. Ibid., pp. 124–5.
21. For detailed calculations on separations, see Tadman, *Speculators and Slaves*, pp. 133–78.
22. See Fredrickson, *Black Image*, esp. pp. 58–68, 90–6; Fredrickson, *White Supremacy: A Comparative Study in American and South African History* (Oxford, 1981): Fredrickson, *Arrogance of Race*, esp. pp. 140–1, 252–3.
23. Ibid., p. 252.
24. Eugene D. Genovese, "Yeomen Farmers in a Slaveholders' Democracy," *Agricultural History*, 49 (1973): 331–42.

25. Ibid., p. 332.
26. Ibid., pp. 333–42.
27. Steven Hahn, *The Roots of Southern Populism: Yeoman Farmers and the Transformation of the Georgia Upcountry, 1850–1890* (New York, 1983); J. William Harris, *Plain Folk and Gentry in a Slave Society: White Liberty and Black Slavery in Augusta's Hinterlands* (Middletown, CT, 1985); Lacy K. Ford Jr., *Origins of Southern Radicalism, 1800–1860* (New York, 1988); Stephanie McCurry, *Masters of Small Worlds: Yeoman Households, Gender Relations, and the Political Culture of the Antebellum South Carolina Low Country* (New York, 1995).
28. Bill Cecil-Fronsman, *Common Whites: Class and Culture in Antebellum North Carolina* (Lexington, KY, 1992); Charles C. Bolton, *Poor Whites of the Antebellum South: Tenants and Laborers in Central North Carolina and Northeast Mississippi* (Durham, NC, 1994).
29. Hahn, *Roots of Southern Populism*, pp. 89–90.
30. Ford, *Origins of Southern Radicalism*, p. 362.
31. Ibid., p. 363.
32. See McCurry, *Masters of Small Worlds*.
33. Cecil-Fronsman, *Common Whites*, p. 29.
34. Ibid., p. 68.
35. Ibid., p. 81.
36. Bolton, *Poor Whites*, p. 184.
37. See Philip D. Morgan, "The Ownership of Property by Slaves in the Mid-Nineteenth Century Low Country," *Journal of Southern History*, 49 (1983): 399–420 and Philip D. Morgan, "Work and Culture: The Task System and the World of Low Country Blacks, 1700–1880," *William and Mary Quarterly*, 35 (1982): 563–99.
38. For a particularly fine study of the attempts of slave-owners to control trading, see John Campbell, "'As A Kind of Freeman'?: Slaves' Market-Related Activities in the South Carolina Up Country, 1800–1860," in Ira Berlin and Philip D. Morgan, eds., *Cultivation and Culture: Labor and the Shaping of Slave Life in the Americas* (Charlottesville, 1993), pp. 243–74.
39. For a fascinating discussion of these stereotypes, and the female slave stereotyped as "promiscuous," "Jezebel," and asexual "Mammy," together with the plantation mistress as "Southern belle" and the planter as "Cavalier," see Elizabeth Fox-Genovese, *Within the Plantation Household: Black and White Women of the Old South* (Chapel Hill, 1988), pp. 290–2.

40. See for example Diane Miller Sommerville, "Rape, Race, and Castration in Slave Law in the Colonial and Early South," in Catherine Clinton and Michele Gillespie eds., *The Devil's Lane: Sex and Race in the Early South* (New York, 1997), pp. 74–89.

41. Martha Hodes, *White Women, Black Men: Illicit Sex in the Nineteenth-Century South* (New Haven 1997).

42. Timothy J. Lockley, "Crossing the Race Divide: Interracial Sex in Antebellum Savannah," *Slavery and Abolition*, 18 (1997): 159–73.

43. For some statistical evidence on "biracial" churches, see McCurry, *Masters of Small Worlds*, pp. 159–67.

44. Betty Wood, "'For their Satisfaction or Redress:' African Americans and Church Discipline in the Early South," pp. 109–23 in Clinton and Gillespie, eds., *The Devil's Lane*.

45. David Brown, "The Logical Outcome of the Nonslaveholders' Philosophy? Hinton Rowan Helper on Race and Class in the Antebellum South," unpublished PhD thesis, University of Hull, 2000. The principal focus of Brown's thesis is a reinterpretation of the writing of Helper, whom he sees as not developing fixed biological ideas of "race" until after the fall of slavery. Before then, Brown argues, he was a societal racist, not a confirmed biological racist. Although seeing blacks as inferior in his 1850s books, he also saw them as having moral and religious rights. Helper refused to accept slavery, and specifically rejected the idea that slavery was justified on "racial" grounds. I am very grateful to David Brown both for his expert advice and for making his work available.

46. Brown, "Logical Outcome," p. 261.

–16–

Imagining Indians: Differing Perspectives on Native American History
Joy Porter

This chapter will explore how historical writers have represented Native Americans[1] over time. It will also consider the notion that current scholarship primarily presents "settler" understandings of the American past – that is, the suggestion that existing American histories are incomplete since there has been no fundamental integration of Indian and Indian-oriented perspectives. Undeniably, there have been significant developments in the writing of Indian history, in particular over the last three decades of the twentieth century, but it is still true that scholarship has in large part failed fully to incorporate Indian points of view. In order to consider ways in which this might be rectified, this chapter will examine how literary scholarship has approached the issue; it will then discuss the burgeoning field of museum studies and its potential impact upon the writing of Indian history; finally, it will speculate over whether transnational perspectives are likely in the future to erode a seemingly entrenched set of disciplinary approaches to the presentation of the Indian past. These matters deserve consideration in this context because, without them, the initial descriptive overview of the contours of Native American history presented below will be insufficient at this juncture. The current growing momentum for change within Indian history is too fascinating to ignore and the issues raised give new context to the histories created in the past about the indigenous peoples of the United States.

Regrettably, the simplest way to view the history of Native America's relationship to American history is to look at it solely in terms of the remarkable persistence of stereotype and misunderstanding.[2] The dominant discourse within American history has failed to displace a number of myths and untruths and, even today, too few historians are fully cognizant of some of the most basic information about the indigenous peoples within the boundaries of the United States. Take, for example, perhaps the single most important factor overall about Native America, its essential diversity, a characteristic which has impacted and will continue to impact upon every aspect of Indian political, social, and cultural life. Before 1492, the American continent was home to over two thousand cultures with their own significantly differing ways of functioning. Their languages were often discrete and unintelligible to their neighbors, they inhabited a great variety of landscapes, they engaged in a range of sometimes interlinked economies, and they all cherished their own shared memories of the past. Only relatively recently have American school history textbooks been required to register these facts. Formerly, they were particularly resistant to taking a longer-term and broadly continental, as opposed to primarily nationalistic, view of the peopling of the United States. Regrettably, too, the history of the American continent prior to the date of "discovery" is still customarily discussed by Euro-American academics as "prehistory," an explicitly Eurocentric term presupposing that American history by definition originates with the non-Indian written record. The persistence of the term "Indian" is yet another case in point. At contact, these diverse groups of native "Americans" did not conceive of themselves or categorize themselves as a single entity – if they knew about each other's existence at all. The collective descriptor "Indian" is, in fact, a non-native invention that can be traced back to Columbus. It is thought to be derived from his original name for the Taino people he first encountered, whom he described as "una gente in Dios," or "Indios," meaning "a people in God."[3]

This chapter will confine itself to the discussion of Indian history from its academic beginnings when the profession of history-writing was first finding its disciplinary feet in the United States. In 1893, Frederick Jackson Turner delivered his famous lecture on "The Significance of the Frontier in American History." In so doing, he positioned the settling of the frontier West, and with it the Indian, firmly in the nation's past. A characterization of Indians as "vanishing" and/or as "noble savages" thereafter continued to solidify within United States history as it did within American life. Early twentieth-century studies focusing on Native Americans consequently dismissed as myth or romantic folklore what was, in fact, a rich native oral tradition. They based the "Indian" research carried out almost exclusively upon European and Euro-American sources laden with mediations of translation, gender bias, and cultural incomprehension. A fascination with frontier conflict, rather than with Indian cultural adaptation or Indian development, dominated the attention of the reading public until the middle decades of the twentieth century.[4]

Before the watershed years of the late 1960s and early 1970s, in fact, Indian history remained limited in approach and roughly divisible into three neat categories: the history of Indian policy, that of frontier conflict, and tribal histories whose narratives usually ended around 1900.[5] Historians dominated the first two categories and anthropologists the third. Anthropology, it should be noted, like history, first developed as a discipline in the 1880s and persistently influenced historical scholarship on Native Americans.[6] Anthropology underwent a fundamental transformation during the Civil Rights era, and so too did understanding of the Indian's historical significance. The early 1970s saw an upsurge in scholarship and a significant shift in scope, methodology, and perspective within Native American history. Studies on Indian policy did not disappear, but, after the early 1970s, debate moved beyond consideration of the construction or merits of specific policy toward consideration of how policy was administered and experienced by native peoples. Scholars, benefiting from institutional developments such as the foundation of the D'Arcy McNickle Center for the History of the American Indian in Chicago, began to move beyond the insidious stereotype of the "vanishing" American. There was a new recognition of Indian cultural continuity, and the process of cultural adaptation came to the fore. As the conflict and consensus paradigm lost intellectual currency, the Indian position changed in terms of the construction of the American past. Instead of casting American Indians as the nation's victims or as marginal "exotics," historians began to address the complexities of Indian-white relations across time. Of course, the harvest of new understandings of the American past that resulted from this shift is by no means complete. Even the outline overview that follows shows that many avenues for multi- and inter-disciplinary analysis remain and that the research completed to date has purchase far beyond "Native American Studies" as it is customarily defined.[7]

Much of the work produced in the 1970s undoubtedly capitalized on the era's countercultural fascination with all things Indian. The book which, perhaps more than any other, helped stimulate this interest was the tremendously popular and one-sided version of Indian-white relations which Dee Brown produced for the Vietnam generation in 1971. Then, in 1972, Alfred W. Crosby began the less commercial but more valuable work of tracing the devastating biological impact of "discovery." This was extended in 1983 when William Cronon further highlighted the clear connections between environmental degradation and native "conquest."[8] Another especially important book appeared in 1975 – *The Invasion of America*, by iconoclastic scholar Francis Jennings. Jennings stripped away ideas about superior European versus inferior Native American culture and stimulated further new understandings of the accommodative complexities of cultural contact. The Smithsonian then laid another bedrock for future work with its encyclopedic summary, *Handbook of North American Indians*, appearing in multiple volumes from 1978.[9]

Frederick Hoxie's 1984 study, *A Final Promise*, is another example of this new approach. It dealt with federal policy, specifically the campaign to allot Indian land. By 1900, Hoxie showed, allotment had brought about the "peripheralization" of Native peoples and relegated them to the margins of American society. Yet another important study in this vein was Laurence Hauptman's 1986 examination of responses to external agency among the Iroquois in New York, Oklahoma, Wisconsin, and Canada. Hauptman revealed a complex understanding of the relationship between the political activism of the Red Power era and internal drives towards cultural rejuvenation.[10]

Some of the work referred to above falls under the category of "Ethnohistory," an approach developed by anthropologists such as Anthony F. C. Wallace during the late 1950s and the 1960s.[11] It was perceived as offering a way of overcoming ethnology's tendency towards synchronism (the assumption of timelessness) by promoting fruitful understandings both of the contexts of particular societies and of change over time. Work in this vein in the late 1970s and 1980s by Francis Jennings, Bruce Trigger, and James Axtell further displaced triumphalist analyses of Euro-American domination over Indians and fostered new evaluations of how the ideals and values that have defined United States history came into being.[12] With the advent of a dedicated journal, *Ethnohistory*, as well as publishing opportunities within other journals such as the *William and Mary Quarterly*, ethnohistory continues to develop. However, even though ethnohistorical texts, such as Richard White's *The Middle Ground* (1991), have received much acclaim, indigenous scholars have bemoaned the non-Indian appropriation of indigenous history and culture that the field overall is said to represent.

For a variety of reasons, the history of Native America in the twentieth century has yet to receive comprehensive attention. Even though Hazel W. Hertzberg paved the way with her 1971 study, *The Search for an American Indian Identity*, and Margot Liberty (1978) and L. G. Moses and Raymond Wilson (1985) have studied specific twentieth-century Native American figures, much work remains to be done. Similarly, the number of studies on the urban twentieth-century Indian experience is limited, even though almost two-thirds of the Indian population now lives off-reservation. Nonetheless, valuable work by Alison R. Bernstein (1991), Donald L. Fixico (1986), Alan L. Sorkin (1978), and Lawrence Hauptman (1981, 1986) has already powerfully mapped some of the ground.[13]

Twentieth-century Indian history has proved a challenge to historians, just as Native American women and their histories have proven difficult to accommodate within dominant feminist thinking. As Kenneth Lincoln has pointed out, Euro-American women have sought gender equality for a century, but tribal women have followed a different agenda. Pre-contact, they were seldom disenfranchised in their own cultures. Indeed, the great majority of pre-Columbian tribes, perhaps ninety percent, functioned as matrilocal, matrilineal, and "mother-right" cultures.[14] Certainly, many Indian women do not award gender issues the same priority as civil and ethnic issues. Perhaps the Brulé Sioux Mary Crow Dog best expressed the primacy of issues relating to national and cultural sovereignty within Indian life when she responded to a white nurse's protest at her "women's work" during the 1973 seventy-one day winter protest at Wounded Knee Creek, South Dakota. Remembering the answer she gave at the site where three hundred Minneconjou Sioux had been butchered in 1890, she said, "We told her that her kind of women's lib was a white, middle-class thing, and that at this critical stage we had other priorities. Once our men had gotten their rights and their balls back, we might start arguing with them about who should do the dishes."[15]

Indian women may generally not have interested white feminists (who have often regarded them as excessively domestic and borne down by childrearing) but one, in particular, has undoubtedly fascinated American historians over time. Within popular and academic discourse alike, the Indian "princess" Pocahontas, alias Matoaka, has dominated attention when it comes to Native women. Useful broader studies of Indian women do exist, by Nancy Shoemaker (1995) and Gretchen Bataille and Kathleen Sands (1984), but it is Pocahontas as a symbol of seventeenth-century cross-cultural interaction who is constantly referred to. She left no verifiable words of her own, and her silence has fostered a range of contrasting interpretations of her role and significance, something charted by Robert S. Tilton in 1984.[16] Encouraged by two Disney films (1995, 2001), interest in Pocahontas continues.

Tension continues to develop between Euro-American versus Indian and Indian-oriented scholarship and there are some issues on which academic debate has been especially acute. One telling example is the highly politicized debate over native population numbers at contact. Russell Thornton (1987) estimated that there were over five million living within the boundaries of the present-day United States alone; Kirkpatrick Sale (1990) suggested it was actually fifteen million for all of the U.S. and Canada; William M. Denevan (1992) estimated that the correct figure for the U.S. and Canada was 3.8 million and, in the same year, A. J. Jaffe suggested it was in fact closer to one million.[17]

Another example of such a disagreement is the wrangle over the Iroquois nation's true relationship to the structure and formulation of American governmental systems, a debate enlivened by a great many, including Daniel K. Richter, James Axtell, Elizabeth Tooker, Francis Jennings, Barbara Graymont, Vine Deloria, and contributors to the controversial *Exiled in the Land of the Free*, edited by Oren Lyons and John Mohawk. The debate rages because, to some, the suggestion that the Iroquois (*Ho-dé-no-sau-nee*, or, People of the Longhouse) and other Indian confederacies helped to shape ideas about democracy in the early United States is, to quote Bruce E. Johansen, "a horror story of multiculturalism and political correctness."[18] Such scholarly conflict seems likely to escalate as Indian academics gain voice and continue to recontextualize non-Indian influence and control over Indian representation in general.

Some commentators have sought to resolve this issue by suggesting that Indians alone should write about Indian history, but this idea is associated with a host of problems. The main reason why the majority of Indian writers are novelists and poets, rather than historians, is that American history presents Indian historians with a number of disciplinary and intellectual challenges. "Indians," as the editor of the *American Indian Quarterly* reminds us, "retain an often emotionally charged commitment to Indian issues above and beyond academia."[19] Their approach, for example, to the impact of scholarship upon tribal peoples, the importance of oral history as a historical tool, the role of ritual and symbolism, and the use of documentation derived from burial ground desecration or from tribal informants who were unaware that their words would be reproduced can all differ radically from that of their non-Indian peers. These issues need to be addressed in much greater depth before the much-touted notion of a "New Indian History" can ever be fully realized.

Indian demands that analyses of American history broaden their perspective and begin to include Indian versions of events are not about to disappear. A number of respected, indeed award-winning, histories have been specifically singled out by Indians as being either predominantly fictive and/or offensive to tribal peoples. Richard White's *The Middle Ground* has given much offence, in particular to the Winnebagos and Wyandots; Ramón A. Gutiérrez's *When Jesus Came, the Corn Mothers Went Away* (1991) has been dismissed by the Pueblo as being wholly unrepresentative of the thinking of the people it describes, and William T. Hagan's biography of famous Comanche Quanah Parker (1993) has been criticized for ignoring the rich seam of Comanche oral history concerning its subject.[20]

As well as targeting specific histories, Indian scholars continue to make powerful arguments over the inclusion of Indian material within the discipline generally. They argue that Indian history should not be seen as special and exotic, but rather as truly foundational to American history itself. For some, like Donald L. Fixico, it is nothing less than an ethical duty to include North American Indian history in the North American experience, both in terms of the actual production of history and its dissemination in the classroom and beyond.[21] When such thinking causes the issue of how to incorporate Indian history and Indian versions of the past within dominant American historical discourse to be seriously debated, questions about the appropriate role of oral history are quickly generated. But, as Fixico notes, even though Studs Terkel won a Pulitzer Prize in 1984 for his *"The Good War": An Oral History of World War Two*, interviews and oral history still do not enjoy anything like the same status as conventional approaches.[22] This is an ongoing stumbling block, since oral history provides one of the few ways of incorporating more fully the Indian oral tradition into historical writing and of moving beyond the consistent use of sources about Indians produced almost exclusively by non-Indians.

The problem is that an Indian epistemological perspective on history often goes against that of the modern white historian. Consider, for example, Brulé Sioux historian Clyde Dollar's remarks that:

> the idea of an historical fact . . . from the Indian side – is something one has been told by his elders and therefore is not to be questioned. Indeed, among the High Plains people, there is little interest in the subject matter of history per se beyond the repeating of its stories, and a deeply searching pursuit of data and facts on which to build veracity in history is frequently considered rather pointless, perhaps ludicrous, decidedly nosy, an occupation closely associated with eccentric white men.[23]

As Arnold Krupat has explained, this difference is not simply a matter of perspective. Most scholars writing North American history look for facts about the past, not stories and symbolism about it, and have a commitment to what they deem to be plausible according to what they know about the world. They view traditional Indian histories as myth or, at best, as messages that are irrationally bereft of any concern for verifiable fact. This issue, centering as it does upon not just the inclusion of Native experience but also Native constructions of the category of knowledge, was dramatized when controversy erupted in 1987 in northern New York over the commissioning of a new educational resource guide.[24] The problem essentially revolved around the real differences between Indian ideas about the past and Euro-American understandings of what history entailed.

But, of course, if we are to move beyond what some critics have termed a settler understanding of history in America, we must find a way to engage with these categories of knowledge, as well as with Indian and non-Indian critics of Indian characterization in representations of the whole American past.[25] For a lesson on how to incorporate Indian and Indian-oriented perspectives, it is necessary to consider another field. If American history has so far failed to take advantage of Native American insight and perspective, then American literary studies, and especially the problems to do with reconstructing the canon that were so pressing in the 1980s, may be a useful disciplinary example. Much of the shift in perspective within American literary studies can be traced to the late 1960s. Indians have always been central to the stories America tells about itself, but after 1968, when Kiowa N. Scott Momaday won a Pulitzer prize for his novel *House Made of Dawn*, a process of change was accelerated which further problematized the Indian relationship to American literature. It became almost impossible to ignore Indian complaints that Euro-American literature was incomplete, that it had plagiarized aspects of native culture, and that it had placed them "outside of the tribal genres and the Indian character" while at the same time ensuring that a white protagonist always remained central.[26]

Such claims were symptomatic of a more general new literary awareness of cultural difference and of a powerful impetus to move beyond any convenient ghettoization of culturally different concerns. This contributed to the precipitation of a literary crisis. As Annette Kolodny commented in 1985: "In the wake of all the new information about the literary production of women, Blacks, Native Americans, ethnic minorities, and gays and lesbians; and with new ways of analyzing popular fiction, non-canonical genres, and working-class writings, all prior literary histories are rendered partial, inadequate, and obsolete."[27] The same rhetoric of crisis is still evident today, although not every commentator goes as far as Mary Poovey, who recently suggested that literary studies has altogether "lost an object of analysis deemed worthy of study" as a result of this sea-change.[28]

Indisputably, over the last thirty years of the twentieth century, Indian literature (written in English for publication) blossomed. The impact of novels by writers such as Leslie Marmon Silko, Louise Erdrich, James Welch, and Gerald Vizenor has been significant. First and foremost, it highlighted how, within the then-dominant American literary tradition, the Indian had served as an inarticulate symbol for all that non-Indian culture deemed absent or lost. Second, the critical response to this work was also noteworthy. In 1992, for example, Arnold Krupat outlined something of a literary corollary to ethnohistory in his book *Ethnocriticism: Ethnography, History, Literature*. Having learned from ethnohistory, he built into his book an awareness of the problems inherent in ethnocriticism. He acknowledged the difficulty in engaging in text-based criticism when so many Native literatures are oral and performative. He recognized the need for an awareness of the cultural assumptions underlying Native stories and questioned the notion of an "esthetic universalism" as a necessary prerequisite to the critique of Native texts.[29] But even with Krupat's awareness and his sharp attention to the processes of translation, it remains very much to be seen whether ethnocriticism will continue to develop because of these very issues.

At least the days when Native American literature was routinely relegated to the status of children's stories, however, look to be very much over. If there really is an "Indian soul" to America, as D. H. Lawrence suggested,[30] it seems that American literature and American literary criticism is now determined to tend to it.

An important site for the debate over the authority and content of American Indian history during the 1980s and 1990s has been within museums as institutions and within the field of museum studies. It seems likely that this body of scholarship, sometimes referred to as "museological studies," will continue to add to the push for change in the representation of the Indian past within print history. During the 1980s, interest in the history of museums accelerated and a new body of research and discussion yielded a richer understanding of the social, cultural, and institutional significance of this history than had existed previously. As Susan A. Crane pointed out in a recent edited collection, *Museums and Memory*, this development coincided with an international boom in museum construction and attendance.[31] Scholars focused upon what Daniel Sherman and Irit Rogoff in their collection *Frameworks for a Critical Analysis in Museum/Culture* have called "the signifying processes through which museums endow objects with meaning."[32] The historical development of museums was identified as being intimately connected with the formation of a bourgeois public sphere and museums were revealed as being specific sites for the expression and presentation of cultural identity. Display clearly had a politics of its own, and scholars were able to make a series of arguments about "difference" (that is, about race, class, gender, and sexuality) within the museum context. In particular, natural history museums and museums of ethnology were seen to be using representational strategies which presented indigenous or "primitive" peoples, and indeed Nature itself, in a specific way. The museum transformed Nature and "exotic" cultures into objects, so that they became available for consumption by modern audiences.

Entire cultures, within nineteenth- and early twentieth-century museum schemes in particular, were frozen in time through the act of display. "Primitives" were presented as being irrevocably "of the past," rather than as being living and breathing contributors to the ongoing present. American museums had presented Indians as part of the evolutionary past and had ossified diverse Indian cultures into static, too often homogenous, representations that fitted into a broader triumphalist national narrative. A range of texts established and then further developed these arguments, including George W. Stocking Jr.'s edited *Objects and Others: Essays on Museums and Material Culture* (1985), Thomas Schlereth's *Cultural History and Material Culture* (1990), and Ivan Karp and Steven D. Lavine's *Exhibiting Cultures: The Poetics and Politics of Museum Display* (1991). Journal contributions made powerful interventions to the debate about museums, one of particular significance being Donna Harraway's discussion of "Teddy Bear Patriarchy: Taxidermy in the Garden of Eden, New York City, 1908–1936." Harraway unpacked the meanings behind New York museum taxidermic display, explaining the triumphalist message behind the creation of replicated "exotic" wild animals caught forever at the moment of contact with an all-powerful hunter.[33] Another excellent piece was produced by David Jenkins, in a discussion entitled "Object Lessons and Ethnographic Displays," which encapsulated many key aspects of museum debates.[34]

James Clifford made some of the most powerful arguments about twentieth-century ethnography, literature, and art in his book, *The Predicament of Culture* (1988). He looked in conceptual detail at what happens whenever "marginal peoples come into a historical or ethnographic space that has been defined by the Western imagination," declaring firmly that "The time is past when privileged authorities could routinely 'give voice' (or history) to others without fear of contradiction." His work used as a launching point Frederick Jameson's remark, in *The Political Unconscious: Narrative of a Socially Symbolic Act*, that "Croce's great dictum that all history is contemporary history does not mean that all history is *our* contemporary history." Clifford explained how, after 1950, those that had previously been spoken for and represented by others were no longer prepared to allow that representation: "peoples long spoken for by Western ethnographers, administrators, and missionaries began to speak and act more powerfully for themselves on a global stage. It was increasingly difficult to keep them in their 'traditional' places." This was all part of a larger reality, the "predicament of culture" which produced a prevalent feeling of "lost authenticity, of 'modernity', ruining some essence of source." This was not something new, but it was a condition that had to be better recognized. Nostalgia, especially nostalgia for "pure products" or peoples representative of authentic tradition, had irredeemably lost its charm.[35]

This awareness of the politics of museum display has resulted in a series of new approaches within contemporary museums, one example being the Northwest Coast collection of material from the Museum of the American Indian displayed at the IBM Gallery in New York from October 10 to December 29, 1984. Here, an exhibit of what has been termed "traditional masterpieces" ended, significantly, with works by living Northwest Coast artists. To some, such changes seem small, but the IBM Gallery display was symptomatic of the larger ongoing reconsideration of "primitive peoples" and their representation which has been described in the works referred to above. Increasingly, museums now recognize that Indian peoples cannot be excluded from their representation, that their cultures are far from static, and that their contribution to the present and future deserves recognition.

If literary studies and museums can provide useful precedents, what more can be learned from new fields of academic growth closer to American history itself? Could historians, for example, find direction in the growing tendency to foreground transnational perspectives in the quest to better accommodate Indian and Indian-orientated concerns within United States history and Indian history as it is customarily defined?

Although World History, for example, is by no means new, it does seem set to take on a new significance in the twenty-first century, a development not unrelated to current pedagogical changes within the United States. As Professor Peter Stearns of Carnegie Mellon University recently pointed out, the United States has become increasingly aware of the dangers of parochiality in terms of its history curricula. There is now something of a consensus that too many U.S. students have confined their historical studies to their own country, an emphasis deemed inappropriate at a time when transnational corporations and globalization generally are taking center stage. At the same time, there has been widespread pressure for more comparative teaching as a result of American demographics, with an ever-expanding number of students being of non-European origin. Introductory World History courses, with an emphasis upon global themes such as migration, the spread of disease, and patterns of commercial exchange, have been increasingly introduced at prestigious U.S. institutions of higher education. Moreover, World History, with its focus upon the tensions operating between a number of significant civilizations over time, has come to be seen as an expanding research area.[36]

Given their connections across so many disciplinary and area boundaries, Indian and Indian-oriented scholars may turn out to be particularly well-placed to develop as multidisciplinary and interdisciplinary practitioners within World History, although the field is still dominated by non-Indian American-based scholars such as William H. McNeill and Theodore H. Von Laue.[37] In spite of this, the work of some World historians may significantly advance the debate on whether or how Native American concerns can be better integrated within the dominant discourse of American history. Take for example Ashis Nandy's discussion of "History's Forgotten Doubles." Nandy, a Bengali, harks back to Gandhi's *Satyagraha* in order to make a call for transcendence of the dominant Western approach to the past. He points out that, until relatively recently, historical consciousness had much less purchase across the globe. Other, diverse modes of constructing and experiencing the past once predominated and today millions, including many Native Americans, still live outside "history." They understand the past in a fashion antithetical to modern Western understandings of history. Especially in societies where myth is central to organizing the experience of the past, what Nandy calls "principled forgetfulness" is practiced. This means both that the past is not remembered completely or objectively and that the remembered past is not divorced from its ethical meaning in the present.

Nandy goes on to compare the inability of Western historical consciousness to comprehend history on anything other than its own terms with Freud's point about the human mind being unable to fantasize itself as dead. He calls not so much for the inclusion of alternative histories, but for an alternative *to* history, demanding our acknowledgement that there is "no perfect equivalence between history and the construction of the past."[38]

Such a radically self-reflexive agenda for history as Nandy's may ultimately help to create further space for Native American formulations of the past. However World History develops in the future, and whatever its disciplinary purchase and relationship to U.S. history, some of sort of fundamental perspective change seems unavoidable. Scholars and theorists are currently struggling to entrench a new paradigm that will accommodate changes within the current era, such as a globalizing economy and the much-discussed decline of the nation state. With the development of the transnational corporation, the state has lost some of its status as the primary unit of economic, political, and cultural activity and analysis. Consequently, there has been much discussion about the need to get away from American parochialism and exceptionalism in favor of some new perspective, be it critical internationalism, globalism, or transnationalism.[39] Whatever new paradigm eventually holds sway, it seems likely to be one which will take greater cognizance of the United States's position in the world. The impact of the 1993 NAFTA agreement creating a trade association between the United States, Canada, and Mexico, for example, may serve to foster analyses of the United States from a continental rather than national perspective.[40] In general, historians seem set to express a new series of concerns over global economic, political, and cultural issues, and institutions. Key issues, such as the implications of global population increase and the North/South wealth differential, may well soon penetrate more deeply within disciplinary discourse.[41]

As these developments take shape, so too do critiques. For example, although the notion of transnational identity has many attractions, especially for those concerned with indigenous issues, commentators such as Kandice Chuh have made the point that transnationality can be chosen or imposed in a coercive fashion. After all, a Japanese transnation was imagined and used to justify the internment of (Japanese) American citizens during World War II.[42] Frederick Buell, too, has usefully warned against reifying globalization as a phenomenon which is in any sense singular, uncontradictory, or, for that matter, coherent. He also suggests that, even though much is obviously changing, much also remains the same. The Clinton presidency, he argues, turned around American fears about a globalizing world economy, styling it instead as "the new frontier for American business and society." It reconstructed multiculturalism/ postcolonialism/postnationalism, Buell maintains, as nothing less than a new form of national consensus, as something which actually reflects the dominant ideology of transnational corporations.[43] For some, the whole notion of "American" history is at risk in the midst of this debate. Thus, when Janice Radway, president of the American Studies Association, stood up to deliver her 1998 address, she questioned the assumption of unity and coherence at the heart of the idea of a distinctly "American" history. She asked whether the very name of the Association did not "enforce the achievement of premature closure through an implicit, tacit search for the distinctively 'common ground.'"[44] Others, such as British historian Tony Badger, have been more concerned with fostering, within Europe, a break away from the historiographical standards set by historians in the U.S.[45]

What might all this mean for Native American history? How will Native American claims fare in this new discursive environment in which terms such as "nationhood," "tradition," and "cultural identity" are now decentered and contested? According to Donald A. Grinde, the answer will be decided by Native American historians themselves. Only their much-extended input will ever create what is needed – "a truly co-equal discourse between Indian and Non-Indian."[46] His thoughts are echoed by others currently providing erudite Native intellectual and political leadership, for example Taiaike Alfred, the Kahnawake Mohawk. As Alfred reminds his readers, "The formation of a new indigenous intelligentsia that understands the essence and commonality of the traditional teachings is crucial to re-forming [American] politics and society."[47] Even though Native American history blossomed in the last thirty years of the twentieth century, Native American critiques of American history still remain at the margins of the discipline. It seems likely that in future it will become progressively harder to avoid a more comprehensive acknowledgement of such critiques. This will highlight the disjuncture at the heart of American history, in which colonial displacement has accompanied a national rhetoric about liberty and democracy. Change in this direction seems destined to make greater discursive space for the Native American voice and, in the process, stimulate truly transformative understandings of the world's most powerful nation.

Notes

1. In this chapter, "Native American" and "Indian" are terms used interchangeably. The former has claims to greater accuracy but, although the latter is a misnomer, it is in some senses preferable, not least because the majority of Indian peoples, whether they are tribally enrolled or not, use it themselves. Writers on Native American issues sometimes choose to use exclusively the distinct names designated by groups or bands themselves, but this still leaves unresolved the

problem of how to talk about native peoples collectively within and beyond the boundaries of the United States. Arguably, this approach also denies the way in which native peoples – especially since the late 1960s – have reinscribed the term "Indian" through pan-Indian or intertribal activities. Recently, increasing dissatisfaction has been voiced over the provenance of words such as "tribe" and "chief" by commentators such as Jimmie Durham. See Durham, "Cowboys and . . . Notes on Art, Literature, and American Indians in the Modern American Mind," in M. Annette Jaimes, ed., *The State of Native America: Genocide, Colonization, and Resistance* (Boston, 1992), p. 433 and Leroy Vail, ed., *The Creation of Tribalism in Southern Africa* (London, 1989).

2. See, for example, Robert F. Berkhofer Jr., *The White Man's Indian: Images of the American Indian From Columbus to the Present* (New York, 1979).

3. See Berkhofer, *The White Man's Indian*, pp. 3–4 and Taiaiake Alfred, *Peace, Power, Righteousness: An Indigenous Manifesto* (Oxford, 1999), pp. xvii. In reviewing the misnomer "Indian" and its survival into the twenty-first century, it is as well perhaps to keep in mind Indian scholar and spokesman Vine Deloria's remark while giving testimony on the 1868 Red Cloud Treaty. He pointed out how it was just as well that Columbus was not "looking for Turkey." See Kenneth Lincoln, *Indi'n Humour: Bicultural Play in Native America* (New York, 1993), p. 23.

4. The University of Oklahoma Press did, however, set a precedent in the 1930s and 1940s by beginning its *Civilization of the American Indian* series and publishing important tribal histories such as Grant Foreman's *The Five Civilized Tribes* (Norman, 1932) and Angie Debo's *The Road to Disappearance* (Norman, 1941).

5. See Frederick E. Hoxie, "The View From Eagle Butte: National Archives Field Branches and the Writing of American Indian History," *Journal of American History*, 76 (1989): 173.

6. Anthropology had its origins in the museum movement. One of its most significant early publications within the United States was by social evolutionist Lewis Henry Morgan. See Morgan, *The League of the Ho-dé-no-sau-nee or Iroquois*, Rochester, NY, 1851; reprinted as *League of the Iroquois* (New York, 1962).

7. For a more expansive overview, see Joy Porter, "Native American History," in K. Boyd, ed., *Encyclopedia of Historians and Historical Writing*, vol. 2 (London, 1999), pp. 858–61.

8. Dee Brown, *Bury My Heart at Wounded Knee: An Indian History of the American West* (New York, 1971); Alfred W. Crosby, *The Columbian Exchange: Biological and Cultural Consequences of 1492* (Westport, CT, 1972); William Cronon, *Changes in the Land: Indians, Colonists and the Ecology of New England* (New York, 1983). More recently, Native academics began to make further important contributions to the debate on Columbus and "discovery" in books such as John Yewell, Chris Dodge, and Jan DeSirey, eds., *Confronting Columbus* (Jefferson, NC, 1992) and Carole M. Gentry and Donald A. Grinde Jr., eds., *The Unheard Voices* (Los Angeles, 1994).

9. Francis Jennings, *The Invasion of America: Indians, Colonialism and the Cant of Conquest* (Chapel Hill, 1975); William C. Sturtevant, ed., *Handbook of North American Indians* (Washington, DC, 1978–).

10. Frederick E. Hoxie, *A Final Promise: The Campaign to Assimilate the Indians, 1880–1920* (Lincoln, 1984); Laurence M. Hauptman, *The Iroquois Struggle for Survival: World War II to Red Power* (Syracuse, 1986).

11. Anthony F. C. Wallace, *The Death and Rebirth of Seneca* (New York, 1970).

12. Ethnohistory did not begin with Wallace. It can be traced back at least to Alfred Goldsworthy Bailey's *The Conflict of European and Eastern Algonkian Cultures, 1504–1700* (Saint John, N.B., 1937). For an evaluation of ethnohistory over time and comments about its future development in the "fast, new academic market" see "The Ethnohistory of Native America" by James Axtell (once dubbed the "High Priest" of ethnohistory) in Donald L. Fixico, ed., *Rethinking American Indian History* (Albuquerque, 1997), pp.11–28; Bruce Trigger, *The Children of the Aataentsic: A History of the Huron People to 1600*, 2 vols. (Montreal, 1976); James Axtell, *the Invasion Within: The Contest of Cultures in Colonial North America* (New York, 1985); Richard White, *The Middle Ground: Indians, Empires, and Republics in the Great Lakes Region, 1650–1815* (Cambridge, UK, 1991).

13. Hazel W. Hertzberg, *The Search for an American Indian Identity: Modern Pan-Indian Movements* (Syracuse, 1971); Margot Liberty, *American Indian Intellectuals* (St. Paul, MN, 1978); Lester George Moses and Raymond Wilson, eds., *Indian Lives: Essays on Nineteenth and Twentieth Century Native American Leaders* (Albuquerque, 1985); Alison R. Bernstein, *American Indians and World War II: Toward a New Era in Indian Affairs* (Norman, 1979); Donald Lee Fixico, *Termination and Relocation: Federal Indian Policy, 1945–*

1960 (Albuquerque, 1986); Alan L. Sorkin, *The Urban American Indian* (Lexington, MA, 1978); Lawrence Hauptman, *The Iroquois and the New Deal* (Syracuse, 1981); idem, *The Iroquois Struggle for Survival.*

14. Lincoln, *Indi'n Humor*, pp. 25, 179.

15. Mary Crow Dog, with Richard Erdoes, *Lakota Woman* (New York, 1990), p. 131.

16. Nancy Shoemaker, ed., *Negotiators of Change: Historical Perspectives on Native American Women* (London, 1995); Gretchen M. Bataille and Kathleen Mullen Sands, *American Indian Women: Telling Their Lives* (Lincoln, 1984); Robert S. Tilton, *Pocahontas: The Evolution of an American Narrative* (Cambridge, UK, 1994).

17. Russell Thornton, *American Indian Holocaust and Survival: A Population History Since 1492* (Norman, 1987); Kirkpatrick Sale, *The Conquest of Paradise: Christopher Columbus and the Columbian Legacy* (New York, 1990); William M. Denevan, ed., *The Native Population of the Americas in 1492* (Madison, 1992); A. J. Jaffe, *The First Immigrants From Asia: A Population History of the North American Indians* (New York, 1992).

18. Daniel K. Richter, *The Ordeal of the Longhouse: The Peoples of the Iroquois League in the Era of European Colonization* (Chapel Hill, 1992); Barbara Graymont, *The Iroquois in the American Revolution* (Syracuse, 1972); Oren Lyons and John Mohawk, *Exiled in the Land of the Free: Democracy, Indian Nations, and the U.S. Constitution* (Santa Fe, NM, 1992); Bruce E. Johansen, *Native American Political Systems and the Evolution of Democracy* (Westport, CT, 1996), p. ix. See also Johansen's *Native America and the Evolution of Democracy: A Supplementary Bibliography* (Westport, CT, 1996).

19. Devon A. Mihesuah, "Who Should Write About Indians?," *American Indian Quarterly*, 20 (1996): 103.

20. White, *The Middle Ground*; Ramón A. Gutiérrez, *When Jesus Came the Corn Mothers Went Away: Marriage, Sexuality, and Power in New Mexico, 1500–1846* (Stanford, CA, 1991); William T. Hagan, *Quanah Parker: Comanche Chief* (Norman, 1993). See Devon A. Mihesuah, "Award Winners and Comfortable Fictions," *American Indian Quarterly*, 20 (1996): 96.

21. Studs Terkel, *"The Good War": An Oral History of World War Two* (New York, 1984); Donald L. Fixico, "Ethics and Responsibilities," *American Indian Quarterly*, 20 (1996): 33.

22. See William T. Hagan's remarks "On Writing the History of the American Indian," *Journal of Interdisciplinary History*, (1971–72): 149.

23. Clyde Dollar, quoted in Arnold Krupat, "America's Histories," in *American Literary History*, 10, 1 (1998): 125.
24. Gail Landsman and Sara Ciborski, "Representations of Politics Contesting Histories of the Iroquois," *Cultural Anthropology*, 7 (1992).
25. For a very much fuller discussion of "Native Views of History," see Peter Nabokov, in Bruce G. Trigger and Wilcomb E. Washburn, *The Cambridge History of the Native Peoples of the Americas*, vol. 1, part 1 (Cambridge, UK, 1996).
26. Elizabeth Cook-Lynn, "American Indian Intellectualism and the New Indian Story," *American Indian Quarterly*, 20, 1 (1996): 59.
27. Annette Kolodny, "'The Integrity of Memory': Creating a New Literary History of the U.S.," *American Literature*, 57, 2 (1985): 291.
28. Mary Poovey, "Beyond the Current Impasse in Literary Studies," *American Literary History*, 11, 2 (1999): 355.
29. Arnold Krupat, *Ethnocriticism: Ethnography, History, Literature* (Berkeley, 1992), pp. 174–200.
30. Lincoln, *Indu'n Humor*, p. 38.
31. Susan A. Crane, ed., *Museums and Memory* (Stanford, CA, 2000), p. 1.
32. Daniel Sherman and Irit Rogoff, "Introduction," *Frameworks for a Critical Analysis in Museum/Culture: Histories, Discourses, Spectacles* (Minneapolis, 1994), p. xiii.
33. George W. Stocking Jr., ed., *Objects and Others: Essays on Museums and Material Culture* (Madison, WI, 1985); Thomas Schlereth, *Cultural History and Material Culture: Everyday Life, Landscapes and Museums* (Ann Arbor, MI, 1990); Ivan Karp and Steven D. Lavine, eds., *Exhibiting Cultures: The Poetics and Politics of Museum Display* (Washington, DC, 1991); Donna Harraway, "Teddy Bear Patriarchy: Taxidermy in the Garden of Eden, New York City, 1908–1936" in idem, *Primate Visions* (New York, 1989).
34. David Jenkins, "Object Lessons and Ethnographic Displays", *Comparative Studies in Society and History*, 36, 2 (1994).
35. James Clifford, *The Predicament of Culture: Twentieth Century Ethnography, Literature and Art* (Cambridge, MA, 1988), pp. 5, 7, 6, 4; Frederick Jameson, *The Political Unconscious: Narrative of a Socially Symbolic Act* (Ithaca, 1981).
36. Peter Stearns, "History Education in the USA: Defining Issues," Lecture delivered at the *History 2000* Conference, Bath Spa University, April, 1999.

37. William H. McNeill, *The Pursuit of Power: Technology, Armed Force, and Society since A.D. 1000* (Chicago, 1982); Theodore H. Von Laue, *The World Revolution of Westernization: The Twentieth Century in Global Perspective* (Oxford, 1987).

38. Ashis Nandy, in Philip Pomper, Richard H. Elphick and Richard T. Vann, *World History: Ideologies, Structures and Identities* (Malden, MA, 1998), pp. 162, 166, 167.

39. See Jane C. Desmond and Virginia R. Domíngues, "Resituating American Studies in Critical Internationalism," *American Quarterly*, 48, 3 (1996): 475–90; Benjamin Lee, "Critical Internationalism," *Public Culture*, 7 (Spring, 1995): 591; Gayatri Chakravorty Spivak, *Outside the Teaching Machine* (New York, 1993), p. 262; Paul Giles, "Virtual Americas: The Internationalization of American Studies and the Ideology of Exchange," *American Quarterly*, 50, 3 (1998): 523–47; Frederick Buell, "Nationalist Postnationalism: Globalist Discourse in Contemporary American Culture," *American Quarterly* 50, 3 (1998): 548–91.

40. The North American Free Trade Agreement, according to Peter H. Schuck, is "likely to be enlarged eventually to include Chile and perhaps other hemispheric nations, as well as being extended to include other areas of economic activity." Schuck in Christian Joppke, ed., *Challenge to the Nation-State: Immigration in Western Europe and the United States* (Oxford, 1998), p. 196.

41. World population has almost doubled since 1961 to 5.77 billion and, in 1992, 20 percent of the world's people living in the richest countries received 82.7 percent of the world's income, while only 1.4 percent went to the 20 percent of the world's population in the poorest countries. Figures taken from the *United Nations Human Development Report 1997*, quoted in Timothy Gorringe, *Fair Shares: Ethics and the Global Economy* (London, 1999), pp. 47, 63.

42. Kandice Chuh in Priscilla Wald, "Minefields and Meeting Grounds: Transnational Analyses and American Studies," *American Literary History*, 10, 1 (Spring 1998): 216.

43. Frederick Buell, "Nationalist Postnationalism": 553, 581.

44. Janice Radway, "What's in a Name?", Presidential Address to the American Studies Association, November 20, 1998, *American Quarterly*, 51, 1 (1998): 2, 3.

45. Tony Badger, paraphrased in Mel van Elteren, "American Studies in Europe: Its Vital Role in Internationalizing the Field," *Journal of American Culture*, 20, 4 (1997): 94.

46. Donald A. Grinde Jr., in Michael K. Green, ed., *Issues in Native American Cultural Identity* (London, 1995), p. 218.
47. Taiaiake Alfred, *Peace, Power and Righteousness*, p. 135.

–17–

Class in American History:
Issues and a Case Study
John Ashworth

At first glance, the history of the United States seems to offer poor pickings for a historian concerned to assert the importance, and especially the primacy, of class. Here we have a nation whose people have, for much of their history, espoused an ideology or set of values at the center of which is a belief not in "class" but in "classlessness." Indeed, the ideology of Americanism, sometimes referred to as "the American Dream," has claimed that a key distinguishing feature of American society has been its exceptional fluidity, a fluidity which has prevented, in most periods at least, the emergence of deep class divisions or of intense class-consciousness.[1]

This has left Marxism, which more than any interpretative tradition has sought to argue for the primacy of class, in difficulties where the United States is concerned. One might fairly easily imagine a history of France, for example, where class was uppermost, stressing the revolutionary upheavals which have punctuated that country's history. Similarly in the case of Britain, a nation which is often described as "class-ridden" by commentators and analysts on all points of the political spectrum. But for the United States? Here the challenge is, it would appear, of a different order.[2]

As a result, Marxism has languished in American historiography. There have been, perhaps, two eras when its impact has been greatest. The first was the 1930s. With the capitalist world economy in deep crisis, it was scarcely surprising that a set of theories which emphasized the vulnerability of capitalism to such crises and which offered, at least in outline, an alternative set of economic, social, and political structures and institutions, should acquire a new popularity. It would be quite wrong, however, to claim that Marxism conquered American history in the 1930s. Indeed, there was probably not a single area where a Marxist interpretation achieved dominance. Yet the contrast with previous decades was sharp indeed. In intellectual circles at least, in the 1930s Marxism acquired a new respectability, and American historical writing was, perhaps for the first time, significantly influenced by it.[3]

If the depression of the 1930s gave a boost to Marxism, there was another vitally important source of strength. This was, of course, the Soviet Union, a nation which officially claimed inspiration from Marx and Marxism. Of course, the two factors were linked in that the Soviet system seemed to some to offer a viable alternative to liberal democracy, and one which might escape the ravages of the depression. By the 1930s, then, a pattern had been established: Marxism's impact on American history would be directly related to the success (or the perceived success) of communist movements abroad and inversely related to the success (or perceived success) of the economy at home.[4]

As a result, the advances of the 1930s proved short-lived. With the commencement of the Cold War, American hostility to the Soviet Union reached new heights. Moreover, peace in 1945 did not bring about the economic collapse that many commentators had predicted. Instead, the western economies entered a golden age of expansion and growth, which brought unparalleled prosperity to millions of Americans. As a result, Marxism abruptly collapsed in American intellectual circles in general and in American historical writing in particular.[5]

The second period of prominence for Marxism came in the 1970s and 1980s. Although the domestic political ferment of the 1960s clearly played a part,[6] it was again, perhaps, the economic downturn of the 1970s – heralded by the emergence of "stagflation" – that was critical. Similarly, intervention in Vietnam, the failure of which became apparent to all by the mid-1970s, encouraged the critical questioning of American foreign policy that had begun in the 1960s. As in the 1930s, however, there was still no widely accepted Marxist overview of American history and probably still not a single area in which Marxists held the field. Indeed, in the 1970s and 1980s the same domestic and international events and processes produced an accretion of strength for the Right, symbolized by the election of Ronald Reagan in 1980. As in the 1930s, a polarization had occurred.[7]

That the success of Marxism in U.S. history was still tied to the success of communism in the international arena was dramatically confirmed in the 1990s. The collapse of the Soviet Union and the dismantling of the Soviet bloc saw a corresponding disintegration of American Marxism. Other factors were, of course, present. The economic successes of the mid- and late 1990s clearly played a major part.[8] Similarly the challenge from other intellectual theories, most notably feminism and post-structuralism, were important. Yet, the end of the Cold War has surely been the decisive factor. According to some commentators, it has brought with it an "End of History" and a permanent triumph of the liberal capitalist system of which Marxists were severe critics and whose demise they had regularly predicted.[9]

Inevitably this has damaged Marxist historiography throughout the western world. But one might argue that the impact in the United States has been especially severe. The 1970s and 1980s now seem, in retrospect, a golden age of Marxist history in the United States. But this renaissance, if such it can be termed, was strangled before it even had the opportunity – whether it had the capacity is another matter – decisively to reshape our understanding of U.S. history. As a result, the traditional view that Marxism specifically (and interpretations that stress class in general) cannot generate a plausible overview of the American past is once more difficult to combat.

Yet before reaching this conclusion, it might be appropriate to pause and consider a prior question. Clearly, one cannot pass a judgment on the potential for class as an explanatory factor in American history without having posed and answered a fundamental question: what is meant by "class?"

In general, historians, American scholars among them, have understood class in two different though by no means unrelated ways. The first of these might be referred to as "class as economic interest group," the second as "class as class-consciousness." Plainly these are anything but irreconcilable since one consequence of distinctly demarcated economic interest groups might well be class-consciousness on the part of their members. Nevertheless it may be appropriate to consider the two separately.

The leading exponent of the class-as-economic-interest-group approach to U.S. history is probably not a Marxist historian at all, but instead "progressive" scholar Charles A. Beard. Beard did not merely argue for significant economic divisions at certain times in the American past, he claimed rather that they were a key driving force in American history as a whole. Beard's periodization of American history and his provocative claims about the role of economic forces are too well known to require anything but the briefest exemplification. Thus, the struggle over the Federal Constitution in the late 1780s was, he claimed, despite appearances not fundamentally a disagreement over abstract theories of governance; rather, it was a confrontation between different economic interest groups, specifically pitting those representing "personalty" (primarily financial and mercantile wealth) against the defenders of "realty" (landed property). To take a second example: Beard maintained that the Civil

War saw the agents of newer forms of industrial wealth (which happened to be located in the North) triumph, in what he termed "the Second American Revolution," over the older forms of agrarian wealth (still dominant in the South).[10]

The interpretations of Beard and his disciples are not, of course, the only ones to have stressed the role of class or economic divisions in American history. In certain eras, scholars, some Beardian, some Marxist, and some belonging to neither school, have succeeded in showing that deep divisions existed within American society, divisions with roots that sometimes were unmistakably economic and which, on some occasions, generated major political confrontations and upheavals. Even the slightest acquaintance with American history allows an accurate guess as to which eras and groups have been most easily identified. Thus, the Jacksonian era has been pronounced as one in which class conflict was rife, and the 1890s and 1930s, both decades scarred with economic recession and widespread social unrest, have also easily qualified for inclusion.[11] So far as specific groups are concerned, it is probably accurate to say that two have attracted most attention. It would not surprise even those unfamiliar with U.S. history to learn that labor unions have been targeted, since conflicts between labor and capital have occurred in every developed nation. Less familiar to historians of European countries, however, are the other group, antebellum Southerners, and especially the antebellum slaveholding elite.[12]

At this point the other widely employed definition of "class" comes into play. For these groups, it has been claimed, have displayed a considerable degree of class-consciousness. In the case of labor and members of labor unions, this claim will once again generate little surprise (though this is not to say that there is agreement among historians on the degree of class-consciousness among workers in any period of American history). The case of the slaveholders of the South, however, may at first glance be less plausible. Here the claim is that they constituted a group conscious of their shared characteristics and their social role and determined to defend both against other "classes" either in the South (slaves, non-slaveholding whites) or in the North (antislavery militants of whatever persuasion or political hue).

This is not the place to assess the claims or the overall success of these historiographical endeavors. However, we should note that, even if the entire project, every one of these attempts at emphasizing the role of class in American history, could be counted a success, acute problems would still remain. Even if it could be conclusively demonstrated that there were eras when class conflict and class-consciousness were uppermost, what of the other eras in the American past? Even if it could be shown that labor and slaveholders were suffused with class-consciousness, what of other groups? And what of other forms of consciousness besides class? After all, slaveholders were, to say the least, conscious of race too, to say nothing of gender. The same also applies, all too often, in the case of workers and their representatives.

In short, it is not clear how the attempts to make "class" a key and even *the* key player in the history of certain groups and eras can generate an overview of American history in which "class" is accorded the primary role. Why should the eras of conflict be more significant that those in which a consensus seems to have prevailed? Is it being claimed that Americans since the revolution or since the Pilgrims have been more aware of class than they have of race or gender? If the fate of a Marxist or a "class" interpretation depended on affirmative (and, an objective outsider might reasonably complain, dogmatic) answers to these questions then its future would be at best extremely uncertain.[13]

Thus, a new theoretical beginning must be made. This is not to say that the existing works by Marxists and non-Marxists alike have no relevance. On the contrary, they are the building blocks out of which a Marxist interpretation of American history can be fashioned. But the new beginning needs to be in the form of a new theoretical foundation, a theorization of class that is new to historians, even of the Marxist persuasion.

Fortunately, an enormous amount of work which is of value has been done by Marxists in disciplines other than history. It is important to note here the epistemological distinctiveness of history within the academy. Historians have traditionally been skeptical of the theories generated by political scientists, sociologists, and social theorists. One might have thought that Marxist historians might have escaped this deficiency, since Marx himself was nothing if not a social (and economic and political) theorist. Such, in fact, is rarely the case. Faced with the challenge from non-Marxists that their commitment to "theory" is already excessive – by virtue of their attachment to Marxism itself – most Marxist historians have turned their backs upon work done in other disciplines. There are some valid reasons for this. All too often, theoretical work seems to lack immediate relevance to any period, social group, or problem with which the historian is grappling. Indeed, it is fair to say that if the historian is typically concerned with empirical phenomena to the exclusion of all theoretical issues, many theorists have displayed precisely the opposite weakness: a scorn for all empirical controls and checks upon their theoretical contrivances.[14] The obvious and safe conclusion, it might be suggested, is that there is a happy medium to be found.

Yet the result of this absence of dialogue is that there is for most historians, and certainly for the present writer, no fully elaborated theory of class that can readily be summoned up and, after a quick inspection, prepared for a campaign of investigation into the American past. The many valuable contributions made by those in other disciplines offer guidelines and hints, warnings and reminders, rather than fully serviceable theories. Thus, the best way forward is for the processes of theorization and historical analysis to proceed in tandem with each informing and refining the other. What follows is the result of the process as I have experienced it. I shall begin with some general remarks on class. Then I will offer some very general suggestions on the consequences of this for United States history as a whole. Finally, I will suggest how this understanding of class can inform a concrete historical analysis: the coming of the Civil War.[15]

The Marxist approach to history and to social analysis emphasizes the role of the economy. Roughly speaking, one can suggest that unless a people control their own economy, their economy will control them.[16] That is to say, they will be at the mercy of a series of unsought but non-random processes, processes that cannot occur independently of human action but which nevertheless do not occur as a result of purposive action. These processes can therefore be termed structural. Thus, in a capitalist economy, there are certain processes which seem to be, in the long run at least, irresistible. For example, no capitalist society has freed itself from the reality of periodic economic recession.[17] While there may be groups who benefit from these recessions (receivers of bankrupt companies, for example, and, more generally and more problematically, employers[18]), their gain is not the cause of the recession. Rather the causes are structural: men and women have entered into certain relationships which, independently of their purposes, so affect their actions that unsought, but non-random, outcomes ensue.

A capitalist economy has other characteristics. It revolutionizes technology at a far more rapid rate than any other, it generates larger and larger units of production ("globalization" being the modern manifestation of this process), and it tends to bring a larger and larger area of life within the ambit of the market.[19] Now, it is apparent that no two countries possess identical economies; equally, a single developed country's economy, in the modern era at least, is in a state of continual flux. But this does not mean that there is an infinite number of economic types and that economies cannot be classified. Marxism – or at least most varieties of Marxism – seeks to classify these economies above all by reference to the type or mode of production that they exhibit. Thus, a capitalist economy or mode of production is (frequently) characterized as one in which the dominant way of producing goods and services requires the employment by some men and women of other men and women in return for a wage.[20] A slave system or mode of production, by contrast, involves instead the actual ownership of some men and women by others. Many Marxists would then argue that these two systems are likely to evolve differently because of the different structures or relations of production which they exhibit.

At this point, class enters into the picture. The relations of production between the dominant class (employer or slaveholder) and the dominated class (worker or slave) are held to be of primary importance in determining the economic structure of the society concerned and, to a significant degree therefore, its probable pattern of evolution. It is clear, however, that in the real world there is no such thing as a "pure" capitalist society or a "pure" slave one. All societies have their own distinctive features. Thus, capitalism in Europe evolved out of a feudal past and continues to this day to bear the imprint of that past. The United States, on the other hand, though lacking a feudal past, does not possess a "pure" capitalist system either. Its history has been shaped by many factors that, while not necessary to the development of capitalism, nevertheless influenced that development considerably. The availability, for much of the nation's history, of huge areas of land at comparatively low prices is one of the more obvious of these factors. This does not correspond to a capitalist ideal any more than would the opposite – an acute scarcity of land. Therefore, the analysis of any actual economy/society must be a complex process which combines abstract analysis of the type under consideration (slave, capitalist, feudal, etc.) with respect for, and attention to, the deviations from any norm which that society/economy exhibits.

In the case of the United States, there are further complexities. If a capitalist economy is one in which wage labor is widespread, then how does one categorize the family farms which were predominant in the nonslaveholding parts of the nation (and even in some of the ostensibly slaveholding areas too) in the seventeenth and eighteenth centuries and the first decades of the nineteenth? Moreover, what is the relationship between slavery, capitalism, and the (precapitalist) forms of production based on these family farms? There is no established Marxist answer to these questions. Rather they must, once again, be tackled with a combination of theoretical and empirical work.[21]

Thus, to reduce class to economic interest groups or to class-consciousness is a vulgarization of Marxist theory. Class is, instead, a relationship in which human beings enter into certain relations with others. Whether the result is a society divided into deep and visible economic interest groups is a contingent issue, as is the question whether class-consciousness is intense, moderate, or nonexistent. These are by no means unimportant questions, but the success of the Marxist enterprise does not depend on a specific answer to them.[22] Instead, the role of class is to be evaluated by reference to two more specific, though still very broad claims: that the economy is of primary importance in determining the development of the society (including its politics and the belief systems operative within it) and that the relations between different classes at the point of production are, in turn, of primary importance in determining its economic structure.[23]

Clearly, it is premature to attempt an evaluation of Marxism as an aid to understanding the American past. Despite the undoubted achievements of some American historians working within the Marxist tradition, the enterprise has scarcely begun. Paradoxically, however, the relative weakness of class-consciousness in the American past and the difficulty in sustaining the claim that economic divisions have been paramount, ought to have encouraged Marxists to move toward a more structural view of class. In this sense, then, the weakness of traditional notions of "class" in the history of the United States might therefore prove ultimately a spur rather than an impediment to further analysis.[24]

So what might be a possible agenda for Marxist historians of the United States? If the claim for the primacy of the economy is valid, then it follows that attempts to explain social change will normally seek to refer to the political economy of the society in question. A fundamental task is to determine the trajectory of development, together with the factors and processes that explain it, of American society as a whole. This may, and indeed generally will, mean a concentration on some groups and some institutions rather than on the entire society, but such studies are likely to be more mindful than orthodox history of what might be termed the social totality. There will usually be an attempt to relate the history of these groups to the political economy of the society in question. Thus, in the case of the history of ideas, the Marxist historian will adopt a contextual as well as a textual approach – one in which the complex relationship of the ideas or text under consideration with the society from which it has sprung is close to the center of analysis. In the case of political history, the likelihood is that the realm of inquiry will be extended to include the often tangled social roots of the political system and its usually complex relationship to economic processes and developments.

It is, of course, true that not just Marxist historians but others as well have been, and continue to be, engaged in scholarly activities of this type. One does not need to be a Marxist, after all, to seek to understand the social underpinnings of politics, for example. But the key issues concern the role of class and the role of the economy. Most Marxists, but few non-Marxists, are committed to the notion that class and the economy should be accorded causal primacy in the study of the human past.[25]

Clearly, it is not possible here to defend so grand a claim as this. Instead, I shall look at one event in the history of one nation, albeit the most important event in the history of the most powerful nation in the world today. In the summary that follows, the object is not to defend all or indeed any of the specific propositions relating to the coming of the American Civil War – that task is already the object of two large volumes – but rather to offer an interpretation in which primacy is accorded to class and economy. The task, therefore, is to defend and make more concrete the alternative notion of class that has already been advanced and to suggest how it may be made operational.[26]

The Civil War that broke out in April 1861 was the product of many developments in political, social, and economic spheres. I should like to suggest, however, that it was ultimately the product of a fundamental incompatibility between the Northern and Southern labor systems. This incompatibility arose as the Northern labor system underwent an important shift: it became not merely a free labor system, which it had been for many decades, but to a significant degree a wage labor system, which it had never been before.[27]

My argument is that the growth of the wage system posed problems for those who employed wage laborers. Similarly in the South, those who owned slaves continued, as they always had, to experience difficulties in controlling them. Thus the two ruling groups or classes experienced problems – or needed to forestall potential problems – of control. Now these problems were by no means insuperable. The South was not, in 1861, on the verge of a servile rebellion that would bring down the regime. Nor was the North on the verge of a social revolution that would see the proletariat overwhelm the employing elite. But the key fact is that the ruling class in each section was constrained by the pressure from below. Each could contain the threat from the subordinate class – but only by making concessions and adjustments. And those concessions and adjustments meant that coexistence with the other section became increasingly difficult and finally impossible.

To understand this process it is necessary to look more closely at antislavery sentiment in the United States. Why did slavery provoke so much hostility? Although many specific objections were raised against it, they can be placed, without undue oversimplification, into three categories: the political, the moral, and the economic. Rather than simply list the arguments, however, we need to rank them and to identify their ultimate causes.

First, the political. Here the slogan was "The Slave Power."[28] It was claimed that the slaveholders of the South constituted, in effect, an aristocracy which controlled the South and also aspired to control the entire nation. These political arguments were extremely important in the decades before the Civil War. However, we should note that they acquired their importance only because of two underlying factors: one was the danger of slave rebellion itself, which fueled Southern fears and which, slaveholders reasoned, required a restriction of the civil liberties of whites as well as blacks, nonslaves as well as slaves. (These restrictions then, in turn, fueled the "Slave Power" allegations.) Yet this danger had been present since the beginning of slavery in the Americas. But its significance was greatly enhanced in the mid-nineteenth century, because of the second factor: attacks from the North (and from Britain) which convinced slaveholders that they needed to tighten their control over their own states and over the federal government. Thus, the idea of a "Slave Power" and the political arguments against slavery generally acquired their potency only because of, first, the vulnerability of the slave regime to insurrection (which, as I shall suggest, was itself a class conflict whether actual or potential) and, second, the other attacks on the institution from outside – that is to say, the economic and moral arguments. The political arguments, therefore, even if we found that they were made more frequently than any other, are in this sense derivative of the other arguments – and of the inherent weakness of slavery itself.

In the minds of abolitionists and of some Republicans, the moral argument against slavery was uppermost. As Harriet Beecher Stowe made clear in *Uncle Tom's Cabin*, the single most important antislavery work of the nineteenth century, the outrage on the family was the worst evil of slavery. And the attempt to deprive slaves of the right to follow their conscience, with all that entailed, was probably second. But, of course, slavery had always been vulnerable to these charges. So again we need to ask: why this concern with families and conscience at this time? Why were these values now held by large numbers of Northerners to be sacrosanct to the extent that they had to be sustained even thousands of miles away and even at the price of political crisis, social upheaval, and internecine war?

The key fact is that economic changes in the North were weakening traditional sources of socio-moral stability. Paternalism, for example, was undermined by the shift of production outside the home. In an increasingly rootless society, there was an urgent need to find alternative sources for social cohesion and individual stability. How else was moral order to be sustained? Abolitionists argued that the family and the conscience were to be the supports for the new social order. But slavery undermined the family and silenced the conscience (of slave and slaveholder alike). And, therefore, to a society which increasingly esteemed these values, slavery became increasingly unacceptable.

The moral case against slavery, then, acquired its urgency because of the economic changes experienced in the society from which abolitionism sprang. In this sense, therefore, the moral argument is secondary too, not because it acquired its force as a result of the economic argument but because its power derived from the economic changes in Northern society.[29]

This brings us to the economic indictment of slavery. Here the focus was on the slave's alleged lack of incentive. Slavery was believed to disrupt an economy. It impeded diversification and retarded growth and development. Virtually all opponents of slavery in the United States held this view. All abolitionists appear to have subscribed to it, though they did not emphasize it as much as the moral indictment. Republicans, with their milder but still ultimately devastating form of antislavery, gave the argument still more emphasis, though it is a moot point whether it received as much stress as the political case against slavery.

What the Republicans and abolitionists wanted to do was to remake the South in the image of the North, morally, politically, and economically. Once again, therefore, the case against slavery was grounded in, and was validated by, the North's confidence in the superiority of its economic system – its diversification, development of cities, and industry – all of which were held to be the product of free, in contrast to slave, labor. Here, then, was the principal source of hostility to slavery: Northern commitment to free labor with all the economic, social, and moral consequences that that implied. The fact that other arguments besides the free labor one were deployed – and may even have been deployed more frequently than that based on free labor – does not alter this conclusion.[30]

However, when we refer to free labor, we need to be careful. For what antislavery spokesmen and women envisaged was an economy in which wage-earning played a critical part. Some Republicans believed that the wage earner ought, in time, to become self-employed and then ultimately, perhaps, an employer. Other Republicans and perhaps all the abolitionists, however, argued that it was perfectly proper for a wage earner to remain a wage earner for life, with no stigma attaching to him as a result. This was a new departure. Throughout history, wage-workers have been regarded as closer to slaves than to free and independent citizens. In nineteenth-century America, the status of the wage earner was drastically altered.[31]

As wage-labor relations spread, how were they to be understood? How were they to be legitimated? The answer was by emphasizing the freedoms that the wage-worker possessed. Even if he lacked land or other forms of productive property he was still independent and estimable, in that he had a home, "a family that is not marketable" in the words of Henry Ward Beecher, the opportunity to rise in society, and the freedom to follow the dictates of his own conscience. Moreover, the freedoms of the wage-worker would confer incalculable societal benefits. An economy of free laborers (many of whom were wage-workers) was one in which economic growth and development were assured.[32]

So when we look at the antislavery argument in the United States as a whole, with its economic, political, and moral components, we find an interdependence between them. Each fortified and was fortified by the others. Yet this was an asymmetrical interdependence in that two factors were paramount. One was the vulnerability of slave society to slave rebellion (whose effects we shall examine in a moment); the other was the confidence of the North in its free labor system. And it is no coincidence that this confidence was growing at a time when wage labor was assuming increasing economic importance and when the wage laborer was achieving an unprecedentedly high social status. As the North acquired the characteristics of a wage-labor and not merely a free-labor economy, so its previous tolerance of slavery gradually became a deep and bitter resentment. As free labor increasingly became wage labor, so the values of Northern society inspired a powerful crusade against slavery. This, in conjunction with the vulnerability of slavery to its own workforce, drove the crusade against slavery to its final apocalyptic triumph.

It is, therefore, legitimate to suggest that, among the causes internal to the North of the antislavery movement, the economic ones were paramount. But to repeat: this is not to say that the economic arguments were necessarily those most often cited or those uppermost in the minds of antislavery spokesmen and women. Moreover, the economic factors were also, in essence, based upon class. For the need to accommodate the growing numbers and, thus, the growing class of wage earners led Northerners increasingly to espouse values that ultimately would preclude peaceful coexistence with the South. Pressure from below, in other words, whether actual or potential, led Northerners to stress the advantages of wage labor and this, in turn, generated an ever-deeper hostility to the South.

Within the South, an analogous process was operating. Just as the relations between employer and worker deserve pride of place in explaining the growth of antislavery, so at the center of the analysis of the Old South should be placed the relationship between master and slave. Clearly this was, in the literal sense, a class relationship, involving a dominant and a dominated group.[33] Once again, the conflict and the potential for conflict between the two groups was decisive. Many modern scholars have tried to demolish the claim that it was precisely this – the control problem – which constrained Southern industrialization and urbanization. But they have failed and it is still perfectly plausible to argue that the difficulties of controlling slaves in cities and in industry ensured that the South remained agricultural and rural.[34] And when we talk of "control," we are referring to slave resistance, which in turn means class conflict and the potential for it.[35]

Slave resistance, actual or potential, in fact took many forms and had many consequences. Resistance to enslavement made some slaves run away; it made others, albeit a tiny minority, plot insurrection and it meant that masters needed to maintain draconian controls. Among these controls was, on the plantation, the threat of breaking up slave families and preventing, so far as possible, slaves becoming literate. Within the political arena, it meant preventing discussion of slavery, seeking to insulate the South from the dangerous currents of antislavery and shoring up the regime in the localities where it was most vulnerable.[36]

The struggle between master and slave generated a series of responses and counter-responses. But it was the impact on the North that was ultimately decisive. Thus, the underdevelopment of the economy fueled the Northern fear that slavery retarded the nation's economic growth. The fugitive slave issue generated enormous controversy in the North and helped intensify antislavery sentiment there. The denial to slaves of literacy and of legalized marriage confirmed the perception of slavery as an anomaly in the progressive nineteenth century. And the refusal to allow slavery to be discussed – as well as the drive for additional slave territory in the West – nourished the Northern fear of a "Slave Power."

Whether this interpretation of the origins of the Civil War, presented here in highly abbreviated form, is or is not acceptable, it should be noted that it does not rest on a claim that there was intense class-consciousness on the part of any group in the entire United States. Whether slaveholders (or slaves) were more conscious of class than of race (or of gender) is an interesting question, but the fate of this interpretation does not in any way rest upon a specific answer to it. As far as the North is concerned, the Republicans, who were obviously key players in the sectional struggle, were sincerely committed to the view that Northern society was uniquely classless. Theirs was, in a sense, the antithesis of a class-consciousness. Yet the fact that this perception of their own society was so flawed – the opportunities for social mobility were never anything like so great as Lincoln and his fellow partisans believed – should alert the historian to the deeper processes at work. The flawed conception of the worker as proto-capitalist was itself a recognition that he was, at least potentially, a threat to the social order.[37] In other words, "class" helped generate an ideology of classlessness – and thus operated to reduce class-consciousness![38]

Similarly, it operated to reduce the likelihood of class or economic divisions in the North. And, more generally, the structural view of class advanced here does not necessitate a claim that there were deep divisions between rich and poor in either the North or the South, or that the battalions of labor were on the march against those of capital, or that the forces of "personalty" were mobilized against those of "realty." As in the case of class-consciousness, whether American society was or was not divided along "class" lines with certain interest groups or classes overtly pursuing their class interests within the political arena or at the workplace is an important matter. But the interpretation advanced here does not hinge upon a specific answer to it.

Instead class should be understood as a richer, more subtle concept. Its effects are sometimes visible, but usually in a highly mediated form, in a society's trajectory of development, in its politics or in its moral and religious principles. Class poses problems of adjustment and, usually, the adjustment can occur without the need for revolutionary upheaval and transformation. But the adjustments are themselves important and (as in the United States prior to the Civil War) sometimes hugely so. Class creates not only conflict but also – which may be equally important in prompting the process of adjustment – the potential for conflict. Class precludes certain kinds of economic development, even as it makes others more probable. It sometimes generates class-consciousness and divisions between economic interest groups but equally often it creates, in a far more subtle way, fault lines in a society whose impact must be traced with great care and sensitivity – not least because millions of lives can sometimes be lost as a result of them.

Should we therefore accord class a special role in American history? There is reason to believe that we should. But this can only be done on the basis of the definition I have suggested. For, if we restrict class to class divisions, then we have no reason to privilege class over, say, race. The claim that class has divided Americans more deeply than race seems highly dubious. Similarly, if we equate class with class-consciousness, then we shall have to defend the rather improbable claim that Americans have been more conscious of class than of, for example, gender. But if, instead, we adopt a structural view of class, then we shall claim for it a central role in determining American society's trajectory of development, in posing key problems of control and adjustment, in facilitating certain modes of thought and behavior and inhibiting others. In short, we shall claim for it a crucial causal role in explaining the continuities and discontinuities generated by the historical process. Can the same be said for gender or for race as explanatory categories? No historian or social theorist has yet made the case and scarcely any have tried. It is, perhaps, for this reason that class should be accorded primacy in the study of American history.

Notes

1. Although these opinions have been prominent in most periods of American history, they perhaps reached a peak of popularity among historians and the general public alike in the 1950s. See Daniel J. Boorstin, *The Americans, The National Experience* (New York, 1965); Richard Hofstadter, *The Progressive Historians: Turner, Beard, Parrington* (New York, 1968); Bernard Sternsher, *Consensus, Conflict, and American Historians* (Bloomington, IN, 1975).
2. The writer who most fully emphasized the distinctiveness of Americans and of American history in this respect was probably Louis Hartz. See Hartz, *The Liberal Tradition in America: An Interpretation of American Political Thought Since the Revolution* (New York, 1955).
3. Prior to the 1930s there had, of course, been occasional lone voices such as that of Algie M. Simons. See Simons, *Social Forces in*

American History (New York, 1912). Marxist writings of the 1930s and early 1940s include: Louis M. Hacker, *The Triumph of American Capitalism: The Development of Forces in American History to the End of the Nineteenth Century* (New York, 1940); Herbert Aptheker, *The Negro in the Civil War* (New York, 1938); idem, *Negro Slave Revolts in the United States, 1526–1860* (New York, 1939); idem, *The Negro in the Abolitionist Movement* (New York, 1941).

4. A very good survey of the impact – or lack of it – of Marxism on American historical writing is Ian Tyrrell, *The Absent Marx: Class Analysis and Liberal History in Twentieth-Century America* (New York, 1986).

5. A full explanation of the collapse of Marxism in these years would, of course, need to take account of other factors. Thus, the McCarthy witch-hunt was of obvious importance. Similarly, the appeal of alternative theories borrowed from psychology and sociology should not be underestimated.

6. It is striking that the American reformist movements of the 1960s – the Civil Rights Movement, the Great Society and War on Poverty programs, and feminism – had few if any links with Marxism (though, undoubtedly, some who later turned to Marxism were dissatisfied veterans of these causes).

7. It is probably fair to say that, in the late 1970s, the Left benefited more within the academy, the Right in the political arena.

8. Yet the economic uncertainties of the early 1990s should warn us against too mechanical a view of the relationship between economy and intellectual fashion.

9. Francis Fukuyama, *The End of History and the Last Man* (New York, 1992).

10. Charles A. Beard, *An Economic Interpretation of the Constitution of the United States* (New York, 1913); Charles A. Beard and Mary R. Beard, *The Rise of American Civilization* (New York, 1930).

11. So far as the Jacksonian era is concerned the key work is probably still Arthur M. Schlesinger Jr., *The Age of Jackson* (Boston, 1945). For the 1890s, see for example Norman Pollack, *The Populist Response to Industrial America* (Cambridge, MA, 1962); Lawrence Goodwyn, *The Populist Moment: A Short History of the Agrarian Revolt in America* (New York, 1978). For the 1930s, see for example Kenneth Finegold and Theda Skocpol, *State and Party in America's New Deal* (Madison, WI, 1995).

12. Among many histories of the labor movement see Sean Wilentz, *Chants Democratic: New York City and the Rise of the American*

Working Class, 1788–1850 (New York, 1984). For the slaveholders, the works of Eugene D. Genovese are of paramount importance. See for example *The World the Slaveholders Made: Two Essays in Interpretation* (Middletown, CT, 1988), *The Political Economy of Slavery: Studies in the Economy and Society of the Slave South* (New York, 1965), and (with Elizabeth Fox-Genovese), *Fruits of Merchant Capital: Slavery and Bourgeois Property in the Rise and Expansion of Capitalism* (New York, 1983).

13. These questions have been posed less often than one might have thought, largely as a result of the (excessive?) specialization that characterized American historical writing in the last thirty years or so of the twentieth century. There have been few attempts to establish an overview in the way that Hofstadter and Beard attempted during their careers.

14. It is perhaps not necessary to add that this applies – and perhaps with still greater force – to non-Marxist theorists too.

15. It is possible to acknowledge only a few of the influences that have shaped my understanding of class in history. Among the most important are Perry Anderson, *In the Tracks of Historical Materialism* (Chicago, 1984); idem, *The Origins of Postmodernity* (London, 1998); Roy Bhaskar, *The Possibility of Naturalism: A Philosophical Critique of the Contemporary Human Sciences* (London, 1998); Andrew Collier, *Critical Realism: An Introduction to Roy Bhaskar's Philosophy* (London, 1994); G. E. M. De Ste. Croix, *The Class Struggle in the Ancient Greek World: From the Archaic Age to the Arab Conquests* (Ithaca, NY, 1989); Stuart Hall, et. al., *Policing the Crisis: Mugging, the State, and Law and Order* (New York, 1978); Eric J. Hobsbawm, *The Age of Capital, 1848–1875* (New York, 1975); idem, *The Age of Empire, 1875–1914* (New York, 1989); idem, *The Age of Revolution, 1789–1848* (New York, 1996); Russell Keat and John Urry, *Social Theory as Science* (London, 1982); Gregor McLennan, David Held, and Stuart Hall, eds., *The Idea of the Modern State* (Milton Keynes, 1984).

16. This is scarcely to claim, however, that all such attempts will be successful.

17. Though this does not seem to prevent commentators from claiming otherwise each time there is a period of a few years without recession.

18. This example is more problematic because the employer gains when wage rates fall but loses when demand for the product also falls (as a result of the falling wages of other workers).

19. I need hardly add that this brief summary is not intended to exhaust the characteristics of a capitalist economy.

20. Capitalism is, thus, not to be equated merely with the market or with commerce. For if all capitalist societies are commercial, not all commercial societies are capitalist.

21. There are some valuable insights in Steven Hahn, *The Roots of Southern Populism: Yeoman Farmers and the Transformation of the Georgia Upcountry, 1850–1890* (New York, 1983).

22. It follows also that a "favorable" answer is no more conclusive than an unfavorable one.

23. I should perhaps add that these claims would not necessarily be endorsed by all Marxists. It should be stressed that Marxism is a living body of ideas, not a fossilized set of dogma.

24. Here the contrast with Britain is especially telling. The plausibility of an emphasis on class-consciousness has encouraged British historians such as E.P. Thompson to adopt what is ultimately, I believe, an unsustainable theory of class. Unfortunately, Americans in the 1970s and 1980s sought all too often to adapt his work to an American environment. See especially Herbert G. Gutman, *Work, Culture, and Society in Industrializing America: Essays in American Working-class and Social History* (New York, 1977).

25. There are no works which precisely recommend themselves in this connection. For European or world history Eric Hobsbawm's trilogy on the nineteenth century comes as close as anything – see Hobsbawm, *Age of Revolution*, *Age of Capital*, and *Age of Empire*.

26. See John Ashworth, *Slavery, Capitalism and Politics in the Antebellum Republic*, vol. I, *Commerce and Compromise, 1820–1850* (Cambridge, UK, 1995) and vol. II, *Towards a Bourgeois Revolution* (forthcoming).

27. It is perhaps worth noting that the argument developed here is at odds with Marx's own understanding of the Civil War and of the South. See Eugene D. Genovese, "Marxian Interpretations of the Slave South," in Genovese, *In Red and Black: Marxian Explorations in Southern and Afro-American History* (London, 1971), pp. 315–53.

28. The leading exponent of the view that this was the primary source of antislavery is Michael F. Holt. See Holt, *The Political Crisis of the 1850s* (New York, 1978). See also William E. Gienapp, *The Origins of the Republican Party, 1852–1856* (New York, 1987).

29. For an extended discussion of the relationship between economic and moral change see the essays by David Brion Davis, Thomas

Haskell and John Ashworth in Thomas Bender, ed., *The Antislavery Debate: Capitalism and Abolitionism as a Problem in Historical Interpretation* (Berkeley, 1992).
30. The key work on the relationship between the free labor North and antislavery is Eric Foner, *Free Soil, Free Labor, Free Men: the Ideology of the Republican Party before the Civil War* (New York, 1970). See also Foner, "Free Labor and Nineteenth Century Political Ideology," in Melvyn Stokes and Stephen Conway, eds., *The Market Revolution in America: Social, Political, and Religious Expressions, c. 1800–1880* (Charlottesville, 1996), pp. 99–127, and Foner, *Slavery and Freedom in Nineteenth-Century America* (Oxford, 1994).
31. Christopher Hill, "Pottage for Freeborn Englishmen: Attitudes to Wage Labour," in Hill, *Change and Continuity in Seventeenth-Century England* (London, 1974), pp. 219–38.
32. See Amy Dru Stanley, "Home Life and the Morality of the Market," in Stokes and Conway, eds., *The Market Revolution*, pp. 74–96.
33. It is perhaps necessary to add that most historians nevertheless refuse to acknowledge that it was a class relationship.
34. I have discussed this at some length in *Slavery, Capitalism and Politics*, vol. I, pp. 80–121, 499–509. Also see Fred Bateman and Thomas Weiss, *A Deplorable Scarcity: The Failure of Industrialization in the Slave Economy* (Chapel Hill, 1981) 159–63; Paul A. David et al., *Reckoning With Slavery: A Critical Study in the Quantitative History of American Negro Slavery* (New York, 1976); Robert W. Fogel and Stanley L. Engerman, *Time on the Cross, The Economics of American Negro Slavery*, 2 vols. (London, 1974); Robert W. Fogel, *Without Consent or Contract: The Rise and Fall of American Slavery* (New York, 1989); Claudia Goldin, *Urban Slavery in the American South 1820–1860: A Quantitative History* (Chicago, 1976); Gavin Wright, "Slavery and the Cotton Boom," *Explorations in Economic History*, 12 (1975): 439–51; idem, *The Political Economy of the Cotton South: Households, Markets, and Wealth in the Nineteenth Century* (New York, 1978); idem, "The Efficiency of Slavery: Another Interpretation," *American Economic Review*, 69 (1979): 219–26; idem, "Cheap Labor and Southern Textiles Before 1860," *Journal of Economic History*, 39 (1979): 655–80; idem, *Old South, New South: Revolutions in the Southern Economy Since the Civil War* (New York, 1986).
35. Once again, it should be stressed that there is no claim here that slaves were, or were not, class-conscious. Again this is a significant but secondary question.

36. See James Oakes, "The Political Significance of Slave Resistance," *History Workshop*, 22 (1986): 89–107.
37. I do not wish to suggest that there was any form of conspiracy involved here.
38. It is, I hope, by now apparent that my rejoinder to the claims of the "consensus" theorists of the 1950s would be not so much to deny the existence of the consensus (in many eras at any rate) as to explain it as (in large part) a product of class.

–18–

Conflict by Consent: Popular Commitment, Community Participation, and the War for the Union

Peter J. Parish

The army of Civil War historians has never been content to rest on its laurels for long, and, despite the protests of historians with different agendas, scathingly denounced by Eric Foner for attempting to "read the Civil War out of American history,"[1] it is still on the march. However, despite the sheer weight of their barrage of books and articles and essays, their coverage of the target has been patchy and uneven. While some topics in the Civil War years have been done to death, and then dug up and restored to life, only to be done to death once again, other topics have been neglected or even ignored. This uneven coverage is a reflection of the compartmentalization of Civil War historiography. High dividing walls have too often kept apart laborers in adjacent areas of Civil War study, and have tended to seal off the war from the longer-term processes of nineteenth-century American history. One major task now facing historians of the war period is to break down these barriers.[2]

The most obvious of these divides has too often been between the military history of battles and campaigns, and the broader political, social, and economic context within which the war was fought. Traditional military historians have pressed more and more detail into their accounts of battles great and not so great, and their biographies of generals distinguished and undistinguished alike, with little or no reference to the world beyond the barracks and the battlefield. However, much to their credit, military historians have recently been redefining their subject and extending its boundaries, by examining armies as institutions, by paying more attention to the lives and attitudes of ordinary soldiers, and by relating methods of waging war to the development of society as a whole. For their part, political historians have too often neglected the importance of what was happening on the field of battle, and exposed themselves to the criticism once leveled at Charles Sumner that he regarded the war itself as an "unfortunate and most annoying, though trifling, disturbance, as if a fire-engine had passed by."[3]

There are other great divides cutting across Civil War historiography. It has been too easy for some historians to overlook the fact that there were two sides in the war. Students of the Confederacy in particular have tended to insist that all the problems of the South at war can and must be explained purely from within the Confederacy, and without reference to Lincoln, Grant, and Sherman, the power of the Union armies and the persistent commitment of the Northern people to the struggle.[4] To take another example, economic and social historians are inclined to dismiss the Civil War as a mere blip on their wide-screen view of nineteenth-century American development.[5] Similarly, inward-looking American scholars have commonly failed even to notice the significance of the war as a major international event. If the war had ended in the temporary, let alone the permanent, break-up of the United States, it would surely have commanded much more attention as a world event.[6]

It is far beyond the scope of this chapter, and the ambition of its author, to propose some grand new over-arching synthesis which can offer shelter for all these various compartments under one roof. The aim here is much more modest: to identify just one among many possible themes or topics that might serve as a connecting link between a number of areas of Civil War study. What might happen if we placed alongside each other a number of current historiographical preoccupations that focus on, or at least straddle, the Civil War years? First, there is the fascinating work on the common soldier in the Civil War, by Gerald Linderman, Reid Mitchell, James I. Robertson, Joseph T. Glatthaar, James McPherson, Joseph Allan Frank, and others,[7] which has revealed so much about the way of life, the outlook, the bonds of comradeship, and the commitment to the cause of the men in uniform. Secondly, one might turn to a quite different body of work: the many studies of local communities in the mid-nineteenth-century decades, from Michael Frisch on Springfield, Massachusetts, through Stuart Blumin on Kingston, New York, on to Don Doyle on Jacksonville, Illinois, and John Mack Faragher on the Sugar Creek valley in Illinois, and, to take an example of a different kind, Grace Palladino on the anthracite region of Pennsylvania.[8] There are studies, too, of the larger cities at war, including Thomas O'Connor on Boston, Matthew Gallman on Philadelphia, and Ernest McKay and Iver Bernstein on New York.[9] A third, and at first sight unrelated, body of work has directed attention to the attitudes and reactions of various sections of opinion to the issues of the conflict – for example books by Earl J. Hess, Randall

Jimerson, and Anne C. Rose, and the collection of essays on gender and the Civil War edited by Catherine Clinton and Nina Silber.[10]

Each of these specific topics – the common soldiers, local community studies, analyses of public opinion – has obvious links with wider-ranging themes bearing upon the mid-nineteenth-century condition of American democracy and nationalism, education and literacy, the print media, and propaganda. All of these topics point toward an increasing focus on the Civil War as "the people's war," to borrow the title of Phillip Paludan's overview of the subject, which he in turn borrowed from Abraham Lincoln.[11] This was the first modern war fought by, indeed within, a society that was democratic (by the standards of its time), politically aware and engaged, and with a high rate of literacy. Here is a theme that covers North and South, soldiers and civilians, politics and society, military, political, social, economic, and intellectual history. What was to be the role of the citizen in such a war? For young men, it might well be to fight, whether as volunteers or draftees, but for large sections of the population, it might involve taking on new work, producing the goods needed to sustain the war effort, paying higher taxes, buying government bonds, accepting shortages and sacrifices and limitations on freedom, and giving political, moral, and emotional support to the war.

Popular commitment to the cause, or at least popular acceptance of the war, was essential in a conflict of this kind, in this kind of society. Writing of the attitude of common soldiers, James McPherson has made the point that "without their willing consent there would have been no Union or Confederate armies, no Civil War."[12] This notion of "conflict by consent" can profitably be extended from the soldiers to the mass of the civilian population. Close attention to civilian morale and popular support for the war may lead toward answers to many important questions – not only the role of the citizen in such a conflict, the challenges facing a democratic society at war, the links between home front and battlefront, the character and limits of dissent, and the means by which popular support was promoted and manipulated, but even that oldest and most durable of the chestnuts of Civil War historiography: why did the North win and the South lose?

There is a powerful case for saying that Northern morale and popular commitment were absolutely crucial to the outcome of the war. The likeliest way – perhaps the only realistic way – for the South to win its independence was not by conquest of the North but by conducting the war with sufficient pertinacity to convince Northern leaders and people that the attempt to force unwilling Southern states back into the Union was futile. The South could achieve its goal whenever the North decided to call it a day – and whether or not that would happen depended upon the strength and durability of Northern morale and commitment to the cause, both military and civilian.

The analysis of questions of morale and commitment can be divided into four segments, divided by North and South in one dimension, and by soldiers and civilians in the other. Historians have by no means ignored this topic, but they have shown a strange order of priorities in tackling it. Understandably, perhaps, they have devoted more attention to soldier than to civilian morale – and reference has already been made to some of the excellent work on this subject.[13] Less justifiably, they have also tended to focus more on the South than on the North. Southern motivation seems more straightforward and simpler to explain, when Southerners were fighting in defence of hearth and home. And yet, there has been a long-running debate on whether ultimate Confederate defeat was or was not caused by "loss of will" or "collapse of morale." The loss-of-will thesis was powerfully restated by Beringer, Hattaway, Jones, and Still in their collaborative volume on *Why the South Lost the Civil War*, but it has been challenged by, among others, Gary Gallagher in his *The Confederate War*, in which he locates the fundamental cause of Confederate defeat in the overwhelming strength of the North. The real question, he suggests, is how the Confederacy managed to survive so long in face of a much more powerful opponent.[14]

Curiously enough, concentration on the soldiers and on the South has meant relative neglect of what is surely the most important of the four "segments" of the morale question – the popular commitment of Northerners to the war. The side with the greater numbers and resources still needs the sustained will to win. This question is the main concern of the remainder of this chapter, along with some comparison, implicit or explicit, with the situation in the South. Incredibly, in the earlier study by Hattaway and Jones of *How the North Won the Civil War*[15] (note the word "how" rather than "why") there is not one reference in the index to morale. In their later volume on the Confederacy, there are fifty-eight references in the index to morale. However, it is a fact of fundamental importance that Northern will and commitment were sustained, at least adequately and often robustly, over four long years. This is all the more remarkable when one calls to mind that no one expected the kind of war that the Civil War became. The war escalated dramatically in scale, costs, casualties and suffering – and sheer war-weariness, frustration, and disillusionment posed a recurring danger to morale. After all, for long periods, the war went disappointingly, or downright badly, for the North; James McPherson, for example, identifies four periods of crisis for the

North,[16] when the will to persevere was severely tested by the potentially very depressing combination of relentless escalation of the conflict and recurrent dismay at battlefield reverses. Some 350,000 Union soldiers died during the war, and the combined total for both sides was over 600,000 – and that in a total population of just over thirty millions.[17] (As a proportion of the total population, the equivalent in today's United States would be five million dead soldiers.) Here surely was a massive threat to morale – but Northern commitment to the cause did hold out. This must be a subject worthy of serious investigation.

The issue here is not the *initial* motivation that inspired devotion to the Union and determination to defend it, but rather the *sustaining* motivation[18] that enabled Northerners to cope with the twin challenges of repeated setbacks and relentlessly rising casualties. First, in order to set the scene, it may be worthwhile to list a number of significant contributory factors that do not in themselves provide full or fundamental answers. For example, there is the simple but vital ingredient of luck – or "contingency" if it requires a more dignified label.[19] It does seem that relief from the worst crises of Northern confidence always seemed to arrive in the nick of time – at Antietam in September 1862, at Gettysburg and Vicksburg in July 1863, and at Atlanta in September 1864. Then again, some commentators attach importance to what might be called the "comfort factor." With very rare and brief exceptions the war was not fought on Northern soil. In most Northern communities, much of daily life went on as normal, and many people prospered during the war. However, this argument could cut both ways, and distance from the front line could have bred indifference rather than commitment. Indeed, in the South, it has been suggested that it was precisely those areas most directly and immediately threatened by invading Union forces that gave the strongest and most enduring support to the Confederate cause.[20]

Again, Northern morale was sustained by superior leadership, especially in terms of sensitivity to public opinion and ability to contain internal dissent or discontent. Whatever conclusion might emerge from a broader comparison of wartime presidential leadership, Abraham Lincoln surely outshone Jefferson Davis in this role. There is a wider argument too, famously expounded by Eric McKitrick, about the role of political parties in the North in focusing loyalty, containing discontent, and channeling political disagreement into familiar patterns. This argument has now attracted a good deal of criticism, but it surely retains some merit.[21] What is beyond challenge is the greater facility to focus loyalty on an established – if often remote – national government, rather than on a new Confederate government, desperately trying to establish its identity and its credibility, while its impact on the lives of its citizens rapidly assumed painful and unpopular forms, ranging from rising taxes and impressment of property to conscription into the army and even interference with the ownership of slave property.

One further and more deep-rooted Northern advantage derived from differences between North and South in social structure and economic development, and in the distribution of their respective populations. The North was simply a more advanced society, with many, many more towns and cities, linked together by much better communications. These communities provided focal points of collective activity and a more immediate sense of participation in the wider national effort. The North had the material resources – the railroads, the telegraph lines, the printing presses – and the political, intellectual, and cultural environment in which such activities could be promoted and could flourish. These advantages served to stiffen Northern morale and they certainly facilitated attempts to promote the Northern cause. They also lead directly into the central concern of this discussion.

One key to the nature and the strength of the sustaining motivation of the Northern people may be found in the links between home front and battlefront. How and why did people at the grass-roots level feel involved and engaged in the war? In a federal system, with very limited central government and emphasis on local self-rule, the relationship between the local community and wider national concerns was crucial. It had been so since the founding of the republic – but was never more so than during the Civil War. How did the link between the local and the national operate under all the stresses and strains of civil conflict, and how did it sustain popular involvement and commitment? The United States in the 1860s, North as well as South, was a very localized society; the federal government was distant and, for most aspects of daily life, irrelevant. Somehow, broader regional and national causes had to be made meaningful at the local level.

A number of historians have attempted to establish and define this essential link. Phillip Paludan has suggested that the federal government was acceptable precisely because it was so limited – but it was still important. The Union was the guarantee of the local community and its freedom; local self-rule and national unity were interdependent.[22] In one of his essays on Union soldiers in the Civil War, Reid Mitchell translates the broad concept of links between local community and national loyalty into very specific terms:

When a Northern recruit joined the army to protect American institutions his idea of those institutions came from his own, usually limited, experience. The institutions, the values for which he fought were those with which he had grown up. Democracy meant the town hall; education meant the schoolhouse; Christianity meant the local church. As for broader concepts – freedom, Constitution, democratic rule – so frequently had they been mediated by local figures that even they might be thought of as community values. In the North, localism aided rather hindered national patriotism. The Northern soldier fought for home and for Union, for family and for nation. For him, the Civil War experience made sense only in relation to both the domestic and the civic components of his world.[23]

In his book on Jacksonville, Illinois, Don H. Doyle entitled his chapter on the Civil War years "Localism as Nationalism." He sees the relationship between the two as a two-way process. While nationalism provided a "badly-needed adhesive for a disparate local community," community organizations and activities fed into and sustained the national war effort. In his survey of the Northern home front, Matthew Gallman describes the Civil War as a "national war fought by local communities." He places great emphasis on localism, voluntarism and what he calls "private activism," and argues that these were all well-established American traditions that were now channeled into support for the war effort.[24]

This concept of a national war fought by local communities may be tested by taking three examples as case studies: first, the recruitment of the huge citizen armies that fought the war; secondly, the network of voluntary bodies of all kinds that sustained life at the community level; and thirdly, the propaganda campaign in support of the Union cause. All three illustrate the themes of localism as nationalism, and private activism for public purposes.

The most direct contribution of home front to battlefront lay in the stimulation and organization of the flow of manpower into the armies. Something between one and a half million and two million separate individuals served in the huge, and overwhelmingly volunteer, armies that waged the war for the Union. The surge of volunteers in the early months of the war, and again in early 1862, was the product of individual enthusiasm, local initiative, and community effort. By midsummer 1862, when the reality of a protracted conflict had become apparent, the supply of volunteers was drying up. In any event, it is generally accepted that there is a limit to the percentage of any population of men of military age who will be genuine, unaided, uncoerced volunteers. The North had reached that stage by the latter part of 1862.

There was no master plan to tackle this problem, but what emerged over a period of months was a policy that combined the carrot and the stick. The latter was provided by the Enrollment Act of March 1863 which established the draft. As a direct means of putting conscripts into the army, the draft was hopelessly ineffective. Estimates vary, but the total number of draftees who actually served in the army was probably less than 50,000; in addition there were something like 118,000 substitutes provided by those who chose to avoid service themselves. A man whose name was called in the draft could avoid the call-up either by finding a substitute or by paying a commutation fee of $300. Such provisions may now seem bizarre but they conformed to widespread practice at the time, and they reveal the chief purpose – and effect – of the draft, which was to stimulate volunteering. When a draft was called, each congressional district was assigned a quota, and only any shortfall in that quota not filled by volunteers was to be supplied by draftees.[25]

If the goad, or stick, of the draft was to be effective, it had to be matched by a range of incentives – the carrot. There were repeated appeals to local pride, as communities, jealous of their reputations, strove to avoid the shame of the draft. For the individual of military age but no great military enthusiasm, the advantages of volunteering included choosing one's own regiment (often a local regiment), enhancement of one's reputation and popularity with family and friends and neighbors, and, above all, financial gain. The large carrot dangled before possible volunteers was provided by the network of bounties raised from state and local funds, and also from private sources. Large sums of money were involved, running into many millions of dollars. In Wisconsin, some $12,000,000 was raised for bounties and for aid to soldiers' families – one-third from the state, and the rest from counties and towns. This total was equivalent to $150 for every man, woman and child in the state.[26]

Individuals could accumulate considerable sums from the bounty system. In Jacksonville, Illinois, where there was a desperate determination to avoid the shame of the draft, a volunteer could receive more than $500. By 1864, a volunteer in Springfield, Massachusetts, could receive $875 from a combination of local, state, federal and private sources – a sum equivalent for many of them to a few years' wages. In addition, Springfield raised $80,000 for the relief of wounded soldiers, many of them just passing through the town, and the Soldiers' Rest Association became a major inclusive and extensive community activity, unprecedented in the town's history.[27] Expenditure on provision for the wives and families of soldiers added to expenditure on bounties, and local communities were burdened with higher taxes and heavy debts in their efforts to cope with soaring increases in spending levels.

The bounty system led to fierce competition between communities to attract volunteers, and the shady activities of bounty jumpers and bounty brokers. Some young men invested in draft insurance policies to pay for a substitute if their name should come up in the draft. All of this may strike the twenty-first century mind as a ramshackle, inefficient, extravagant, and often squalid way to fill the ranks of the army – and so it often was. Yet it did the job, and equally importantly, it adhered to the principles of localism, individual choice, and community action that were part and parcel of nineteenth-century American culture. By a combination of mass meetings to arouse popular feeling, financial inducements, and community pressure, towns such as Springfield and Jacksonville, and many others, filled their quotas and avoided or deferred what was felt to be the disgrace of resorting to the draft to fill the district quota. In one study of a Massachusetts town during the war, it is suggested that community support for the war effort took different forms in response to changing circumstances. During the first half of the war, the emphasis was simply on encouraging volunteers to come forward; later, when the limit of normal volunteering had been reached, community effort switched to raising funds for bounties, and searching for men wherever they could be found in order to meet the quota without resort to the dreaded draft.[28]

There may be little that is uplifting about this whole process, but it clearly demonstrates localism as nationalism, and private activism for public purposes, in energetic action. In her book on Victorian America and the Civil War, Anne Rose suggests that the war resolved the dilemma in many Northern minds between pursuit of selfish material goals and higher moral objectives. She writes that: "In wartime society . . . private glory promised to be consistent with the public good, and all effort seemed to be redeemed by association with ennobling ideals such as liberty and union."[29] She did not have in mind anything quite so mundane as volunteering for the army, but her words can be aptly applied to that situation.

Voluntary societies of all kinds were another power-house of the war effort at the local community level – and there is an element of irony about their key role. The whole elaborate Northern network of voluntary societies had no equivalent on anything like the same scale in the South. Indeed it was an indicator of that meddlesome, interfering, do-good Yankee Puritan tradition which the South loathed and despised. But that network added muscle and nervous energy to the Union war effort. Such societies and associations provided the mechanism for a huge amount of non-governmental community effort during the war, and presented a classic case of private activism for public purposes.

These organizations varied widely in size, purpose, and degree of formality or informality, from sewing circles and Ladies' Aid societies through church groups and philanthropic societies to propaganda agencies such as the Union Leagues and Loyal Leagues. One of their most important functions was to mobilize women and organize their partici-pation in the war effort. Women were very prominent in the work of many societies, including church groups and the local groups that supported the work of the United States Sanitary Commission. The Commission has attracted a good deal of attention and some criticism from historians, but it was an exception to the general rule, first in that it was a nationwide organization, and second in that it was a very unusual hybrid, as a part-public part-private body. It was established on the initiative of a number of wealthy and influential figures in New York and other eastern seaboard cities, and was then given government approval to engage in the vital task of providing field hospitals, medical services, and creature comforts for soldiers in the field. It raised funds by means of huge Sanitary Fairs in various cities. These were major social events, in which women, children, and whole families joined in raising money for the cause, and where crowds heard speeches from politicians, churchmen, and other local worthies.[30]

Although the Sanitary Commission was a national agency, it depended on the grass-roots work of local branches and local societies. This network of voluntary local effort, channeled into a great national endeavor, offers a conspicuous example of localism as nationalism, and voluntarism in support of national public purposes. The Commission and its local satellite organizations clearly formed an important connection between home front and battlefront, the local community and the war for the Union. Inevitably there were tensions at times between local groups and the national leadership, and it was mainly the latter that has been criticized, by George Fredrickson for example, as the agency of a conservative elite seeking to impose its moral order on the wider society.[31] However, although debate may continue about the ulterior motives of its leaders, the Commission did play a key role in stimulating and sustaining popular support for the war effort. It really did connect at the local level. Gallman makes the point that "rather than a highly centralized structure, wartime benevolence took a chaotic form reminiscent of antebellum America."[32] In his remark-able book on *Children and the Civil War*, James Marten cites the recollec-tions of a man who had been a child in a small town in upstate New York during the war. He was taken by his mother to meetings of the local chapter of the Sanitary Commission, "where young and old would meet, and pick lint and sew bandages, singing at our work those sad old war songs such as 'Tenting Tonight,' 'The Vacant Chair,' and 'Dear Mother, I've Come Home to Die.'"[33] Even if one may harbor some doubts about the boost to morale delivered by some of these songs, the role of such gatherings as examples of localism as nationalism in action is surely clear enough.

The role of the Churches and of such agencies as the Sanitary Commission spills over into a third example of the local/national connection: the propaganda campaign in support of the Union cause. In a society with a high level of both political engagement and popular literacy, there was a constant need to define the issues, sustain public support, and bolster morale. Once again, however, direct government action was not the main vehicle for this purpose, and the administration preferred to work indirectly through unofficial agencies. There was no Ministry of Information, no Committee on Public Information, and no phalanx of government spin doctors. Equally, there was remarkably little censorship or restriction of public debate. A few newspapers were briefly closed down, and thousands of dissenters or allegedly disloyal citizens, particularly in the border states, were held without trial, usually for short periods only.[34]

In general, political debate continued unabated throughout the war, and attacks on the administration and the conduct of the war were uninhibited. In 1864, a presidential election campaign was fought with all the vigor and the extravagant rhetoric that is characteristic of such contests. Politicians and political parties – as distinct from the federal administration – were of course extremely active in the propaganda campaign. Abraham Lincoln himself was no mean performer as a do-it-yourself spin doctor: "shaping public opinion," says Phillip Paludan, "continued to be perhaps his most vital duty."[35] He faced a particularly delicate task in seeking to persuade a reluctant Northern public to accept the evolution of a war to save the Union into a struggle also to free the slaves. He handled it with much subtlety and some equivocation, a remarkable sense of timing, and constant efforts to soothe and reassure those whom he could not completely convince.[36]

However, Lincoln's methods of persuasion were very different from those of his more recent successors. He could not, of course, exploit the opportunities offered today by radio, television, and the internet, and it is also true that he made very few public speeches during the war – the Gettysburg Address was very much an exception to the general rule – and seldom left Washington, except to visit the army in Virginia. But he kept open house at the White House, and spent many hours talking to visitors who thronged the corridors waiting and hoping for a chance to meet the president. He also kept close contacts with the press, or at least with favored journalists and editors, and some of his carefully-crafted letters on major public issues were reprinted in the newspapers all across the country, and often also published as pamphlets.[37] Lincoln may not have been everyone's idea of how a president should look and behave, but he had certain natural advantages. Writing of the antebellum presidency, Michael J. Heale sets out the qualities of the ideal presidential candidate: "The primary or archetypal candidate . . . was the quintessential American republican: self-reliant and self-made, a transcendent patriot, a staunch nationalist, a champion of human liberty. As befitted an American republican, he was close to the people, simple and unaffected in his ways."[38] This reads like an accurate description of Abraham Lincoln – and Lincoln knew how to connect with people at the local grass roots.

The political parties were, of course, in the thick of the propaganda battle, at both the national and the local level. The Republicans strove to establish and reinforce the link between partisanship and patriotism, loyalty to the party and to the Union – and it assumed the name of the National Union Party in 1864. The Democrats sought to prove their credentials as a loyal party of opposition, and as defenders of the constitution against what they saw as executive usurpation or tyranny. However, for propaganda and morale-boosting purposes, the parties, like the administration, chose to rely heavily on non-governmental, private, or at worst, semi-official bodies, operating at both national and local level. Mid-nineteenth-century America was essentially a print culture, and apart from direct personal contact through speeches, debates, and public meetings, the printed word was the main vehicle for the dissemination of information, misinformation, and messages of inspiration and encouragement. The Northern public was deluged with newspapers, pamphlets, tracts, handbills, and broadsides from a variety of sources. Much of the political propaganda came from Union Leagues and Loyal Leagues in the major cities, which tended to merge the Republican party political agenda into the war aims of the Union. The Leagues churned out masses of material, especially during the second half of the war, and generally overwhelmed the opposition propaganda campaign, orchestrated by the Society for the Diffusion of Political Knowledge. The Board of Publications of the Philadelphia Union League, one of the most active organizations, distributed over one million copies of pamphlets in 1863 and again in 1864. The New England Loyal Publication Society operated rather differently but equally effectively. It gathered articles from newspapers and other sources, and printed them in broadsides that were then distributed to many smaller newspapers, particularly in the Midwest, for appropriate use by them.[39] Here is a prime example of the interaction of the national, the regional and the local.

There were other organs of propaganda and inspiration, and the Churches were conspicuous among them. Again, there was no policy imposed from the top, but Churches and individual churchmen produced a flood of sermons, tracts, articles, and reports discussing the war issues and boosting support for the cause. If the churches performed a particular function, it lay in justification of the war, and definition of its objectives. In general, they moved from initial justification of a defensive war to save the Union to identification of wider and deeper purposes in the conflict – emancipation of the slaves, creation of a more perfect Union, and the moral regeneration of America. The war was gradually transformed from a necessary evil into a national blessing. There is remarkably little evidence of agonizing or protest at the carnage and suffering caused by the war (although there was some concern about the morality of fighting on a Sunday). Rather, churchmen sought to understand the place of the war in God's plan for America – a punishment for national sins perhaps, or an opportunity for national purification and rededication. Few preachers doubted that God did have such a plan. The Methodist bishop, Matthew Simpson, confidant of Abraham Lincoln, was quite unequivocal on the subject: "If the world is to be raised to its proper place, I would say it with all reverence, God cannot do without America."[40]

As with the two earlier examples, the propaganda campaign illustrates the interconnected themes of voluntarism, non-governmental organizations serving public purposes, and local activism in support of the national cause. Throughout this discussion, comparison or contrast with the experience of the Southern Confederacy has been implicit rather than explicit. It may suffice simply to suggest that the thicker texture of Northern social, institutional, and intellectual life, with its elaborate networks of societies and organizations, and its remorseless circulation of the printed word in all its many forms, made an important difference to the fortunes of the two sides. In the North, these various ties bound locality and nation together with increasing effectiveness. In the South, with no comparable institutional back-up to that which existed in the North, the same ties existed, but never so strongly, and they began to fray and eventually to snap under intense pressure during the latter stages of the war.

Of course, the bonds between locality and nation do not in themselves explain why the North eventually won the Civil War. But the strength and resilience of those bonds were an essential pre-condition of Northern success. Studies of the American home front during the two world wars of the twentieth century suggest that the same pattern of localism, voluntarism, and private activism, so evident during the Civil War, reappeared in these different circumstances, although the direct interventionist role of the federal government has obviously become much greater. This element of continuity serves to return the discussion to the wider issues raised at the outset.[41]

Study of the home front – and especially of civilian morale, popular commitment, and the means of promoting them – can shed light on other issues, quite apart from how and why the North won the Civil War. It has already been suggested that it may help to break down artificial barriers between various fields of Civil War study. Beyond that, it may serve a broader purpose by helping to integrate Civil War history more effectively with major, long-running issues in the history of the United States during the nineteenth century. The list of such issues is a long one; it would include the character and limitations of American democracy, the evolution of American nationalism, the role of voluntary agencies and associations (about which De Tocqueville wrote so forcefully more than twenty years before the war),[42] the improvement in the means of communicating information and ideas, the interrelated effects of political participation and widespread literacy, the role of women in the local community and in many of the voluntary organizations, the influence of evangelical Protestantism in American public life, and the relationship between the local community and the national identity in a federal system.

The four years from 1861 to 1865 were a truly exceptional phase of American history. But that is no reason to isolate the war years from the study of the rest of nineteenth-century America. On the contrary, a period of exceptional strain in the history of a society may offer unusual opportunities for the scrutiny and analysis of many of its characteristics – both its strengths and its weaknesses. The particular circumstances of the war years can and should be used as a powerful lens through which to observe the structure and development of nineteenth-century America. In short, study of popular attitudes and commitment during the Civil War offers just one among a number of possible approaches to tackling some of the continuing challenges facing Civil War historiography. Far from being "read out" of American history, the Civil War is, or at least should be, expanding the agenda that confronts historians still brave enough to enter the field.

Notes

1. Eric Foner, *Politics and Ideology in the Age of the Civil War* (New York, 1980), pp. 3–12.

2. There is an authoritative recent appraisal of the condition of Civil War historiography in James M. McPherson and William J. Cooper, eds., *Writing the Civil War: The Quest to Understand* (Columbia, SC, 1998), a collection of twelve essays by many of the leading current practitioners in the field. Invaluable as it is, the volume also exemplifies both the uneven coverage and the compartmentalization of Civil War historiography. The twelve essays are neatly divided: four on military matters, four on political and constitutional history, and four on social and economic history (including two on the specific topics of gender and the ending of slavery).

3. George F. Hoar, *Autobiography of Seventy Years* (New York, 1903), Vol. I, p. 212, quoted in David Donald, *Charles Sumner and the Rights of Man* (New York, 1970), p. 146.

4. The problem is exemplified in Gary Gallagher, *The Confederate War* (Cambridge MA, 1997). Although his conclusion is that the South was ultimately overwhelmed by the massive strength of the North, Gallagher's analysis is almost exclusively devoted to the internal history of the Confederacy. There is a thoughtful appraisal of "internal" and "external" explanations of Confederate defeat in James McPherson's essay, "Why Did the Confederacy Lose?" in McPherson, *Drawn With the Sword: Reflections on the American Civil War* (New York, 1996), pp. 113–36.

5. During the 1960s and 1970s there was a vigorous debate on the economic impact of the Civil War, triggered by an article by Thomas C. Cochran, "Did the Civil War Retard Industrialization?" *Mississippi Valley Historical Review*, 48 (1961): 197–210. Cochran challenged the received wisdom of that time by answering "yes" to his own question, and he was broadly supported by a number of other statistical-minded economic historians, including Stanley L. Engerman, "The Economic Impact of the Civil War," *Explorations in Entrepreneurial History*, 3 (1966): 176–99. Other historians, such as Allan Nevins, and more recently James McPherson, have relied less on quantification and have taken a broader view, with a continuing emphasis on the economic stimulus provided by the war, in both the shorter and longer term. It seems clear that no simple yes-or-no answer to Cochran's question can be applied to all sectors of the American economy. For a thoughtful review of the subject, see Phillip Shaw Paludan, "What

Did the Winners Win? The Social and Economic History of the North during the Civil War," in McPherson and Cooper, eds., *Writing the Civil War*, pp. 175–87. Social historians have generally paid inadequate attention to the Civil War. In Maris A. Vinovskis, ed., *Toward a Social History of the American Civil War: Exploratory Essays*, (Cambridge and New York, 1990), the editor deplores this neglect, but the essays in the volume offer a series of often interesting snapshots rather than a sustained investigation of the subject.

6. There is a substantial body of literature, by both American and non-American scholars, on the diplomacy of the Civil War, especially on British relations with both sides. On the other hand, American historical writing often shows little awareness of the international context, and there has been comparatively little work on the international echoes of the great issues involved in the Civil War, including democracy, majority rule versus minority rights, nationalism, federalism, the multiple meanings of liberty, and the question of race. Richard J. M. Blackett, *Divided Hearts: Britain and the American Civil War* (Baton Rouge, 2001) is an important study of British attitudes to the war, which breaks a good deal of new ground.

7. Gerald F. Linderman, *Embattled Courage: The Experience of Combat in the American Civil War* (New York, 1987); Reid Mitchell, *Civil War Soldiers: Their Expectations and their Experiences* (New York, 1988) and *The Vacant Chair: The Northern Soldier Leaves Home* (New York, 1993); James I. Robertson, *Soldiers, Blue and Gray* (Columbia, SC, 1988); Joseph T. Glatthaar, *The March to the Sea and Beyond: Sherman's Troops in the Savannah and Carolinas Campaigns* (New York, 1985); James M. McPherson, *For Cause and Comrades: Why Men Fought in the Civil War* (New York, 1997); Joseph Allan Frank, *With Ballot and Bayonet: The Political Socialization of American Civil War Soldiers* (Athens, GA, 1998).

8. Michael Frisch, *Town into City: Springfield, Massachusetts, and the Meaning of Community, 1840–1880* (Cambridge, MA, 1972); Stuart Blumin, *The Urban Threshold: Growth and Change in a Nineteenth Century American Community* (Chicago, 1976); Don Harrison Doyle, *The Social Order of a Frontier Community: Jacksonville, Illinois, 1825–1870* (Urbana, IL, 1978); John Mack Faragher, *Sugar Creek: Life on the Illinois Prairie* (New Haven, CT, 1986); Grace Palladino, *Another Civil War: Labor, Capital, and the State in the Anthracite Regions of Pennsylvania* (Urbana, IL, 1990). Some of these studies, notably Frisch, Doyle, and Palladino, pay much more attention to the Civil War than others.

9. Thomas H. O'Connor, *Civil War Boston: Home Front and Battlefield* (Boston, 1997); J. Matthew Gallman, *Mastering Wartime: A Social History of Philadelphia during the Civil War* (Cambridge and New York, 1990); Ernest A. McKay, *The Civil War and New York City* (Syracuse, NY, 1990); Iver Bernstein, *The New York City Draft Riots: Their Significance for American Society and Politics in the Age of the Civil War* (New York, 1990).

10. Earl J. Hess, *Liberty, Virtue and Progress: Northerners and their War for the Union* (New York, 1988); Randall C. Jimerson, *The Private Civil War: Popular Thought during the Sectional Conflict* (Baton Rouge, LA, 1988); Anne C. Rose, *Victorian America and the Civil War* (Cambridge and New York, 1992); Catherine Clinton and Nina Silber, eds., *Divided Houses: Gender and the Civil War* (New York, 1992).

11. Phillip Shaw Paludan, *"A People's Contest": The Union and the Civil War, 1861–1865* (New York, 1988).

12. McPherson, *For Cause and Comrades*, p. 16.

13. See Note 7, above.

14. Richard E. Beringer, Herman Hattaway, Archer Jones and William N. Still, *Why the South Lost the Civil War* (Athens, GA, 1986), especially chapters 14, 16, 17; Gallagher, *The Confederate War*, especially pp. 3–13, 157–72.

15. Herman Hattaway and Archer Jones, *How the North Won: A Military History of the Civil War* (Urbana, IL, 1983).

16. James M. McPherson, *Battle Cry of Freedom: The Civil War Era* (New York, 1988), pp. 857–58.

17. Of course, exact casualty figures were not known at the time, and all manner of wild guesses and rumors circulated in the press and elsewhere. It is also true that well under half of the dead were actually killed on the field of battle; the remainder died of disease or from the after-effects of wounds and the attentions of the surgeons. However, through casualty lists in newspapers or posted in public places, or by knowledge of deaths among family, friends, and the local community, people on the home front were scarcely unaware of the scale of the bloodletting.

18. This distinction is defined in McPherson, *For Cause and Comrades*, p. 16. He acknowledges his debt to John A. Lynn, *The Bayonets of the Republic: Motivation and Tactics in the Army of Revolutionary France, 1791–1794* (Urbana, IL, 1984), p. 12.

19. Among the present generation of historians of the Civil War, James McPherson has placed particular emphasis on contingency; he has

argued that there was nothing inevitable about the course and conclusion of the war, and that, at various points, there was a very fine line between military success and failure. See his *Battle Cry of Freedom*, passim, and also some of the essays in his *Drawn With the Sword*, especially chapter 8, "Why Did the Confederacy Lose?" and chapter 15, "What's the Matter with History?"

20. See, for example, William Blair, *Virginia's Private War: Feeding Body and Soul in the Confederacy* (New York, 1998), especially pp. 141–6.
21. Eric McKitrick, "Party Politics and the Union and Confederate War Efforts," in William Nisbet Chambers and Walter Dean Burnham, eds., *The American Party Systems: Stages of Political Development* (New York, 1967). Mark E. Neely, "The Civil War and the Two-Party System," in James M. McPherson, ed., *"We Cannot Escape History": Lincoln and the Last Best Hope of Earth* (Urbana, IL, 1995) is extremely sceptical about the McKitrick thesis, but much of his critique seems to be based on a misinterpretation of McKitrick's argument.
22. Phillip Shaw Paludan, "The American Civil War Considered as a Crisis of Law and Order," *American Historical Review*, 77 (1972): 1013–34. See also Paludan, *A People's Contest*, pp. 10–15.
23. Reid Mitchell, "The Northern Soldier and his Community," in Vinovskis, ed., *Toward a Social History of the Civil War*, p. 92.
24. Doyle, *Social Order of a Frontier Community*, p. 228, and more generally pp. 227–41; J. Matthew Gallman, *The North Fights the Civil War: The Home Front* (Chicago, 1994), p. 188. Gallman's brief book is much the best recent overview of the Northern home front. For another illuminating study of a local community at war, see Thomas R. Kemp, "Community and War: The Civil War Experience of Two New Hampshire Towns," in Vinovskis, ed., *Toward a Social History of the Civil War*, pp. 31–77.
25. For an analytical study of the draft and its operation, see James W. Geary, *We Need Men: The Union Draft in the Civil War* (DeKalb, IL, 1991). See also Geary, "Civil War Conscription in the North: A Historiographical Review," *Civil War History*, 32 (1986): 208–28.
26. Richard N. Current, *The Civil War Era, 1848–1873* (*History of Wisconsin*, William Fletcher Thompson general editor, Vol. II), (Madison, WI, 1976), p. 335.
27. Doyle, *Social Order of a Frontier Community*, p. 235; Frisch, *Town into City*, pp. 65, 59. For excellent accounts of the whole process of recruitment at the local level in one New England town and one

Midwestern state, moving from volunteering to quotas, drafts, and bounties, see ibid., pp. 60–6, and Current, pp. 296–335.

28. Emily J. Harris, "Sons and Soldiers: Deerfield, Massachusetts and the Civil War," *Civil War History*, 30 (1984): 166–8.

29. Rose, *Victorian America and the Civil War*, p. 70.

30. For descriptions of some of the great Sanitary Fairs, see Gallman, *The North Fights the Civil War*, pp. 170–2; Gallman, "Voluntarism in Wartime: Philadelphia's Great Central Fair," in Vinovskis, ed., *Toward a Social History of the Civil War*, pp. 93–116; and McKay, *The Civil War and New York City*, pp. 240–4.

31. George Fredrickson, *The Inner Civil War: Northern Intellectuals and the Crisis of the Union* (New York, 1965), pp. 98–112.

32. Gallman, "Voluntarism in Wartime," p. 110.

33. James Marten, *The Children's Civil War* (Chapel Hill, NC, 1998), p. 6.

34. Mark E. Neely, *The Fate of Liberty: Abraham Lincoln and Civil Liberties* (New York, 1991) provides a realistic assessment of Lincoln's use of arbitrary arrests.

35. Phillip Shaw Paludan, *The Presidency of Abraham Lincoln* (Lawrence, KN, 1994), p. 222.

36. Paludan, *Presidency of Lincoln*, pp. 142–58 and 162–6; Peter J. Parish, *The American Civil War* (London and New York, 1975), pp. 226–61.

37. For two outstanding examples of Lincoln letters of this kind, see Roy P. Basler, editor, *The Collected Works of Abraham Lincoln* (New Brunswick, NJ, 1953), Vol. VI, pp. 260–9 and 300–6. There is a useful brief discussion of Lincoln's relations with journalists in Allen C. Guelzo, *Abraham Lincoln: Redeemer President* (Grand Rapids, MI, 1999), pp. 364–5. Evidence of Lincoln's friendship with one journalist may be found in Michael Burlingame, ed., *Lincoln Observed: Civil War Dispatches of Noah Brooks* (Baltimore, 1998). See in particular the editor's introduction, pp. 1–12. Don E. Fehrenbacher and Virginia Fehrenbacher, ed., *Recollected Words of Abraham Lincoln* (Stanford, CA, 1996) brings together a huge number of reports and recollections by a wide variety of people of their meetings with Lincoln.

38. Michael J. Heale, *The Presidential Quest: Candidates and Images in American Political Culture, 1787–1852* (London and New York, 1982), p. 168.

39. Frank Freidel, ed., *Union Pamphlets of the Civil War*, 2 vols. (Cambridge, MA, 1967) is a superb collection. See the editor's introduction (Vol. I, pp. 1–24) for an illuminating discussion of the

work of the publication societies and the content of the pamphlets. In a forthcoming work, my former student Adam Smith has important things to say about the propaganda campaign, particularly during the election campaign of 1864.

40. George R. Crooks, *The Life of Bishop Matthew Simpson of the Methodist Episcopal Church* (New York, 1891), p. 382. On the general question of the support of the Protestant Churches for the war effort, see two essays by Peter J. Parish, "The War for the Union as a Just War," in David K. Adams and Cornelis A. van Minnen, eds., *Aspects of War in American History* (Keele, 1997) and "From Necessary Evil to National Blessing: The Northern Protestant Clergy Interpret the Civil War," forthcoming.

41. Comparison with the experience of twentieth-century wars might fruitfully be extended a good deal further. In the case of World War I, there has been innovative work on the home front, particularly in Britain but also in other European countries. See, for example, Joanna Bourke, *Dismembering the Male: Men's Bodies, Britain and the Great War* (London, 1996) and Niall Ferguson, *The Pity of War* (London, 1998), especially chapters 7 and 8. Bourke focuses on questions of masculinity and the male body in a study of the cultural impact of war which goes well beyond the scope of this chapter. In asking why so many men volunteered, Ferguson lists recruitment techniques, female and peer-group pressure, economic motives, and simple impulse. All of these, except perhaps the economic motive, could equally apply to young volunteers in the first half of the Civil War. Bourke and, especially, Ferguson also discuss the role of propaganda, and Ferguson points out that, in World War I as in the Civil War, much of the propaganda effort was organized not by the government but by other agencies and individuals. Just as Civil War historians have generally failed to take note of recent work on the European home front in 1914–1918, British and European historians have failed to absorb the lessons of the American Civil War as a precursor of the home front experience during the Great War.

42. Alexis De Tocqueville, *Democracy in America*, 2 vols., Vintage edition, Phillips Bradley, ed. (New York, 1954), Vol. II, pp. 114–28.

–19–

By Way of DuBois: The Question of Black Initiative in the Civil War and Reconstruction

David Turley

The huge scale and dramatic character of the Civil War has made it a permanent source of passionate interest to many outsiders as well as to Americans. It has never failed to draw either historical commentary or popular fascination. Reconstruction, however, has only achieved greater salience as a subject of historical inquiry in recent years. The "Second Reconstruction" of the civil rights era altered the social and political realities of segregation and political disfranchisement that had underpinned the long-established view of the first Reconstruction as a disastrous experiment in civic and political equality. The consequence has been a highly sophisticated body of work transforming our sense of the period at the national level as well as in particular localities.[1]

One of the most striking developments in the literature of the Civil War and Reconstruction in the last generation has been the attention that both black and white scholars have paid to the role of African Americans in helping shape the movement of events. The first, early twentieth-century, phase of professional scholarship on the Civil War and Reconstruction, identified with Columbia scholars William A. Dunning and John W. Burgess, assumed a "grant" of freedom to the slaves by the Lincoln administration that the president intended should be followed by a policy of reconciliation toward the white South. With Lincoln's assassination, Radical Republicans in Congress thwarted Johnson's attempts at continuity and forced corrupt and oppressive regimes on the whites in the South. Although, in this interpretation, the participation of African Americans as voters and officeholders along with "carpetbaggers" and "scalawags" constituted a self-evidently malign element, the Dunningite tradition largely presented black people not as agents of oppression but as ignorant and feckless tools that the whites who were aligned with them manipulated for their own ends.[2]

As differing revisionist and post-revisionist interpretative frameworks later gained widespread acceptance, this disregard of African American initiative and agency ceased. Interpreting Republican policy as pursuing widely supported objectives of political democracy and civic equality between the races, revisionist historians in the 1960s and 1970s also gave credit to freed people as active both in their own cause and, more generally, in that of social and educational progress in the South. More recently, although some post-revisionists have concluded that the changes of the 1860s and 1870s had rather little effect on the racism, social inequality, and economic constraints confronting the former slaves, there has been no return to the image of a quiescent and malleable freed people. The argument instead has been directed at the relative failure of black and white activism in the period to bring about substantial change.[3]

Recognizing the seeming permanence of the interpretative shift stressing African American initiative, scholars have also grasped that its most important historiographical origin was in the writings of W. E. B. DuBois. Foner paid tribute to the eventual impact of DuBois's "monumental study." The emphasis on the agency of slaves in the analytical essays of the historical team composing the Freedmen and Southern Society Project – which has so enriched the study of the black role in the Civil War and its immediate aftermath – builds on DuBois's pioneering work. In addition, both Edward L. Ayers and David R. Roediger have linked the modern recognition of the importance of slaves' actions in pushing emancipation to the top of the political agenda during the war to DuBois's work. Part of the purpose of this chapter is to follow through and analyze the precise character of these recognized interpretative connections. It is also to indicate where historians have taken fresh directions.[4]

Perhaps it is even more important to explore the *conceptual* relevance of DuBois's *Black Reconstruction* (1935) to later historical writing on the Civil War and Reconstruction. Historians have noticed his use of the idea of the "general strike" and this will be explored further. But this idea itself is only one aspect of his more general insistence that the role of blacks in the period can only be fully understood when the implicit bargain between the propertied and employing class and significant elements of white labor is recognized. This was a bargain that operated to the detriment of African Americans, and perhaps ultimately of white labor, too. DuBois's analysis consequently involved "mixing race and class by design." This focus has been used in a number of significant writings that examine the situation of African Americans and the limits on the impact of their activism.[5]

But DuBois's historical work needs to be approached in another way both to grasp its character fully and to understand how it illuminates later historical work. Some of that subsequent writing does not have the black role in the period as its direct subject, yet in the light of DuBois's work it emerges as relevant. It has to be recognized that, to DuBois himself, his historical work was also a *political* intervention. *Black Reconstruction* was the culmination of over three decades of his historical writing on the consequences of emancipation. In applying to the Rosenwald Fund in 1931 to finance research for the project, he himself linked it to earlier work, specifically to the second chapter of *The Souls of Black Folk* (1903), his paper to the 1909 meeting of the American Historical Association and the subsequent article in the *American Historical Review* (July, 1910), and the fifth chapter of his *The Gift of Black Folk* (1924). He could additionally have added, among other items, a 1913 contribution to *Survey* and various shorter, overtly polemical, pieces in *The Crisis*. DuBois had no doubt that his recurrent historical discussion of the topic was pertinent to the continuing circumstances of African Americans. His early twentieth-century attempts to counter the Columbia school's denigration of blacks' participation in public and economic life after emancipation occurred as Jim Crow was fastened firmly upon the South. *Black Reconstruction* was composed in the depths of economic depression and during the political controversies and hopes, including the rise of labor, of the early New Deal years. Its representation of black efforts in the Civil War and Reconstruction as part of a striving for political and economic, as well as racial, democracy spoke to contemporary circumstances. Equally, his characterization and explanation of the failures of the struggle coincided with his own increased emphasis on the contemporary need for African Americans to make attempts at separate economic and social development and his consequent break from the NAACP in 1934.[6]

From DuBois's perspective, there had never been any clear separation between the different expressions of his intellectual activity. Writing about the past, contesting existing versions of it, and writing about the present were all aspects of an intended seamless intellectual critique of the black situation in American life. During the ventures into the history of Reconstruction he undertook at the end of the first decade of the twentieth century, DuBois was simultaneously working on social scientific analyses of contemporary black life. Earlier, he had juxtaposed historical writing with contemporary social analysis and other varieties of representation of black life and culture in *The Souls of Black Folk*. Similarly, he used the columns of *The Crisis* to attack the historical interpretations of Ulrich Bonnell Phillips while cheek-by-jowl exposing recent incidents of racial prejudice. Had DuBois needed any encouragement to see his historical work and his politics as intimately connected, he received it both organizationally and from respected friends and colleagues. The Board of Directors of the NAACP, convinced of the project's political relevance, had funded him to research and write a history of black troops in World War I, though it now exists only in various drafts. He told the Rosenwald Fund that the doyen of African American literary figures, James Weldon Johnson, had suggested that DuBois's proposed history of blacks in Reconstruction would fulfil "a great need ... to complete and offset recent studies."[7]

The reception of the book on its appearance in 1935 – and the nature of some of the criticism directed at it – can only have confirmed DuBois in seeing historical reinterpretation as one front in a cultural and intellectual war with significant stakes for the future. Although, as is well known, the *American Historical Review* failed to review the volume, it was quite widely noticed and by no means completely unfavorably. The point to be addressed here, however, is not the general reception but some of the criticisms made. The professionalization of historical research placed a premium on archival study. DuBois and his helpers did none of this, and his book was sharply criticized on this count. The desire to get the work completed as rapidly as possible was one factor in the reliance on official and other institutional reports, a smattering of newspapers, and extensive secondary literature – DuBois himself complained during the course of the book's preparation that historical and social research could go on forever. There would also have been difficulties in getting into Southern archives. But he distrusted existing books based too heavily on archival work in unpublished manuscripts since, in his view, they often amounted to little more than the translation into print of the prejudices to be found in the papers of the Southern white ruling class. In this context, official and other reports were likely to offer somewhat more balanced evidence.[8]

The implications of a close connection between DuBois's scholarship and his politics should not be misunderstood. It does not follow that his historical work was simply reductive propaganda to serve current political and agitational ends. Indeed, it is suggested here that the history he wrote and DuBois's thinking about how best to engineer progressive racial and social change in the 1930s are likely to have informed each other. The struggles of the Depression era gave prominence to the links between race and class and particularly to the relation of black workers and tenants to white workers and tenants, especially their politics and institutions. DuBois's historical studies must inevitably have influenced his contemporary reflections but, equally, those reflections probably reinforced the historical significance of dealing with actual and possible cross-racial class and political alignments that could have (or did) help sustain black initiatives in the 1860s and 1870s. However well or inadequately DuBois treated these alignments in *Black Reconstruction*, his political logic reinforced the historical logic to open up these issues on terms different from those of the earlier historiographical renderings of blacks as abject appendages of self-interested whites. That, in turn, indicates that writing focused primarily on actual and potential allies of African Americans in the period deserves some consideration in relation to the question of black initiative.

The next part of this chapter considers DuBois's views on forms of black initiative during the war and afterwards. This includes his use of the idea of the "general strike" and its implications as well as his ways of relating race and class, particularly in regard to the alignments of black and white labor and the failures of interracial collaboration. In the case of each topic in turn, summary and commentary will be offered on more recent work in relation to DuBois's treatment of the same themes.

DuBois's attribution of initiative to African Americans owed something to what David Levering Lewis has termed an "alternative tradition" of black memoirs and historical accounts of the period. These extended from the writings of John R. Lynch, drawing upon his own participation in events in Mississippi, to the state monographs of A. A. Taylor in the 1920s. Yet only in 1965, when James M. McPherson published extracts from sources linked by narrative and commentary in *The Negro's Civil War*, did black agency assume a prominent place in white historical discourse on the war. In other words, this prominent feature of *Black Reconstruction* was paralleled in the intervening years only in the books of other black scholars, such as Benjamin Quarles and Dudley T. Cornish.[9]

DuBois devoted a number of pages to the flight of slaves from their masters during the war and placed considerable significance upon it. The nature of his argument underlined the element of calculation on the part of the slaves. They did not await their freedom passively but nor, he suggested, did they immediately rush towards Union forces. Rather, what the slaves did was "to wait, look and listen" and act only when they were sure what was to their benefit. Once "it became clear that the Union armies would not or could not return fugitive slaves, and that the masters with all their fume and fury were uncertain of victory," slaves, eventually to the number of half a million, left the plantations. This process DuBois termed "a general strike." Its effects were crucial: "This withdrawal and bestowal of his [the former slave's] labor [on the Union] decided the war."

The logic here was the same as that articulated by Frederick Douglass in the early stages of the war: the South was able to maximize its forces in the field because it relied on the slaves to produce both food and cash crops and to provide military labor. The South's loss of the slaves and the Union's acceptance of their aid was thus a double blow on behalf of freedom.[10]

The argument itself did not rest upon the notion that some extended form of organization was needed to bring about the general strike once individuals and groups had decided to act. DuBois had no explanation that he could document for the initial phases of such widespread mobilization, though, once such a substantial movement had begun, knowledge of it was bound to spread. He could only advance without comment the phrase from one of his sources, "a mysterious spiritual telegraph," as providing the impetus leading to the initial appearance of fugitives at Fortress Monroe in the early weeks of the war. Thereafter, he posited a kind of mass spontaneous action to account for the flow of fugitives, regarding this tide of humanity – in a phrase from one of his documents – as "a mere inarticulate decision of instinct."[11]

There is, however, an ambiguity in his presentation of why the slaves left the plantations. "The slave entered upon a general strike against slavery," DuBois declared in beginning his narrative of slave flight, with the result that the slaveholders' regime collapsed in military defeat. But there is here an elision between *effect* and *intention* that is clarified nowhere else in *Black Reconstruction*. The book provides little on the nature of the *consciousness* of the fugitives, apart from an instinct for freedom that was a result of "unlettered reason." Of course, within the broadly Marxist tradition that constituted DuBois's frame of reference in 1935, the concept of *class* action as the dynamic arising from the systemic exploitation of both black and white workers transcended any concern with individual or group intentions. And this is indeed DuBois's approach. The "truth" that ought to have been recognized from the outset of the war was that "The Southern worker, black and white, held the key to the war; and of the two groups, the black worker ... held an even more strategic place than the white." Equally, there is warrant in the analyses of other Marxist writers for making use of the notion of mass spontaneity as the basis for a "general strike." Rosa Luxemburg, for example, wrote of workers becoming aware of their objectives during the very course of the struggle that engaged them. She offered instances from Russian history at the end of the nineteenth century of spontaneous general strikes in St. Petersburg and Rostov-on-Don that supposedly owed nothing to central organization. Georges Sorel, in his syndicalist phase, spoke of the "general strike" in the context of "spontaneous, non-rationalized activity on the part of the proletariat." I have no evidence that DuBois was a close student of either Luxemburg or Sorel, but the point is to emphasize that he was not unique within this style of social analysis in relying on popular spontaneity as an explanation for events.[12]

The historians of the Freedmen and Southern Society Project have devoted close attention in recent writing to the causes and significance of slaves leaving the plantations during the Civil War. Their work has clarified some of the ambiguities left by DuBois. The system of bondage in districts experiencing the loss of a significant body of fugitives began to be undermined quite early in the conflict. As time went on, even in areas at some distance from Union forces, African Americans were able to negotiate improvements in their conditions because the owners or their agents feared losing their slaves. These findings expand on the sketch that DuBois provided.

On the question of causation, however, recent work goes much further. It elaborates on the variables that slaves had to consider and that often prompted them to escape. Some encountered tougher discipline after the war began and reacted against it. Those sent off to do military labor picked up knowledge of possible escape routes which they either took advantage of or passed on to others. The practice of "refugeeing" – sending slaves out of their home districts and deeper into the Confederacy away from enemy lines – or even the prospect of it, could have the effect of hastening slave flight. The disruption of the slave family or the stripping away of the limited security of slave community that might well be involved in these forced movements into the interior add dimensions to slave escapes. Later scholars have been more alert to them than DuBois because they have benefited from the whole body of work on family and community developed in reaction to the theses of Stanley Elkins.[13]

Later in the war, sheer survival in the face of material deprivation became a motive for the flight of some slaves. The recognition in *Black Reconstruction* of the significance of the non-return of fugitives in maintaining or increasing the flow of escapees has been expanded and given additional nuances through more detailed research on how the fugitives were received in different local environments. This has taken into account the attitudes of various army commanders, as DuBois did, but also of the responses of ordinary soldiers, and how changing policy made in Washington filtered down to localities.[14]

Recent scholarship has not been content with invocations of instinct or "spiritual telegraphs" in explaining the large-scale slave mobilization involved in flight. Networks of communication among slaves have been explored by Leon Litwack and others. Slaves overheard the conversations of whites and their reading aloud of newspapers. A minority could read for themselves. Those who had had occasion to travel around on their master's or Confederate business picked up news on the progress of the war and the location of Yankee forces. Black preachers, despite the presence of whites, apparently found ways to hint at developments in the war: worshippers knew what to make of prayers that the Yankees be driven back North.[15]

As slavery disappeared or eroded in areas of the Confederacy now occupied by Union troops, former slaves began to work land in ways that they preferred. DuBois recorded their partially successful attempts on the South Carolina Sea Islands to purchase land, some of it bought cooperatively and then divided into family-worked blocs. He described the takeover of land late in the war by the government at Davis Bend, Mississippi, the division of the place into districts, and the self-government and economic self-management of the former slaves with their own sheriffs and judges under the general supervision of the military. DuBois maintained, on the basis of such examples, that the former slaves had thereby demonstrated their capacity for looking after themselves and running their communities.[16]

Later studies on the period of transition from slavery to a wage and tenant economy in South Carolina, such as those of Willie Lee Rose and, more recently, Julie Saville, reveal complexities beyond DuBois's analysis as a result of their focusing in detail on local interactions. On the Sea Islands during the Union occupation beginning in late 1861, the struggle facing the freed people, as they saw it, against both government officials and private purchasers of the abandoned estates was to mitigate or avoid the pressures to introduce "free labor" in the form of wage labor. Where rights of preemption to blocs of forfeited estates were available to the former slaves for purchase – in the eyes of white reformers the best alternative to wage labor – many lacked sufficient funds for a deposit. Even when freedmen had the resources, many resisted a relationship of absolute ownership to a bloc of land which might also have the effect of cutting them off from traditional access to marsh and woodland areas elsewhere on the estates. Such access had allowed foraging, pasture for animals, opportunities for hunting, and other conveniences. Many of the ex-slaves simply wished to raise food crops and keep stock without interference in the manner of their previous "informal economy." Here was but one local set of circumstances in which *de facto* freedom, the free labor objectives of Northerners, and the former slaves' inherited assumptions from the old order did not mesh.[17]

The historical debate about the *political* effects of black agency during the war has so far concentrated on its impact on the emergence of emancipation as Union policy. As already noted, DuBois made considerable claims for the significance of mass slave flight. The conclusion that it brought victory to the North required that the "general strike" be linked to intervening steps. Thus, the initiative taken by the fugitives created a new situation. "With perplexed and laggard steps," DuBois contended, "the United States Government followed the footsteps of the black slave." This was true, he indicated, in the changing sentiment and actions of Congress in 1862 and in terms of Lincoln's growing realism about the moral, political, and military circumstances of the war. DuBois represented the president as implicitly accepting the "double blow for freedom" argument since Lincoln saw black military enlistment as an intended aspect of the decision for emancipation.[18]

The principal terms of later debate about the role of the slaves in bringing on the decision to make emancipation a Union objective are all present in DuBois's discussion. The most emphatic support for the interpretation of emancipation as mainly the self-liberation of the slaves has come from Ira Berlin and his colleagues in the Freedmen and Southern Society Project. The struggle for freedom, they maintain, was essentially won by black initiative in the countryside rather than in Washington. The main alternative emphasis has come from James M. McPherson, who accepts that the action of the slaves was significant and that a good number gained their own freedom, but also argues that military victory for the Union was a prerequisite for freeing the majority. The difference in these positions is over the relative weight to be given to slaves' actions as against political and military decisions by the Lincoln administration. Neither approach fails to attribute some significance to the other and nor did DuBois, though his stress is clearly on black initiative.[19]

A major reason for this emphasis is the importance he placed on black military involvement in the second half of the war. For DuBois, the black soldiers demonstrated the truth of the "double blow for freedom" perspective that black activists had espoused from the beginning of the conflict. They demonstrated their worth through their military actions, efforts as military laborers, guides to Union troops, and spies bringing back intelligence. Equally important to the argument for the crucial character of the black military role is DuBois's suggestion that the provision of the 200,000 or so African Americans enabled the redeployment of Union forces making it possible successfully to pursue Grant's strategy, but this is not an argument substantiated in any detail. *Black Reconstruction* also examined the impact of black soldiering on the troops themselves and on white troops and civilians and fellow African Americans who encountered them. Though this area of research has been taken further in succeeding decades, DuBois established the grudging respect the soldiers gained from whites and the translation of suspicion into enthusiasm among slaves in the South as the arrival of black soldiers marked their freedom.[20]

Berlin and his colleagues doubtless had this in mind when they saw the commitment to emancipation and the substantial enlistment of black troops as transforming the character of the war. These changes gave the war a potentially revolutionary social dimension, opening up the possibilities of citizenship and fostering a sense of black self-worth and pride. More particularly, the work of the Freedmen and Southern Society Project has thrown light on the importance of black enlistment in Maryland, Kentucky, and Missouri, where it was enthusiastically and hugely embraced by the slaves as virtually the only way to freedom in slave states that had remained within the Union. The historians of the Project have also documented how the slave owners' largely unsuccessful attempts to prevent their slaves enlisting created a scarcity of agricultural labor, turned the balance of the labor market against them, and allowed the slaves who remained the opportunity to bargain for better conditions. DuBois had paid only a small amount of attention to the peculiar path to freedom of the slaveholding but loyal states.[21]

Scholars have linked the success of black military service at various levels to the question of black suffrage as a critical aspect of Reconstruction. DuBois, like later students of the issue, recognized the significance and the peculiarity of the suffrage controversy as it emerged in Louisiana in the latter months of the war. The existence of an educated, legally-free mixed-race minority "who have fought gallantly in our ranks" (Lincoln's words) raised the possibility of limited enfranchisement, though DuBois's treatment of the episode stressed white obduracy rather than shifting Northern attitudes. Yet the discussion also introduced the major organizing theme for his narrative of Reconstruction – the struggle for forms of democracy, political but also economic. From his earliest writings on the topic onwards, DuBois repudiated the common conclusion that the eventual achievement of black suffrage had led only to "failure." He was alert to the relative suddenness of the end of slavery and how little time the contending parties had to adjust to radically new circumstances – hence, in part, Southern white obduracy and the bitterness surrounding the whole suffrage issue.[22]

Among today's historians, Gavin Wright has also emphasized that the rapidity and initial completeness of the collapse of slavery created peculiarly harsh circumstances facing freed people and their allies in striving for political equality and economic opportunity. Southern whites consistently tried, through Black Codes, vagrancy laws, convict labor systems, and violence, to minimize any concession to African Americans' new status. In the later period of Radical supremacy, there were far greater possibilities for freed people to work with Southern Republicans for democratic advance, but scarcely ever without the rigid hostility of most Southern whites.[23]

This perception shaped DuBois's treatment of the Reconstruction years in his narratives of developments in the various states. He positioned himself essentially as a defender of the Radical governments in the South. He understood the governments as alliances between blacks, "carpet-baggers," and "scalawags," but he defended them generally for their extension of public schools and social policies. Incidents of corruption were noted, some of them implicating African Americans, but he chall-enged the veracity of reports from Redeemer legislatures about many alleged frauds – and thereby the earlier historiography that had largely taken the Redeemers' perspective as its own. In this broad defence of the political conduct and progressive policies of the Radical governments, DuBois laid the groundwork for the generalizing revisionist texts of the 1960s, particularly those of John Hope Franklin and Kenneth Stampp. But, given his earlier attention to black initiative during the war, it is surprising that he said comparatively little about the balance of power and responsibility between African Americans and their allies in the Radical governments. His mainly political account was framed in terms set by the scholarly and political opponents whose conclusions he wished to challenge. Above all, he stressed the important break constituted by universal male suffrage and what governments based upon it achieved, despite the determination of opponents to undermine their basis and challenge their legitimacy. Recent writing also recognizes the significance of democratic developments but raises more questions than DuBois about the relation of leaders to followers. According to Thomas Holt, state-level leadership in South Carolina was drawn not from rural freed people but from the old free black elite, especially from Charleston. Even local black officeholders in the period of Radical ascendancy, according to Foner, were more likely to be ministers and artisans and incoming Northerners than they were local country people. Precisely how well office-holders represented the outlook of people like this is a question that has emerged in some analyses of local agrarian societies.[24]

An impressive body of scholarship now exists on black experience in Reconstruction that, while not ignoring politics, approaches political connections through social and religious networks. DuBois paid some attention to the black Church and school, which he saw as mitigating some of the problems of the period, and concluded that the Freedmen's Bureau was sometimes a positive factor. In education, he saw the demand and activity of African Americans as the dynamic force that drew on the resources of the Bureau and missionary bodies. It was a view of the Church and the school as institutions that fed black aspirations but also provided some protection against outside pressures. Some recent commentary on the black Church, especially the African Methodist Episcopal Church, whose boast was that they had sent more ministers and missionaries to the South after the war than anyone else, has seen it as a cohesive community force in this time of change. Sometimes it also engaged directly with political and social issues. The minister, where he was not so already, emerged as adviser, instructor, and educator on public issues as well as religious and moral questions (many would not have acknowledged the distinction between them). Sometimes, however, the politics was too much for members of the congregation and they demanded that there should be no more "dry and cold" sermons on public issues.[25]

Black Reconstruction, in the balance of its treatment of Reconstruction, has less to say about the complexities of rural economic change than some more recent treatments. This is surprising in a man who had been a keen student of, and prolific writer about, the rural sociology of African American life in the 1890s and early 1900s. It reflects the trade-off between his reliance on publicly accessible printed sources, orientated towards the politics of the era, that enabled fairly rapid publication and gave historical depth to issues of civic inequality and the limitations imposed by such sources in the treatment of less obvious changes hidden in their local variety. Besides, the historiographical battle was primarily on the political front. DuBois's very general discussion of the land problem focused on the failure of the federal government and the Freedmen's Bureau to provide on a permanent basis land acquired from Confederates, except in small amounts to a tiny minority. Johnson's pardon policy, the unwillingness of Northerners to see government redistribute private property, and the determination of white Southerners to get land back, he argued, pushed the majority of freed people into wage labor and tenancy agreements. A small minority that managed to get together some capital was able to build up holdings, but a community of independent peasant farmers was at no point a likely outcome.[26]

Later historical research on economic change in the Southern countryside indicates a mosaic of outcomes. In the cotton regions, sharecropping was a widespread conclusion to the freedman's desire for sufficient land to maintain his family. This was disappointing to many after the hopes of wartime and the expectations of land redistribution in 1865. It was, however, an alternative to the perceived dependency of wage labor and drew on a family work force, though it might often have to be supplemented by some work for wages. Yet modern scholarship has gone well beyond these general conclusions to elucidate local variations in shares, the extent and character of provisioning, arrangements over marketing, and the possibilities of croppers bringing marginal land into regular cultivation to escape complete engagement in share arrangements. We thus have a clearer, if complicated, picture of the intricate legal, customary, and power relations shaping the efforts of the freed people to obtain a secure tenure and to improve their conditions in much of the old Cotton Kingdom during Reconstruction.[27]

The different requirements of large-scale sugar production in Louisiana, maintained as it was through new inflows of capital, were fulfilled through *continuity* in the now-waged gang labor system. In stark contrast, the low country rice area departed furthest from prewar arrangements. Black community cohesiveness, lack of planter resources to keep the infrastructure of the rice plantations going, and some examples of cooperative land purchases by freed people all contributed to greater access and more African American control of land than almost anywhere else in the United States at the end of Reconstruction. Both the socioeconomic dimension of change and the distinctive directions of such change have become preoccupations of the historical literature for which there is little precedent in *Black Reconstruction*.[28]

Finally, we turn to DuBois's thesis about the relation between race and class. The concept of the "general strike" was one aspect of DuBois's view that the slaves and freed people should be understood as a proletariat in more or less conscious struggle with their masters/employers/landlords. There was, of course, a larger proletariat that included white workers but DuBois was clear that, even before the Civil War, white labor saw itself as completely separate from black labor. His comment on the outlook of ordinary white people who had moved West was, he believed, more generally applicable: "[The white laborer] was an advocate of extreme democracy and equalitarianism in his political and economic philosophy, [but] his vote and influence did not go to strengthen the abolition-democracy, before, during, or even after the war. On the contrary, it was stopped and inhibited by the doctrine of race." DuBois recognized that there could be advantages to whites in defining themselves in antagonism to blacks: "they were compensated in part by a sort of public and psychological wage. They were given public deference and titles of courtesy because they were white." Therefore, he concluded, it was not only the class and racial determination of planters, employers, and landlords but also the racism of the white proletariat that undermined the class unity and potential strength of workers in their struggles after the war, rendering any general self-liberation of labor impossible.[29]

Although not all historians who raise the issue of the relations of white and black labor invoke DuBois, a number do. The point of discussing the relation of black and white labor does not come from any reductive, and unhistorical, sense that black and white proletarian unity was ordained and somehow thwarted. Rather, it begins to open up analysis of the social relations of freed people beyond those with the former master or landlord, a procedure beginning to reveal more complex post-emancipation societies in, for example, Brazil and Cuba. Summaries of recent work indicate the relevance in north-eastern Brazil of changes in opportunities for the employment of freed people at different times and the significance for their social relations of varying possibilities of physical movement.[30]

In the period of Radical ascendancy in Washington and in the South, there was a strand of conviction in the Republican party, made explicit at the national level by Thaddeus Stevens, that Reconstruction constitutionalism incorporated a commitment to aid the poor, those disadvantaged by class as well as race. Drawing explicitly on the spirit of DuBois, William Forbath has argued that, in making a reality of citizenship, white laborers as well as freed people needed the suffrage but also education and perhaps redistributed land. While it is possible to interpret the Black Codes of 1865–66 as designed in part to maintain the separation between white and black workers, Stevens clearly hoped to convince white laborers that they, too, could fall victim to some of the provisions. Something like a possible cross-race laboring class alliance was in vague formulation here. And Radical Republicans in the South periodically aided what David Montgomery has termed "the everyday struggles of rural black workers." White labor organizations existed in Southern cities in the 1860s and 1870s and black delegates from Richmond attended a black National Labor Congress in 1869 that urged Republicans to be more radical in land distribution. Yet there was little evidence of rural white Southerners, apart from "scalawags," offering themselves as allies of the freed people. The social and political institutions that gave some coherence to rural black sentiment – the Churches, the Union Leagues, and the Republican party – either were by definition exclusively black or were ideologically unattractive to ordinary white Southerners.[31]

Eric Foner's discussion of the white labor movement's attitude to black concerns concludes that it had little or no interest in incorporating them in a labor program. David Roediger's emphasis is slightly different, but neither he nor Foner explains the lack of an alliance simply in terms of the racism of white labor. Roediger shows a particular concern with variable situation and context, perhaps to avoid reifying "racism." He is also alert to signs of contradictory impulses behind the rhetoric of white labor. The influence of fears of "swamping" as a result of emancipation during the war sometimes recurred after 1865. But, while shifts in white attitudes to African Americans as a result of their participation in the war did not transform the suspicion of many white laborers towards possible black competitors, in some cases it may have complicated them. And the idea of *emancipation* was taken up by some labor spokesmen to characterize their own objectives. However, despite these qualifications, and despite limited evidence about contradictory discourses in the pro-labor press on "the policy of elevating the black man," there is little to gainsay DuBois's sense, on this issue as more generally, that Reconstruction was a "tragedy." The needs and hopes of black and white laboring people were thwarted, substantially because they found themselves positioned in opposition to each other.[32]

Notes

1. W. R. Brock, *An American Crisis* (New York, 1963); Hans L. Trefousse, *The Radical Republicans: Lincoln's Vanguard for Racial Justice* (New York, 1969); Michael L. Benedict, *A Compromise of Principle: Congressional Republicans and Reconstruction, 1863–1869* (New York, 1974); Howard N. Rabinowitz, *Race Relations in the Urban South, 1865–1890* (New York, 1978); William Gillette, *Retreat from Reconstruction, 1869–1879* (Baton Rouge, 1979); Michael Perman, *The Road to Redemption: Southern Politics, 1869–1879* (Chapel Hill, 1984); George C. Rable, *But There Was No Peace: The Role of Violence in the Politics of Reconstruction* (Athens, GA, 1984); Dan T. Carter, *When the War Was Over: The Failure of Self-Reconstruction in the South, 1865–1867* (Baton Rouge, 1985); Eric Foner, *Reconstruction: America's Unfinished Revolution, 1863–1877* (New York, 1988).

2. William A. Dunning, *Reconstruction, Political and Economic 1865–1877* (New York, 1907); John W. Burgess, *Reconstruction and the Constitution 1866–1876* (New York, 1902).

3. John Hope Franklin, *Reconstruction After the Civil War* (Chicago, 1961); Kenneth M. Stampp, *The Era of Reconstruction, 1865–77* (New York, 1965); Harold M. Hyman ed., *New Frontiers of American Reconstruction* (Urbana, IL, 1966).

4. Foner, *Reconstruction*, p. xxi; Ira Berlin et al., *Slaves No More: Three Essays on Emancipation and the Civil War* (Cambridge, UK, 1992); Edward L. Ayers, "Worrying about the Civil War" and William E. Forbath, "Caste, Class and Equal Citizenship," both in Karen Halttunen and Lewis Perry, eds., *Moral Problems in American Life: New Perspectives on Cultural History* (Ithaca and London, 1998) pp. 145–65, 167–98.

5. W. E. B. DuBois, *Black Reconstruction in America, 1860–1880*, introduction by David Levering Lewis (New York, 1992 edn., originally published 1935); Forbath, "Caste, Class"; David R. Roediger, *The Wages of Whiteness: Race and the Making of the American Working Class* (London, 1991) pp. 11–13.

6. W. E. B. DuBois, Memorandum to the Rosenwald Fund, January 9, 1931, Rosenwald Fund Archive, Box 409 f.5 Special Collections, Fisk University.

7. W. E. B. DuBois, "The Economics of Negro Emancipation in the United States," *The Sociological Review*, October 1911; DuBois, "The Rural South," *Papers and Proceedings of the American Economic Association*, December 1911; DuBois, Memorandum to the Board of Directors [of the NAACP] from Dr. DuBois, May 12, 1931, James Weldon Johnson MSS., W. E. B. DuBois Coll., ser. 3, Box 5, f.109, Beinecke Library, Yale University.

8. David Levering Lewis, "Introduction" to *Black Reconstruction*; DuBois to Edwin R. Embree, June 3,1933, Rosenwald Fund Archive, Box 409 f.5; DuBois to Joel E. Springarn, February 22, 1933, James Weldon Johnson MSS., Joel E. Springarn Coll., ser. 1, Box 1, f. 12.

9. John R. Lynch, *The Facts of Reconstruction* (New York, 1913); Alrutheus A. Taylor, *The Negro in South Carolina during the Reconstruction* (Washington, DC, 1924); idem, *The Negro in the Reconstruction of Virginia* (Washington, DC, 1926); James M. McPherson, *The Negro's Civil War: How American Negroes Felt and Acted During the War for the Union* (New York, 1965); Benjamin Quarles, *The Negro in the Civil War* (Boston, 1953); Dudley Taylor Cornish, *The Sable Arm: Negro Troops in the Union Army, 1861–1865* (New York, 1956).

10. DuBois, *Black Reconstruction*, pp. 57–83; McPherson, *Negro's Civil War*, pp. 39–40.

11. DuBois, *Black Reconstruction*, pp. 63–4.

12. DuBois, *Black Reconstruction*, p. 63; Rosa Luxemburg, *Leninism or Marxism* [1904] in Rosa Luxemburg, *The Russian Revolution and Leninism or Marxism*, introduced by Bertram D. Wolfe (Ann Arbor, MI, 1961), pp. 90–2; H. Stuart Hughes, *Consciousness and Society: The Reorientation of European Social Thought, 1890–1930* (New York, 1961), p. 162.

13. See Stanley Elkins, *Slavery* (Chicago, 1959).

14. Berlin et al., *Slaves No More*, pp. 13–22; Leon F. Litwack, *Been in the Storm So Long: The Aftermath of Slavery* (London, 1980), pp. 32–6.

15. See, for example, Litwack, *Been in the Storm*, pp. 23–5.

16. DuBois, *Black Reconstruction*, pp.72–4.

17. Willie Lee Rose, *Rehearsal for Reconstruction: The Port Royal Experiment* (New York, 1964), pp. 311–15 for acceptance of wages only until freedmen got land; Julie Saville, *The Work of Reconstruction: From Slave to Wage Laborer in South Carolina, 1860–1870* (Cambridge, UK, 1996), pp. 45–50, 121–5; Berlin et al., *Slaves No More*, pp. 98–100.

18. DuBois, *Black Reconstruction*, pp.81–3.

19. Berlin et al., *Slaves No More*, pp. 29–30, 42–3, 111–20; James M. McPherson, *Battle Cry of Freedom: The American Civil War* (London, 1988), pp. 494–504, 557–8, 881.

20. DuBois, *Black Reconstruction*, pp. 91–121.

21. Berlin et al., *Slaves No More*, pp. 47–9, 51–3, 65–6, 206.

22. DuBois, *Black Reconstruction,* pp. 153–9; DuBois, "Reconstruction and Its Benefits," *American Historical Review*, 15 (July, 1910): 781.

23. Gavin Wright, "Economic and Political Consequences of Emancipation," in Frank McGlynn and Seymour Drescher, eds. *The Meaning of Freedom: Economics, Politics, and Culture After Slavery* (Pittsburgh and London, 1992), pp. 89–90.

24. DuBois, *Black Reconstruction*, pp. 381–486; Thomas Holt, *Black over White: Negro Political Leadership in South Carolina During Reconstruction* (Urbana, IL, 1977), pp. 95–170; Foner, *Reconstruction*, pp. 362–79; Saville, *The Work of Reconstruction*, pp. 155–60.

25. DuBois, *Black Reconstruction*, pp. 637–69; Foner, *Reconstruction*, pp. 282–3; Litwack, *Been in the Storm So Long*, pp. 450–71; Saville, *The Work of Reconstruction*, p. 165.

26. DuBois, *Black Reconstruction*, pp. 368–9, 386, 600–4.

27. Roger L. Ransom and Richard Sutch, *One Kind of Freedom: The Economic Consequences of Emancipation* (New York, 1977); Jay R. Mandle, *Not Slave, Not Free: The African American Economic Experience since the Civil War* (Durham, NC and London, 1992).

28. Rebecca J. Scott, "Defining the Boundaries of Freedom in the World of Cane: Cuba, Brazil, and Louisiana after Emancipation," *American Historical Review*, 99, no. 1 (February 1994): 70–102; Foner, *Reconstruction*, pp. 164–75, 399–411; Berlin et al., *Slaves No More*, pp. 174–81; Saville, *The Work of Reconstruction*, pp. 125–7.

29. DuBois, *Black Reconstruction*, pp. 17–31, esp. 28.

30. Rebecca J. Scott et al., *The Abolition of Slavery and the Aftermath of Emancipation in Brazil* (Durham, NC, 1988); idem, "Fault Lines, Color Lines, and Party Lines: Race, Labor, and Collective Action in Louisiana and Cuba, 1862–1912," in Frederick J. Cooper, Thomas C. Holt, Rebecca J. Scott, *Beyond Slavery: Explorations of Race, Labor, and Citizenship in Postemancipation Societies* (Chapel Hill and London, 2000), pp. 61–106; Kim D. Butler, *Freedoms Given, Freedoms Won: Afro-Brazilians in Post-Abolition São Paulo and Salvador* (New Brunswick, NJ, 1998).

31. David Montgomery, *Citizen Worker: The Experience of Workers in the United States with Democracy and the Free Market during the Nineteenth Century* (Cambridge, UK, 1993), pp. 123–5; Forbath, "Caste, Class," esp. pp. 167–74.

32. Foner, *Reconstruction*, pp. 477–80; Roediger, *The Wages of Whiteness*, pp. 170–84.

Index

Index

Index

Center for the Study of Southern Culture 311

Century of Struggle: The Women's Rights Movement (Flexner) 224, 225

Chafe, William H. 164, 167

Chandler, Alfred 182

Channing, Edward 27

Charleston, invasions of 45–6

Chartier, Roger 246–7

Cherokee 34

  Christianity 97

Cherokee Women (Perdue) 233–4

Cheseborough, David 104

Chinese Americans: Western history 289

  women 234

Chuh, Kandice 359

Cincinnati, poverty in 48

Cinema Journal 272, 275

citizenship: voluntary tradition 146

Civic Ideals Conflicting Visions of Citizenship in U.S. History (Smith) 205

civil liberties and rights: anticommunism and 133

  historiography 317–19

  new look at Reconstruction 407–8

  women's votes 226–7

civil rights movement 9

  anticommunism 145, 157, 159–60

  CIO as early force 156–8

  historiography 28, 30, 156–69

  McCarthyism 139

  Montgomery bus boycott 165, 168

  religion 215

  role of the NAACP 158–61

  segregation 161–9

  Southern identity 314

  women 166–8

Civil War: black military service 415–16

  bounty system 395

  divisions in historiography 387–8

  incompatible North-South labor systems 375–81

  influence of *Gone With the Wind* 265

  institutional support for North 16

  military and civilian volunteers 393–7, 399–400

  morale and commitment 389–93

  Northern advantages 391–2

  propaganda and inspiration 397–400

  religion 101, 103–5

  sobering for historians 26

  splits Southern history 315, 317

Clark, Charles 248

Clark, Christopher 6–7

  "Reshaping Society: American Social History from Revolution to Reconstruction" **45–64**

Clark, Elizabeth 213

Clark, J. C. D.: *English Society* 94

class: economic divisions 369–70

  experience of Revolution 33–4, 36, 37

  film audiences 272

  historiography of working class 187–8

  ideology of "classlessness" 15–16, 367

  incompatible North-South labor systems 375–81

  Marxist historical approach 371–5

  non-elite whites and slaves 336–42

  plebian biographies 31–2

  social consciousness 370–1

  women and children workers 55

"Class and the Construction of 'Race': White Racism in the Antebellum South" (Tadman) **327–42**

The Classical Hollywood Cinema (Bordwell, Thompson and Staiger) 273

Clay, Henry 76, 81

Cleveland, Grover 73

Clifford, James: *The Predicament of Culture* 356–7

Clinton, Bill 136

Clinton, Catherine 389

coal mining 286

Coclanis, Peter 310

Cody, Iron Eyes 292–3

Cohen, Lizabeth 121

Cohen, Miriam 228

Cold War: effect on Western historiography 286 *see also* anticommunism; McCarthyism; Soviet Union

colonial history: historiography 27

  the South 316

Colorado, University of 297

Colored People (Gates) 311–12

Comanches 352–3

The Coming of the Book (Febvre and Martin) 246

Index

Index

Index

Index

Index

Index

Index

religion 100, 102–3
and Sally Hemmings 309
Jeffrey, Julie Roy: *Frontier Women* 229–30
Jenkins, David: "Object Lessons and Ethnographic Displays" 356
Jennings, Francis 350, 352
The Invasion of America 349
Jensen, Joan 229, 230
Jesus of Nazareth: millennium celebrations 199–200
Jews and Judaism 102
Jim Crow *see* race and racism
Jimerson, Randall 388–9
Johansen, Bruce E. 352
John, Richard 79
John Birch Society 131
Johns Hopkins University: historians 26
Johnson, Andrew 418
Johnson, Charles S. 164
Johnson, Curtis 96
Johnson, James Weldon 410
Johnson, Lyndon B. 134
Johnson, Paul 98
Johnson, R. C. 165
Jones, Archer: *How the North Won the Civil War* (with Hattaway) 390
Why the South Lost the Civil War (with others) 390
Jones, Jacqueline: *Labor of Love, Labor of Sorrow* 229
Jordan, Winthrop 328
The Journal of American History 216, 276, 307
Journal of Southern History 307
Jowett, Garth: *Film: the Democratic Art* 270
Juster, Susan 96, 105

Kammen, Michael 2
Kann, Mark E.: *A Republic of Men* 232, 233
Karp, Ivan: *Exhibiting Cultures: The Poetics and Politics of Museum Display* (with Lavine) 356
Keeran, Roger 156
Kelley, Florence 214
Kelley, Robin 156, 186
Kelly, Joan 226

Kennedy, David: *Freedom from Fear* 118
Kennedy, John F. 134, 140
Kerber, Linda 24, 32, 208
No Constitutional Right to Be Ladies 205
The Women of the Republic 213, 233
Kessler-Harris, Alice 228, 235
Keynes, John Maynard 125
Kimmel, Michael S. 232
Kindem, Gorham A. 271
King, Desmond 161
King, Richard 310
King, Rodney 291
King Jr, Martin Luther 318
focus of scholars 156
launch protests 165
a "new age" 169
whites in background 162
Wilkin's jealousy of 160
Kirk, John 159
Klehr, Harvey 135–6, 137
Klein, Laura: *Women and Power in Native North America* (with Ackerman) 298
Kleinberg, S. Jay 11, 228
The Shadow of the Mills: Working Class Families in Pittsburg 234
Women in the United States 226
"Women's History and Gender" **223–37**
Kloppenberg, James T. 5, 10–11
"Intellectual History, Democracy and the Culture of Irony" **199–217**
Kluger, Richard 158
Knack, Martha: *Native Americans and Wage Labor* (with Littlefield) 302
Knight, Arthur: *The Liveliest Art* 268, 269
Kolodny, Annette 354
Korean War 144
Korstad, Robert 156, 157, 158
Kousser, Morgan 165
Kraditor, Aileen: *The Ideas of the Woman Suffrage Movement* 225
Krupat, Arnold 353
Ethnocriticism: History, Literature 355
Ku Klux Klan 145, 168
Kuhn, Thomas 209
Kuklick, Bruce 100

labor: black and white 328

Index

Index

early American newspapers 248–9
ideal and reality of public sphere
259–60
ideology of impartiality 252–4
partisan 257–9 *see also* books and
publishing
men: freemasonry 60–1
frontier settlement 57–8
gender history 232, 234
patriotic posturing 141–2
Mennonites 95
Merritt, Russell 272
Methodists 93
Canadian 105
early expansion 94–5
evangelical surge 103
Metz, Christian 272
Mexico: NAFTA 359
Western history 285, 288
Meyer, Melissa 293
The Middle Ground (White) 350
Middletown (Lynd and Lynd) 266
migration: family and social networks 57,
59–60
religion of immigrants 104
wage workers 63
military: effect on rural economies 46
Mill, John Stuart 212
millennium celebrations 199–200
Miller, Perry 206
Miller, Randall 104
A Million and One Nights (Ramsaye) 267,
269
mining: the West 286, 288
Mississippi, University of 311
Mitchell, Clarence 161
Mitchell, Reid 388, 392–3
Mohawk, John: *Exiled in the Land of the
Free* (ed. with Lyons) 352
Molho, Anthony: *Imagined Histories* (ed.
with Wood) 4–5
Momaday, N. Scott: *House Made of
Dawn* 354
Monroe, Marilyn 274
Montejano, David: *Anglos and Mexicans
in the Making of Texas* 294
Montezuma, Carlos 298
Montgomery, David 181
Montgomery bus boycott 155–6, 165

decisive shift 169
NAACP's lukewarm response to 160
women's involvement 168
Morgan, Edmund S. 212, 328
American Slavery, American Freedom
30
Birth of the American Republic 29
Morgan, Philip 339–40
Mormons 94, 95
Moses, L. G. 350
Mothers of Invention (Faust) 309
*Motion Pictures: The Development of An
Art* (Fulton) 269
movies *see* films
The Movies (Griffith and Mayer) 268–9
Mullin, Bruce 100
Mulvey, Laura: "Visual and Other
Pleasures" 272
Murray, Judith Sargent 215
Murrin, John 33
Museum of the American Indian 357
Museums and Memory (Crane) 355
museums and museum studies: Native
Americans 355–7
music: rhythm and blues 168
Myrdal, Gunnar 164
myth 358

Naison, Mark 156
Nandy, Ashis: "History's Forgotten
Doubles" 358
Nash, Gary 31
Nash, Roderick 294
Nation of Islam 162
National Alliance of Postal Employees
161
National Association for the Advancement
of Colored People (NAACP) 9, 163
anticommunism 159–61
civil rights movement 158–61
DuBois and 409, 410
opposition 164
purged of militant elements 157
react to *Birth of a Nation* 265–6
support for dissent 166
National Association of Colored Women
166
National Council of Negro Women 168
National Labor Congress 420

Index

Index

Index

Index

Index

Index

Thompson, E. P. 2, 271
Thompson, Kristin: *The Classical Hollywood Cinema* (with Bordwell and Staiger) 273
Thornton, Russell 351
Thornwell, J. H. 100
Tillman, Ben 309
Tilton, Robert S. 351
Tise, Larry 331
Tocqueville, Alexis de: democracy 212, 214
  Jacksonian era 70
  outside viewpoint 217
  voluntary tradition 145–6, 400
Tomlins, Christopher 181
Tooker, Elizabeth 352
trade unions *see* labor organization
transport: Jacksonian era 79–80
  market revolution thesis 72
treason 25
Trigger, Bruce 350
Trudeau, Gary 30
Truman, Harry S: anticommunism 132, 133, 134, 138–9, 143
Trumbull, John 253, 255
Truth, Sojourner 100
Tuck, Steven 159
Turley, David 16
  "By Way of DuBois: The Question of Black Initiative" **407–21**
Turner, Frederick Jackson 13
  defining "frontier" 289
  frontier thesis 285, 286, 288, 348
  re-read 287
Turner (Frederick Jackson) Award 190
Tushnet, Mark V. 158
Tyler, Alice Felt 76
Tyson, Tim 160, 168

Ulrich, Laurel Thatcher 97
Uncle Tom's Cabin (Stowe) 376
Union Leagues 396, 398
unions *see* labor organization
United Packinghouse Workers 158
Universal Negro Improvement Association 9
Universal Negro Improvement Association (UNIA) 161–2
urban life: Depression era 124

North and South 313, 379
  poverty 48
  social change 46–7
Uricchio, William 273

Valeri, Marck 102
Van Buren, Martin 81
Van Deburg, William 168
Vance, Rupert 310
Varon, Elizabeth R. 56
  We Mean to be Counted 77
  women of Jacksonian era 75, 76, 77
Vassiliev, Alexander 137
Venona Project 137, 138
Vietnam 30
Vincent, Theodore 162
Virginia: early press 248–9
  leading families 55
"Visual and Other Pleasures" 272
Vogel, Lisa 228
voluntary tradition 146
  during Civil War 393–7, 399–400
  de Tocqueville 145–6, 400
Von Eschen, Penny 160

The Wages of Sin (Jacobs) 273
Waldstreicher, David 258
Walker, Vanessa Siddle 169
Wallace, Anthony C. 350
Ward, Brian 168
Warner, Michael D.: *Letters of the Republic* 250–2
Warren, James, and family 53
Warren, Mercy Otis: *History of the Rise, Progress and Termination of the American Revolution* 25
Washington, Booker T. 156, 164, 165
Washington, George 25
Washington Post (newspaper) 287
Watson, Harry L. 70, 71
We Mean to be Counted (Varon) 77
Weatherill, Amanda 235
Weber, Max: "ethnic status" 329
  outside viewpoint 217
  religion and economics 206
  social change 124
Weem, Mason 25
Weinstein, Allen: *The Haunted Woods* 137
Weld, Theodore 79

Index